BRITISH SPECIAL PROJECTS

FLYING WINGS, DELTAS AND TAILLESS DESIGNS

BILL ROSE

FONTHILL

Fonthill Media Language Policy

Fonthill Media publishes in the international English language market. One language edition is published worldwide. As there are minor differences in spelling and presentation, especially with regard to American English and British English, a policy is necessary to define which form of English to use. The Fonthill Policy is to use the form of English native to the author. Bill Rose was born and educated in London and now lives in Norfolk; therefore British English has been adopted in this publication.

www.fonthillmedia.com
office@fonthillmedia.com
First published in the United Kingdom
and the United States of America 2020

British Library Cataloguing in Publication Data:
A catalogue record for this book is available from the British Library

ISBN 978-1-78155-805-8

Typeset in Minion Pro 10pt on 13pt
Printed and bound in England

Unless otherwise noted, all illustrations and photographs used in this book belong to the Bill Rose Collection.

Contents

Introduction

Futuristic in appearance and still the subject of development for military and civil applications, the flying wing, blended wing body (BWB), delta and various tailless designs never fail to generate professional and public interest.

The lines separating these types of aircraft can be rather indistinct as their features often overlap, but the starting point was the flying wing. Its origins can be traced back many centuries to the days before manned flight was considered possible. In those pre-industrial times, birds were the principle inspiration for heavier than air flying devices, although nobody understood how this might be accomplished. It is also the case that nature chose a very efficient way to transport certain shapes of small tree seeds over considerable distances utilising the wind and this caught the attention of most pioneering inventors.

Historians tend to attribute the earliest design for a manned aircraft to Leonardo da Vinci (1452–1519) who produced a detailed drawing of a man-powered ornithopter (flapping wing device) in about 1485. His concept was totally unworkable, but it helped to promote interest in the possibility of manned flight which persisted throughout the centuries that followed. As things turned out, it would be the Montgolfier brothers who finally achieved this in 1783 using a hot air balloon.

Although, the idea of building a heavier-than-air flying machine remained in the realms of fantasy, the inventor Sir George Cayley (1773–1857) began constructing and testing small gliders in about 1804 at Brampton, Yorkshire. By 1853, he had completed a glider capable of carrying a pilot and this was reportedly flown on several occasions by his coachman (possibly John Appleby) or his butler. However, these experiments were never officially documented and whether or not Cayley deserves to be credited for making the first flight of a heavier than air craft possible remains a matter of some debate.

A decade after Cayley's death, the British designers James William Butler and Edmund Edwards proposed a superficially very simple flying wing concept that stemmed from nothing more complex than a paper dart. They envisaged a large, man-carrying aircraft with the same shape, powered by some form of steam propulsion. The design was patented (UK Ref: 2115), although their ideas were (in some ways) too far ahead of their time and totally unrealistic.

As the possibility of heavier-than-air flying machines continued to gain credibility, the brilliant French experimenter Alphonse Pénaud 1850–1880) demonstrated sustained flight by flying a small, hand-launched model aircraft called the Planophore in Paris on 18 August 1871. The Planophore used a rear mounted propeller driven by an elastic band and it travelled for a distance of 131 ft (40 m). Having shown that powered flight was possible, Pénaud went on to design a series of astonishingly advanced flying wing aircraft that never actually flew, but set the standard for all future proposals. It is also worth noting the pioneering work undertaken by the French inventor Louis Pierre Mouillard (1834–1897). He reportedly made a short, although uncorroborated flight of 90 ft (27 m) at an altitude of 30 ft (9 m) in his fourth glider near Cairo, Egypt, on 3 January 1878.

Towards the end of the nineteenth century, the well-known German engineer Otto Lilienthal (1848–1896) began flying gliders and is widely acknowledged as having flown the first manned glider in 1891. Sadly, his last glider flight killed him.

Regardless of who deserves credit for making the first manned aircraft flight, Lilienthal was swiftly followed by his associate Igo Etrich (1879–1967), who built gliders directly based on the winged liana seed, which would prove very influential with future designers.

Powered flight would be next big step forward and British inventor Percy Sinclair Pilcher (1866–1899) prepared to fly an aircraft powered by a small 4 hp (3 kW) engine at Stanford Hall, Leicestershire. Unfortunately, there was a mechanical fault with the engine, so he decided to make an unpowered glide-flight for his investors, but was killed when the airframe broke up shortly after take-off. This was some four years before the Wright Brothers made their first flight in North Carolina and Pilcher might have slightly altered the course of history if things had gone differently for him.

The application of an internal combustion engine to a tailless design was soon taken up by pioneers like French engineer René Arnoux and the British designer John William Dunne (1875–1949), who are both known to have studied the behaviour of winged seeds. The stage was now set for considerable development of the powered flying wing, although various technical issues and inadequate engine performance would seriously impede progress.

However, the First World War would lead to substantial aviation advances, with aircraft recognised as valuable military assets. Once hostilities ceased, the German engineer Hugo Junkers (1859–1935) turned his attention towards building a more efficient type of aircraft designated the JG-1, carrying passengers and cargo within the wing. Junkers had already patented a flying wing aircraft in 1910 and was a strong supporter of this configuration, envisaging future giant transporters capable of carrying 1,000 passengers. Unfortunately for Junkers, the design was deemed to have contravened post-war conditions for aircraft construction set out by the Allies and the JG-1 proposal was scrapped. Nevertheless, tailless aircraft would continue to be developed in Germany during the years that followed, by individuals like Dr Alexander Martin Lippisch (1894–1976), who was possibly one the greatest aircraft designers of the last century and is widely credited with development of the delta wing, which he named after the 3-sided Greek letter. Also working on sleek gliders for recreational purposes that would set standards, were the Horten Brothers. I will just mention that these pre-war pioneers and of course their predecessors like Lilienthal would provide most of the know-how that was used in the 1960s to build the hang gliders we are familiar with today. This regeneration of interest in low cost flight was made possible by the combination of a flexible kite wing created by Francis and Gertrude Rogallo in the USA, and a flight control method using weight shift devised by John Dickensen in Australia.

However, returning to this book's main theme of military and research aircraft, a major turning point arrived during the Second World War, when the potential of the flying wing was recognised in Germany, America and Britain. Aside from this type of aircraft's usual elegance, the advantages of high lift and low drag were obvious. With constantly improving engine performance adding further capability, there was an eagerness to develop prototypes into fast, agile fighters and long-range bombers.

Funding was now available for relatively exotic concepts and the Germans pressed ahead with development of the Me 163 tailless rocket powered interceptor that entered service before the war ended and saw combat. During this time, German scientists and engineers would make enormous progress with designs of various jet powered flying wings and deltas, that pushed the boundaries of intercontinental operations and supersonic flight. Nevertheless, this was uncharted territory and there were aerodynamic compromises and many handling problems. Testing often showed that elegant original concepts for flying wings required vertical stabilisers and tail fins, while fuselage sections would end up protruding beyond the fore and aft boundaries of the wing.

Although a swept (flying) wing is usually considered normal (for reasons such as control and stability), it is also possible (for specialised requirements) to use a straight, forward swept, swivelling (in an oblique manner) or variable geometry configuration. While the classic flying wing is unsuitable for development as a supersonic aircraft because of its substantial wingspan and high aspect ratio, there are exceptions to the rule and this is where the swept thin wing delta takes over.

From the earliest wind tunnel tests, it was clear that the delta wing provided a path to supersonic performance. But there was another issue of maintaining lift at low speeds, which requiring a high angle of attack. As a consequence, this would eventually encourage the development of leading-edge root extensions (LERX) and the double delta.

When hostilities ceased, Alexander Lippisch was immediately recruited by the Americans, but they decided not to secure the services of German flying wing pioneers Reimar Horten (1915–1994) and his older brother Walter (1903–1998), although both would briefly work for the British. Reimar Horton was arguably the more creative of the two and was employed by Fairey in the design department, but the staff were generally hostile towards him and Reimar Horten finally returned to Germany. That said, the British and Americans drew heavily on Horten and Lippisch's research work to build a series of ambitious high performance experimental prototypes, leading to advanced fighters and strategic bombers. Eventually, one particular line of British development produced the Fairey Delta 2 (FD.2), an experimental supersonic aircraft that set a new World Air Speed Record on 10 March 1956 of 1,132 mph (1,811 kph), which held good for over a year. The aircraft was further modified for specialised wing development that proved invaluable when designing the supersonic Concorde airliner and the FD.2 also directly inspired the famous French Mirage fighter. During this period, the British contemplated long range ballistic missiles, orbital satellites and a manned space capability. It was generally unrealistic wishful thinking, well beyond the technical ability of the era and financially impossible for the UK. But the idea of building spaceplanes and a manned RAF space fighter led to some very interesting ideas based on the use of a delta wing.

These paper studies were generally all unworkable, with many becoming 'what if' topics within the ranks of aviation experts and enthusiasts. Needless to say, there is no prospect of any future revival in this area. Furthermore, there is little chance of any UK aerospace company considering any major aerospace projects without international partners and this was clearly demonstrated by involvement in development of the American F-35 Lightning II, which is now the UK's primary multi-role stealth, strike fighter.

Today, most of the major aerodynamic problems that plagued flying wings, deltas and tailless aircraft have been eliminated, or worked around and the arrival of advanced computer control systems have made the previously impossible, possible. A modern aircraft takes years to design, requires serious funding, a lengthy period in development and a full order book. Of course, we can still expect to see new types of civil and military aircraft crossing British skies in the future and many will utilise sleek configurations derived from flying wing and delta shapes. Most will be manned, but this could eventually change to machines piloted by ground controllers and eventually on-board artificial intelligence.

Civil BWB aircraft will not be capable of greater speeds than most existing aircraft in the same class, but they will transport greater payloads over longer ranges at reduced cost. This will also attract military customers with initial applications for tactical airlifters, tankers, command and observation platforms, manned and unmanned BWB bombers and perhaps specialised craft equipped with directed energy weapons or carriers of unmanned combat aircraft.

This book is primarily concerned with UK military aerospace projects and it is possible that I have omitted a few obscure designs, which tends to be an ongoing problem with any written work of this nature. However, I have tried to show the immense influence exercised over all post-war military aircraft and spacecraft design by research and development undertaken in wartime Germany. This would have a lasting effect with engineers and scientists around the world.

While I have explored many of the less well known UK military aviation concepts and projects from the last century, this book makes no real attempt to provide a detailed technical appraisal of the flying wing, delta or tailless designs. Again, there are many excellent publications available covering these areas.

Bill Rose
Norfolk
2020

Many individuals provided assistance with background material and technical advice for this book, but I would like to especially thank:

Chris Farara
Chris Gibson
Tony Buttler
Dr Iain Murray
Martin Müller
Alexi Malinovsky
John Luc Seligman-Brown

1

Early Flying Wings

The development of tailless aircraft in Britain has an interesting history, but a good starting point for this book is with the pioneering work of John William Dunne (1875–1949). Dunne was born in county Kildare, Ireland and the oldest son of General Sir John Hart Dunne KCB. From an early age, he became interested in science, technology and the idea of manned flight. Having served with the Imperial Yeomanry as a trooper during the Second Boer War and as a second lieutenant in the Wiltshire Regiment (also in South Africa), Dunne was finally invalided out due to ill-health and returned to England. He then became a friend of the author H. G. Wells and they undoubtedly discussed many ideas for future manned flight, while Dunne spent a much of his time designing and building small models of tailless aircraft.

Despite his health issues, Dunne remained a serving army officer and his interests caught the attention of Colonel John Capper who commanded the newly formed Army Balloon Factory at Farnborough. In June 1906, Dunne was assigned to work for Capper, where he was given a free hand to develop his aircraft designs further. Dunne was soon responsible for the design of a manned glider with V shaped swept wings, designated D.1, which could be adapted to utilise propeller propulsion.

Dunne's work was considered top secret and in July 1907, the D.1 was transported by rail to Blair Atholl, a small, remote village in the Scottish Highlands, where flight testing could be undertaken on the Duke of Atholl's estate. A series of short flights followed, with Capper managing to crash the glider into a stone wall. Luckily, the damage was modest, so the glider was repaired and fitted with two small 12 hp (8.9 kW) Buchet engines and propellers.

Unfortunately, the modified D.1 crashed on take-off, but it was considered to have demonstrated good stability and a decision was taken to build and test another glider called D.2. As things worked out, D.2 was never built and Dunne moved on to the manned D.3 glider, followed by the D.4, which utilised crude wingtip control surfaces and was fitted with a 25 hp (18.6 kW) REP engine driving two propellers. Both aircraft were tested at Blair Atholl during 1908, undertaking fairly successful short flights and as a consequence, Dunne began work on his improved D.5. However, the War Office in its infinite wisdom decided to cut funding for further aircraft development and Dunne left the Army Balloon Factory in 1909. He then set up the Blair Atholl Aeroplane Syndicate Ltd and completed the D.5, now powered by a 60 hp (44.7 kW) Green engine.

This American built Burgess-Dunne D.8 flying wing biplane was completed in 1914. The photograph shows the aircraft without any forward canvas wind shielding, suggesting it was undertaking a test flight. Some details such as undercarriage design vary slightly between D.8 aircraft. One of the aircraft built in the UK is understood to have briefly served with the Royal Flying Corps during the First World War, although records are vague.

The revised design accommodated the pilot and a passenger in tandem and Dunne first flew it on 11 March 1910, generating considerable public interest. Meanwhile, Dunne was putting the finishing touches to a monoplane adaptation of the D.5, not surprisingly called the D.6. This design had a wingspan of 36 ft (10.97 m), a wing area of 230 ft^2 (21.36 m^2), a length 21 ft (6.4 m) and was powered by a 60 hp (44.8 kW) Green engine driving a single propeller. Trials were undertaken at Sheppey and D.6 was followed by the very similar, but slightly more compact D.7 powered by a 70 hp (52.2 kW) Gnome engine, which flew in 1912.

However, the monoplanes failed to compete with the original design and Dunne now concentrated on developing a more refined version of his tailless biplane called the D.8, which would prove to be his most successful model. Powered by an 80 hp (59.7 kW) Gnome engine with accommodation for two, the War Office ordered a pair of these aircraft on 19 March 1913. Information about the D.8 had also spread across the Atlantic and caught the attention of Starling Burgess, who worked under contract for the Wright Brothers. Subsequently, Burgess travelled to England to meet Dunne in September 1903 and they soon struck a deal that would allow Burgess to manufacture the D.8 under licence at Marblehead, Massachusetts, with the provision that he could undertake modifications and improvements as necessary.

Burgess, saw the potential for adaptation as a floatplane and the first of these new Burgess–Dunne aircraft would fly on 28 January 1914, powered by a 100 hp (74.6 kW) Curtiss OXX V-8 engine. However, this test flight ran into trouble and the aircraft was damaged, but a modest re-build followed and Clifford L. Webster made the first successful flight on 4 March 1914,

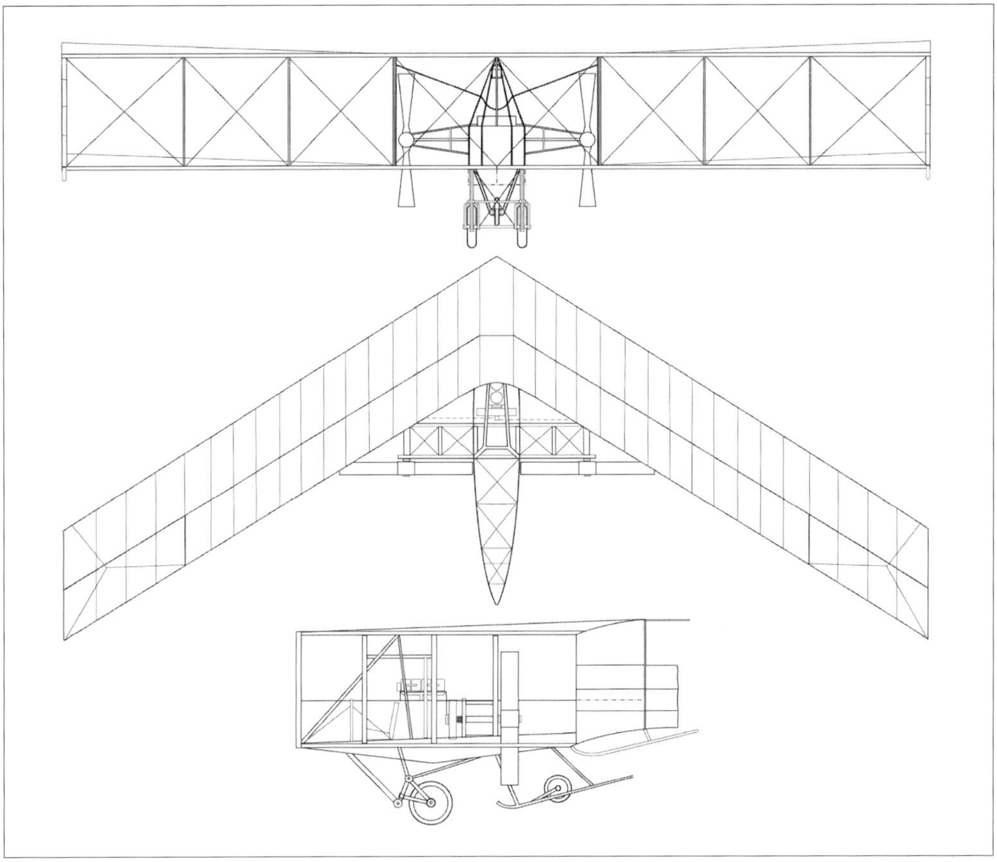

3 view drawing of a Dunne D.5 Flying Wing Biplane from 1910.

The second Burgess-Dunne BD-5 floatplane purchased by the US Navy (serial AH-10) above Pensacola.

John Dunne seated at the controls of his D.5 at Eastchurch, Kent in June 1910.

A Burgess-Dunne BD-6 beached at Pensacola. (*US Navy Photo*)

demonstrating good stability and handling. This immediately led to orders from the US and Canadian military and the first of the Burgess–Dunne production aircraft now called the BD-5 was delivered to the US Navy in October 1914. This modified floatplane carried a crew of two and was fitted with a 90 hp (67.2 kW) Curtiss engine. It received the official serial AH-7.

The aircraft purchased by the US Army, featured a conventional undercarriage, was powered by a 120 hp (89.6 kW) Salmson engine and was formally accepted on 30 December 1914. In early 1915, it was fitted with floats and utilised by coast artillery. Both of these aircraft would remain in service until 1916. The second of five Burgess–Dunne aircraft purchased by the US Navy (serial AH-10) would be flown by Lt Patrick Bellinger on 23 April 1915, who set a new US altitude record for a seaplane, reaching 10,000 ft (3,050 m) above Pensacola. It is also worth noting that the Burgess–Dunne seaplane purchased by the Canadian government became the country's first military aircraft.

In turn, Dunne would inspire Geoffrey Terence Roland Hill (1895–1955) to produce a series of advanced designs that were all flown and tested prior to the Second World War. His ultimate objective was to design a superior utility aircraft and a new type of agile fighter based on the flying wing, but this never came about in his lifetime. Hill was an engineer and a pilot who became preoccupied with the problem of stalling and this led him to design a small flying wing glider with a 31° leading edge sweep and all-moving wingtips called the Pterodactyl Mk 1. It was built in a shed at Hill's home in Surrey with some Air Ministry financial support over an 18-month period.

With a 49.5 ft (15 m) span, the aircraft was almost entirely constructed from wood and supported by a two main wheels, a small rear skid and stabilizing skids below the wings. The glider was finished with a fabric covering, stitched by Hill's wife and Hill flew it for the first time on 31 December 1924 at the Sussex Downs. By this time, he was planning to install a small Bristol Cherub engine rated at 33 hp (24.6 kW) and improve the undercarriage, which would have a wider track and a braked tail wheel. The modifications took some time to complete, but the Pterodactyl (adapted to a two-seater) completed a short powered flight at the Royal Aircraft Establishment (RAE) Farnborough during November 1925. Hill now required the support of an aircraft constructor to continue work on this promising design and in 1926 he joined Westland Aircraft at Yeovil. This was largely orchestrated by the Air Ministry, who were impressed with the Pterodactyl and Hill now headed the company's tailless aircraft department, assisted by Stanley A. R. Richards, who was appointed as his chief draughtsman.

In the following years, Hill was responsible for designing a small, relatively advanced flying wing known as the Pterodactyl Mk 1A, 1B and 1C. This aircraft (J9251) was powered by a 36 hp (26.8 kW) Cherub engine, driving a two-blade propeller. This was deemed inadequate and the revised aircraft called the Mk 1B was fitted with an 82 hp (61 kW) Armstrong Siddeley Genet five-cylinder radial engine. The modifications to this aircraft continued and it was re-designated again as the Mk 1C after changes to the undercarriage and rudders. The aircraft was flown by Westland and then transferred to RAE Farnborough, making its last flight in July 1930. It is believed that the Mk 1C was broken up sometime after this. Hill also proposed the Pterodactyl Mk II and Mk III prototypes, but these designs were never built. However, he was encouraged by Westland's senior management to develop a Pterodactyl with commercial applications and this resulted in the Mk IV.

Mainly built from plywood and ash, the Mk IV featured a short enclosed cockpit with accommodation for the pilot, two passengers and their luggage. The aircraft was powered by rear mounted 120 hp (89.4 kW) de Havilland Gipsy III air-cooled four-cylinder engine driving a two-blade propeller in a pusher configuration. The wing was based on an RAF 34 aerofoil section and rather unusually,

Underside view of the Pterodactyl Mk 1 (J8067) flown by Geoffrey Hill during a test flight in 1925. (*Westland*)

The Pterodactyl Mk 1 on display at Hendon on 3 July 1926. It led a display of new aircraft types under test by the RAE.

Pterodactyl Mk 1C in flight with its revised tandem wheel undercarriage and underwing skids. (*Westland*)

The Pterodactyl Mk 1C piloted by Harald Penrose is readied for a test flight in June 1930. (*Westland*)

The Pterodactyl Mk IV in flight. (*Westland*)

there was provision for a small amount of variable geometry, making it possible to shift the centre of gravity to compensate for different loads. Hill later took out a UK patent on this feature. Control of the aircraft was achieved using wingtip rudders and elevons. The aircraft's undercarriage followed earlier layouts, with two tandem wheels below the fuselage and skids beneath the wings.

Both main wheels were supported by a single pneumatic leg, with the front wheel being steerable and the rear fitted with a brake. The Mk IV was flown for first time in June 1931 by Harald Penrose OBE (1904–1996), who had just been appointed as Westland's chief test pilot. He reported that the aircraft was superior in most respects to the Mk 1C. Issued with the serial K1947, the Mk IV was displayed at Hendon that same year. However, despite a promising start, the Mk IV suffered from engine overheating problems and it was decidedly underpowered. The situation was probably rectifiable, but these were economically challenging times and Westland abandoned plans to pursue further development of the Mk IV. As a consequence, the Mk IV continued to appear at air shows, painted in various unusual schemes and was finally decommissioned in autumn 1938.

When the Mk IV programme was cancelled, Hill turned his attention to the possibility of building a two-seat fighter version of the Pterodactyl, which was assigned Air Ministry Specification F3/32. Not surprisingly, this design was known as the Mk V and construction began in 1932. Duralumin and steel were used for most of the fuselage and main wing, providing increased strength. Control surfaces were similar to those used on the previous aircraft and Hill decided to add short unswept lower wings for strengthening purposes, making the Mk V a sesquiplane. The undercarriage used tandem wheels located beneath the centre of the fuselage and skids below each lower wingtip with small trailing wheels. The Mk V was powered by an experimental and rather troublesome Rolls-Royce water-cooled, supercharged 600 hp (447 kW) Goshawk 1 engine, mounted in a forward position driving a wooden two-blade tractor propeller. This provided a maximum speed in level flight of about 190 mph (306 kph) and a service ceiling of 30,000 ft (9,144 m). Empty, the Mk V weighed 3,534 lb (1,602 kg) and fully loaded; it was about 5,100 lb (2313 kg). The wingspan was 46.66 ft (14.2 m), with a wing area 396 ft^2, (36.78 m^2) and the overall length was 20.5 ft (6.24 m). As a fighter, the aircraft would be equipped with two forward firing (synchronised) .303 in (7.69 mm) Vickers machine guns and a .303 (7.69 mm) Lewis machine gun in the rear cockpit. The Mk V would also be capable of carrying a small bomb load.

The prototype was ready for taxiing trials in 1933 and during flight tests undertaken by Penrose in 1934, the performance was said to be comparable to a Hawker Demon. Longitudinal stability was superior to earlier Pterodactyls, but the Mk V failed to win support for further development and the project was abandoned in 1935, with the Mk V being broken up for scrap in 1937. Although disappointed, Hill continued to work on the Pterodactyl design, producing further tailless aircraft concepts that included the Mk VI fighter with a pusher propeller, a larger Mk VII flying boat and a multi-engined Mk VIII passenger plane. Nevertheless, the Westland programme had effectively come to an end with the Mk V's cancellation.

The Pterodactyl Mk V piloted by Harald Penrose during a test flight. (*Westland*)

Pterodactyl Mk V with access panels removed to show the Rolls Royce Goshawk engine. Only 20 of these were built by RR at Derby. (*Westland*)

The Pterodactyl Mk V flown by Harald Penrose after several modifications. The Mk V was a fighter variant, developed to meet Specification F.3/32. A sesquiplane in configuration, with a small, unswept lower wing, the aircraft was fitted with two forward firing machine guns and carried a rear gunner who enjoyed a completely unrestricted view. (*Westland*)

Pterodactyl Mk V in military configuration showing its sleek engine exhaust system. (*Westland*)

The Pterodactyl Bombers

In 1939, Professor Geoffrey Hill was recruited by the Air Ministry to oversee various specialised military research projects and his first assignment involved a programme to assess methods of allowing an aircraft to cut enemy barrage balloons cables without stalling. In addition to his consultative work, Hill became the chief scientific liaison officer between the British and Canadian governments in 1942. At the beginning of this period, he started a private design project for an advanced tailless bomber with initial plans being completed on the 22 July 1942.

His first proposal was a boomerang shaped flying wing, with a straight central leading edge and the outer wing sections swept (at the leading edge) by approximately 44°. The wingspan was 140 ft (42.6 m) with a wing area of 3,350 ft^2 (311 m^2) and the overall length appears to have been about 50 ft (15.24 m). The wing would have a central depth of 7.5 ft (2.28 m), making a pressurised crew compartment of adequate size possible. Quoted weight is 85,000 lb (38,555 kg), which was presumably an all-up estimate.

Hill envisaged six forward positioned piston engines mounted in side-by-side pairs, driving three rear mounted pusher configuration contra-rotating propeller assemblies via lengthy drive shafts. The use of turbojets was also considered and Hill believed this design could easily be modified when jet propulsion became a practical proposition. Estimates of performance are not quoted in any available documentation.

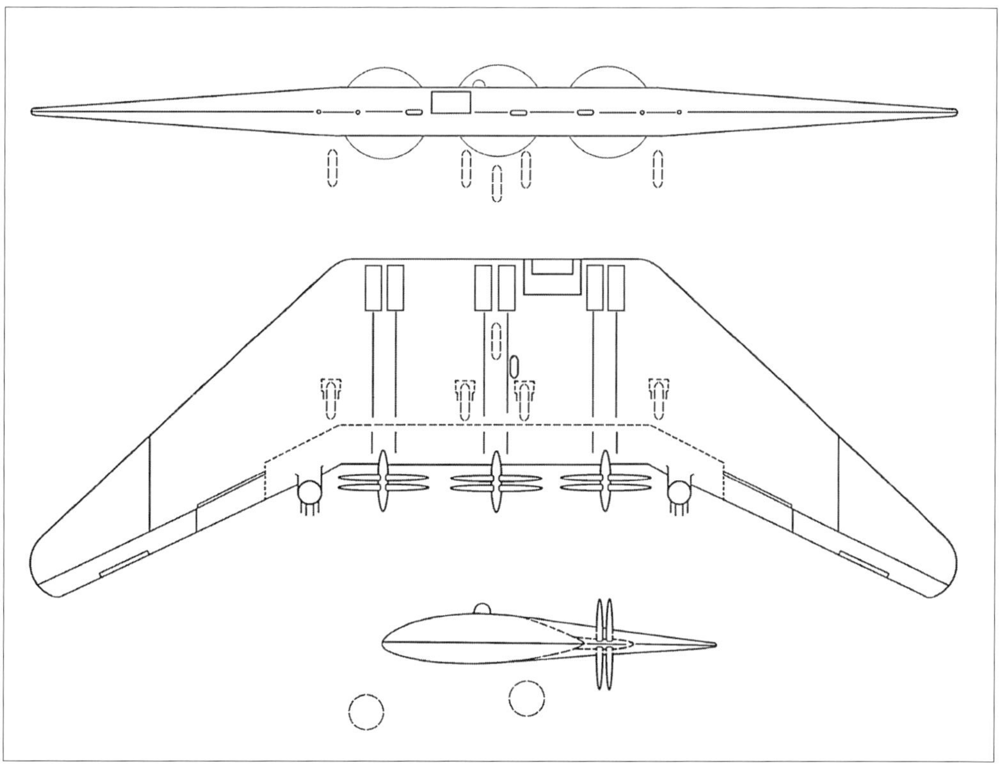

A proposed six engined, three contra-prop Pterodactyl flying wing bomber, with an estimated weight of 85,000 lb (38,555kg).

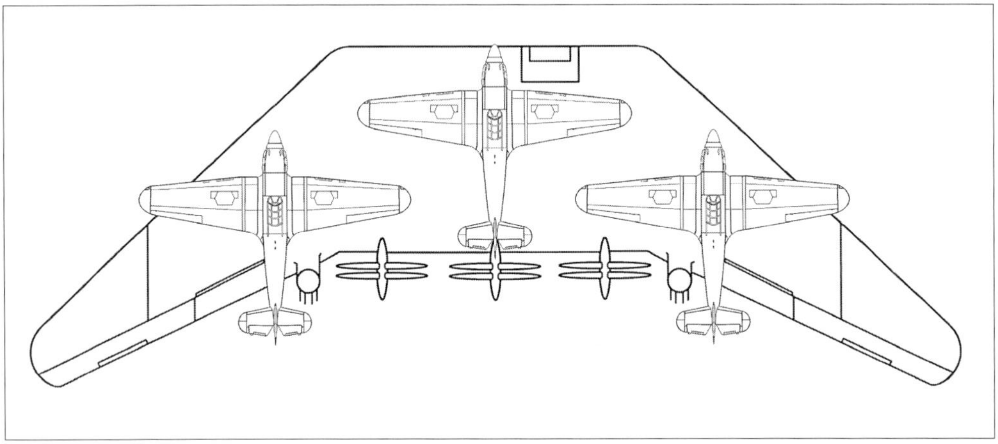

Unquestionably the most unusual version of the six engined Pterodactyl flying wing bomber was a carrier for up to three fighters mounted on pylons above the wing. Intended for special long-range operations, the fighters would be on their own after separation, having to reach a suitable landing zone after their mission had been completed.

The Pterodactyl bomber would be supported on a rather unusual fully retractable undercarriage comprising of four large main wheels, positioned across the underside of the wing at the centre of gravity and a single nose wheel. During take-offs and landings, the pilot would sit in a capsule located towards the centre of the aircraft, which Hill called the 'Dustbin.' It would be extended below the wing to afford the pilot a better view of the runway and the front wheel would be used as a positioning aid. For normal flight, the pilot would sit behind a windshield in the leading edge of the wing, positioned slightly starboard of centre. Hill also planned to seat the navigator alongside the pilot at the front of the aircraft, with extra windows allowing downward observation. The bomber would be equipped with four (forward and rearward facing) remote controlled machine gun turrets. Details of bomb carriage are unknown, although it is possible that Hill envisaged two separate bays. There were no vertical fins with control surfaces, although in addition to elevons and flaps, Hill considered ideas such as movable wing tips.

A proposed development of this design was an aircraft carrier, able to transport up to three piston-engined fighters (probably Spitfires or Hurricanes) above the wing. This would make it possible to operate at ranges much greater than might normally be available. Presumably the fighters would return to base under their own power, or the pilots would bail out at a pre-arranged location? There was also to be a smaller version of the Pterodactyl bomber with a wingspan of approximately 100 ft (30.4 m) and a length of about 38 ft (11.5 m). It would have an anticipated weight of approximately 45,000 lb (20,411 kg). This design differed in having four separate unspecified piston engines, each driving a tail-mounted propeller. The fully retractable undercarriage would be slightly simpler than the larger bomber, using three separate main wheels and a single nose wheel. It appears that Professor Hill did not consider the retractable pilot's capsule necessary for this aircraft. Rear facing remote controlled machine gun turrets were mounted outboard of the propellers on each trailing edge and a single forward firing gun turret was positioned on the leading edge, to the port side of centre. The control surfaces appear similar to the larger design.

These concepts were undoubtedly submitted for official consideration, but went no further as they were probably viewed as too unconventional. Professor Hill continued to work on the

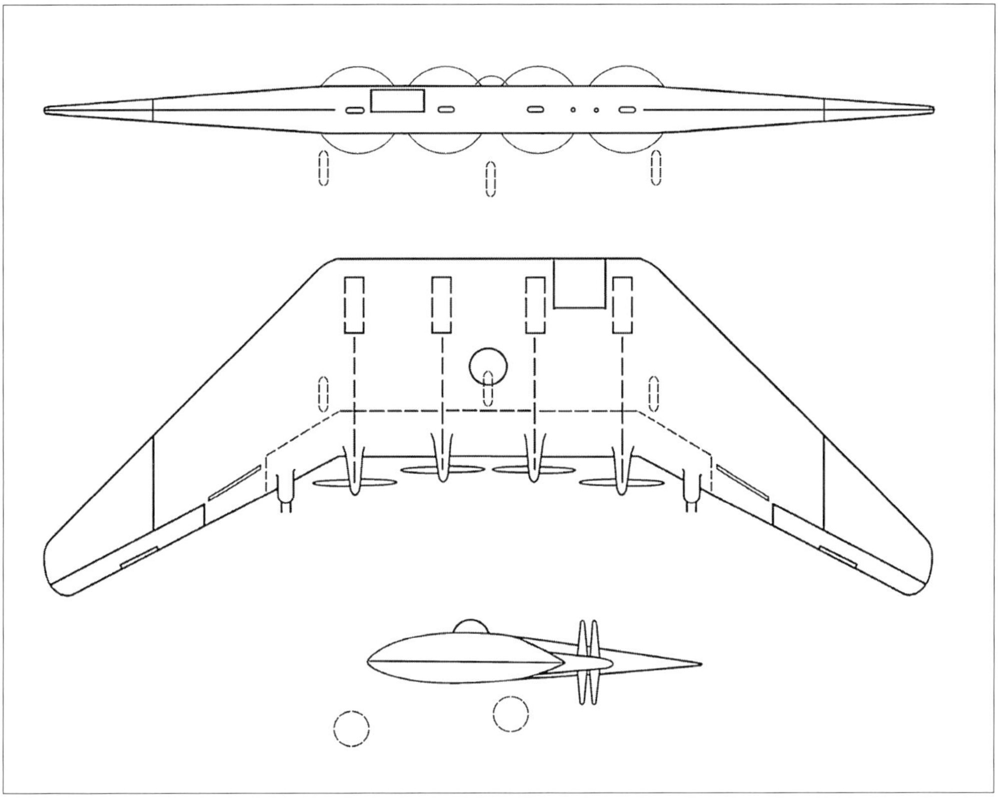

Professor Hill's wartime proposal for a four engined, propeller driven flying wing Pterodactyl Bomber weighing 45,000 lb (20,411kg).

design, which he now envisaged as a large transatlantic airliner suitable for post-war operations. This proposal was known as the Pterodactyl Mk VIII and Hill managed to gain the interest of Short Brothers in Belfast. Powered by five Rolls-Royce Griffon engines driving pusher propellers, the airliner was to have a cockpit section protruding from the central leading edge. Nothing came of this project.

However, during the Second World War, when Hill was based in Canada and working as Britain's scientific liaison officer, the National Research Council (NRC) expressed an interest in building a small research glider based on his experience with the Pterodactyl series. This led to tests of several wind tunnel models, including a 1/10 scale model being tested by the US National Advisory Committee for Aeronautics (NACA—the forerunner of NASA) at the Langley free-flight tunnel. A full-sized flying wing mainly built from wood was completed in 1945. In appearance, the glider was a typical Hill design, with a straight central leading edge and outboard wing sections swept back at 43°. The glider was fitted with two separate side-by-side cockpits, wingtip rudders and a retractable tricycle undercarriage. Painted in bright yellow, the glider was first flown in 1946 and the RCAF undertook tests using a Dakota tow plane at Namao, Edmonton and Arnprior, Ontario. Often referred to as the NRC Pterodactyl, the design was considered a success and trials continued until 1950, when the project ended.

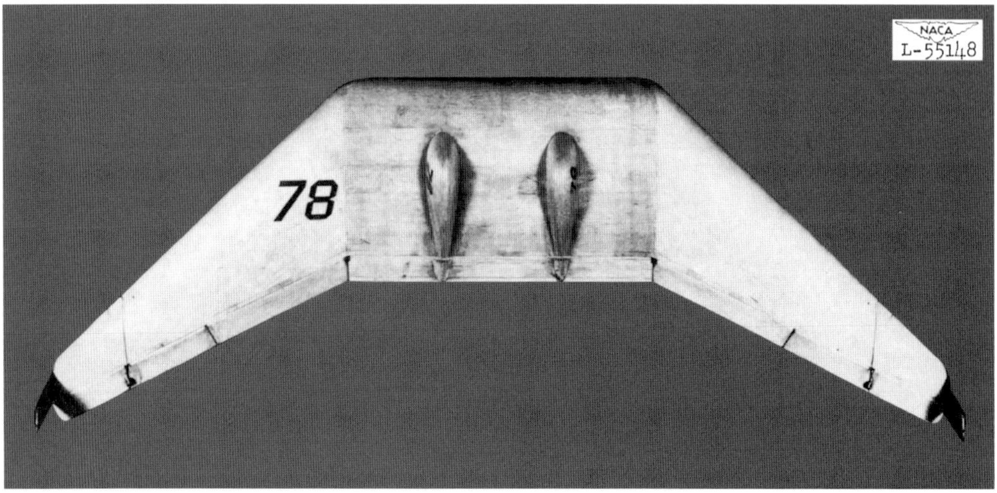

A 1/10 scale model of the Canadian National Research Council glider designed by Geoffrey Hill and wind tunnel tested by NACA at Langley. (*NASA/Bill Rose*)

The GAL Gliders

In late 1942, the Director of Scientific Research decided to form the Tailless Aircraft Advisory Committee (TAAC) to oversee development of new designs. The Germans were known to be interested in developing tailless military aircraft and considerable research was taking place in America. Once established, the TAAC invited a number of aircraft contractors to submit plans for tailless aircraft that could be used for research purposes. Many companies that included de Havilland, Saunders Roe, Hawker and Fairey declined to take part, leaving General Aircraft Ltd (GAL) and Armstrong Whitworth as participants, along with Handley Page, who were already preparing to fly an experimental aircraft called the Manx.

Designers at GAL worked under the direction of Frederick Francis Crocombe (1901–1987), with input from Professor Geoffrey Hill. The company had been interested in developing tailless aircraft since the mid-1930s and their proposals were submitted to the TAAC. Soon after this, a series of GAL swept-wing prototypes received official approval for construction. They would be used to explore low-speed handling characteristics and initially, it was planned to build six prototypes, but this was quickly reduced to four. Two would be gliders designated GAL.56 and the other two were powered versions referred to as GAL.57, which would use single Lycoming R-680-13 radial engines in a pusher configuration.

It was essential that construction was cost effective, easily achieved and common parts were used wherever possible. This was necessary to avoid diverting too many resources away from war production. For the same reason, it was also decided to use one type of centre section with standardised attachment points for wing anchorage. However, it soon became apparent that there would be problems interchanging wings with different configurations on a universal body and a decision was taken to abandon the powered versions and build four different gliders, taking the simplest route to keep the project on course. It was also agreed that GAL test pilots and observers would conduct most of the initial test flights. Refinement and construction was then

The third GAL.56 glider "Maximum V" (TS513), which made its maiden flight on 30 May 1947 at Lasham.

passed to an engineering team at the Hanworth factory, Feltham, Middlesex, which was headed by a Czech engineer called Otto Wels (no connection to the pre-war German politician), who specialised in flight control systems.

Each central section utilised a tubular steel framework covered in plywood and the wings were mainly of wooden construction, supported by a single spar. Off-the-shelf landing gear was used for the GAL.56, with the main wheels being Dowty units designed for the Lysander and the tail wheel normally used on a Bisley. The serials TS507, TS510, TS513 and TS515 were allocated on 21 October 1944, although it was finally decided not to proceed with construction of TS515. Each GAL.56 accommodated a pilot and observer in the centre section, with the main difference between these models being the wing design. Fins with rudders were fitted to the wingtips and it was eventually decided to add anti-spin parachutes in wingtip containers for emergency use. No overall name was assigned to the glider project, but the models were referred to by their wing configuration.

The first to be completed during autumn 1944 was the GAL.56/01 (TS507) 'Medium V' which identified its 28.4° leading edge sweep. An RAF-34 aerofoil section was used and it had a modified contour to enhance the elevon performance. The wingspan was 45.33 ft (13.8 m), length was 19 ft (5.79 m) and it was 8.75 ft (2.66 m) high. The aircraft undertook taxiing trials at Aldermaston during November 1944 and made its first flight on 17 January 1945 at RAF Dunholm Lodge in Lincolnshire. This location had been assigned to GAL as a facility to store Hamilcar heavy gliders and it was chosen for testing because the GAL.56 was a secret project and there was less chance of the trials being observed by anyone.

For the flight at Dunholm Lodge, an Armstrong Whitley V bomber was used to tow the glider into the air and test pilot Robert Kronfeld was at the GAL.56's controls. He reported that the aircraft handled fairly well except in extreme conditions and after making 48 flights at Dunholme Lodge, TS507 was transferred to RAE Farnborough in June 1945. However, when the RAE's chief test pilot Captain (RN) Eric Melrose 'Winkle' Brown (1919–2016) flew the GAL.56, he was far from impressed with it, describing it as very difficult to control and noted that he, 'could not relax for a second, beginning right away with takeoff.'

The second aircraft known as GAL56/04 (TS510) was designated 'Medium U'. It differed from the first aircraft in having a parallel chord centre section and swept outer leading edge of 28.4°.

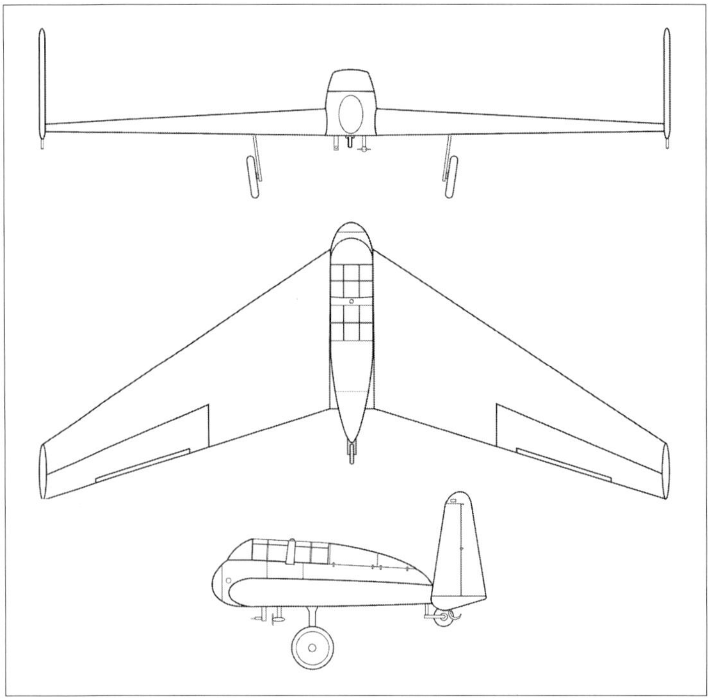

General arrangement of the GAL.56 (TS507) Medium V glider, with a 28.4° leading edge sweep.

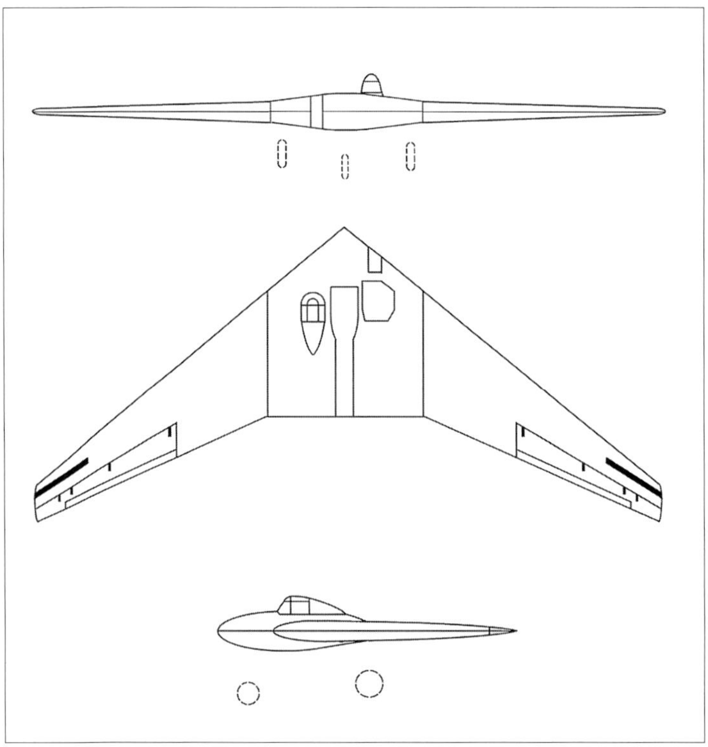

The final and most advanced glider in the GAL experimental series was the GAL.61 (TS515). It was completed in 1948 and shown at the SBAC Air Show at Radlett during the same year. It was then prepared for testing at Lasham, but never flown.

The GAL.56 "Medium U" (TS510) glider piloted by Flight Lieutenant Robert Kronfeld, after release from a Halifax tow aircraft.

The wingspan was 51 ft (15.54 m), height 21 ft (6.4 m) and the length 10 ft (3 m). Medium U had been given the reference TS510D and it flew for the first time on 27 February 1946 at Aldermaston and was then moved to Lasham. It was damaged in an accident during 1949 and subsequently scrapped. The third GAL.56/03 (TS513) was called 'Maximum V' and featured a 36.4° sweep. It flew for the first time on 30 May 1947 at Lasham. This version of the glider featured additional nose flaps and only the front or rear set could be used during a flight. This was set beforehand and it was also possible to adjust the wing dihedral on the ground. The wingspan of 'Maximum V' was 45.33 ft (13.8 m), with a length 23.5 ft (7.16 m) and a height of 9 ft (2.74 m) high.

All three gliders were exhibited at the September 1947 SBAC show held at Radlett Aerodrome and the second GAL.56 'Medium U' was demonstrated by Robert Kronfeld (1904–1948), after a Halifax towed it into the air. But the programme was dealt a severe blow on 12 February 1948 when Kronfeld was killed while testing GAL56/01 (TS507). Kronfeld had left Lasham Airfield with his observer Barry McGowan and they were towed behind a Halifax until reaching 16,000 ft (4,876 m) where separation took place. The purpose of the flight was to carry out stall tests, but having made a normal recovery from his first stall the glider entered a steep dive and became inverted. Kronfeld told McGowan that he had lost control of the glider and his observer immediately bailed out. The altitude was about 1,000 ft (300 m) and his parachute opened at about 100 ft (30 m) making it a close call. Regrettably, Kronfeld stayed in the aircraft until it hit the ground.

A significantly more advanced GAL experimental glider was nearing completion at this time, called the GAL.61. It was re-assigned the original serial TS515 that was intended for use with a fourth GAL.56 prototype. GAL.61 featured a raised cockpit in the centre of the aircraft, with a prone position for an observer within the wing. The wing had the same 36.4° leading edge sweep as the GAL.56 Maximum V and in overall appearance, it loosely resembled the powered Northrop N-1M flying wing.

GAL.61 had a wingspan of 51.9 ft (15.8 m), an overall length of 24.66 ft (7.5 m) and a gross weight of approximately 5,174 lb (2,346 kg). A fully retractable undercarriage was fitted as standard equipment and the GAL.61 was a true flying wing in all respects. There were no vertical stabilisers and the aircraft used elevons and wingtip drag rudders for control. GAL.61 was completed by mid-1948 and displayed at the 1948 SBAC Air Show at Radlett. It was then returned to Lasham for testing, but approval to begin test flights was never granted and the project was finally cancelled in mid-1949. Although it was the most interesting of the four gliders, GAL.61 was abandoned and is thought to have been broken up for scrap in 1950.

Baynes BAT

After leaving school, Leslie Everett Baynes (1902–1989) became immediately involved with the aviation industry. He worked for the Aircraft Engineering Company in Hendon, North London, became a designer for Shorts at Rochester and then devised the very successful Scud 1 light sailplane. This led him into a manufacturing partnership with F. D. Abbot, forming the company Abbot–Baynes Sailplanes Ltd of Farnham, Surrey. In 1935, a powered version of the Scud was built to meet a request made by Sir John Carden who ran a company developing armoured vehicles. As a consequence of this order, a new partnership was formed, called Carden–Baynes Aircraft, with a factory located at Heston, Middlesex where powered aircraft were manufactured.

Baynes and Carden began producing a sailplane (which was essentially a Scud 3) equipped with a small retractable 249 cc Villiers engine. The unit was mounted above the aircraft in a pusher configuration and a small tank carried enough fuel to run the engine for about 30 minutes. At the start of the Second World War, Baynes had become a scientific advisor to the Alan Muntz Company in Heston and he took responsibility for organising their aircraft division. At this time there were no suitable transport aircraft and the army was looking for ways to airlift military cargo and equipment to operational areas.

In 1941, Baynes designed an unpowered 'Carrier Wing' capable of transporting a light tank to a combat zone, which was generally referred to as the Baynes Aerial Tank (BAT). Taking the form of a towed glider, it would transport a light armoured vehicle, which was expected to be the Armstrong Whitworth Mk VII Light Tank developed in 1938 and later known as the Tetrarch. This vehicle had a combat weight of 16,800 lb (7.62 Metric tons) and carried a crew of three. A similar American tank with almost the same weight was developed in 1941 and a number eventually entered British service (as the M22 Locust). Baynes may have also considered carrying this vehicle. The swept wing would have a 100 ft (30 m) span with vertical stabilisers at the wingtips. It was proposed that just before landing, the tank's engine would be started, allowing it to go into action immediately after touchdown.

The Baynes BAT received enthusiastic official support and it was decided to build a one-third-scale, proof-of-concept tailless manned glider, with a wingspan of 33 ft 4 inches (10 m) and using a single main spar. A small cockpit accommodated the pilot and the undercarriage was a lower centrally located skid and wingtip skids. A wheeled trolley was used for ground handling and take-offs.

A nacelle replaced the area beneath the glider where the tank would be carried. On the full sized version, the wing would be released at the moment of touchdown and drawn away from the tank. A contract was issued to Slingsby Sailplanes at Kirkbymoorside for the manufacture of

Artwork showing the Baynes BAT during a test flight.

a prototype. Built almost entirely from wood, the glider was completed during spring 1943 and issued with the serial RA809. The first test flight took place in the summer of 1943 at Airborne Forces Experimental Establishment (AFEE), Sherburn-in-Elmet, Yorkshire.

The Baynes BAT was towed into the air behind an Avro Tutor, with Robert Kronfeld at the controls. Kronfeld later reported that, 'In spite of its unorthodox design the aircraft handles similarly to other light gliders with very light and responsive controls and is safe to be flown by service pilots in all normal attitudes of flight'.

Captain Eric Brown was far less enthusiastic about the Baynes BAT when he tested it, finding the controls disappointing. Why this difference of opinion arose is hard to say, but the tests were still judged successful. Unfortunately, there were ongoing problems concerning tank suitability and it had been realised that landing faster than the tank's maximum speed was a serious issue. This led to the idea of fitting an undercarriage to the BAT, but it was considered over-complex and the Baynes BAT was then moved onto the back burner.

At the same time, a heavy glider was being developed by General Aircraft called the GAL.49 Hamilcar, which had been designed from the outset to carry a substantial payload that included a Tetrarch or Locus light tank. While the Hamilcar eventually entered service, the Baynes BAT never progressed to a full-sized carrier wing glider. It was then transferred to the Royal Aircraft Establishment at Farnborough, who made good use of the glider for stability tests that continued after the war. In late 1946, the Baynes BAT was formally disposed of as surplus equipment, being purchased by British Light Aircars of Redhill, Surrey.

It seems that the BAT was then moved to Croydon Airport, where it was last seen behind a hangar in 1958, apparently in poor condition. Soon after this, the glider was scrapped. Baynes,

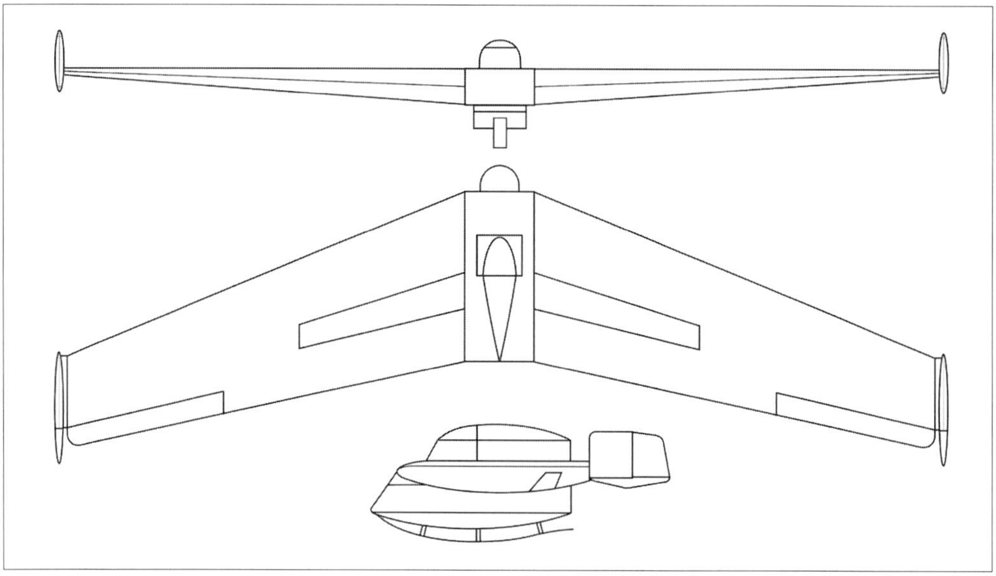

3 view drawing of the Baynes BAT.

known to his friends and family as 'Baron' worked on many other interesting wartime projects that included an unusual tilt-rotor aircraft design and he was responsible for design work on converting Lancasters to carry the Barnes Wallis bouncing bomb used to breach several dams in the Ruhr Valley during May 1943.

Handley Page Manx

In the late 1930s, Dr Gustav Victor Lachmann (1896–1966) who headed the Design Office at Handley Page Aircraft turned his attention towards the possibility of improving aircraft performance by a significant reduction in drag. He favoured the flying wing design and the company chairman Frederick Handley Page (1885–1962) fully supported this research and agreed to authorise the construction of a small experimental aircraft. The initial assembly was contracted out to Dart Aircraft of Dunstable, Bedfordshire, a small specialist company, building gliders and replica light aircraft. Work proceeded well and the airframe was returned to Handley Page at Radlett, Hertfordshire, during September 1939, for completion. But the aircraft was found to be substantially overweight and there were serious problems with the type of glue used during assembly. As a consequence, the aircraft underwent a detailed programme of modifications, including a re-build of the main spar. It is likely that this had some bearing on the fact that Dart Aircraft ceased trading at the end of 1939.

Constructed mostly from wood, this aircraft received the semi-official name Manx (after the tailless cat). It has been claimed that the company designation HP.75 may not have been applied until 1945, although the official serial H-0222 was issued at an early stage in this project. The Manx was fitted with two rear-mounted de Havilland Gipsy Major II 4-cylinder piston engines, each rated at 140 hp (104 kW) and fitted with two blade propellers acting as pushers.

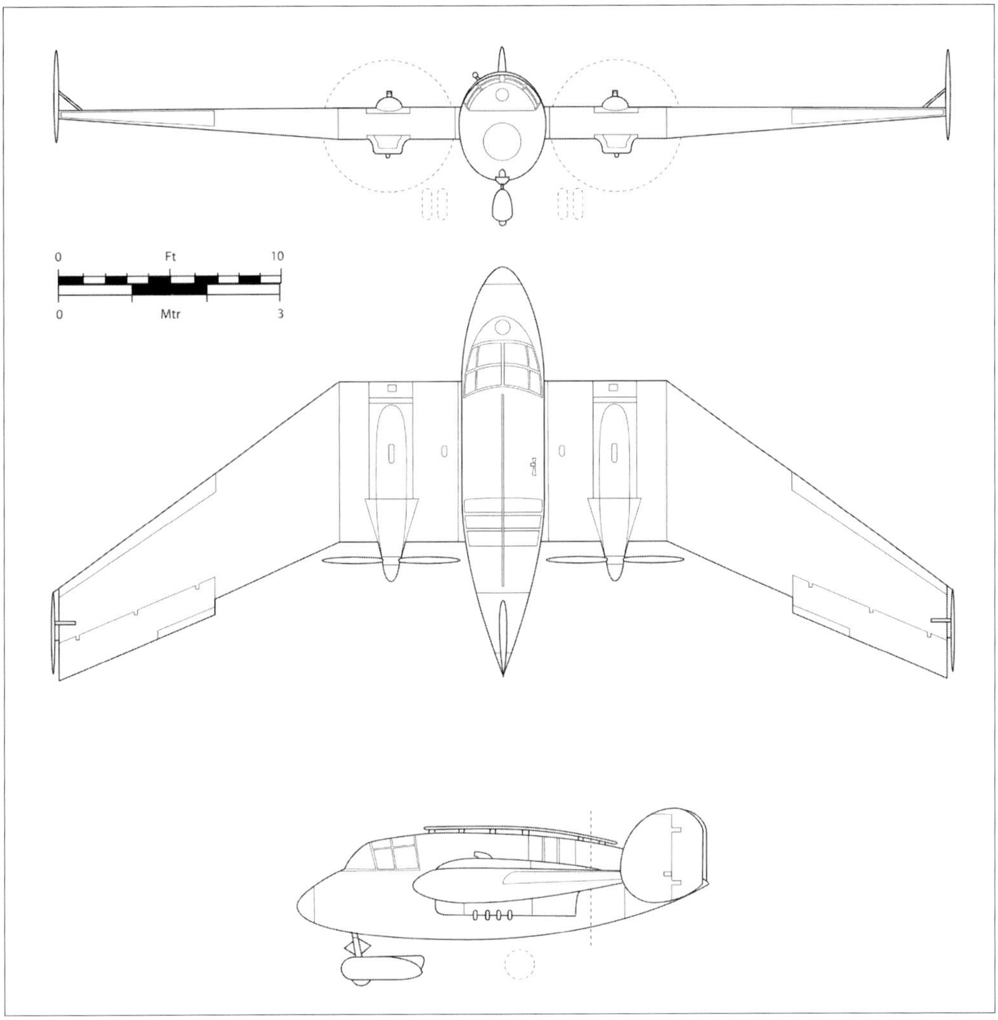

General arrangement of the tailless HP.75 Manx experimental aircraft. (*Chris Gibson*)

The overall wingspan was 39.83 ft (12.1 m), with a wing area of 245 ft^2 (22.76 m^2), a length of 18.25 ft (5.5 m) and empty weight of 3,000 lb (1,360 kg).

Maximum take-off weight was estimated at 4,000 lb (1,814 kg) allowing a maximum speed of approximately 146 mph (234 kph) and a service ceiling of about 10–12,000 ft (3,000–3,650 m).

The central section of the wing where the engines were housed on either side of the cockpit was straight and the outer leading edge section of the wing was swept back by 35° and this part of the wing accommodated elevons and leading edge slots. An upright fin and rudder was attached to each wingtip and an additional fin was located on the upper rear of the fuselage to enhance directional stability.

The distinctive fuselage section accommodated a two-man crew with the flight observer sitting directly behind the pilot and facing rearward. The Manx was equipped with a tricycle under-carriage, with the rear wheels able to retract, but the nose wheel fixed. This was normally fitted

The HP.75 Manx at Radlett in September 1942, prior to taxiing trials.

with a streamlined fairing to reduce drag. Taxiing trials began at Radlett in late 1940, although tests became long and drawn out, with more pressing wartime work often taking priority.

The company's senior test pilot James Richard Talbot (1909–1945) was now involved with these trials, along with Edgar Alexander 'Ginger' Wright (1914–1945) who was a Handley Page test pilot that headed the Observer's Office. On 12 September 1942, during high speed taxiing trials, the Manx became momentarily airborne, achieving a height of about 12 ft (3.65 m), but on touchdown, it was evident that the nose wheel had been damaged and several modifications were made.

Further attempts to fly the Manx followed and it finally became airborne on 11 June 1943, with Talbot at the controls, although the cockpit canopy became detaching soon after take-off and the flight was immediately terminated. As trials continued on an intermittent basis, Robert Kronfeld was invited to test fly the Manx. He was now an RAF squadron leader, still primarily assigned to GAL as the company's senior test pilot. Kronfeld made at least two flights in the Manx and reported that the aircraft handled well in comparison to other tailless designs he had flown. By late 1945, the Manx had logged up 30 test flights lasting for a total of around 17 hours.

Many of the missions had been flown by Talbot and Wright, but both were killed on 3 December 1945 when a prototype Hermes 1 airliner they were flying crashed shortly after leaving Radlett Aerodrome. This loss had a direct impact on the Manx programme, which saw one more test flight in April 1946 and then, the aircraft was placed in storage. The Manx was an interesting design, which was briefly considered for development as a twin-engined transport aircraft, or possibly a light bomber, with a canard configuration. Nothing came of this and the Manx remained in storage until 1952, when it was broken up for scrap.

Mainly built from wood and powered by two rear-mounted de Havilland Gipsy Major II 4-cylinder piston engines, the experimental HP.75 was given the semi-official name Manx (after the tailless cat).

The HP.75 Manx in flight.

Napier Tailless Fighter Proposal

This intriguing design for an advanced tailless fighter was probably produced towards the end of the Second World War, with details being sparingly disclosed in July 1946. Apparently, the concept originated at Napier's Engine Installation Development Establishment at Luton Municipal Airport, although Napier became a subsidiary of the English Electric Company in 1942, so it seems possible that they received some assistance from the parent company's aircraft division. The single seat fighter was designed around an advanced 24-cylinder, liquid cooled supercharged engine, which appears to have been the ultimate development of the Napier Sabre series. Assigned the reference E-122, it is not clear if a prototype engine was actually built and tested. This would have occupied a central position in the airframe, with a shaft coupling to a forward set of contra-rotating propellers. A large forward annular radiator would occupy the area directly behind this unit.

With the engine expected to produce a maximum output of around 3,350 hp (2,498 kW); this would in theory allow a top speed approaching 500 mph (800 kph). The aircraft would be equipped with four wing-mounted cannon and supported on a fully retractable undercarriage. Virtually no other details of this project are known, although it has been suggested that the fighter was intended for carrier use. However, by 1946, the era of propeller driven combat aircraft was drawing to an end and Napier's tailless fighter design was filed away and completely forgotten about.

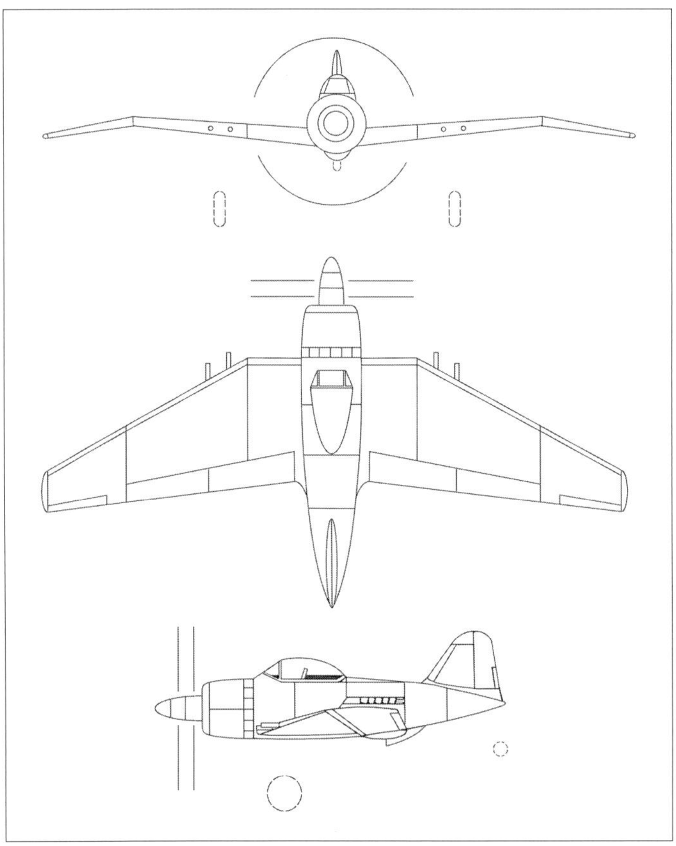

Anticipated appearance of the Napier tailless fighter.

Dunne D.5
Crew: 1
Wingspan: 46 ft (14.02 m)
Sweep (leading edge): 58°
Wing area: 527ft^2 (49 m^2)
Length: 20.37 ft (6.18 m)
Height: 11.5 ft (3.51 m)
Gross weight: 1,550lb (703 kg)
Powerplant: 1 × Green D4, 4-cylinder piston engine, rated at 60 hp (44.7 kW)
Maximum speed: 45 mph (72 kph)

Dunne D.8
Crew: 2
Wingspan: 46 ft (14.02 m)
Wing area: 545 ft^2 (50.6 m^2)
Length: 25.75 ft (7.85 m)
Empty weight: 1,400 lb (635 kg)
Gross weight: 1,900 lb (862 kg)
Powerplant: 1 × Gnome 7-cylinder rotary engine, rated at 80 hp (60 kW)
Maximum speed: 56 mph (90 kph)
Rate of climb: 500 ft/min (2.5 m/s)

Westland Pterodactyl Mk 1A
Crew: 2
Wingspan: 45.5 ft (13.8 m)
Wing area: 200 ft^2 (18.5 m^2)
Length: 17 ft (5.18 m)
Height: 6.66 ft (2 m)
Empty weight: 900 lb (408 kg)
Gross weight: 1,080 lb (490 kg)
Powerplant: Bristol Cherub engine rated at 33 hp (24.6 kW). 82 hp (61 kW) Armstrong Siddeley Genet five-cylinder radial engine
Maximum speed: 70 mph (112 kph)
Ceiling: N/A

Westland Pterodactyl Mk IV
Crew: 3
Wingspan: 44.33 ft (6.8 m)
Wing area: 259 ft^2 (24 m^2)
Length: 19.5 ft (5.94 m)
Height: 7.5 ft (2.2 m)
Empty weight: 1,320 lb (598 kg)
Gross weight: 2,100 lb (952 kg)
Powerplant: de Havilland Gipsy III 120 hp (89.4 kW) air-cooled four-cylinder engine driving a two blade propeller in a pusher configuration
Maximum speed: 113 mph (182 kph)
Rate of climb: 750 ft/min (228 m/min)
Landing speed: 54 mph (86 kph)
Ceiling: 15,000 ft (4,572 m)

Westland Pterodactyl Mk V
Crew: 2
Wingspan: 46.33 ft (14.2 m)
Wing area: 369 ft^2 (34 m^2)
Length: 11.66 ft (3.55 m)
Height: 11.66 ft (3.55 m)
Empty weight: 3,535 lb (1,603 kg)
Gross weight: 5,100 lb (2,313 kg)
Powerplant: Rolls-Royce supercharged Goshawk 1 engine, rated at 600 hp (447 kW)
Maximum speed: 165 mph (190 mph)
Landing speed: 66 mph (106 kph)
Ceiling: 30,000 ft (9,144 m)

NRC Pterodactyl Glider
Crew: 2
Wingspan: 46.66 ft (14.22 m)
Sweep (leading edge): 43°
Length: 18 ft (5.48 m)
Height: N/A
Flying weight: 4,150 lb (1,882 kg)
Maximum speed: 140 mph (225 kph)
Landing speed: 60 mph (97 kph)
Ceiling: 10,000 ft (3,048 m)

Hill Pterodactyl Flying Wing Bomber (3 contraprop version)
Crew: 4-6?
Wingspan: 140 ft (42.6 m)
Sweep (outer leading edge): 44°
Wing area: 3,350 ft^2 (311 m^2)
Length: 50 ft (15.24 m)
Height: N/A
Empty weight: N/A
Gross weight: 85,000 lb (38,555 kg)
Powerplant: 6 × unspecified piston engines
Maximum speed: N/A
Ceiling: N/A
Range: N/A
Armament: Forward and rearward remote control machine gun turrets. Internal bomb load

GAL.56 'Medium V'
Crew: 2
Wingspan: 45.33 ft (13.8 m)
Sweep (leading edge): 28.4°
Wing area (net): 317ft^2 (29.45m^2)
Wing area (gross): 350 ft^2 (32.5 m^2)
Aerofoil section: RAF 34 Modified
Chord—root: 11.33 ft (3.45 m)
Chord—tip: 43.5in (1.1 m)
Dihedral—normal: 0.5 deg
Aspect ratio: 5.8

Length: 19 ft (5.79 m)
Height: 8.75 ft (2.66 m)
Flying weight (two crew + max ballast): 4,400 lb (1996 kg)
Stalling speed: 58 mph. E.A.S. (93.3 kph)
Maximum towing speed: 150 mph. E.A.S. (241 kph)

GAL.61
Crew: 2
Wingspan: 51.92 ft (15.8 m)
Sweep (leading edge): 36.4°
Length: 24.33 ft (7.5 m)
Flying weight: 5,174 lb (2348 kg)

Baynes BAT
Crew: 1
Wingspan: 33.33 ft (10.15 m)
Sweep (leading edge): 22°
Wing area: 160 ft^2 (14.86 m^2)
Aspect ratio: 7:1
Length: 11.33 ft (3.45 m)
Empty weight: 763 lb (346 kg)
Gross weight: 963 lb (437 kg)
Cruising Speed: 90 mph (145 kph)
Maximum speed: 120 mph (193 kph)
Stalling speed: 40 mph (64 kph)

HP.75 Manx
Crew: 2
Wingspan: 39.83 ft (12.1 m)
Wing area: 245 ft^2 (22.76 m^2)
Length: 18.25 ft (5.5 m)
Empty weight: 3,000 lb (1,360 kg)
Gross weight: 4,000 lb (1,814 kg)
Powerplant: 2 × de Havilland Gipsy Major II 4-cylinder in-line piston engines each rated at 140 hp (104 kW)
Maximum speed: 146 mph (234 kph)
Ceiling: 10–12,000 ft (3,000–3,650 m)

2

Jet Bomber Projects

While researching material for this book, I came across a surprisingly unusual article in an old copy of *Flight* magazine (13 May 1943). It outlined the future use of flying wings powered by gas turbines. It was written by (George) Geoffrey Smith MBE (1885–1951), who was not only a qualified engineer and an authority on jet engine development, but the editorial director of *Flight* magazine. What made this article stand out was the general limitation on wartime public discussion of advanced aeronautical concepts. This was a period of paranoia about giving away secrets and Smith actually served as a member of the Inter-Services Press Committee on Defence Notices, which decided what kind of military information could be released into the public domain. Designs of jet powered flying wings were at the cutting edge of aviation engineering during the Second World War, but it can only be concluded that Smith must have felt that he was talking about things that belonged some way in the future and presented no threat to national security.

There is certainly no question that Smith had his finger directly on the pulse of technical developments and this article outlined the numerous advantages of a flying wing, developed from work already undertaken by Dunne, Lippisch and Northrop. He mentioned a wingspan of 120 ft (36.5 m), a pressurised cabin and several different four engine propulsion layouts combining jets and propeller, but clearly favoured the turbojet, which he suggested would allow cruising at around 550 mph (885 kph) and an operational altitude of 40,000 ft (12.192 m). His proposal would utilise a tricycle undercarriage and the use of jet engines housed within the wing would considerably reduce the need for ground clearance.

While the article made various references to future transport and passenger applications, it remains hard to visualize these designs as being primarily considered for that purpose and it is almost as if Smith had more than just an inkling of the need for an entirely new type of high performance long range bomber in the near future. This certainly became true in the immediate period after the Second World War, when the requests went out to aircraft manufacturers for cutting edge designs that would become the V-Bombers. Perhaps Smith was simply expressing his hopes for the future of commercial aircraft, but the article still stands out as unusual for the period.

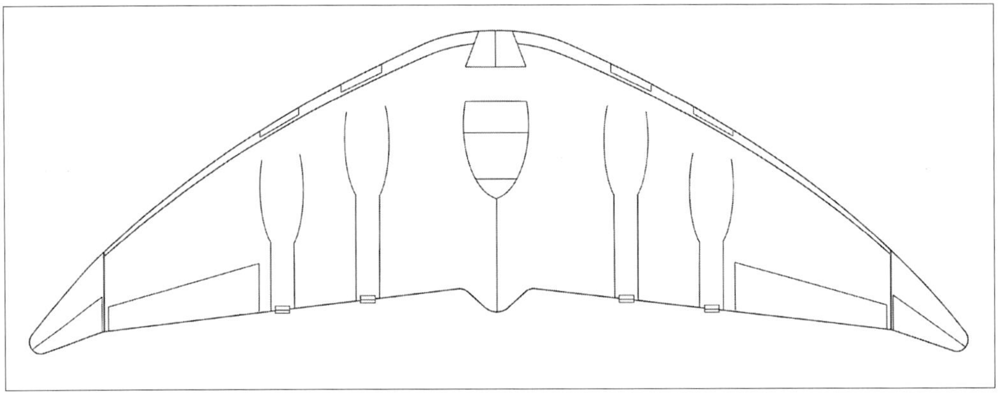

This is the general appearance of a flying wing designed by Geoffrey Smith during the Second World War. Various propulsion layouts were considered and this version was to be powered by four turbojets within the wing, exhausting at the trailing edge.

Armstrong Whitworth Flying Wings

In 1942, the Directorate of Scientific Research approached Armstrong Whitworth Aircraft (AWA) to develop an aerofoil section for wind tunnel laminar flow experiments. Northrop were working on a long-range flying wing bomber for the USAAF and NACA was undertaking extensive research into laminar flow aerofoils. So it seems that the British were hoping to take advantage of US developments for a future jet propelled tailless bomber. As a result of the official UK request, Armstrong Whitworth's chief designer John 'Jimmy' Lloyd (1888–1978) began work on proposals for a military flying wing aircraft. Lloyd produced an initial design study of an advanced flying wing jet bomber for the RAF, which carried the company reference A.W.50 and he was authorised to continue with this work, supported by MAP (Ministry of Aircraft Production).

Lloyd envisaged the use of a smooth surface for the aircraft's skin, fabricated from a fairly thick alloy, strengthened by rolled corrugations of lighter gauge metal to maintain adequate rigidity. At the centre of the aircraft was a cockpit affording fairly good visibility, with a slightly raised crew section and a tail mounted, rear-facing, remotely controlled turret containing two 20 mm cannon. In addition, it was also proposed to equip the aircraft with two forward facing 20 mm cannon located in the wings between the engines.

Propulsion would be provided by four advanced Metropolitan-Vickers (Metrovick) F.2/4 Beryl axial flow turbojet engines. This design was producing 3,500 lb (15.5 kN) of static thrust by 1944, but the F.2/4 remained too unreliable for use in any production aircraft. Lloyd hoped that the ongoing problems with the F.2/4 would be largely resolved by the time the A.W.50 was ready for production and improved thrust might be available.

The engines would be located within the wings on each side of the cockpit drawing air from four separate inlets along the leading edge of the wing. Split-flaps would be used, plus wing tip fins equipped with rudders and A.W.50 was to be equipped with a fully retractable tricycle undercarriage. Lloyd's initial plans were for an aircraft with a wingspan of 120 ft (36.6 m), a wing area 2000 ft^2 (185.8 m^2) and an overall length of 45 ft (13.8 m). The estimated maximum speed was 470 mph (756 kph) at sea level and 480 mph (772 kph) at 30,000 ft (9144 m), with a rate of climb slightly better than 3,000 ft/per min (914 m/per min). The anticipated service

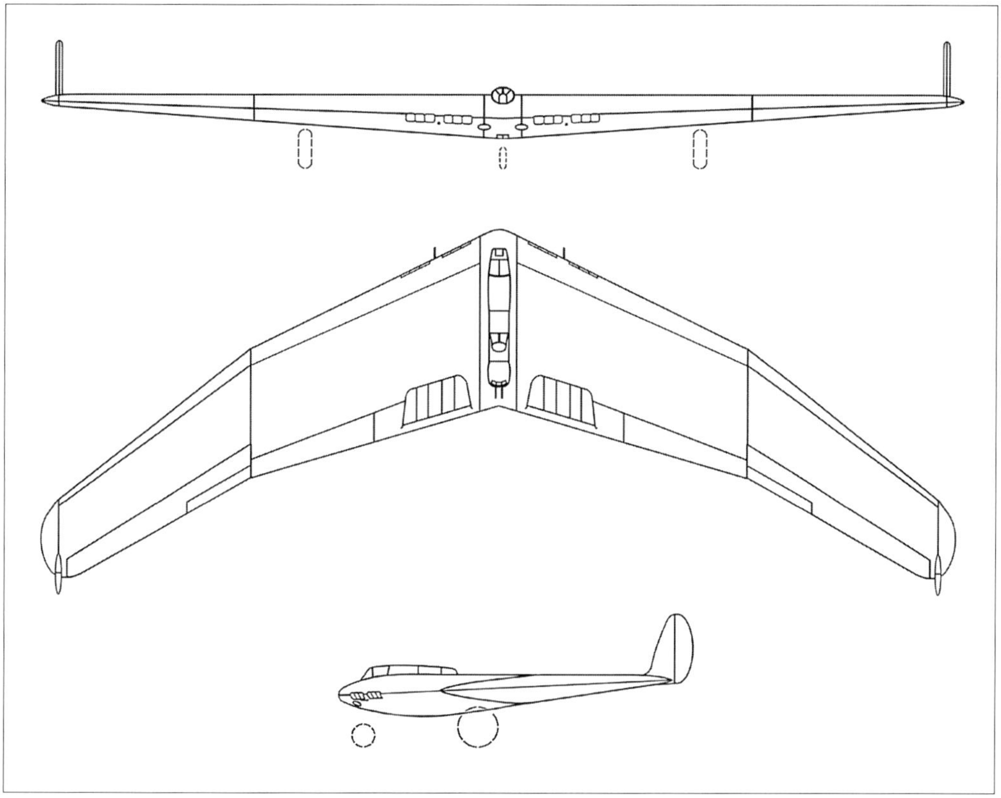

An initial Armstrong Whitworth design study for an advanced RAF flying wing jet bomber, with the company reference A.W.50.

ceiling is unknown, but range was expected to be about 1,500 miles (2,424 km). Gross weight was 49,765 lb (22,573 kg), with the bomb load accounting for approximately 12,000 lb (5,443 kg) of this figure. However, within months, the design underwent a significant revision, with the wingspan being reduced to 112.5 ft (34.3 m) and the wing becoming thinner. As a consequence, the centre section became recognisable as a fuselage and the rear gun turret was removed, leading to nominal changes in weight and performance. A smaller two-engined experimental version of this aircraft was considered at some point during the early design phase, but engine problems appear to have ruled this out.

Lloyd also envisaged a larger six-engined civil airliner for use when the war ended and is on record as saying that he anticipated the development of several different designs for jet-powered flying-wing aircraft. With wind tunnel tests showing promise, it was decided to build a one-third-scale size, glider test the aerodynamics as there was little data to draw on regarding the behaviour of flying wing aircraft at low speeds or at unusual attitudes.

Initially, this glider was assigned the company reference A.W.51 and design work started in May 1943, with the project altering to A.W.52. This finally became A.W.52G, with the last letter referring to its status as a glider. Assembly began at the start of March 1944, although proceedings were relatively slow as priority was being given to more pressing war production work. However, wind tunnel testing continued and A.W.52G was finally completed in early 1945. It

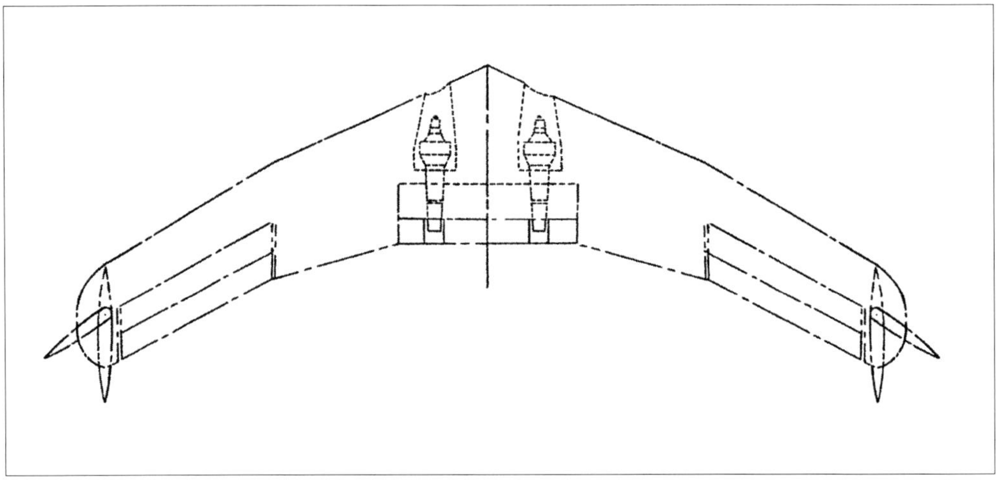

One of John Lloyd's early designs for an experimental twin-jet aircraft which appeared in a UK Patent (2,474,685) filed during 1944 and released into the public domain in 1949. This would eventually lead to the AW.52.

A staged company photograph of the AW.52G, with crew members and staff. The attachment to the trailing edge of the port wing is a frame for the pitot comb used to measure airflow.

An unobstructed view of AW.52G from above.

was then assigned the official serial RG324, but by this time, the original flying wing bomber had been cancelled. Nevertheless, A.W.52G was seen as a useful research tool and on 2 March 1945, it was towed into the air behind a Whitley bomber. This first flight was undertaken by the company's test pilot Charles K. Turner-Hughes (1908–1973), who reported no unexpected handling difficulties.

Spruce and plywood (used for the single box spar and ribs) formed much of the construction, with the outer skin fabricated from Plymax (a thin sheet of duralumin bonded to a thicker sheet of plywood). This allowed a very smooth finish that met the requirements for effective laminar flow. The central cockpit area accommodated a pilot and rear seated observer, with conventional flight controls, aside from a large handbrake style lever used to actuate additional hydraulically-operated, horizontal control surfaces called 'correctors.' These were used to counteract a significant change in trim when elevator or flap movements took place. In addition to the other control surfaces a substantial hydraulically operated one-piece slotted flap with a length of 15.33 ft (4.67 m) was positioned along the entire trailing edge of the central wing section. Also anti-spin parachutes housed in canisters were fitted on each wingtip as a precaution during testing.

A.W.52G utilised a fixed tricycle undercarriage with brakes and a non-steering nose-wheel. The wingspan was 53.83 ft (16.41 m), with a wing area of 443.04 ft^2 (41.16 m^2). Overall length was 19.33 ft (5.89 m); the height was 8.33 ft (2.54 m). The gross weight of the aircraft was approximately 6,000 lb (2,724 kg). The A.W.52G would normally glide at around 100–120 mph (160–190 kph), with a maximum permitted speed of 250 mph (400 kph) and stall occurring at about 60–65 mph (96–104 kph). With considerable interest in boundary layer control, an experimental system was devised to draw in air through a slot forward of the elevons. The idea was to reduce the possibility of wing tip stall at lower speeds and to achieve the suction, small wind powered pumps were fitted to each of the main wheel struts.

Encouraging trials of the glider continued throughout 1945, and it was usually flown by company test pilots Charles Turner-Hughes or Eric George Franklin. Some refinements were made to the glider as the project progressed and it was then decided to build two somewhat larger experimental jet powered flying wings. The project would receive the company reference A.W.52 and approval under the original MAP specification E.9/44 by the Ministry of Supply (MoS). The new aircraft would be approximately three quarters the size of Lloyd's initial design for the A.W.50. Its gross weight would be about 34,000 lb (15,422 kg) and two Rolls-Royce turbojets would provide propulsion. The overall appearance, the larger jet powered A.W.52 was similar to the glider, although the centre of the wing now contained a recognisable fuselage section that protruded forward.

The two turbojet engines were buried in the wing on each side of the cockpit section and the aircraft's internal structure was very different to the A.W.52G, with metal being used throughout. The first A.W.52 (TS363) was completed in Armstrong Whitworth's assembly shop at Whitley, Coventry by early 1947. It had already been revealed to the public as a mail carrying aircraft, although this appears to have been largely public relations spin.

Like the glider, this aircraft had an initial sweep of 17.5°, followed by 34° to the wingtip, which provided the distinctive boomerang shape. The A.W.52 had a wingspan of 90 ft (27.4 m), a length: 37.33 ft (11.4 m) and a height of 14.33 ft (4.4 m). Empty, the aircraft weighed 19,662 lb (8,919 kg), with a gross weight of 34,154 lb (15,492 kg) and the aircraft accommodated two crew members.

The engines chosen for the first aircraft were Rolls-Royce Nene 2 turbojets, each rated at 5,000 lb (22.2 kN) static thrust. The estimated maximum speed of the A.W.52 was about 500 mph (800 kph), with a ceiling of about 35–40,000 ft (10–12,000 m) and a range of approximately 1,000 miles (1,600 km).

The first of two AW.52 experimental jet aircraft (TS363), which were originally based on designs for the more substantial AW.50 bomber. Two Rolls-Royce Nene turbojets provided propulsion; each rated at 5,000 lb (22.24 kN) static thrust.

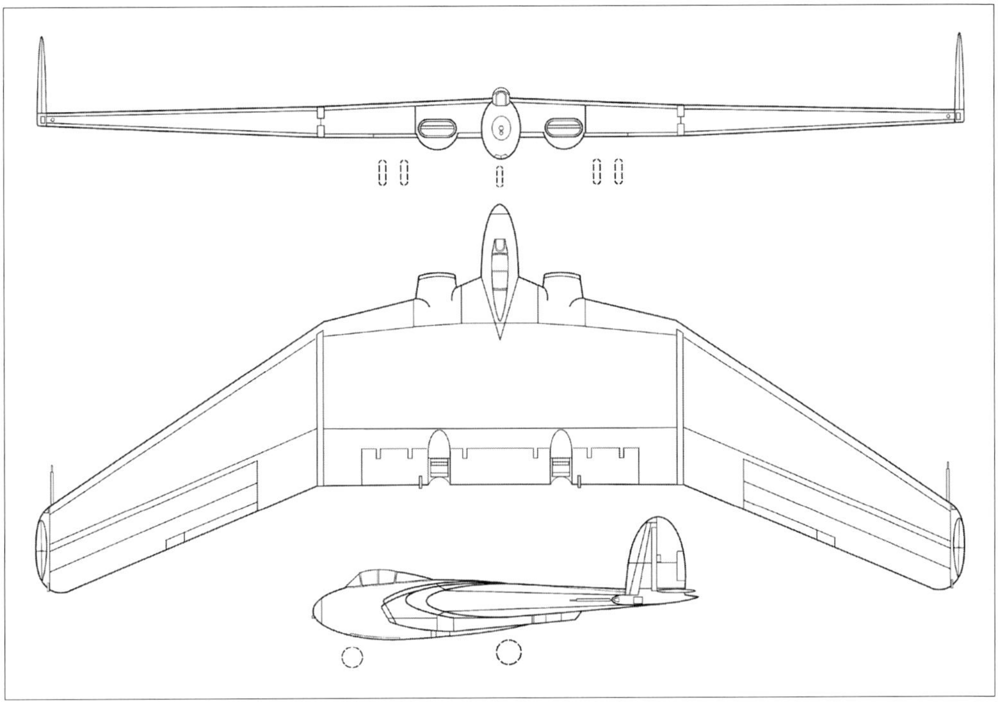

AW.52 General arrangement.

The aircraft featured a pressurised cockpit and the pilot was equipped with a Martin Baker Mk 1 ejector seat, although not the passenger. A.W.52 was fitted with a thermal de-icing system using exhaust from the engines, a boundary layer control system connected to the engine air intakes and pressure balanced controllers. A fully retractable tricycle undercarriage supported AW.52 on the ground and the nose-wheel was steerable.

Like the A.W.52G, the A.W.52 was equipped with vertical wingtip fins and rudders and canisters were attached that contained anti-spin parachutes for emergency use. The trailing edge of the flying wing was occupied by a substantial Fowler flap, which was contoured to allow for each jet exhaust pipe. After a period of tests and minor modifications, the aircraft was partly dismantled and transported by road to the RAF Experimental Establishment at Boscombe Down. Having been re-assembled, A.W.52 spent the next couple of months undertaking ground tests and taxiing trials until a break in the weather allowed the first flight to be made on 13 November 1947.

The trial was undertaken by Armstrong Whitworth's test pilot Eric Franklin, who reported that the aircraft handled as anticipated. Following this success, the A.W.52 was returned to A.W.'s Bitteswell Airfield (no longer in existence) for further testing. The second A.W.52 (TS368) was completed in the Whitley workshops during the summer of 1948 and differed slightly by having two less powerful Rolls-Royce Derwent 5 engines, each producing 3,500 lb (15.56 kN) of static thrust. Rolls-Royce engines appear to have been chosen for reasons of reliability, although it remains unclear why Derwent turbojets were fitted to the second aircraft in preference to the similar Nene units. TS368 first flew on 1 September 1948 and flight-testing with both aircraft continued until 30 May 1949.

On this date, John Lancaster was undertaking a series of trials in the vicinity of the Bitteswell Aerodrome with TS363. After entering a dive at about 320 mph (510 kph), Lancaster encountered severe pitch oscillation and realising that the aircraft was about to break up, he ejected, becoming the first British pilot to use this system in an emergency.

The second A.W.52 was transferred to the RAE Farnborough in October 1950, where testing continued until September 1953, when Armstrong Whitworth left the programme. As a consequence, the RAE decided to conclude operations.

Exactly how useful the Armstrong Whitworth flying wing programme proved to be, remains debatable, as it has been described as disappointing. Laminar flow turned out to be largely unworkable, control of the aircraft was often difficult and take-off and landing distances proved unsatisfactory. In May 1954, the second jet powered A.W.52 was broken up for scrap and it is thought that the glider met a similar fate.

A.W.56

In late 1946, the UK Air Staff requested proposals for an advanced medium range jet bomber. Known as Operational Requirement (OR) 229, this set out the RAF's future needs for a fast, high-altitude aircraft, capable of delivering a 10,000 lb (4,535 kg) bomb to a release point 1,500 nautical miles (2,776 km) distant. Although the primary objective was the carriage and delivery of a single atomic bomb, no British nuclear weapon had been developed at this time and a second requirement designated OR.1001 (later given the codename Blue Danube) was issued by the Air Staff to develop a plutonium bomb.

Both the aircraft and the bomb represented a significant technical challenge and the RAF were seeking a bomber that was capable of sustaining a speed of 500 knots (926 kph) at an altitude of 50,000 ft (15,240 m), with a gross weight of 100,000 lb (45,359 kg). Bearing in mind the state of aerodynamic knowledge and gas turbine technology at that time, this was a very tall order.

Armstrong Whitworth responded to OR.229 with an initial submission and not surprisingly, the designers drew heavily on their flying wing and laminar flow research. After the MoS issued the more precise Specification B.35/46 in early 1947, Armstrong Whitworth submitted detailed plans for a swept-wing tailless jet bomber, incorporating a host of advanced features with the company reference A.W.56.

From the outset, Armstrong Whitworth believed that a tailless configuration would generate fewer aerodynamic problems at transonic speeds. They also proposed a series of wing slots that would allow boundary layer control at all speeds, leading to theoretically effective laminar flow. Experiments to determine the viability of laminar flow had been sponsored by Armstrong Whitworth and were being conducted at RAE Farnborough with a modified Hurricane fighter (Z3687) at this time. Initial results had been disappointing, but research continued, with a modified Gloster Meteor Mk III jet fighter and AWA's flying wing programme.

The Armstrong Whitworth laminar flow wing for the A.W.56 was to have a span of 120 ft (36.58 m) and an area of 2,611 ft^2 (242.56 m$^{2)}$. The overall length of the aircraft was initially 80 ft (24.38 m) with an unconfirmed height of 32 ft (9.75 m) and a gross weight of 113,000 lb (51,256 kg). To meet the performance requirement of B.35/46, five Rolls-Royce AJ65 Avon turbojets would be used for propulsion, each rated at 6,500 lb (28.9 kN) static thrust. Four engines would be installed in the wing roots with air intakes on each side of the cockpit and another engine would be located in the tail, with its own dorsal air inlet located mid-way along the fuselage. With a rather optimistic maximum speed of 640 mph (1,030 kph) the aircraft was anticipated as having a ceiling in excess of 50,000 ft (15,240 m).

The A.W.56's fuselage section would be built using fairly conventional materials and construction methods, although the two-spar wing would be covered with an unusual multi-layer skin similar to that developed for the experimental A.W.52 flying wing. The aircraft would utilise a fully retractable tricycle undercarriage and a flight control system developed for the A.W.52 was planned, using two tandem control surfaces called a 'corrector' and a 'controller'.

The 'corrector' acted as a longitudinal trim control and the 'controller' was similar in function to an elevon. A crew of five would man the aircraft, housed in a pressurised nose section, with access to the bomb bay to allow in-flight arming of a nuclear weapon.

No ejector seats were planned, but it was proposed that the entire nose section would be jettisonable in an emergency and could be lowered to the ground by four substantial parachutes. As an alternative to a nuclear weapon, the A.W.56 could carry a variety of conventional stores with a maximum weight of 20,000 lb (9,071 kg). Another interesting design feature, was the bomb bay doors which opened by sliding fore and aft. This was considered an effective way of minimizing impact on the aircraft's speed and trim.

A long-range mission would involve the aircraft initially climbing to an altitude of 40,000 ft (12,192 m) and then progressively climbing to 50,000 ft (15,240 m), which would be attained after approximately 2 hours and 30 minutes. It was suggested that the Avon engines might be

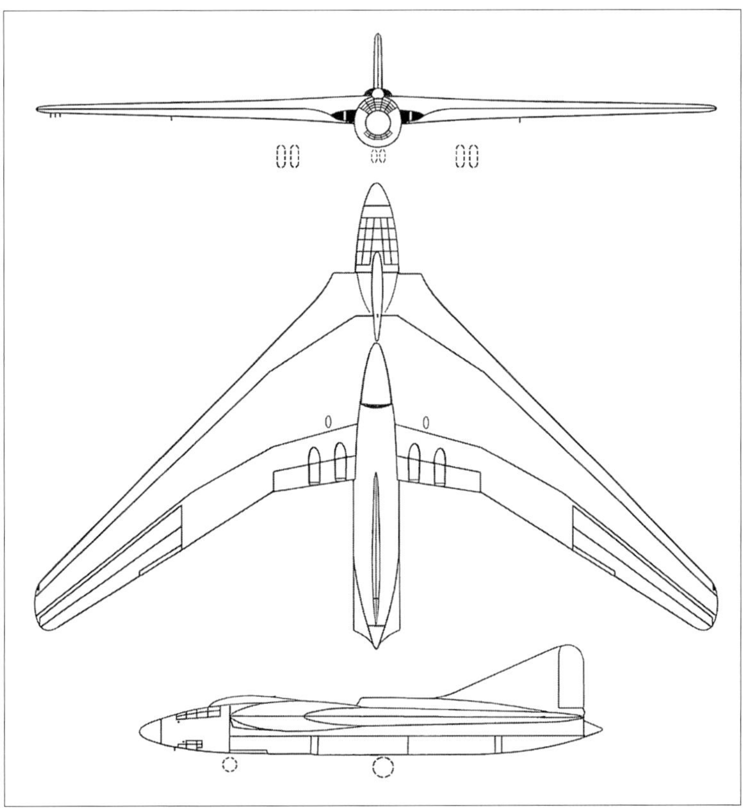

The initial design of the AW.56 jet bomber, produced to meet MoS Specification B.35/46 in early 1947.

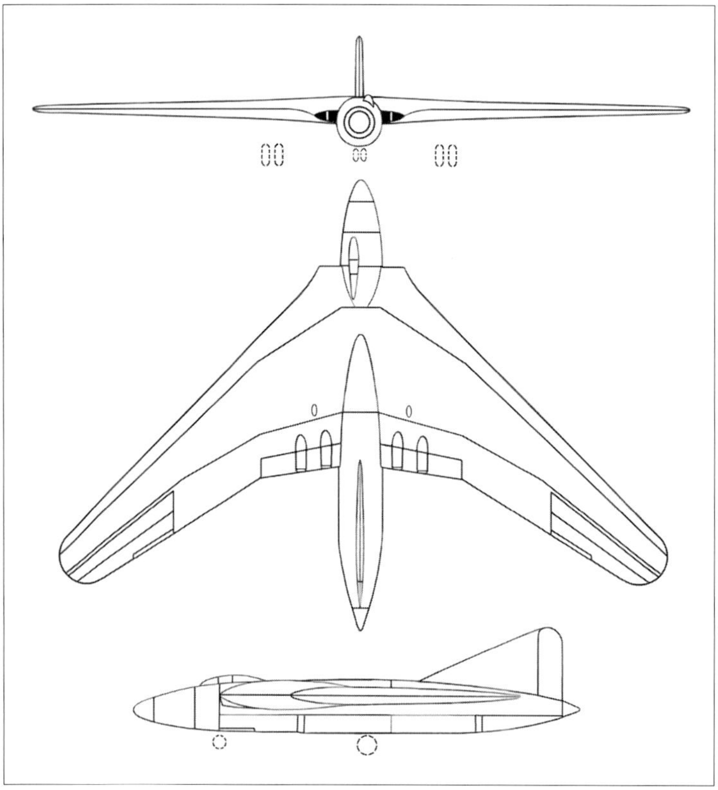

The revised AW.56 design, using four of the new Rolls-Royce RB.77 jet engines and undergoing changes to the cockpit and various aerodynamic features.

replaced by Metrovicks F.9s, which would offer improved thrust, lower fuel consumption and the ability to climb directly to 50,000 ft (15,240 m).

However, the requirements for a new bomber were lowered after the Tender Design Conference took place and this led to a significant revision of the A.W.56 proposal, resulting in a slightly smaller aircraft. The re-designed A.W.56 would be fitted with the new Rolls-Royce RB.77 engines, allowing the use of four rather than five units. This meant that the tail engine was removed, leading to better streamlining and a noticeable weight reduction. This improvement would provide the A.W.56 with performance similar to the proposed F.9 powered version. Another alteration to the revised aircraft was the use of a raised cockpit canopy for the pilot. Offset to the port side, this would have improved visibility considerably. AWA anticipated full completion of this second design within two years and testing of the first prototype about five months later. But the design was finally rejected by the MoS in favour of the Avro 698 and Handley Page H.P.80, which became the Vulcan and Victor.

The RAE Atom Bomber

In the immediate aftermath of the Second World War, the RAE was assigned the task of developing proposals for a guided missile carrying an atomic warhead. Unfortunately, it would be some years before Britain had its own nuclear bomb and it was already clear that this type of weapon

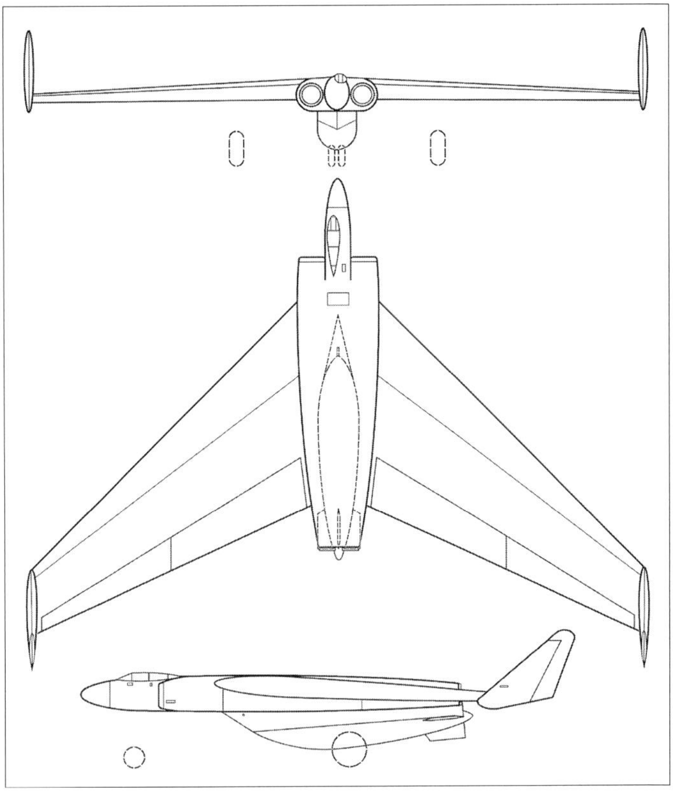

General arrangement of the Minimum Conventional Bomber, which was proposed by the RAE in the early 1950s as the simplest and most cost effective means to deliver an atomic weapon to a target. Conventional describes the aircraft, not its special payload.

would be substantial in size and impossible to mate with a V-2 size rocket. For the remainder of the 1940s, an RAE team worked on a range of concepts under the project name Menace, but almost everything they considered was beyond the technical ability of that period. The Air Ministry wanted an unrealistic range, impossibly accurate guidance and sufficient speed and altitude to avoid interception.

Developing a strategic rocket or cruise missile capable of carrying a large, heavy atomic warhead was considered a real challenge with prevailing technology and the UK lacked sufficient financial resources for such a project. By 1950, they had almost given up, but then decided to revert to a manned aircraft for the task. This led to the 1951 proposal for a flying wing called the Minimum Conventional Bomber. In this case, the word conventional described the design of the aircraft, not the special payload. This was the Blue Danube single 15 kt (nominal) yield fission bomb. It had a weight of 10,000 lb (4,535 kg) and an overall length of 24 ft (7.3 m). The aircraft was intended to be simple and cheap to manufacture, so as a result, it would have an unpressurised cockpit, no ejector seats and be powered by two Rolls-Royce Conway jet engines that were still in development. These would theoretically allow the aircraft to cruise at Mach 0.86 at around 47,000 ft (14,325 m), with a range of perhaps 450 miles (724 km). Overall length was approximately 55.5 ft (16.9 m), height, about 15 ft (4.5 m), an estimated wingspan of 66 ft (20 m), with a leading edge sweep of 45°. However, the design failed to generate any enthusiasm with the Air Staff and the RAE team then returned to studying possible designs for guided missiles.

Handley Page HP.80

A considerable amount of data gathered during the HP.75 Manx project found its way into the design of an advanced flying wing jet bomber known as HP.80. The company were aware that the RAF sought an advanced replacement for its existing piston engined bombers and they submitted a provisional proposal based on this concept to the Air Ministry in February 1946. It was Handley Page's first major post-war military project, undertaken by Dr Gustav Lachmann and his deputy, Godfrey H. Lee (1913–1988).

Their HP.80 design featured a smooth cylindrical fuselage with an integral pressurised forward cabin. The wings would have a leading edge sweep of 45° with upturned fins at the tips and propulsion provided by four advanced turbojets located in the wing roots. The Air Ministry responded to Handley Page's submission by issuing Air Staff Requirement OR.229 that made various specific performance requests and this was followed in March 1947, by the Air Ministry's Specification B.35/46, which set out exactly what they expected from a new bomber. As a consequence, Dr Lachmann reconfigured the aircraft's wing to improve performance, drawing on ideas he had been working on for several years and wartime German research (mostly undertaken by Arado). While the HP.80's new crescent shaped wing was unproven and considered a little risky, initial wind tunnel tests indicated it would function exactly as anticipated. With the sweep and chord decreasing in three phases, this helped to provide a constant limiting Mach number allowing a substantial cruise speed. Dr Lachmann also abandoned the idea of a tailless configuration and added a tailplane section to improve handling.

It was now decided to build a one-third scale, radio controlled glider to test the wing and this received the company designation HP.87. Unfortunately, the glider crashed during the first

This is one of three Handley Page HP.80 wind tunnel models that would eventually evolve into the Victor bomber. In the next stage, a butterfly tail was added, the wing altered to a new crescent shape and the wingtip fins were removed. Various positions were also tested for the four engines.

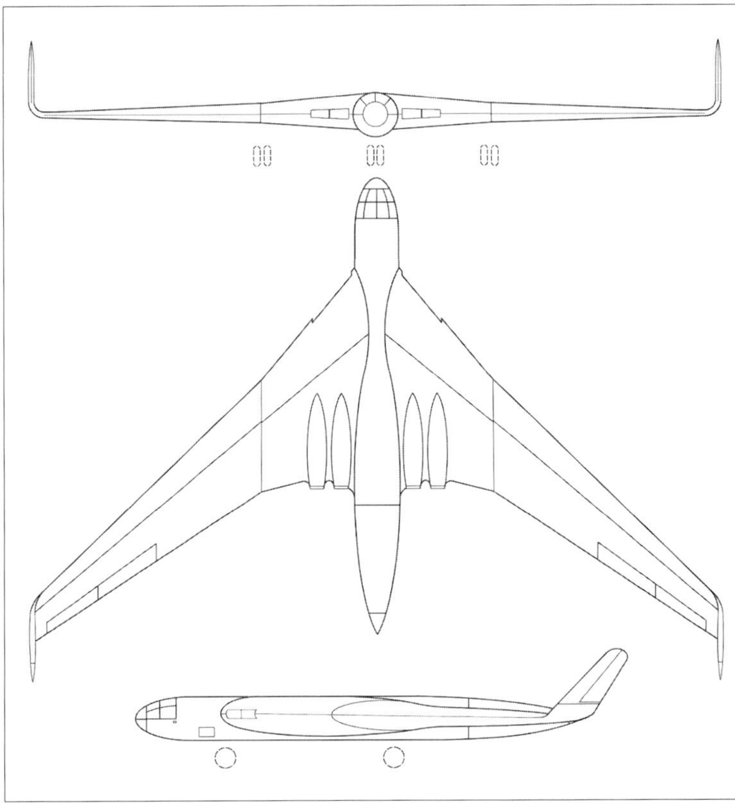

An early Handley Page proposal for a four engined tailless jet bomber concept that would lead to the aerodynamically sophisticated Victor V-Bomber.

test flight. Nevertheless, the Air Ministry remained enthusiastic about the HP.80 project and issued Specification E.6/48 in 1948 for a small manned demonstrator known as HP.88. They also approved construction of two full sized HP.80 prototypes. The HP.88 was initially subcontracted to GAL, who based this aircraft on the fuselage of a Supermarine Attacker jet fighter. HP.88 flew for the first time on 21 June 1951, but proved to be of limited use as the wing's design had continued to evolve and the first HP.80 prototype (WB771) had now reached an advanced stage of construction. HP.88 flew for the next two months, but finally broke up during a test flight, killing the test pilot Duggie Broomfield (1920-1951).

The following year, WB771 was shipped from the factory to Boscombe Down, where the maiden flight was undertaken on 24 December 1952. The second prototype (WB775) undertook its initial flight on 11 September 1954. By this time, the HP.80 had entered production and the Air Ministry formally named it as the Victor B.1. The first of these new V-Bombers would reach the RAF in late 1957.

Short's Flying Wings and V-Bomber Proposal

Short Brothers & Harland of Belfast were eager to participate in the RAF's post-war jet bomber competition (Specification B.35/46) and design work began under a team headed by David Keith-Lucas (1911–1997), with Professor Geoffrey Hill, acting as a scientific consultant. The first

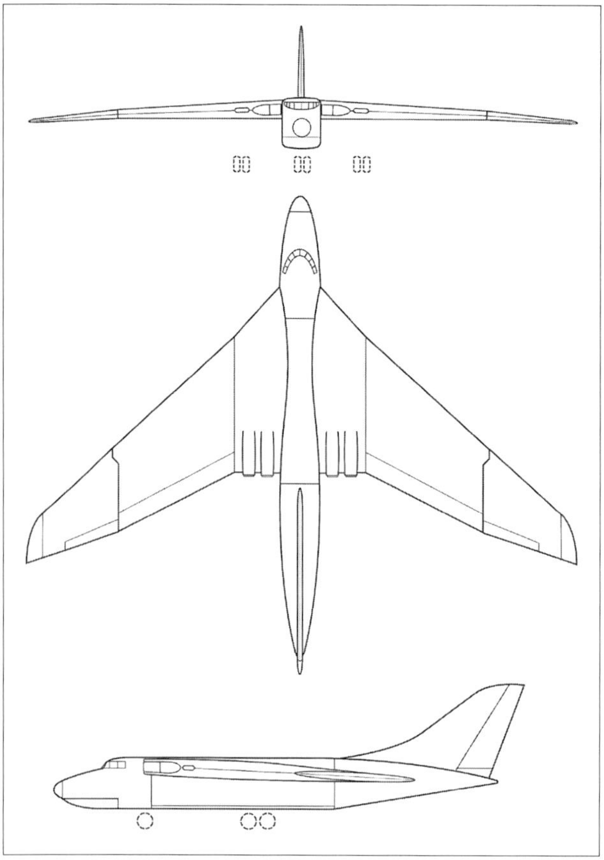

Short Brothers' PD.1 tailless proposal for the RAF's V-Bomber project.

concept to emerge drew on Hill's experience with the Pterodactyl and featured his 'aero-isoclinic' wing. It was an advanced tailless concept, provisionally powered by four Avon turbojets carried in the wing roots, or nacelles above and below the wing. The idea of also installing a fifth engine in the tail with a dorsal air intake was considered, if performance requirements proved difficult to meet. This proposal received the company designation PD.1 and an initial design was submitted to the Air Ministry in 1947, but they swiftly rejected it as technically too ambitious.

On the other hand, there was considerable interest shown in Shorts parallel very straightforward four-engine design called the SA.4 Sperrin, which utilized a broadly similar fuselage to the PD.1 (Preliminary Design #1) but was conventional in all other respects. The SA.4 met the less demanding B.14/46 requirement and was considered worthy of further development as it represented a useful fall back if there was trouble with the designs already selected for development as V-Bombers.

While work proceeded on the construction of two SA.4 Sperrin prototypes and one static test example, Shorts took the decision to privately fund a one-third, scale-sized demonstrator based on the tailless PD.1, which received the company designation SB.1 (serial G-14-5). This was to be a simple glider that clearly demonstrated Hill's unusual 'aero-isoclinic' wing, which was structurally designed to avoid flexing which could cause tip stalling and instability. Hill also replaced the conventional ailerons (which tended to twist the wing), with substantial rotating wingtip control surfaces.

The Short Brothers' SB.1 glider during a test flight.

Having completed wind tunnel testing with several models, the one-man, lightweight SB.1 glider was constructed at Belfast. It was mainly built from wood with some load-bearing steel sections and the emphasis was firmly on keeping construction costs down. The compact glider undertook its first winch-launched flight on 14 July 1951 at RAF Aldergrove, with Shorts Chief Test Pilot Tom Brooke-Smith (1918–1991) at the controls. A similar flight was undertaken during the following day and on 30 July 1951 the SB.1 was towed into the air behind a Short Sturgeon TT2 (VR363) to a height of 10,000 ft (3,048 m). However, during the next flight, SB.1 was caught in the Sturgeon's wake and Brook-Smith had to cast-off at relatively low altitude. He then lost control of the glider and crash-landed. Brook-Smith was injured and SB.1 was virtually a write-off, apart from the wings and tail section. During his recovery, Brook-Smith made a number of important recommendations about the project and as a consequence, the salvaged parts from SB.1 were used to construct a new aircraft called SB.4. This utilised a metal fuselage, with a fixed tricycle undercarriage and the aircraft was powered by two small Blackburn built Turboméca Palas turbojets. Air for the engines was provided by a dorsal inlet, with the exhausts located behind the wing roots.

Like the SB.1, a key feature of this design was the 'aero-isoclinic' wing and it remains unknown if SB.2 and SB.3 were unsuccessful proposals for demonstrators using the same technology. SB.4 (serial G-14-1) was given the name Sherpa (Short & Harland Experimental Research Prototype Aircraft) and Brooke-Smith made a full recovery, being able to continue working on the project and making the first test flight of the SB.4 at Sydenham Airport, Belfast on 4 October 1953.

Trials of the SB.4 Sherpa proved very successful, but the RAF's nuclear bomber programme was settled and the two SA.4 Sperrin prototypes were not needed, being relegated to research duties and eventually scrapped in the late 1950s. Shorts remained hopeful of generating further official interest in a tailless bomber for several years, revising their original concept to be powered by five Avon turbojets. This tailless design used Sperrin style twin-engine nacelles on the inner wing section and an engine mounted above the rear fuselage. They must have visualized a number of applications for this research programme, but Shorts failed to generate any military and commercial interest.

Shorts jet powered SB.4 experimental aircraft demonstrated at Farnborough in 1954.

Shorts SB.4 in flight.

David Keith-Lucas Senior aircraft designer at Short Brothers of Belfast, Northern Ireland.

Eventually, the low-speed Sherpa was passed to the College of Aeronautics at Cranfield, who flew it until the mid-1960s, when it was passed to the Bristol College of Advanced Technology. After that, the aircraft was displayed at the Norfolk & Suffolk Aviation Museum, RAF Bungay and finally secured by the Ulster Aviation Society in 2008. Yet another design proposal to emerge from Shorts during the early 1950s was the PD.13, which used Hill's 'aero-isoclinic' wing. It was a naval strike aircraft intended to meet the Royal Navy's 1952 Staff Requirement NA.39 for a two seat carrier-based design with folding wings for hangar storage. They needed a two-seat fast twin-engined jet with a maximum speed of at least 633 mph (1018 kph), a combat radius of 460 miles (740 km) and the ability to carry payload of 8,000 lb (3,628 kg) which would take the form of conventional bombs, rockets, anti-shipping weapons or one free-fall nuclear bomb.

The PD.13 would accommodate its crew in an unusual configuration with an offset cockpit for the pilot and a fully enclosed fuselage section alongside for the navigator. There are various explanations for why this kind of cockpit layout was adopted for versions of the Canberra and the Sea Vixen, but it appears to have been primarily to improve pilot visibility. Power would be provided by two Rolls-Royce Avons, possibly with some simple form of vectored thrust and the aircraft would be supported by a tricycle undercarriage, with the main wheels housed in nacelles located towards the rear of the wing.

While the PD.13 received serious consideration by the Royal Navy, the contract eventually went to Blackburn for their Project B-103 proposal. Slightly larger, heavier and generally more conventional, this aircraft designed by Barry P. Laight (1920–2012) would become the Buccaneer. There are also indications that Shorts considered a version of the PD.13 for development as a fighter, giving it the name Swallow. Whether this was intended for the Royal Navy or RAF is still unclear, but the concept did not progress very far.

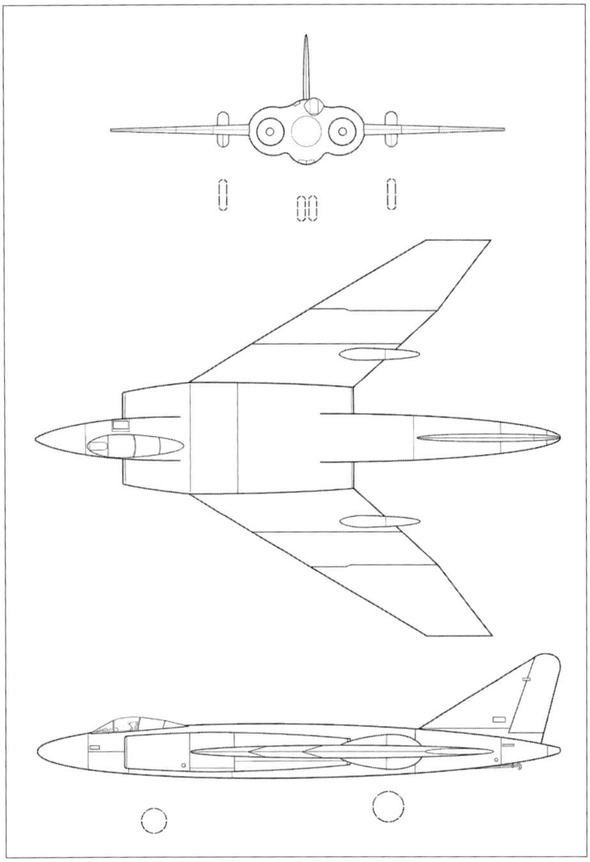

The Shorts PD.13 design for a Royal Navy two-seat, carrier based strike aircraft requirement of June 1952. Despite this proposal generating considerable interest, The Blackburn Buccaneer was finally chosen.

A scale model of the Shorts' PD.13.

Two other little known Shorts studies deserve a mention. The PD.8 was another design by David Keith Lucas that used Hill's 'aero-isoclinic' wing, with a leading edge sweep of 47.5°. The design is thought to originate from around 1951/2 and was intended to be a single seat, twin engined (probably RR Avons), high altitude photo reconnaissance aircraft. Another Shorts concept that progressed little further than the drawing board, was a three engined, supersonic bomber that might have carried the designation PD.12. This also originated in the early 1950s and may have been regarded as a second generation V-Bomber with a brief Mach 2 capability. Unfortunately, very little further information is currently available on either of these interesting concepts.

Short Brothers' PD.8 design for a high altitude spyplane using Hill wingtip control surfaces. The study was completed in May 1952, but went no further. (*Based on Shorts original artwork*)

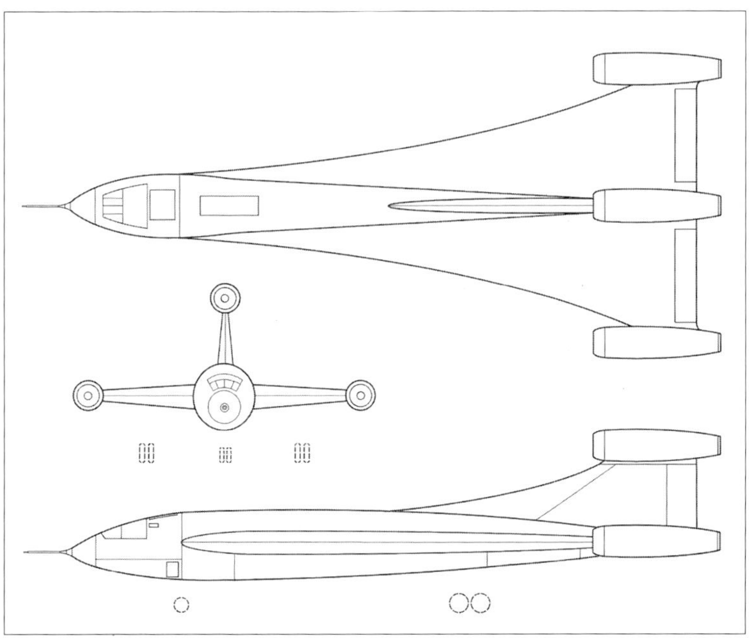

A supersonic bomber project from Shorts, believed to have the company designation PD.12 and dating from around 1953. There appears to be another version of this proposal with a similar fuselage, but a more conventional wing and tail configuration, powered by two engines in wingtip nacelles. At the time of writing, the PD.12 designation has not been properly verified, although the author has been unable to find any alternative references for this design in the company's projects list.

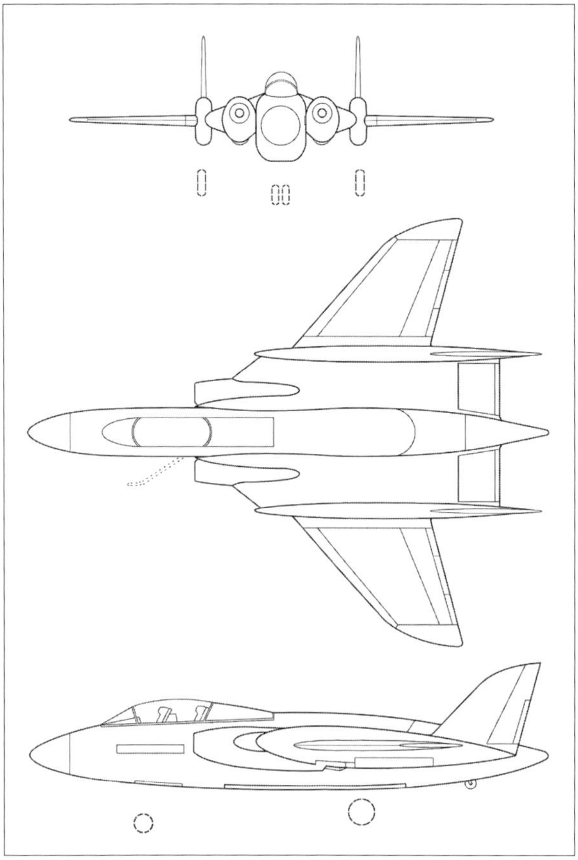

Conceived in the early 1950s alongside the Shorts P.13, the Westland P.148 was a twin-engine naval aircraft with a nuclear strike capability. The Westland M.148 had a number of well considered features like jet exhaust deflection for shorter take-off, but it failed to win acceptance by the Royal Navy.

Westland M.148

Developed in competition with the Shorts PD.13 design for the Royal Navy's new carrier operated strike aircraft of the early 1950s, was the advanced two-seat Westland M.148. It was powered by two Gyron Junior turbojets equipped with deflection exhausts that could be positioned to improve take-off and landing performance. The aircraft obviously featured folding wings for hangar storage and weapons were carried within the bomb bay. This would comprise of a single nuclear weapon, a selection of conventional bombs, mines or rockets. Fuel was mostly contained above the bomb bay and there was provision for in-flight refuelling. A promising design that may have reached wind tunnel testing as a scale model, but failed to match the Buccaneer in terms of projected performance and was never developed further.

Avro's Delta Bomber

In 1944, the Air Ministry produced a paper with the title 'Future Bomber Requirements'. This outlined ideas for aircraft to follow the most successful types in service such as the Avro Lancaster. With the war over, there were new adversaries in the East and the RAF began to seriously consider ideas for an advanced, five-man strategic bomber powered by jet propulsion. This led to an Air Staff Operational Requirement (OR) 229 being issued in late 1946 for a fast, high-altitude aircraft, capable of delivering an atomic bomb with an estimated weight of 10,000 lb (4,535 kg), to a target 1,500 nautical miles (2,776 km) distant. A more detailed official requirement was issued on 7 January 1947 known as Specification B.35/46. The companies responding to this request were quickly narrowed down to Avro, who developed a proposal called the Type 698, along with Handley Page who produced the HP.80 and Armstrong Whitworth's AW.56 design.

The preliminary studies undertaken by Avro's Project Office at Chadderton, Manchester received enthusiastic support in official circles and were given the go-ahead. Handley Page were also contracted to develop the HP.80, which was seen as a fall-back against failure of the Avro design. The advanced Handley Page proposal would eventually become the Handley Page Victor, but the AW.56 was finally rejected for a number of technical reasons. In addition to the selected designs, Vickers-Armstrong had been working on ideas for a jet bomber since 1944 and submitted a proposal for OR.229. Their concept was considered too conservative and met with swift rejection, but the company's chief designer George Edwards managed to maintain interest in his proposal and the Air Ministry finally decided to allow further development on the promise of a prototype by 1951. Subsequently, Specification B.9/48 was issued and the Vickers bomber received the company designation Type 660. Considered as further insurance against development problems with the more advanced Vulcan and Victor, this aircraft would become the Valiant.

Prior to reaching the completion date for OR.229, Avro's design team had considered several ideas that differed considerably from the later Vulcan delta wing bomber. Heading the design office was Avro's Technical Director Roy Chadwick (1893–1947), who created the Avro Lancaster and is now generally regarded as one of Britain's greatest aircraft designers. Initially, Chadwick envisaged a more conventional jet powered bomber that was not totally dissimilar to

Roy Chadwick, one of Britain's leading aircraft designers, who was responsible for a number of aircraft that included the Avro Manchester, Lancaster and initial work on the Vulcan.

the Vickers-Armstrong proposal. It would have a streamlined fuselage, four jet engines buried in the wing roots and a conventional tailplane. Unfortunately, Chadwick contracted shingles in January 1947 and had to leave the bomber project to his staff, which included Bob Lindley, Stuart Davies and Donald Wood.

Influenced by the work that had been undertaken in Germany by Alexander Lippisch on delta configurations, Chadwick's deputy Bob Lindley moved away from the early outlines and began to draw up proposals for a bomber, which was for all intents and purposes a flying wing with no vertical stabilisers. It would use a boundary layer control system and be powered by five centrally located Avon or Sapphire turbojets.

The intake for the jet engines would be a substantial letterbox shaped duct located at the front of the aircraft. One of the most interesting features of this particular design was the directable engine exhaust system, using large upper and lower flaps.

The aircraft would be fitted with two separate cockpits connected by an access tunnel and the forward section would have been capable of tilting to provide better downward visibility under certain circumstances. Lindley also proposed an additional crew area within the leading edge of the port wing. There would be two separate bomb bays at each side of the engine compartment, both allowing enough space for a single large bomb.

Layout of the fully retractable undercarriage is a little unclear from the one available drawing of this early design, but it appears to comprise of two rear-mounted main wheels and two separate nose wheels. The whole package was something of a design *tour-de-force*, combining many new ideas in a largely unproven aerodynamic shape. When Chadwick finally returned to the office, he was not entirely pleased with the direction the project had taken and it seems there were disagreements about what he perceived to have become a science fiction concept. However, Roy

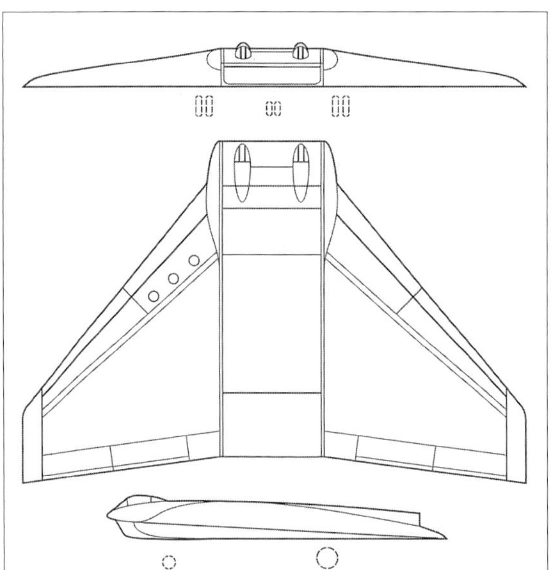

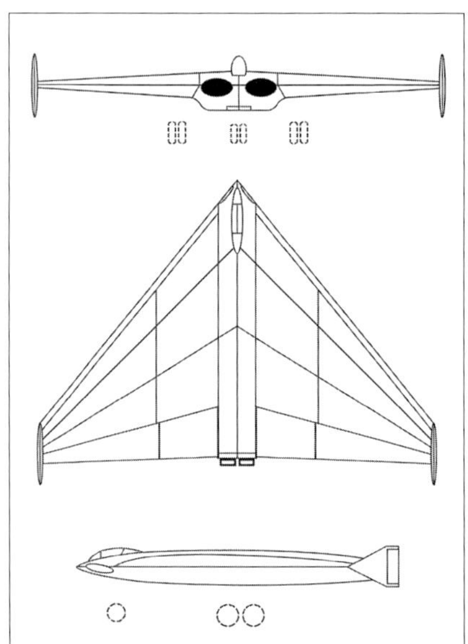

Left: An unusual flying wing design produced during early studies that would lead to the Vulcan bomber.

Right: One of many early configurations for the advanced post-war Avro jet bomber that would become the Vulcan.

Chadwick finally came around to the idea of a flying wing design and soon began to suggest modifications and improvements.

The appearance of the new Type 698 began to move towards a triangular delta-winged shape, although some of the existing features were retained. The forward engine inlet was replaced with two intakes at the leading edge and the rather strange dual cockpit layout was replaced with a single enclosure. Chadwick kept the two bomb bays, but now decided that wingtip stabilisers were necessary.

The undercarriage underwent considerable revision, with the favoured choice being a bicycle arrangement supplemented by outrigger wheels. There were also attempts to design various crew capsule escape systems, but this was seen as too complicated and the idea was finally abandoned. With concerns about weight, Chadwick hoped to reduce the number of turbojets to two, assuming it became possible to build an engine with 20,000 lb (89 kN) static thrust. This two-engined delta wing bomber continued to evolve and a fuselage began to form in the centre of the wing and protrude forward beyond the leading edge, making it easier to produce a pressurised crew compartment and allowing extra space for essential equipment. But it was clear that two engines remained an unrealistic option and the Avro team eventually accepted that four turbojets were necessary.

Modifications continued and the Type 698 now featured upright wingtip fins with rudders and four Bristol BE.10 (later Olympus) turbojets arranged with two of these, staggered above the others. Air intakes for upper and lower engines were located on each side of the forward fuselage section. On 23 August 1947, Roy Chadwick was being carried as an observer on the test flight of an Avro Tudor 11. Incorrect servicing of the ailerons resulted in the aircraft crashing into the ground moments after it left the runway. Both test pilots and Chadwick were killed.

This represented a significant setback to the programme and almost led to cancellation of the contract. But William Farren was appointed as Technical Director and managed to calm concerns, which ensured continuation of work on the design, with official confirmation being received on 27 November 1947.

Longitudinal stability remained a problem and the idea of utilising a horizontal tailplane similar to the Gloster Javelin was briefly considered. This was eventually dropped, but a single upright tailfin was retained. There were also official concerns about the staggered engine layout and this was finally dropped in favour of a less complicated side-by-side arrangement. Work on the jet bomber continued and Avro were awarded a contract to proceed to the hardware stage on 1 January 1948.

The company would now build a full-sized mock-up of the bomber; two scale-sized proof-of-concept demonstrators and two full sized prototypes. The demonstrators were designed as half-sized aircraft called the Avro 710, each powered by two Rolls-Royce Avon turbojets. Preparations began to build the prototypes in 1948, but it was realised that the Avro 710 would be complex and expensive to produce, so construction of this design was stopped. However, Avro had also been working on plans for a smaller single engine experimental delta and attention switched to this, which is described in a later section.

At this time, the design that would be used for the first two full sized prototypes (VX770 & VX 777) was essentially complete, although the RAE had insisted on some significant changes to the wing structure in late 1948, which would delay the start of construction at Chadderton and Woodford until early 1951. Once the first Type 698 prototype (VX770) had been completed and tested on the ground, Wing Commander Roland 'Roly' John Falk (1915–1985) undertook the maiden flight on 30 August 1952. The flight went well, aside from problems with trailing undercarriage doors, which required careful in-flight inspection from a Vampire chase plane and

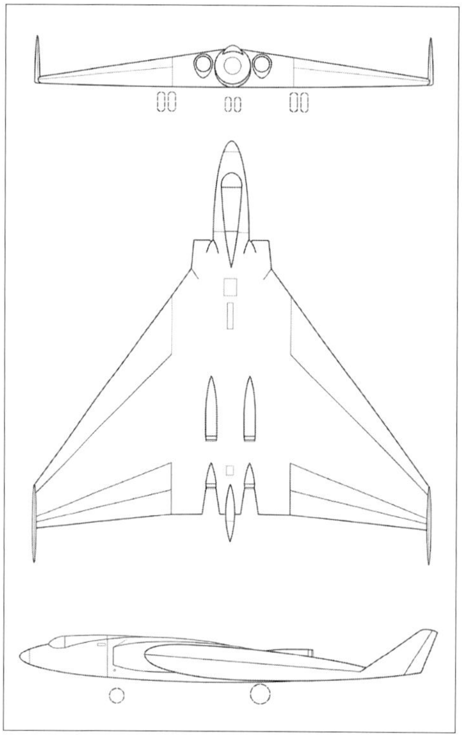

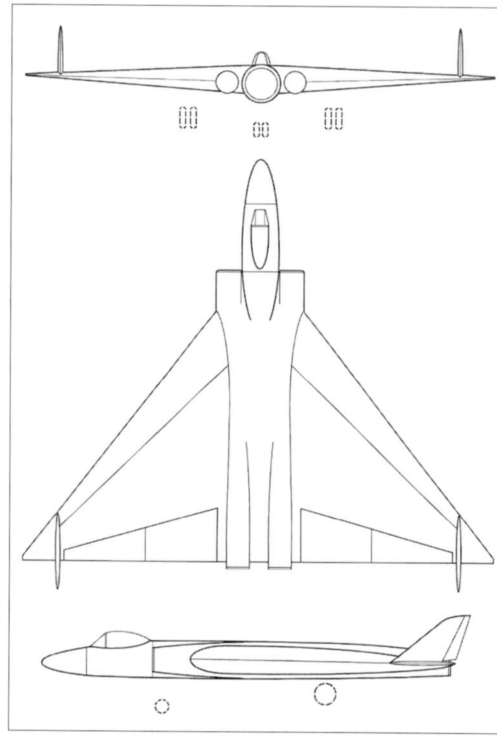

Left: General arrangement of the original four engined Avro 698 proposal with staggered engines.

Right: The experimental Avro 710 was to be twin-engine, half-size test version of the future bomber, but rising costs cut the project short, with a series of Avro 707s taking its place.

a company Avro 707 delta. It was finally determined that this did not interfere with the aircraft's ability to land and Falk put VX770 down on the runway with no problems.

Production aircraft were to be powered with Bristol Olympus engines, but these were not available at that time, so VX770 was fitted with four lower-powered Rolls-Royce RA.3 Avons. In October 1952, it was decided that the new bomber should be given a proper name and a Commonwealth capital city was favoured. Ottawa was the preferred choice, but this idea was soon dropped and Vulcan was selected.

The Vulcan in Service

The first Avro Vulcan B.1 (XA897) was accepted by the RAF during September 1956 and it was decided to send the aircraft to Australia and New Zealand as part of a PR exercise. Unfortunately, the aircraft crashed at the end of this tour while making its final approach to London airport in torrential rain. The second Vulcan B.1 entered service with the RAF in 1957 and during the same year, the first B.2 was tested, although it would be several years before this improved version entered service. The B.2 was equipped with superior engines, in-flight refuelling, an advanced electronic warfare capability, a new electrical system and changes to the wing that reduced turbulence.

The cost of each B.2 was said to have been about £750,000, which was roughly double that of the other V-Bombers. Nevertheless, the RAF appears to have considered it the most capable aircraft of the three and a total of 136 Vulcans would be built, including the prototypes. Subsequently, the B.2 would replace all the B.1s and stood a better chance of penetrating Soviet airspace should the need ever arise. Avro had moved on to development of the Vulcan's proposed supersonic successor, the Avro 730, but 1957 was the year of the UK Defence White Paper, which brought an end to many advanced aviation projects including the Avro 730.

As anyone who has been inside a Vulcan will know, the cockpit area can only be described as rather confined, with limited space to move around. Visibility is somewhat restricted, but many Vulcan pilots felt it was a reasonably agreeable aircraft to fly and it handled quite well. At its operational peak during the 1960s, the Vulcan proved to be a very capable warplane. This became evident when RAF Vulcans took part in the US Operation called Skyshield, which was a series of exercises designed to test the NORAD (North American Aerospace Defense Command) defences against a massive Soviet bomber attack. These exercises were undertaken during three separate periods in 1960, 1961 and 1962. On each occasion, four Vulcan B.2s flew from RAF Lossiemouth, in Scotland and four B.2s from Kindley Air Force Base, Bermuda. The main targets in the US during Skyshield were Washington, New York and Chicago. During the first of these exercises, an RAF Vulcan was intercepted by a McDonnell F-101 Voodoo at 56,000 ft (17,000 m) above Goose Bay, Labrador but it was the only instance of detection during the Skyshield trials.

Two factors played a part in allowing the Vulcans to undertake deep penetrations. The first may have been the Vulcan's slightly reduced radar signature and the second was undoubtedly the use of advanced electronic countermeasures. Skyshield was apparently the largest military aviation exercise of this kind ever undertaken, with civilian air traffic grounded for up to 12 hours. Furthermore, the outcome of the trial raids on major US targets were considered so sensitive that most details remained classified until 1997. Although the Vulcans in Skyshield had flown at high altitudes, above the US bombers participating in these trials, the British now generally favoured using the Vulcans at low level, to reduce the chances of early radar detection further. Nevertheless, it was clear that practice flights would considerably reduce the life expectancy of the airframes. Strategic weapons carried by V-Bombers were free fall nuclear bombs, but it had been obvious for many years that this was an increasingly unattractive option and a stand-off missile was essential to maintain the aircraft's effectiveness and the crew's chances of survival in an all-out war. From as far back as 1954, the MoS had been actively discussing the development of a nuclear tipped stand-off missile with defence contractors that would eventually receive the name Blue Steel.

Vickers seem to have been the preferred company, but Avro finally won the Blue Steel contract, despite their lack of experience with guided weapons. Subsequently, trials commenced at Woomera, Australia in early 1960, using Victor and Vulcan bombers as launch platforms. Nevertheless, the programme was some years behind schedule and the MoS were unhappy that the missile was not already in service. This led to an agreement being reached between Prime Minister Harold Macmillan (1894-1986) and US President Dwight Eisenhower (1890-1969) in March 1960, to purchased 144 Douglas GAM-87 Skybolt missiles that were under development for the USAF. It would also lead to proposals for a further Vulcan upgrade known as Phase 6 (sometimes referred to as the B.3), initially described to Air Staff by Avro in December 1961. Able to carry four, or possibly six underwing Skybolts (or an increased conventional payload), the Phase 6 aircraft would be powered by four improved Olympus 23 engines, there would be

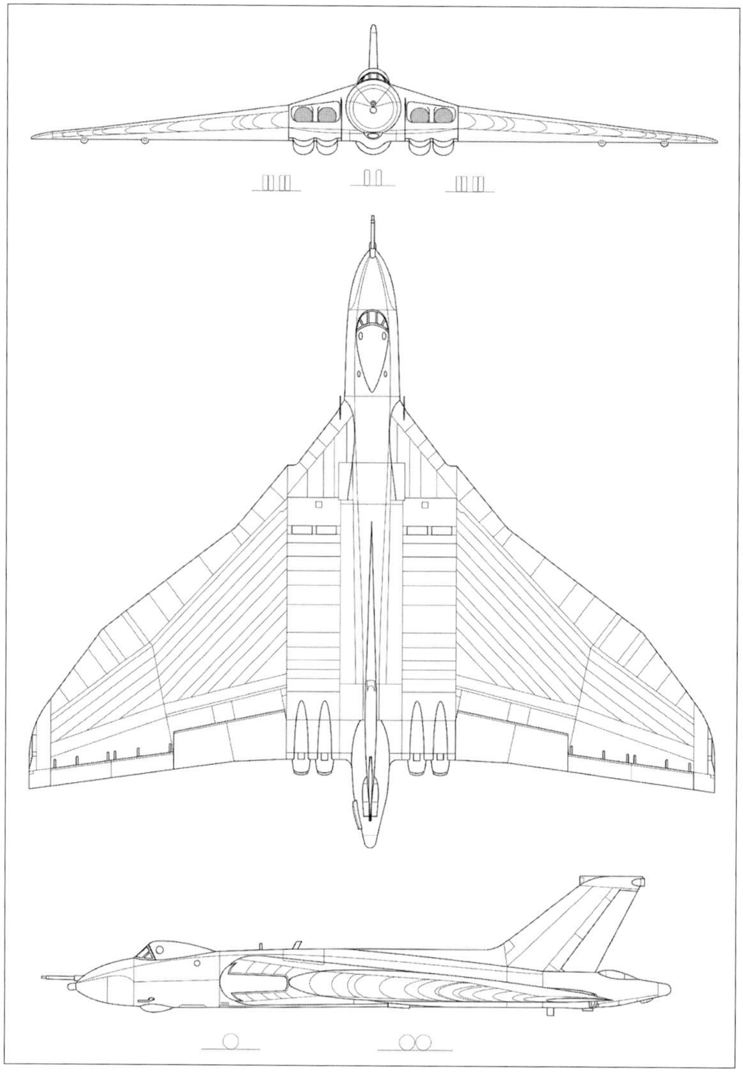

General arrangement of the Avro Vulcan B Mk 2. (*Kaboldy*)

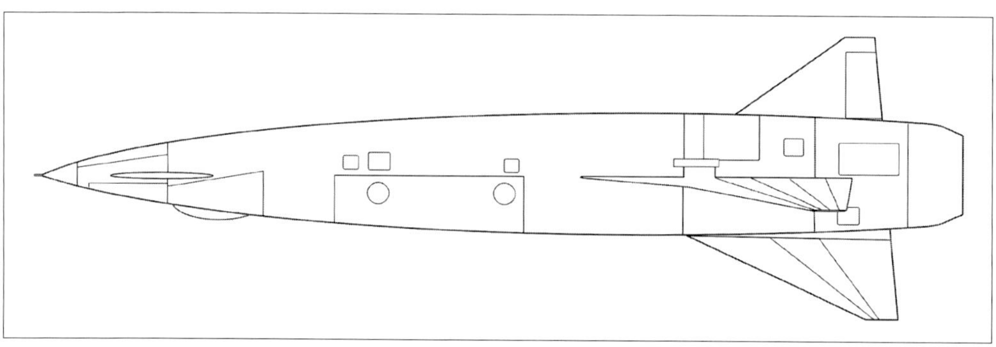

Blue Steel nuclear stand-off missile.

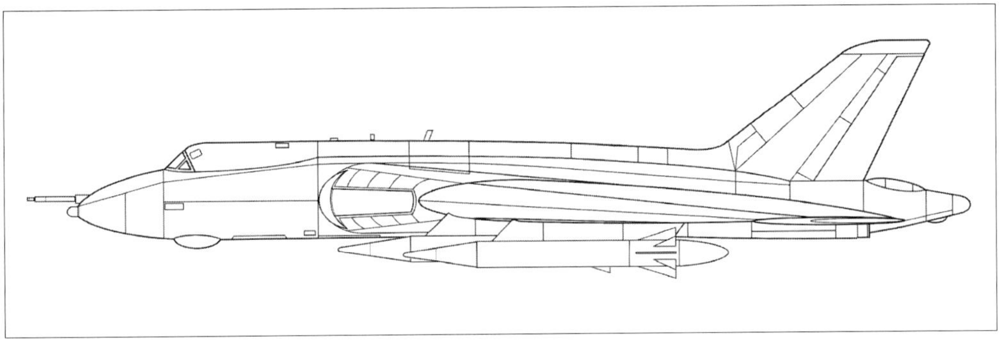

An advanced, uprated Avro Vulcan proposal known as the Phase 6 design, carrying four underwing Skybolt nuclear missiles.

further wing modifications and a host of smaller upgrades, like space for a second crew. A fully armed Phase 6 Vulcan was expected to have an unrefuelled range of about 5,700 miles (9,000 km) carrying a full complement of missiles.

Meanwhile, relations between East and West continued to deteriorate, leading to the Cuban Missile Crisis of 1962, when nuclear conflict seemed possible. In October 1962 the situation became critical and following a meeting between Chief of the Air Staff Sir Thomas Pike (1906–1983) and Macmillan, the RAF prepared for war.

Fully fuelled Vulcans known as Quick Reaction Alert (QRA) aircraft waited on dispersal pans called Operational Readiness Platforms (ORP) at the end of runways at several UK airfields. Each bomb bay contained one free-fall nuclear bomb. These may have been British thermonuclear weapons, or just possibly American B28 or B43 thermonuclear bombs provided under a top secret agreement called Project E and normally assigned to Valiant V-Bombers. The reality was that Britain still had relatively small nuclear stockpile and the American weapons were of a more advanced design.

RAF flight crews were expected to have their aircraft in the air within two minutes, should the order come from Downing Street to scramble. Plans already existed to disperse the RAF's V-Force aircraft to sites across the country and reduce the chances of being knocked out in a pre-emptive nuclear strike, but Macmillan rejected this, as he was concerned that the Soviets might see it as a definite intent to attack.

There can be no doubt that the US played a significant role in these operations and most of the targets assigned to the RAF are thought to have been major military sites in the Baltic region. However, it has not been possible to verify any details which appear to remain secret. Fortunately, the Americans and Russians stepped back from the brink, but it was the highest state of readiness every reached by the V-Force and many experts believe that in almost any re-run of history there would have been a substantial nuclear exchange killing hundreds of millions of people.

Questions were now being asked about the RAF's ability to penetrate Soviet air defences and there was a widespread belief within the RAF that attacking the Russians with existing aircraft would be little more than a series of suicide missions. Blue Steel would enter service in 1963 and there had already been a decision taken in 1960 not to develop a superior longer range ramjet version of Blue Steel. A deal had been struck with the Americans for Skybolt and it seems that the MoS simply wanted to ensure that Blue Steel Mk.1 would continue as a fall-back if any problems arose with the American weapon.

Unfortunately, it was clear that Blue Steel had major problems. It had a limited range, even when launched under optimal conditions, it was extremely unreliable and the aircrews were nervous about being near the weapon due to the very dangerous liquid fuel (HT (high-test) hydrogen peroxide and kerosene) used by its rocket engine. That said, development of Blue Steel and Skybolt continued, with Avro working on both projects.

There were actually a number of proposals to improve the weapon and extend its operational life, or replace it. The most interesting were Avro suggestions for a completely new dart shaped missile, with different propulsion configurations. However, it appears that the cost and anticipated technical problems limited these ideas to initial paperwork proposals. Nevertheless, the RAF was keen to ditch Blue Steel as soon as possible and wanted the solid fuel, longer range Skybolt. But serious technical problems persisted and at the end of 1962, the Americans unexpectedly cancelled Skybolt. This was not quite as bad an outcome for Britain as initially feared, because a deal was then struck to obtain the submarine launched Polaris nuclear missiles for the Royal Navy, while the V-Force would continue to have a limited nuclear capability.

Blue Steel entered service with the RAF in February 1963 and was carried by Vulcans and Victors in a semi-recessed condition beneath the bomb bay. To allow sufficient ground clearance, the missile's lower fin was folded and remained that way until it was ready for launch.

Blue Steel was equipped with a compact, UK adapted version of the American W28, 1.1 megaton thermonuclear warhead given the codename Red Snow. Unfortunately, the move to low level flight reduced the missile's effective range from a little over 100 miles (160 km) to about 25 miles (40 km), which was obviously far from satisfactory. So a number of minor modifications were made to Blue Steel, in order to address the weapon's limited low level capability. While there were some improvements, the weapon was still considered unsatisfactory and changes were made to UK nuclear strike plans, allowing part of the V-Force to continue delivering free-fall nuclear weapons.

In retrospect, Blue Steel was hardly a success. In 1963, the RAF predicted that in a conflict, at least half the missiles would fail to launch, meaning they would have to be dropped onto the targets, assuming this was possible. Handling the weapons on the ground was difficult, demanding and potentially very dangerous, with each missile taking about seven hours to prepare for use.

Records indicate that 48 operational Blue Steel missiles were made available to the RAF for use on Vulcan and Victor bombers. Five additional fully functional missiles were kept in storage, plus twenty further non-nuclear rounds, thought to have been mostly used for training purposes. While the RAF maintained a nuclear strike capability beyond the life of the V-Force, Blue Steel was retired from service in December 1970, with the submarine launched Polaris system becoming the UK's principle strategic nuclear weapon. In 1973, the Vulcans belonging to Number 27 Squadron were assigned to maritime radar reconnaissance (MRR) operations. Their B.2s underwent a series of modest modifications for the new role, becoming B.2MRR aircraft. The AN/APN-171 Terrain Following Radar (TFR) system and the thimble radome were removed and a LORAN-C navigation receiver was added. The H2S Mark 9A radar was retained as suitable for maritime duties, the aircraft's operational camera was adapted and the crew were issued with standard photographic equipment for use when necessary. Some of the aircraft were also fitted with air sampling pods, but whatever they were used for remains secret. However, it seems fair to assume they were looking for evidence of fallout from nuclear testing in fairly remote locations. By the late 1970s, RAF Vulcans were almost at the end of their service life and preparations were underway to replace the V-Bombers with the Panavia Tornado GR.1.

Avro Vulcan XH558 at the Duxford Airshow 2012. (*John 5199*)

An RAF Vulcan B.2 in flight during Air Fete '85. (*Sgt. David S. Nolan, USAF*)

Throughout this period, RAF B.2 Vulcans were deployed overseas, to locations like Cyprus, Malta or Bahrain and it is understood that they were accompanied by stockpiles of conventional and tactical nuclear weapons. Of the 16 Vulcan crashes that took place while the bomber was in RAF service, one occurred at RAF Luqa, Malta of 14 October 1975. The aircraft came down on the nearby town of Zabbar and there was considerable damage and several fatalities. I mention this, having landed at Luqa just prior to the accident and being immediately aware of the Vulcans lined up alongside the runway. With problems in Cyprus due to the Turkish invasion of the north and this very serious incident in Malta, it appears that most of the overseas Vulcan B.2s were progressively withdrawn to the UK.

The Vulcan received a totally unexpected life extension in 1982, following the invasion of the UK's Falkland Islands in the South Atlantic by Argentinean military forces. Clearly the Argentinian Junta did not anticipate a major response, perhaps because of the extreme distance involved. Nevertheless, it was not long before a substantial naval task force was heading south from Britain. This included aircraft carriers with Harriers, although it was decided to attempt a series of long range strikes using five adapted Vulcan B.2s that would be based at the Wideawake airfield on Ascension Island in the mid-Atlantic. In addition, several Victor tankers were assigned to provide in-flight refuelling.

The chosen primary target was Port Stanley Airport, with the aim of putting the runway out of use and the number of raids undertaken by the Vulcans would depend on how well things went from the outset. This operation was given the name Black Buck and it required the Vulcans being prepared for full in-flight refuelling. Crews would need to be brought up to speed, as airborne refuelling of Vulcans was almost a thing of the past and rarely undertaken. Aircraft chosen were those still fitted with Skybolt pylons as one of these was used to carry a AN/ALQ-101 jammer pod. The B.2s were also equipped with a Carousel inertial navigation system, previously used on Vickers Super VC10 airliners.

The first long-range Black Buck mission started out from Ascension on 30 April 1982, made a low level approach on the target and dropped a full complement of 1,000 lb (450 kg) bombs on the airport before leaving the area. The mission lasted 16 hours and covered a distance of about 7,500 miles (12,000 km). Another Vulcan flew as backup and eleven Victor tankers took part. Only one bomb actually struck the runway which was the intended target area, but it seems the general idea was not to severely damage any other features that might be useful to invading British forces.

The second Black Buck raid launched on 3 May 1982, produced similar results and the third mission scheduled to leave on 16 May was cancelled due to difficult weather conditions.

It was now decided to attack the enemy's radar using Martel AS37 missiles, but tests indicated that this weapon was unsuitable for carriage by the Vulcan at high altitude for long periods. The US had been supplying the British with the latest AIM-9L Sidewinder air-to-air missile for use by Sea Harriers and they agreed to also provide AGM-45A Shrike anti-radiation missiles which could be carried on Vulcan pylons. Interestingly, there were discussions about equipping the Vulcans with Sidewinder AAMs for self-defence and making the aircraft suitable for delivering laser guided bombs, but nothing came of either idea.

On 28 May 1982, Black Buck 4 was prepared to undertake the first Shrike attack on the Argentine radar installation at Port Stanley, but this had to be cancelled at short notice due to tanker problems. A few days later, Black Buck 5, with its Westinghouse AN/ALQ-101 jamming pod turned off (to attract Argentine radar), launched two Shrikes against an enemy radar installation but there was no damage to the target. Then on 3 June, Black Buck 6 undertook another

Shrike raid, with one missile hitting the installation, two failing and one refusing to launch. On the return journey, Black Buck 6 was unable to refuel due to a damaged probe and made an emergency landing at Rio de Janeiro, which caused a minor international incident and a formal diplomatic protest. Subsequently, the aircraft was refuelled and allowed to leave, but the Shrike was impounded by the Brazilians.

On 12 June 1982, Black Buck 7 carried out the last Vulcan mission of the conflict, undertaking a ground attack operation against Argentine troops. Shortly after this, a ceasefire was agreed and the war ended. However, it is fair to say that the Black Buck raids were not only costly, but made little contribution to the outcome of the war and British ground forces would have prevailed anyway. Intriguingly, this was not quite the end of the story. According to classified information released in 2012, a series of post-war plans were drawn up by RAF Air Commodore Simon Baldwin to attack targets on the Argentine mainland using Vulcans. These strikes against air bases would be ready for approval if there had been any attempt to re-take the Falkland Islands.

For some months after the Argentine surrender, RAF crews who had taken part in the Black Buck raids undertook night-time training sorties over remote areas of Scotland. In the event of further hostilities, raids would be launched from Ascension Island under cover of darkness. Each aircraft would be fitted with defensive Sidewinder AAMs to supplement electronic countermeasures and they would navigate over enemy territory with terrain following radar. Two Vulcans would be used in each raid. The first aircraft would launch Shrike ARMs to destroy the enemy's radar and the second Vulcan would deliver a full load of free-fall 1,000 lb (450 kg) bombs to the target. Training moved to Goose Bay, Canada, but as things worked out, there was a change of government in Argentina and the threat passed.

The Vulcan was formally retired from RAF service as a bomber in December 1982, although six of the remaining B.2s were converted into tankers, with hose-drum units fitted into the rear fuselage. This would fill a worrying gap before the VC 10 tankers entered service as support aircraft for the new Tornados.

The modified Vulcans were now re-designated as K.2 aircraft and operated by Number 50 Squadron until March 1984, when they were finally disbanded.

Unusual Developments

During the early 1950s, Avro undertook a detailed study for an airliner primarily based on the Vulcan B.1. At the same time Vickers and Handley Page also considered developing the Valiant and Victor into transporters and airliners that could enter service by 1960. The Avro delta design was given the company reference Type 722 and the name Atlantic. It would use the same engines as the Vulcan, an extended fuselage and a similar delta wing. Several passenger layouts were proposed, with rear-facing seats that are generally accepted for military transporters. The Atlantic would have been an impressive looking aircraft that would have set the standard until larger passenger capacity became the main requirement.

It is conceivable that the airlines felt the Atlantic aircraft would be too expensive to fully develop, might not prove to be cost-effective and had limited scope for future upgrades, especially with engines mounted in the wing roots. As things worked out, the Boeing 707 became top dog and commercial aircraft derived from British V-Bombers never materialised.

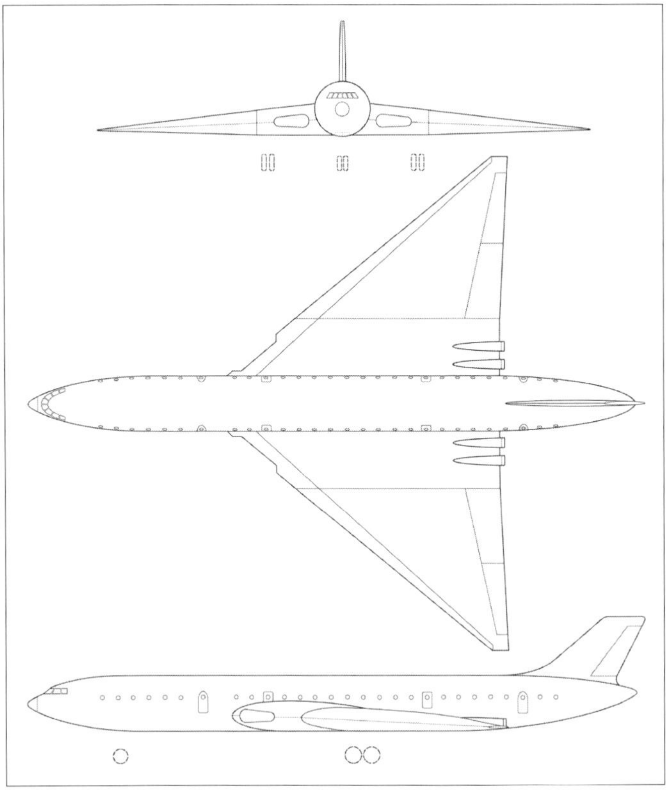

Avro's Atlantic was an airliner, designed in the early 1950s and derived from the Avro Vulcan bomber. Despite its sophistication, the company was unable to secure any commercial interest and the proposal was finally abandoned.

The Vulcan was considered suitable for use as a test bed for new engines under development and the substantial ground clearance below the aircraft proved useful for this purpose. A B.1 (XA894) was substantially adapted to carry a single Olympus 22R turbojet with afterburner (below the fuselage) that was intended for the BAC TSR.2 strike aircraft. Ground testing began during January 1962 at Filton airfield and flight tests soon followed. Things went well, including a demonstration at that year's Farnborough Air show. However, the trials ran into catastrophic problems on 3 December 1962, when the Olympus engine was run up to full power on the runway. At this point, a turbine disc failed and the engine caught fire. The crew of the Vulcan escaped unhurt, but the aircraft was completely destroyed.

There was also a proposal to use a Vulcan for trials of the very advanced Bristol BS.100 vectored-thrust engine intended for the Hawker P.1154 and Republic-Fokker D-24 Alliance VTOL supersonic strike-fighters. Unfortunately, this ambitious engine was cancelled and the trials never took place.

In the mid-1960s, the last remaining airworthy Vulcan B.1 (XA903) was pressed into service by Rolls-Royce as the testbed for another new engine. This was a prototype afterburning Olympus 593 turbojet with French designed variable geometry exhaust system, expected to power the supersonic Concorde airliner. It was housed in a nacelle below the fuselage and trials began on 9 September 1966 in a ten phase series of tests that lasted until the 21 July 1971. The Vulcan was restricted to a maximum speed of Mach 0.98, which reflects the Vulcan's aerodynamic limitations rather than the 593 engine's performance, with it reaching a thrust of 35,190 lb (157 kN) on several occasions which was actually beyond its design specifications. In all, 219 flights were undertaken, with just a few minor incidents and no major emergencies.

With Concorde 001 having flown in 1969, it was time to move ahead to the next engine testing project and XA903 was requisitioned to test the new RB.199 three-spool afterburning turbofan that would power the Panavia Tornado. Trials began at Filton during 1972 and would last for several years, with two engines and 120 hours of flight time allocated to XA903.

There were a few design proposals for the Vulcan that never progressed very far. One attributed to Avro's design office, suggested a method to extend the RAF's nuclear strike range in the event that Blue Steel was scrapped. They proposed a modified B.2 able to carry three Folland Gnat fighters underneath it. Each Gnat would be equipped with extra fuel tanks and a single tactical nuclear bomb. Assuming the Gnats managed to reach their targets the chances of escaping hostile territory were clearly very slim and the whole idea seems to have been rejected at an early stage.

Another proposal was to equip the proposed Phase 6 Vulcan with a much greater conventional bombing capability. Two large underwing pods would be carried, each containing two clusters of 7 × 1,000 lb (450 kg) bombs and a revised bomb bay would accommodate a further 10 × 1,000 lb (450 kg) bombs, providing a very substantial increase in capability over the B.2. Much later in the 1970s, there appears to have been some discussion about adapting B.2s to make use of laser guided bombs, but this failed to materialise.

There were also several proposals to use modified Vulcans as launch vehicles for long range nuclear ballistic missiles, rockets capable of placing satellites in orbit and as motherships for small manned rocket planes. Also, a rather strange VTOL missile launching version. These will be discussed in later chapters.

And finally as a footnote, I will just mention that Vulcans have appeared in several British feature films and TV series. VX890 puts in a brief appearance at the start of a little known Danziger's sci-fi film called *Satellite in the Sky* (1956). There was also a Vulcan used in the James Bond film *Thunderball* (1965). This aircraft seen in the underwater sequences is a mixture of miniatures and a fake (partial) full-sized Vulcan. Those aircraft that appear earlier in flight or on the ground are Vulcan B.1As (XA913 & XH506). UK televisions series that have made use of Vulcan bombers, include *The Avengers*, *The Champions* and *Bugs*.

Avro's Research Deltas

Vast amounts of captured German research material had pointed towards the advantages of the delta wing and its suitability for high-speed flight. This initially led British designers to start work on the Avro 698 bomber, but there was still a considerable knowledge gap and scientists at the RAE were eager to start an evaluation programme with manned aircraft. Avro had proposed a glider to provide initial data for their bomber project, but the RAE was not entirely happy with the idea and wanted to extend their research much further. After discussions with the MoS, Avro proposed the twin-engined 710 scale model of the 698 and a smaller single engined delta with the reference 707.

Specification E.15/48 was issued and preparations to start construction of initial prototypes began in 1948. However, as mentioned earlier, it was realised that there was little purpose to proceeding with the 710 and this was cancelled. Official interest now focused on the single engine Derwent powered 707 which the RAE were eager to obtain for general delta research and to assist with the development of aircraft like the proposed Avro Type 698.

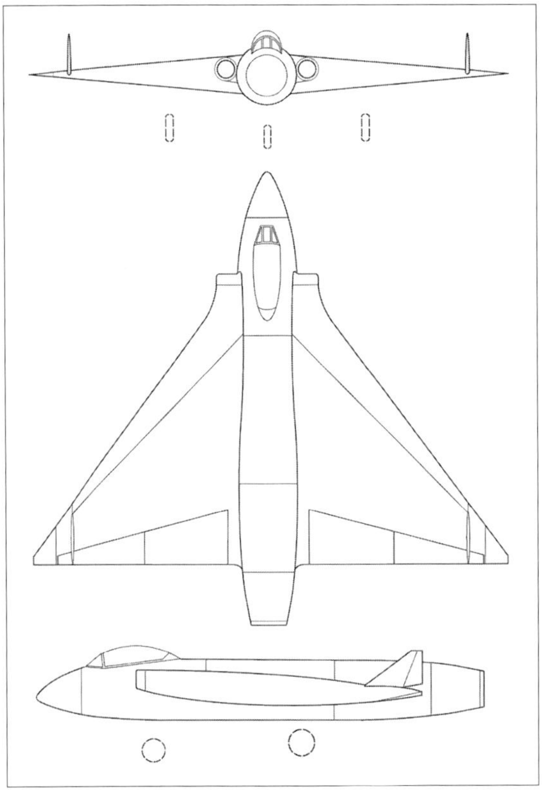

The initial Avro 707 design, proposed in 1948.

While the high-speed potential of the delta was already accepted, it would be necessary to secure a detailed technical understanding of the way it behaved in a range of situations, especially at relatively low speeds.

So, it was soon agreed with the MoS to proceed with a delta wing Avro 707A which was effectively a one-third scale sized version of the Type 698. The number of Avro 707 aircraft ordered by the RAE then increased and five would be built. Despite representing a new type of aircraft, the first Avro 707 (VX784) was, like many prototypes, assembled using a number of readily available off-the-shelf components. The powerplant was a fairly basic Rolls Royce Derwent 5 centrifugal-flow turbojet with a rating of 3,500 lb (15.5 kN) static thrust and this was fed by a dorsal air intake. This was aerodynamically advanced, but otherwise nothing unusual, with quite a few components being provided by the Hawker Siddeley organisation. The aircraft flew for the first time on 4 September 1949 and was then displayed at the 1949 SBAC Farnborough Air Show. But during a test flight from Farnborough on 30 September 1949, Flight Lieutenant Samuel Eric Esler (1918–1949) lost control of the aircraft when entering a low-speed stall near Blackbushe, Hampshire, it crashed moments later and Esler was killed. Apparently the aircraft was not fitted with an ejector seat, although it has been suggested that this probably would not have saved him at low altitude. The accident was almost certainly caused by faulty air brakes which locked open and as a consequence, various modifications were made to the next two 707 aircraft.

The Avro 707B (VX790) visibly differed from the first aircraft having a new nose probe fitted that was 12 ft (3.65 m) longer than planned. There were also changes to the nose gear, cockpit canopy, a slight leading edge sweep alteration and eventually, the installation of an ejector seat. VX790 would make its first flight on 6 September 1950 at Boscombe Down, with Wing Commander 'Roly' Falk at the controls.

However, the 707 project was now somewhat out of sync due to the accident and work on the next aircraft had been delayed as parts being used to construct this aircraft were fitted to VX790. As a consequence, the 707 which followed was given the official serial WD280 and it was known as the Avro 707A. The first test flight was undertaken on 14 June 1951. This aircraft had a number of different features specified by the RAE, which included engine air intakes located in the wing roots and a slightly different leading edge sweep, more in keeping with the full sized bomber. Some changes were made to the control surfaces and a Derwent 8 engine was installed, with WD280 configured for relatively high-speed subsonic flight. After lengthy trials, various modifications were made to the leading edge, bringing it in line with Vulcan upgrades. This aircraft was followed by another 707A (WZ736), which made its initial flight on 20 February 1953.

Flight testing of the 707B at Dunsfold Aerodrome, Surrey generally confirmed that the delta wing handled satisfactorily at low speed. Changes were then made to the dorsal engine intake, which was replaced by a more efficient NACA venturi inlet. However, the new style cockpit canopy was responsible for generating unwelcome air turbulence directly behind it and this directly affected the dorsal air flow, causing engine problems that needed to be resolved. There were also problems with pitch stability and in general terms, more time was spent fixing issues with this aircraft that undertaking research for the 698 project.

On 21 September 1951, the 707B was quite badly damaged during a very hard landing and although it was not a write-off, the aircraft required repair at Woodford. Once it was returned to Boscombe Down, the 707B continued to undertake research flights for the RAE and was also flown by the Empire Test Pilots School (ETPS), until it suffered another, more serious landing accident at Farnborough on 25 September 1956. It was now beyond the point of repair and engineers stripped all the useful components from it, for use with the remaining 707s. In 1960, what remained of the 707B was formally scrapped.

Avro 707B (VX790) on the apron with the NACA dorsal intake and modified canopy. The background of this picture was slightly retouched to aid clarity.

After being transported from Woodford to Boscombe Down, Avro 707A (WD280) began a lengthy series of trials. It differed from the other Avro deltas, in being set-up for high subsonic flight. Its delta wing was closer in configuration to the 698, with cropped wingtips, hydraulically operated control surfaces and wing root air inlets for the engine. The absence of the dorsal air intake also allowed a larger tail fin to be fitted. Like the other aircraft in this series, much time was initially taken up dealing with problems that were generally unconnected with the 698 programme. However, in 1954, WD280 underwent further modifications to the wing's leading edge which was very much connected to the Vulcan upgrade. During 1956, WD280 was retired from RAE service and shipped to the Australian Aeronautical Research Council (AARC) for further flight trials. These would continue for several years, until the aircraft was finally decommissioned in 1967 and sold to a private collector. In 1999, it was purchased by the RAAF Museum, fully restored and is now on display at Point Cook.

The second 707A (WZ736) and the two-seat, side-by-side 707C (WZ744) were built at Avro's Bracebridge Heath Works near Lincoln, which was a large facility normally used as an aircraft service centre. Because of this, WZ736 first flew at nearby RAF Waddington on 20 February 1953 and this was followed by WZ744 on 1 July 1953. The dual-control 707C was intended as a trainer for the Avro 698 bomber, but the Vulcan proved easier to fly than expected and WZ744 would be used for wider research purposes by the RAE. A second 707C had been planned and was assigned the serial WZ739, with the possibility of two more but these follow-on aircraft were cancelled. Both WZ736 and WZ744 were then flown to Woodford and once fully tested, were passed to the RAE at Farnborough and Bedford.

The two aircraft played almost no part in the Vulcan's development and WZ736 was mostly used for advanced throttle development until 1964, while WZ744 was chosen for the development of fly-by-wire systems, remaining in RAE service until 1967. Both aircraft would end up in museums, with WZ736 located at the Manchester Museum of Science and Industry, and WZ744 currently in storage at the RAF Museum, Cosford.

As things worked out, the Avro 707s played a relatively minor role in the Avro Vulcan's development, although their contribution to a better understanding of delta wing aircraft was considerable. They were also used to develop a number of new aircraft systems like fly-by-wire, which are now largely taken for granted.

Aircraft associated with the 707 were the supersonic Avro 720 series of designs, which are discussed in a later chapter and the proposed Avro 727 ground attack-fighter which was conceived to meet a 1954 NATO requirement. This called for a strike aircraft, also capable of operating as a light fighter. It would have a low level maximum speed of Mach 0.95, be able to operate from a modest grass landing strip and could deliver two 500 lb (226.7 kg) bombs.

The principle competitors for this NATO request were the Fiat G.91, Breguet Br 1001, Dassault Mystère XXVI and a version of the Folland Gnat.

Avro's delta wing submission for this very compact, single-seat combat aircraft was to be powered by a Bristol BE.26 Orpheus, that would be uprated to provide 4,850 lb (21.57 kN) static thrust, without an afterburner. The gross weight was set at 10,214 lb (4,633 kg), allowing a maximum speed of Mach 0.97 and an expected ceiling of 46,000 ft (13,020 m). The aircraft would be able to meet the payload requirements easily and could deliver a maximum of two 1,000 lb (453.5 kg) bombs or napalm tanks. It would also be armed with two 30 mm ADEN cannon to undertake the fighter role. The final choice in this contest was announced in early 1958 and it was the Fiat G.91, which would serve with the West German and Italian air forces.

Avro 707A (WD280) in flight above the English countryside during the early 1950s. In 1956, it was transferred to the RAAF. It was retired from service in 1967 and became an RAAF museum exhibit in 1999.

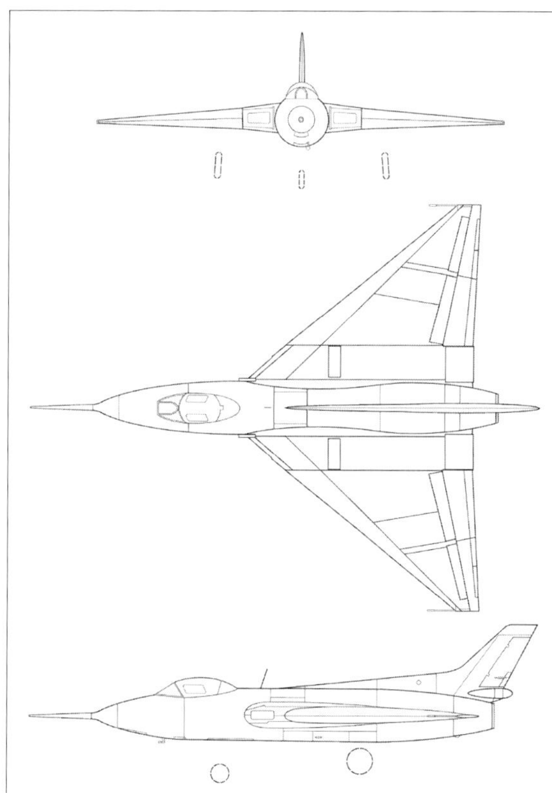

General arrangement of the Avro 707A.

Avro 707C (WZ744) in flight. The aircraft remained in service until 1967, when it became a museum exhibit.

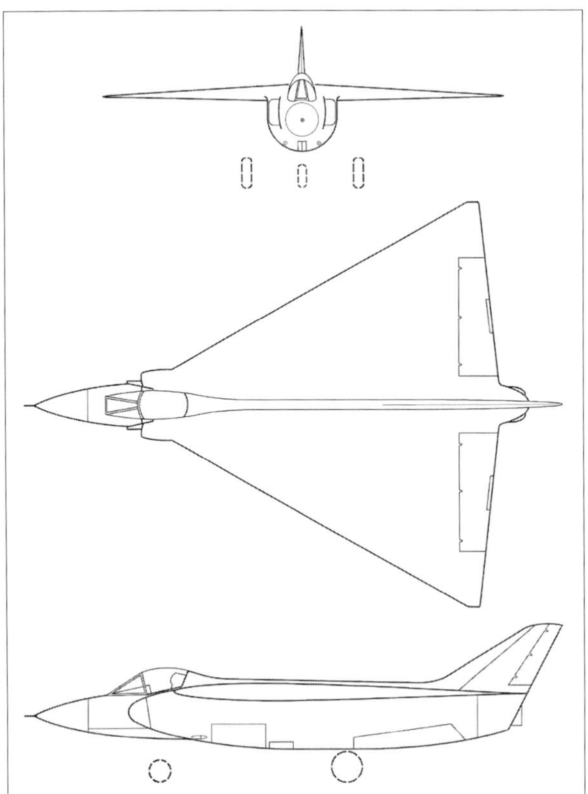

The Avro 727 as proposed in 1954 to meet NATO combat aircraft requirements.

Armstrong Whitworth A.W.50 Bomber
Crew: 6
Wingspan: 120 ft (36.6 m), later reduced to 112.5 ft (34.3 m)
Wing area: 2,000.04 ft^2 (185.8 m^2)
Length: 45 ft (13.7 m)
Height: N/A
Gross weight: 49,765 lb (22,573 kg)
Maximum speed: 470 mph (756 kph) at sea level and 480 mph (772 kph) at 30,000 ft (9,144 m)
Rate of climb: 3,000 ft/per min (914 m/per min)
Ceiling: unknown
Range: 1,500 miles (2,424 km)
Powerplant: 4 × Metropolitan-Vickers (Metrovick) F.2/4 Beryl axial-flow turbojet engines, initially producing 3,500 lb (15.5 kN) static thrust
Armament: provisionally, 2 × 20 mm forward firing cannon and one rear firing remote controlled turret with 2 × 20 mm cannon. Bomb load: 12,000 lb (5,443 kg)

Armstrong Whitworth A.W.52G
Crew: 2
Wingspan: 53.83 ft (16.41 m)
Wing area: 443.04 ft^2 (41.16 m^2)
Length: 19.33 ft (5.89 m)
Height: 8.33 ft (2.54 m)
Gross weight: 6,000lb (2,724 kg) approximate
Powerplant: none
Glide speed: 100–120 mph (160–190 kph) approximate
Maximum permitted speed: 250 mph (400 kph)

Armstrong Whitworth A.W.52 Jet (TG363)
Crew: 2
Wingspan: 90 ft (27.4 m)
Sweep (leading edge): Initial 17.5°, followed by 34° to the wingtips
Wing area: 1,314 ft^2 (122 m^2)
Length: 37.33 ft (11.4 m)
Height: 14.33 ft (4.4 m)
Empty weight: 19,662 lb (8,919 kg)
Gross weight: 34,154 lb (15,492 kg)
Powerplant: 2 × Rolls-Royce Nene 2 turbojets, each rated at 5,000 lb (22.2 kN) static thrust
Maximum speed: 500 mph (800 kph) estimated
Ceiling: 35–40,000 ft (10–12,000 m) estimated
Range: 1,000 miles (1,600 km) estimated

Armstrong Whitworth A.W.56 Tailless Medium Bomber Project (OR.229)
Crew: 5
Wingspan: 120 ft (36.58 m). Revised: 102 ft (31 m)
Wing area: 2,611 ft^2 (242.56 m^2). Revised: 2,250 ft^2 (209 m^2)
Length: 80 ft (24.38 m). Revised: 75 ft (22.8 m)
Height: 32 ft (9.75 m) unconfirmed
Gross weight: 113,000 lb (51,256 kg). Revised: 101,150 lb (45,881 kg)
Powerplant: 5 × Rolls-Royce AJ65 Avon turbojets, each rated at 6,500 lb (28.9 kN) static thrust. Revised: 4 × AJ65 engines, or possibly RR RB.77 at 7,500 lb (33.3 kN) static thrust
Maximum speed: 640 mph 1,030 kph. Revised: 575 mph (925 kph)
Ceiling: 50,000 ft (15,240 m)
Range: carrying a 10,000 lb (4,535 kg) bomb load, initially expected to be 1,724 miles (2,776 km)
Armament: maximum 20,000 lb (9,071 kg) bomb load. Either, one nuclear weapon, two ground penetrating bombs, 3 × 6,000 lb (2,721 kg) bombs, or various smaller free fall bombs

Short PD.1 Bomber
Crew: 5
Wingspan: 114 ft (34.74 m) estimated
Sweep (inner leading edge): 42.25°
Wing area: N/A
Length: 102 ft (31 m)
Height: N/A
Empty weight: N/A
Gross weight: N/A
Powerplant: 4 × Rolls-Royce AJ65 Avon turbojets, each rated at 6,500 lb (28.9 kN) static thrust
Maximum speed: 570 mph (917 kph)
Ceiling 50,000 ft (15,000 m)
Range: 5,000 miles (8,000 km)
Armament: 10,000 lb (4,500 kg) payload—one nuclear bomb

Short SB.4 Sherpa
Crew: 1
Wingspan: 38 ft (11.58 m)
Sweep (leading edge): 42°
Wing area: 230 ft^2 (21.4 m^2)
Length: 31.83 ft (9.7 m)
Height: 9 ft (2.7 m)
Empty weight: 3,000 lb (1,400 kg)
Loaded weight: 3,268 lb (1,482 kg)
Powerplant: 2 × Blackburn Turboméca Palas turbojet, each rated at 350 lb (1.55 kN) thrust
Maximum speed: 170 mph (150 kts, 275 kph)
Cruise speed: 117 mph (102kts, 188 kph)
Ceiling: 5,000 ft (1,500 m)
Endurance: 45-50 min

Short PD.13 Naval Strike
Crew: 2
Wingspan: 38 ft (11.58 m)
Sweep (leading edge): 60° estimated

Wing area: 482 ft² (44.77 m²)
Length: 51 ft (15.5 m)
Height: N/A
Empty weight: 24,000 lb (10,886 kg)
Gross weight: 41,000 lb (18,598 kg)
Powerplant: 2 × Rolls-Royce AJ65 Avon turbojets, each rated at 6,500 lb (28.9 kN) static thrust
Maximum speed: 758 mph (1,220 kph) at sea level. 700 mph (1,126 kph) at 30,000 ft (9,144 m)
Ceiling: 45,000 ft (13,716 m)
Range: 480 miles (773 km)
Armament: rockets, bombs or one free-fall nuclear weapon

Westland M.148
Crew: 2
Wingspan: 43 ft (13.1 m)
Length: 50.10 ft (15 m)
Wing area: 863 ft² (80 m²)
Gross weight: 40,915 lb (18,558 kg)
Powerplant: 2 × PS.43 Gyron Junior turbojets, each rated at 6,830 lb (30.4 kN) static thrust
Performance: max speed: 758 mph (439 kph) at sea level. 709 mph (410 kph) at 30,000 ft (9,144 m)
Dive speed 760 mph (1,223 kph)
Ceiling: N/A
Armament: 1 × tactical nuclear weapon. A maximum of 8,000 lb (3,628 kg) free-fall bombs, mines or rockets

HP.80 (1946 Specification)
Crew: 4-5
Wingspan: 122 ft (37 m)
Sweep (leading edge): 45°
Length: 92 ft (28 m)
Height: 21 ft (6.4 m)
Powerplant: 4 × axial flow turbojets
Maximum speed: 570 mph (917 kph)
Ceiling: 50,000 ft (15,000 m)
Range: 5,000 miles (8,000 km)
Armament: 10,000 lb (4,500 kg) payload. Conventional bombs or one nuclear weapon

Avro Vulcan B1 Bomber
Crew 5
Wingspan: 99 ft (30.2 m)
Wing area 3,554 ft² (330 m²)
Length: 97.08 ft (29.6 m)
Height: 26.5 ft (8.1 m)
Weight: Empty—83,573 lb (37,144 kg)
Weight: Maximum takeoff—170,000 lb (77,100 kg)
Powerplant: Initially 4 × Rolls-Royce Olympus 101 turbojets, each rated at 11,000 lb (49 kN) static thrust. Later aircraft used Olympus 102 or 104 engines
Maximum speed: 625 mph (1,005 kph)
Ceiling: 55,000 ft (16,750 m)
Range: 3,000 miles (4,828 km)

Avro Vulcan B2 Bomber
Crew: 5
Wingspan: 111 ft (33.83 m)
Wing area: 3,964 ft² (368.27 m²)
Length: 99.91 ft (30.45 m). 105.5 ft (32.16 m) with refuelling probe
Height: 27.16 ft (8.28 m)
Normal take-off weight: 179,898 lb (81,591 kg)
Maximum take-off weight: 200,180 lb (90,718 kg)
Powerplant: 4 × Bristol Siddeley Olympus 201 turbojets each rated at 17,000 lb (75.6 kN) static thrust. Alternatively, Olympus 301 turbojets each rated at 20,000 lb (89 kN) static thrust
Maximum speed: 645 mph (1,038 kph)
Ceiling: 55,000 ft (16,750 m)
Absolute ceiling: 64,000 ft (19,507 m)
Range (internal fuel): 3,400 miles (5,471 km)
Ferry range: 4,750 miles (7,644 km)
Armament: 21 × 1,000 lb (454 kg) conventional bombs, or nuclear payload. Provision to carry one Blue Steel air-to-surface nuclear missile, and some aircraft were adapted to carry Douglas Skybolt missiles underwing. Despite Skybolt being cancelled the pylons were late used operationally to carry Shrike anti-radiation missiles and the carriage of Sidewinder AAMs was briefly considered

Avro Atlantic Type 722 Transporter/Airliner
Crew: 4, plus 3 or 4 staff
Passengers: 113 (max)
Wingspan: 121 ft (36.8 m)
Fuselage Width: 12.5 ft (3.8 m)
Length: 145 ft (44 m)
Maximum weight: 200,000 lb (90,718 kg)
Powerplant: 4 × Rolls-Royce Olympus turbojets
Cruising speed: 600 mph Mach 0.80
Cruise altitude: 45,000 ft (13,716 m)
Range: 4,000 miles (6,437 km)

Avro 707
Crew: 1
Wingspan: 33 ft (10.06 m)
Wing area: N/A
Length: 30 ft 6in (9.29 m)
Height: N/A
Powerplant: One Rolls-Royce Derwent 5 turbojet, rated at 3,500 lb (15.5 kN) static thrust
Weights: empty N/A; loaded 8,600 lb (3,901 kg)
Maximum speed: N/A
Ceiling: N/A

Avro 707A
Crew: 1
Wingspan: 34.1 ft (10.41 m)
Wing area: 420 ft^2 (39.02 m^2)
Length: 42.33 ft (12.90 m)
Height: 11.58 ft (3.53 m)
Powerplant: 1 × Rolls-Royce Derwent 8 turbojet, rated at 3,600 lb (16 kN) static thrust
Weights: empty: N/A; loaded 9,500 lb (4,309 kg)
Maximum speed: Mach 0.95 in a shallow dive
Ceiling: N/A
Range: N/A

Avro 707B
Crew: 1
Wingspan: 33 ft (10.06 m)
Wing area: N/A
Length: 42.33 ft (12.90 m)
Height: 11.75 ft (3.58 m)
Powerplant: 1 × Rolls-Royce Derwent 5 turbojet of 3,500 lb (15.5 kN) static thrust
Weights: Empty N/A; loaded 9,500 lb (4,309 kg)
Maximum speed: Mach 0.8
Ceiling: N/A
Range: N/A

Avro 707C
Crew: 2
Wingspan: 34.16 ft (10.41 m)
Wing area: 420 ft^2 (39 m^2)
Length: 42.33 ft (12.90 m)
Height: 11.58 ft (3.53 m)
Powerplant: 1 × Rolls-Royce Derwent 8 turbojet, each rated at 3,600 lb (16 kN) static thrust
Weights: empty 7,873 lb (3,571 kg); loaded 9,826 lb (4,457 kg)
Maximum speed: N/A
Ceiling: N/A
Range: N/A

Avro 727
Crew: 1
Wingspan: 27.25 ft (8.3 m)
Wing area: 360 ft^2 (33.44 m^2)
Length: 37.79 ft (11.51 m)
Height: N/A
Powerplant: 1 × Bristol BE.26 Orpheus (uprated) 4,850 lb (21.57 kN) static thrust
All-up-weight: 10,214 lb (4,633 kg)
Maximum speed: Mach 0.97
Ceiling: 46,000 ft (13,020 m)
Range: N/A
Armament: 2 × 30 mm ADEN cannon, or four .50 12.5 mm Browning machine guns. 2 × 500 lb (226.7 kg) or 2 × 1,000 lb (453.5 kg) bombs or napalm tanks.

3

Post-war Fighters

As the Second World War drew to an end in Europe, a number of American/British (T-Force units) and (a lesser number of) Russian technical intelligence teams were assembled for the specific purpose of locating and securing the Nazi's best kept military secrets. Germany was one of the most scientifically advanced nations in the world and there was clearly much to be gained. Tracking down secret cutting edge aviation projects and the scientists who worked on them, was high on every official list, alongside rocketry, weapons of mass destruction, sophisticated electronic systems and a host of other possibilities. Soon after hostilities ceased, the teams began to locate large amounts of hardware and this was rapidly shipped home for detailed evaluation. In some areas, German technical research and development was well ahead of any other nation and aircraft designers had been contemplating intercontinental jet bombers, vertical take-off fighters and supersonic flight. The degree of progress made was truly impressive and it would strongly influence aviation for at least the next ten years and perhaps somewhat longer.

When allied forces arrived at the Luftfahrtforschungsanstalt (Aeronautical Research Institute, also known as the Hermann Göring Research Institute), which was located at Völkenrode, near Braunschweig, they were astounded by how advanced the facility was. British and American scientists regarded this Institute as the best aeronautical research establishment in the world and it had survived the war untouched. In addition to the massive A3 wind tunnel that was large enough to accommodate aircraft like the Me 109 and Ar 234 jet bomber, there were the A6 and A7 tunnels that had been used to test models at supersonic velocities. Study and removal of equipment and research material continued until 1948, which indicates the scale of what was there. The Americans seized a vast amount of equipment and recruited the best German scientists, while the British took at least one entire wind tunnel and re-assembled it at the RAE Farnborough, along with much of the A9 tunnel, which went to RAE Bedford. After this, a good part of the Institute was blown up, although some of the buildings still survive today.

In addition to the large amounts of hardware and documentation, the Allies now had many of Germany's most capable designers and engineers in their custody, who had managed to avoid capture by the Soviets and chose to end up in American or British hands. This included people like Dr Alexander Lippisch and the Horten Brothers, who played very important roles

Dr Alexander Lippisch, seen here with two models of his delta winged designs, was perhaps one of the most influential aircraft designers of the 20th Century.

A Messerschmitt Bf-109 E3 is being used for wind tunnel trials at the Luftfahrtforschungsanstalt Hermann Goering, located at Volkenrode during 1940. At that time this facility was the most sophisticated of its kind in the world.

in the early development of flying wings and deltas. Indeed, the shadow of their signatures can still be seen on some present day aircraft. Lippisch was already well-known to the Allies, but his work on development of the delta wing proved to be a big step forward and models of his most advanced designs had been wind tunnel tested up to speeds of Mach 2.6 with very encouraging results.

Lippisch had selected a leading edge wing sweep of 60°, which he considered optimal for supersonic flight and this generated immediate interest amongst American and British scientists, who regarded it as a magic number in the quest for greater speed. Once the war ended, Lippisch agreed to work for the Americans and was encouraged to complete construction of his full-sized DM-1 prototype delta winged glider. Much of his research material was made available to the British and the extent of his influence on post-war military aircraft design cannot be overstated.

It is also worth mentioning that one of the final wartime Horten designs, was a proposed supersonic interceptor with the designation Ho XIIIB. Like the Lippisch DM-1 and P.13A, this near delta had a 60° sweep and the pilot was accommodated in the tail fin. However, the favoured propulsion was a BMW 003R turbojet/rocket engine carried beneath the fuselage allowing a brief maximum speed of 1,118 mph (1,799 kph) to be attained at high altitude. It is very hard to avoid concluding that the design was built with some collaboration with Lippisch, but this was always denied by the Hortens.

In the years that followed, German delta wing research would lead to a whole range of American and British aircraft that included the Skyhawk, XF-92, F-102, B-58, Avro Vulcan and Gloster Javelin.

Lippisch's DM-1 glider and a large amount of documentation was shipped to NACA Langley in the US, where various aerodynamic problems were discovered at transonic speeds. Nevertheless, NACA scientists remained sure these issues could be resolved and their findings were passed to Convair, who began development of the experimental XP-92, with assistance from Lippisch.

Lippisch DM-1 prototype glider, recovered by the US Army in 1945.

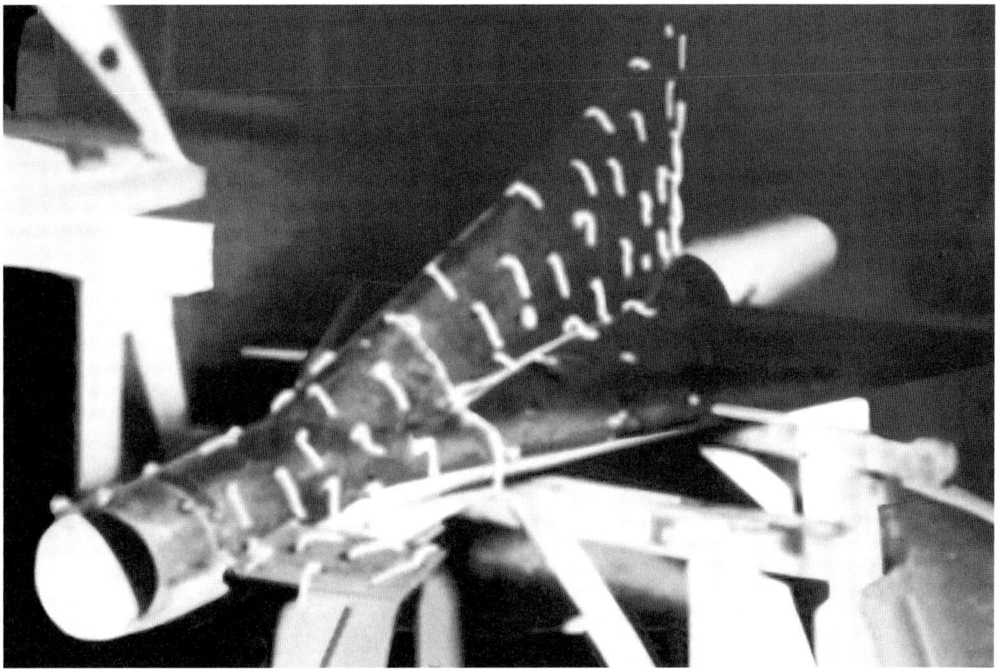

Wind tunnel model of the Lippisch P.13A ramjet interceptor.

This illustration of a Horten Ho XIIIB has been in circulation for decades and appears to show a scale model, possibly built by the Horten Brothers. It has often been described as proof that a prototype was built and flown, although this clearly never happened.

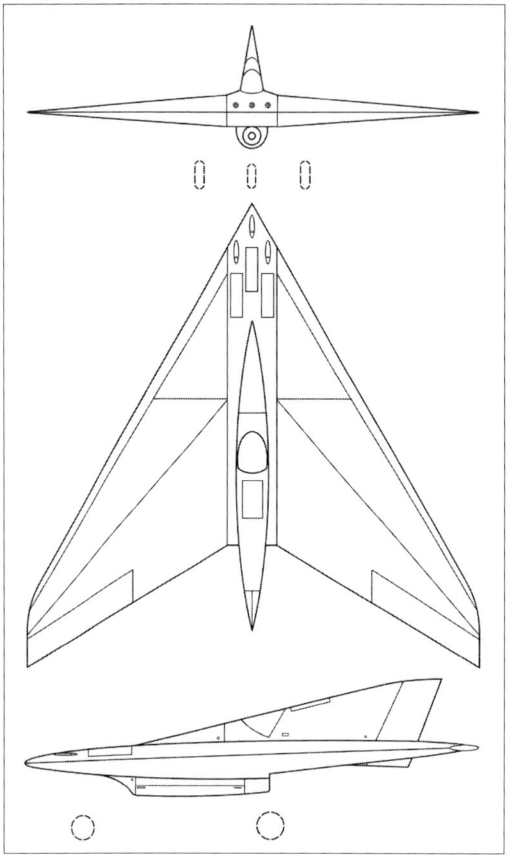

General arrangement of the proposed Horten XIIIB supersonic interceptor, which was based on the Ho XIIIA glider.

Meanwhile, a number of British aircraft manufacturers were provided with seized German research documentation by the RAE and encouraged to investigate the possibility of utilising it to develop new military aircraft. The full extent of this is unknown, but one company who carefully evaluated Lippisch and possibly Horten's work was Martin Baker. Today, they are best known as a manufacturer of ejection seats, but James Martin and Valentine Baker began as small scale aircraft constructors in 1934, producing four prototypes, which were the M.B.1, M.B.2, M.B.3 and M.B.5. However, they failed to secure any contracts and the company's main business remained the manufacture of components for larger aircraft companies. From the outset, Martin Baker had been developing ideas for an ejector seat, but it was 1944 when the Ministry of Aircraft Production officially asked them to design a system that would allow pilots to safely escape from a high-speed fighter. While this would become their main business, Martin Baker continued to work on designs for experimental military aircraft, moving onto jet powered fighters in late 1944. This resulted in the M.B.6, which was a very straightforward concept with a nose intake, forward positioned cockpit, straight wings and a rather crude landing skid arrangement. However, there was little official interest in the design, which seems to have been little more than a slightly larger version of the Gloster E.28/39. Nevertheless, after the war ended, Martin Baker's design office would appear to have obtained details of the most sophisticated German fighter designs produced by Lippisch and possibly the Hortens. This resulted in a significantly more advanced Martin Baker delta winged concept. Some sources have suggested this was designated as the M.B.6, which it obviously was not. There was an M.B.7 design, apparently given the unofficial name Black Bess, but this is understood to have been an advanced propeller driven aircraft, so if the delta was assigned a reference, it could have been the M.B.8, although nobody seems to know.

Work on this single-seat delta concept started during 1945 and continued into 1946. Like the German proposals, it carried the pilot in a section of the large tailfin and utilised a wing with a leading edge sweep of 60°. The big difference was propulsion with the Martin Baker fighter being powered by a single Rolls-Royce AJ65 Avon turbojet drawing air from a nose inlet fitted with a centre cone. A fully retractable tricycle undercarriage and pressurised cockpit with an ejector seat for the pilot were standard. Armament was two 20 mm cannon and no radar equipment was carried. As a daylight interceptor, it would have been directed from the ground, which was not unusual at that time. Anticipated performance was a maximum speed of 640 mph (1,029 kph) at sea level and a ceiling in the region of 50,000 ft (15,240 m). The proposal was originally intended to meet the Air Ministry Requirement F.43/46, but the company never submitted this design for official scrutiny. However, a small display model appeared at the 1947 SBAC Radlett show and at Farnborough the following year. It is believed that a number of models were wind tunnel tested, but nothing came of this concept, which was probably beyond the capability of Martin Baker to fully develop anyway.

Another delta wing design clearly drawing on captured German research material emerged during the early development stages of the Gloster Javelin and was submitted for official consideration in April 1948 to meet Specification F.3/48 (OR228). It is unclear exactly who worked on the design, but Gloster's Chief Designer (Wilfred) George Carter (1889–1969) was in overall charge. This delta interceptor was given the company reference P.275 and although a little less elegant than the Martin Baker design, it was quite advanced for its day.

The pressurised cockpit was located in the tailfin and Carter remarked that it would provide the pilot with a good forward view. Estimated performance was slightly better than the Martin Baker Delta, with a high subsonic maximum speed and the suggestion that it would be capable of reaching an absolute ceiling of 62,000 ft (18,897 m). The engine is not specified in available documentation, but it seems probable that the intended powerplant was a future afterburning version of the Armstrong Siddeley Sapphire. Apparently Gloster also indicated that it would be possible to produce a version of the P.275 that utilised a mixed propulsion system comprising of a turbojet and rocket engine. Supported on a fully retractable tricycle undercarriage, the P.275 had an estimated wingspan of 43 ft (13 m) and a leading edge sweep of 60° like the Martin Baker Delta. Interestingly, the P.275 would employ the Geoffrey Hill type 'all-moving' wingtips for control in place of a more conventional elevon system.

The estimated overall length would have been 49.5 ft (15 m) and the aircraft would be equipped with an airborne interception radar system using a scanner located in the air inlet cone. For armament, the P.275 would be fitted with four wing mounted 30 mm cannon. It is hard to know how far development of this concept progressed, but it seems possible that models were wind tunnel tested. However, the P.275 generated little official interest and it is probable that the Air Ministry simply regarded the design as too unconventional.

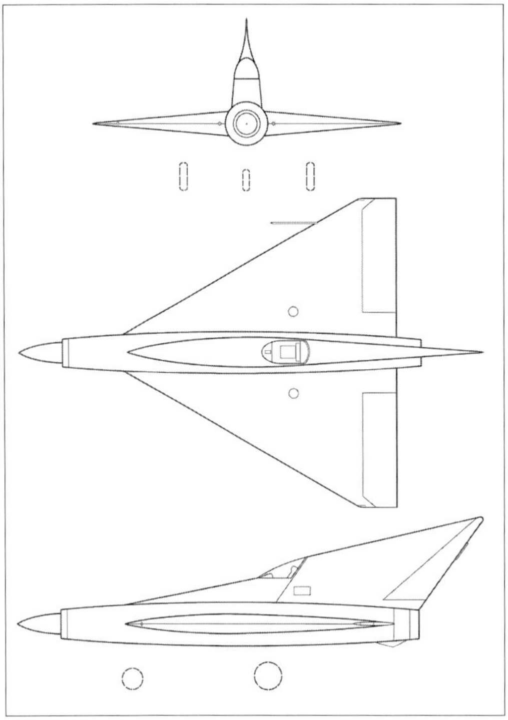

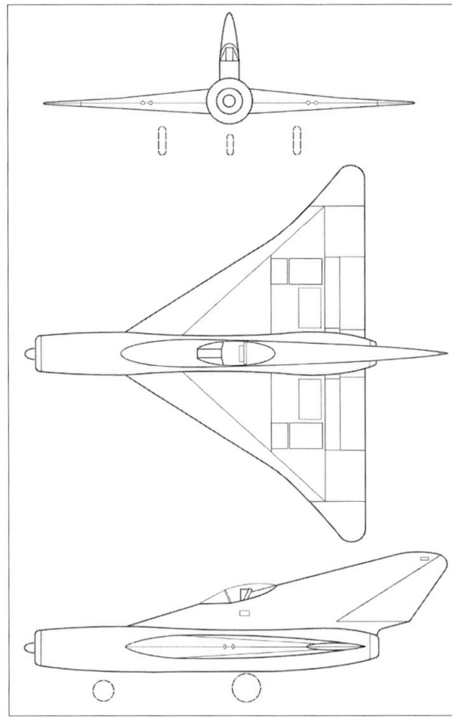

Left: Martin Baker's post-war Delta jet fighter design.

Right: Gloster's P.275 high performance jet fighter proposal of 1948. Similar in some respects to the Martin Baker concept and clearly drawing on Alexander Lippisch's wartime research.

Griffith Takes up the Lippisch Delta

After a lengthy period with the RAE, Dr Alan Arnold Griffith (1893–1963) joined Rolls-Royce, becoming their chief scientist. He was a leading expert on gas turbine engines and took a different approach from Frank Whittle, believing that the future lay with the axial flow designs as opposed to engines using a centrifugal compressor. While the Whittle engine proved to be a considerable success and earned him a knighthood, the axial flow designs produced by Griffith and those developed in Wartime Germany would ultimately prevail.

Griffith would also spend considerable time evaluating aircraft designs for jet engine use and he considered the possibilities this relatively new form of propulsion might provide for vertical take-off and landing (VTOL).

In keeping with the designers who created the Martin Baker Delta and the Gloster P.275, there can be little doubt that Griffith was strongly influenced by the work of Lippisch and/or the Hortens.

Griffith conceived a stretched, one-man delta with an air intake at the nose and another in the tailfin around the cockpit. Leading edge wing sweep, appears to be approximately 70° and Griffith used elevons and a rudder for control. His proposal was a supersonic aircraft that would be fitted with two separate rings of turbojets. The first ring would provisionally contain six engines and was positioned near the nose, with exhaust outlets below the wing's forward section.

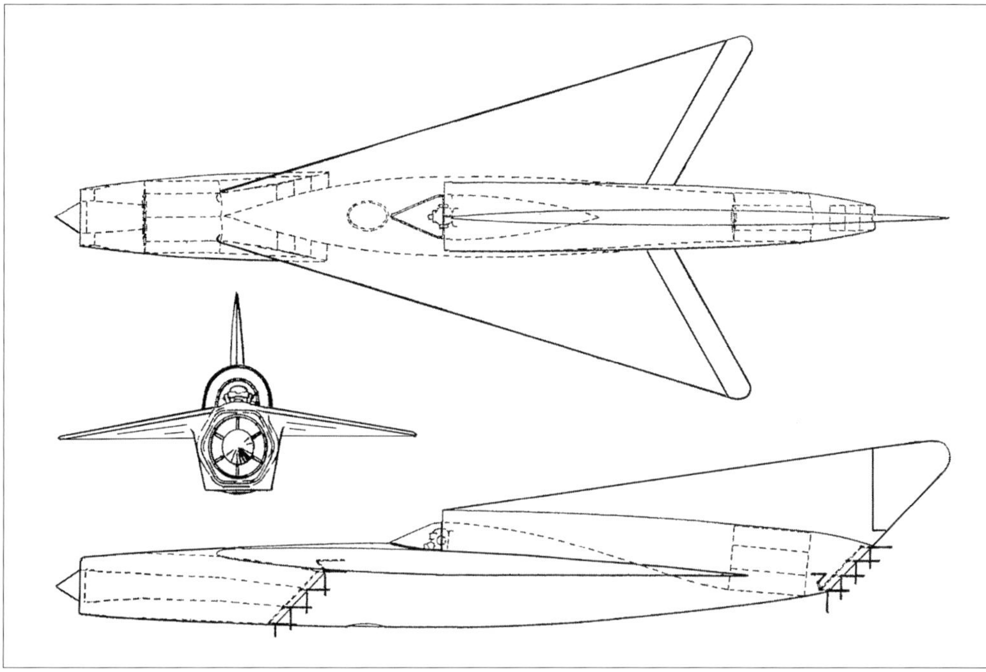

A 1951 Rolls-Royce outline for a supersonic aircraft powered by two rings of six jet engines. This design was produced by Alan Arnold Griffith and appears to be strongly influenced by the wartime work of Alexander Lippisch. It was clearly intended for development as a combat aircraft, but never progressed beyond the concept stage.

A second ring of compact turbojets would be located towards the rear of the fuselage, with air drawn in from the dorsal inlet and engine exhaust at the tail of the aircraft. Flaps would be fitted to front and rear exhaust sections that would direct the flow downwards and provide very short take-offs of perhaps, rather optimistically, VTOL. It is not clear when Griffith began work on this design but it was probably in the late 1940s. Rolls-Royce applied for a patent in November 1951 and this was not released until mid-1956 as GB753656. By that time, aircraft development had moved on quite a bit and the patent was no longer considered sensitive or probably viable from an engineering viewpoint.

Hill's Variable Geometry Tailless Delta

During the Second World War, Germany was at the cutting edge of aviation research and once hostilities ceased, Allied engineers wasted no time securing and evaluating the former enemy's most advanced projects. This included research into supersonic flight and variable geometry wings. Both the America and Britain were already working on research aircraft intended to exceed the 'sound barrier,' but the discovery of a prototype Messerschmitt P.1101 V1 jet fighter with variable wing sweep generated almost as much interest. This aircraft was only designed to have its wing position altered on the ground, but if this could be made to operate during flight it might open the door to good low speed handling with the wings opened out and supersonic speed with them fully swept.

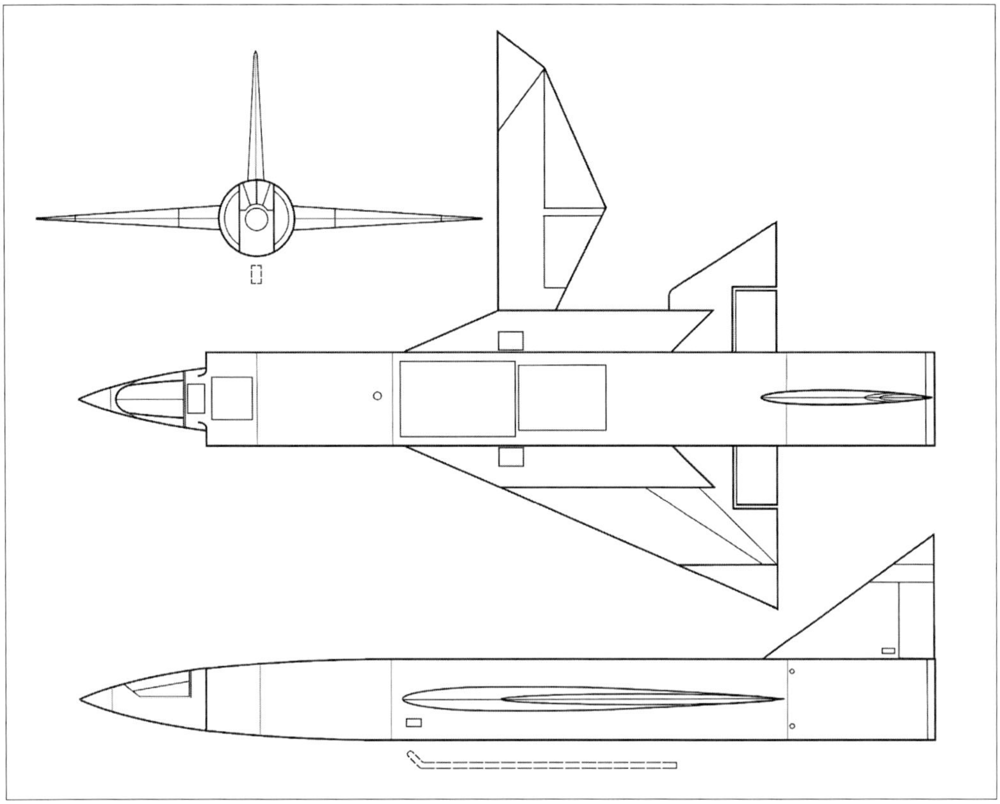

The jet powered Transformable Delta proposed by Geoffrey Hill as a research aircraft capable of supersonic flight.

The Americans were eager to see if the idea could be made to work and the aircraft was shipped to the US and evaluated by Robert J. Woods (1904-1956) and his design team at Bell Aviation, Buffalo, New York. It eventually led to the construction of two similar looking, but more advanced Bell X-5 prototypes, which featured electrically powered wing adjustment during flight and showed the concept was viable.

Professor Hill had begun to experiment with limited variable geometry in the early 1930s with the Pterodactyl Mk IV and his involvement with the NRC Pterodactyl and GAL gliders put him at the forefront of his field. Hill was totally familiar with the Air Ministry Specification E.24/43, for a supersonic aircraft, which had been awarded to Miles (as the M.52). In 1946, the Miles project was cancelled (for financial and almost certainly political reasons), with the Americans eventually carrying out the first rocket powered supersonic flight in October 1947. Nevertheless, considerable interest in building a jet-powered supersonic aircraft persisted in the UK and while he was acting as a consultant for General Aircraft Ltd (GAL), Hill conceived a supersonic tailless research aircraft that shared a similar looking fuselage to the Miles M.52. It was somewhat larger, with almost double the gross weight and would be powered by the high performance Rolls-Royce Avon turbojet that was under development. The pilot was housed in a jettisonable capsule and the undercarriage was a simple low-weight skid that would be extended prior to landing.

The most significant feature of this aircraft was a unique a delta wing that incorporated a variable sweep capability and additional wing tip control surfaces for high speed flight. Described as the 'Transformable Delta,' a preliminary design was submitted by GAL to the UK's Principle Director of Scientific Research on 7 February 1948, who rejected it almost immediately.

Professor Hill now revised the delta wing design, increasing the fully swept leading edge to 66.5° and suggesting that the aircraft would be able to reach Mach 1.38 at 38,000 ft (11,500 m). To maintain longitudinal trim and stability when altering wing sweep, it was proposed that some fuel would have to be pumped into auxiliary forward or rear tanks. The modified design was re-submitted in June 1948, but again met with rejection.

GAL were in the process of amalgamating with Blackburn Aircraft and the senior management fully supported Hill's work, convinced that it could lead to a variable geometry supersonic fighter. Consequently, Professor Hill and company designer Thomas Guppy continued to develop the design of an advanced swing-wing single-seat fighter, which would be powered by an Armstrong Siddeley Sapphire engine. Blackburn-GAL applied for a UK patent for this design in late 1949 and perhaps for security reasons, it remained unpublished for several years, although the original Transformable Delta was briefly described in a July 1951 *Flight* magazine article. Nothing came of either design, although by this time Barnes Wallace was making considerable headway with his own variable geometry research programme and this is discussed in a later section.

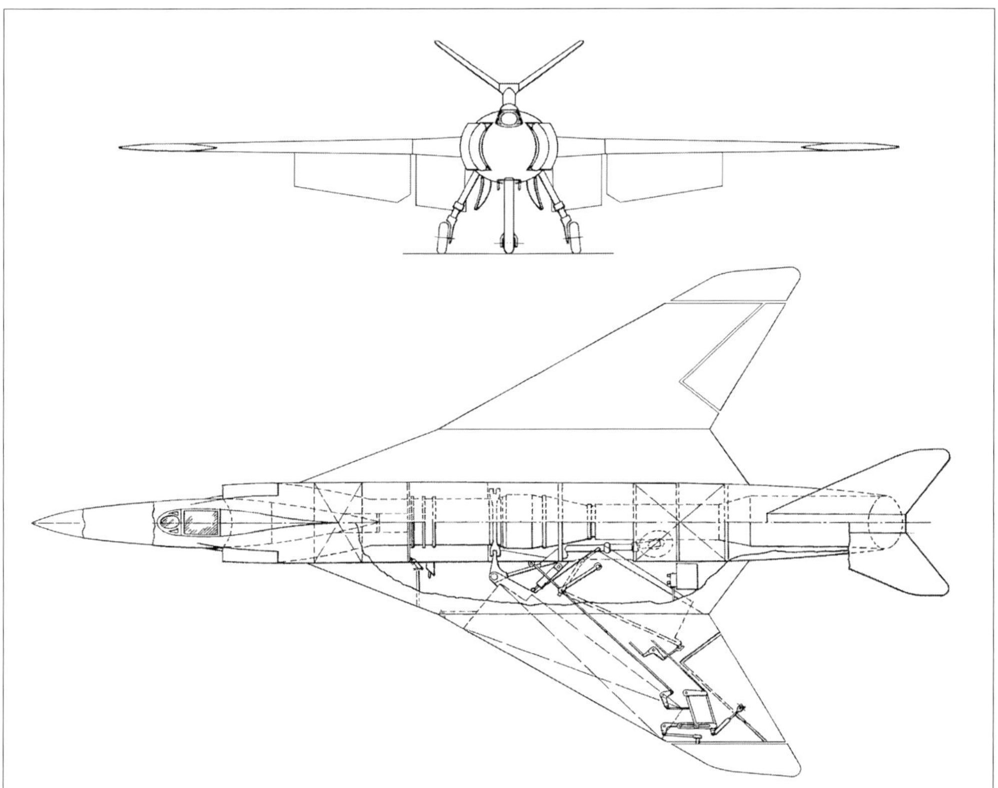

A swing-wing fighter designed by Geoffrey Hill and Thomas Guppy of Blackburn/GAL in the late 1940s and filed as a UK patent in August 1950. (*Adapted from a US Patent Office drawing by Bill Rose*)

The Gloster Javelin

The ancestry of the Gloster Javelin stretches back to the immediate post-war years when the UK Air Ministry asked for new jet fighter proposals from several aviation companies. The first official request known as Specification F.43/46 (OR.228), sought provisional designs for a daylight interceptor directed by ground radar that was capable of reaching enemy bombers at high altitude. The aircraft would have a maximum speed of 575–625 mph (925–1,000 kph) at 45,000 ft (13,716 m) and an ability to reach this height in six minutes. The interceptor would be armed with two 30 mm cannon and have an endurance of at least one hour.

The second requirement known as Specification F.44/46 (OR 227) was for an advanced radar equipped night and all-weather interceptor, with accommodation for a second crew member. Aircraft like the Mosquito had been adapted for this role, but the RAF was looking for a significantly more advanced jet powered design. Subsequently, a number of modified Meteor Mk 11-14 fighters were pressed into service, but this was recognised as a stop-gap from the outset.

Gloster had submitted an early delta winged fighter designed by George Carter, for Specification F.43/46 in February 1947. It received the reference P.234 and is clearly recognisable as an early, single seat incarnation of the Javelin with a butterfly tail. Despite generating considerable interest, it was rejected in favour of the Hawker proposal submitted by Sydney's Camm's team, which evolved into the superb Hunter fighter. At the same time, Gloster produced designs to meet Specification F.44/46, with an aircraft not dissimilar to P.234 but fitted with a different tail

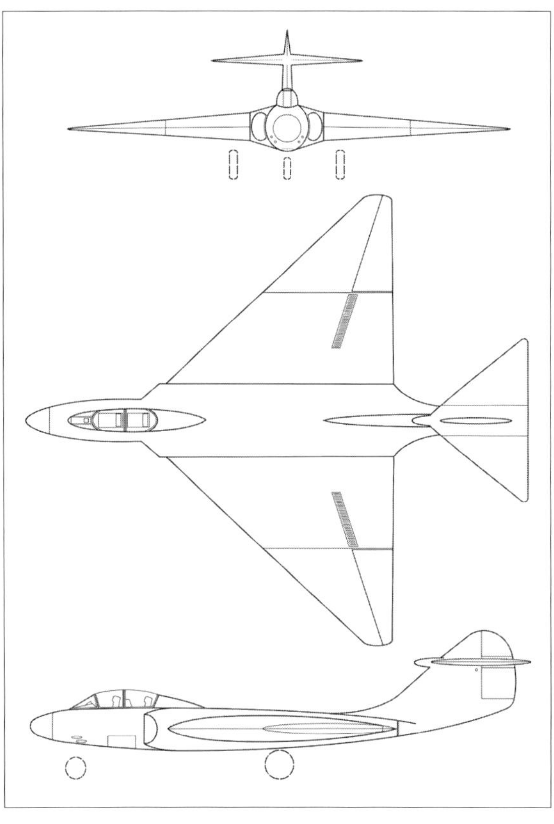

The Gloster P.238 design from 1947. This drawing shows the metamorphosis from Meteor to Javelin as this early post-war fighter project continued to evolve.

arrangement, accommodation for a second crew member and a tricycle undercarriage. Given the company reference P.238, the aircraft bore some resemblance to a Meteor in profile and utilised a large delta wing drawing on German wartime research. Equipped with radar operated by the second crew member, the P.234 was to be armed with four 40 mm cannon below the nose, although a wide range of options were considered. These included 30 mm cannon in varying numbers and different locations, a single 4.5 inch (114 mm) cannon and air-to-air unguided rockets in several packs.

The basic design had now evolved considerably and unlike its predecessor which used two Rolls-Royce AJ.65 (Avon) engines, the P.238 would be powered by two Armstrong Siddeley Sapphire turbojet engines each expected to produce 9,000 lb (40 kN) thrust. The design also continued to undergo aerodynamic changes, with Carter briefly considering a straight wing with slight sweepback, before returning to a delta wing with the P.241 design. It is not clear why this came about, but probably as a result of wind tunnel testing with various scale models.

As work progressed, Specification F.4/48 was issued and discussions began with the Air Ministry for production of fighters. After seemingly endless revisions of the design (now the P.278), the proposed aircraft looked very much like a Gloster Javelin. Now, the Air Ministry decided to move forward with ordering prototypes of the Gloster fighter and the competing de Havilland DH.110, which would eventually become the Royal Navy's Sea Vixen.

Construction of the first Gloster GA.5 prototype (WD804) began in 1949 at Hucclecote. It then took to the air from RAF Moreton Valance on 26 November 1951, with the company's chief test pilot Squadron Leader William A. (Bill) Waterton (1916–2006) at the controls.

The prototype Javelin GA.5 (WD804) during a test flight.

Unfortunately, there were significant problems with flutter and buffeting which persisted and despite many attempts to rectify these faults, both elevators finally detached during a test flight on 29 June 1952. Waterton was again flying WD804 and managed to make a very difficult emergency landing. He walked away from the aircraft uninjured, having first secured vital flight data records, but WD804 was very badly damaged, burst into flames and was completely destroyed.

The second prototype (WD808) first flew on 20 August 1952, but suffered with all the same problems as WD804. It was grounded for almost a year while a team of engineers and scientists worked around the clock to identify and rectify these issues. Nevertheless, this aircraft crashed due to a stall on 11 June 1953 and Peter G. Lawrence (1920–1953) who was flying the aircraft died after ejecting at very low altitude over Long Ashton, Somerset. Prototype (WT827) made its first test flight on 7 March 1953, followed by the fourth aircraft (WT827) which flew on 14 January 1954 and was then handed over to the Aircraft & Armament Experimental Establishment (A&AEE) at Boscombe Down for full evaluation. The final prototype (WT836) first flew on 20 July 1954.

Unfortunately, the Javelin's handing remained bad, so a substantial re-design was undertaken with the aim of rectifying a list of aerodynamic and engine-related shortcomings. Development was now well behind schedule and testing was held up until 22 July 1954, when the first FAW.1 Javelin was flown by Richard F. 'Dicky' Martin (1918–2006).

One of the first aerodynamic improvements, was an alteration to the wing's leading edge, which was now slightly cranked. With an initial inner sweep of 39.5° and the outer section at 33.8° to the clipped wingtips, this helped to rectify stall issues. The wingspan was 52 ft (15.84 m), with a wing area of 927 ft^2 (86.12 m^2) and an overall length of 56.25 ft (17.15 m). Support on the ground was provided by a conventional tricycle undercarriage. Not surprisingly, the airframe was mostly constructed from aluminium alloy, with some steel components and fully loaded, the aircraft weighed 31,580 lb (14,325 kg).

Although Rolls Royce Avon engines had originally been intended for the Javelin, these had now been replaced by a pair of non-afterburning Armstrong Siddeley Sapphire ASSa.6 102/103s turbojet engines, each producing 8,000 lb (35.58 kN) of thrust. These aircraft were also fitted with four 30 mm ADEN cannon and the AI.17 radar unit. Handling was said to be reasonable, despite ongoing issues, but as a consequence, various flight restrictions were introduced, with the aircraft regarded as almost ready to enter service. Maximum speed was 709 mph (1,141 kph) at sea level, with a ceiling of 52,000 ft (15,849 m) and as range was a concern, two ventral 250 gallon (1,136.5 litre) fuel tanks were added. This alteration was probably not a major engineering challenge as an earlier version (P.317) had been proposed as a strike aircraft with four 1,000 lb (453 kg) in exactly the same location. Deliveries of the FAW.1 continued throughout 1955 and a number were diverted away from trials to RAF service, with the majority ending up with squadrons in Norfolk and West Germany. In total, 40 FAW.1s were built.

Meanwhile, improvements to the Javelin continued and this resulted in the FAW.2, which was essentially the same aircraft, but equipped with the American made Westinghouse AN/APQ-43 (AI.22) radar system. 30 FAW.2s were built and they also featured a new larger radome with improved access for maintenance crews. However, the shortcomings of the original AI.17 radar were rectified and in practice there was little significant difference in capability between the British and American systems.

The next Javelin to roll off the production line, was the T.3 trainer. A dual control aircraft, slightly stretched in length, with an elevated rear seat and no radar. Extra fuel was also carried internally. 22 T.3s were built.

Gloster Javelin FAW.1 (XA563) undertakes a demonstration flight at the 1955 Farnborough Air Show. (*Ruth AS*)

Another version of the Javelin, was the FAW.4. It was equipped with the AI.17 radar system and an all-moving tailplane. The first FAW.4 flew on 19 September 1955. 50 aircraft were built, with manufacture shared between Gloster and Armstrong Whitworth. A modest upgrade followed, called the FAW.5, which had modifications to the internal fuel storage and a future ability to carry four Firestreak air-to-air missiles. 64 FAW.5s were built, with manufacture again taking place at Gloster and Armstrong Whitworth. This was followed by the FAW.6, which was fitted with the Westinghouse AN/APQ-43 radar system. 33 of these were built. The next variant was the FAW.7 that undertook its first test flight on 9 November 1956. This aircraft had quite a few improvements over previous versions, utilising more powerful Sapphire ASSa 7 203 engines, each capable of providing 11,000 lb (48.9 kN) of thrust. The fuselage was extended at the rear, there was a new system installed to stabilise yaw, alterations to the flight controls and the addition of four underwing pylons to carry Firestreak missiles. The FAW.5 and FAW.6 had been built with the intention of carrying these missiles, but there were technical issues which delayed it from happening. Now, the FAW.7 would also be capable of carrying additional 100 gallon (450 litre) drop tanks on the missile pylons to extend ferry range. Surprisingly, it was now decided to return to the AI.17 radar, that was considered just as capable as the Westinghouse system. 142 FAW.7s were built, with production spread between the Gloster and Armstrong Whitworth factories.

The last production variant of the Javelin was the FAW.8. This was fitted with afterburning Sapphire ASSa 7LR 204 turbojets providing a modest performance increase to a maximum of 12,300 lb (54.7 kg) thrust above 20,000 ft (6,096 m), although the design of this system made it ineffective at low altitude. In addition, variable engine exhaust nozzles were fitted and the FAW.8s were equipped with the Westinghouse AN/APG-43 (AI.22) radar. The first FAW.8 flew on 9 May 1958. 47 of these aircraft were built before the end of the 1950s and in 1960, Gloster were given the go-ahead to bring 76 of the existing FAW.7s up to FAW.8 standard.

This resulted in these aircraft being re-designated as FAW.9 and the conversion programme was completed in December 1961. Finally, about 40 FAW.9s were equipped with in-flight refuelling probes and these received the designation FAW.9 F/R.

The Javelin never sold to overseas customers and remained in RAF service until 1968. It was the last aircraft the Gloster Aircraft Company produced. 433 Javelins were built, including the five prototypes and there were plans for several specialised versions and a supersonic successor.

One other Javelin proposal that seems to have been give some serious official consideration was P.348, an unarmed photo reconnaissance aircraft. Plans date from early 1952 and the P.348 would have been equipped with a new nose section carrying downward looking cameras. There were also cameras in sections of the wing normally occupied by the cannon. In addition, there would be more space devoted to carrying fuel and larger ventral tanks. Rearward facing radar was proposed, plus various forms of electronic countermeasures. The wingspan was increased, suggesting this aircraft would operate at a high altitude.

However, the Canberra PR.3, which first flew in 1950, proved to be a very capable light bomber and photo reconnaissance aircraft, so there was never any real need for the Gloster proposal, which progressed little further than the concept stage.

Many years later in 1960, Gloster suggested another aircraft originating from the Javelin as a competitor for the NATO Military Requirements 3 (NBMR-3) request for a Short Take-Off & Landing (STOL) strike aircraft. This received the designation P.505. They also worked on a

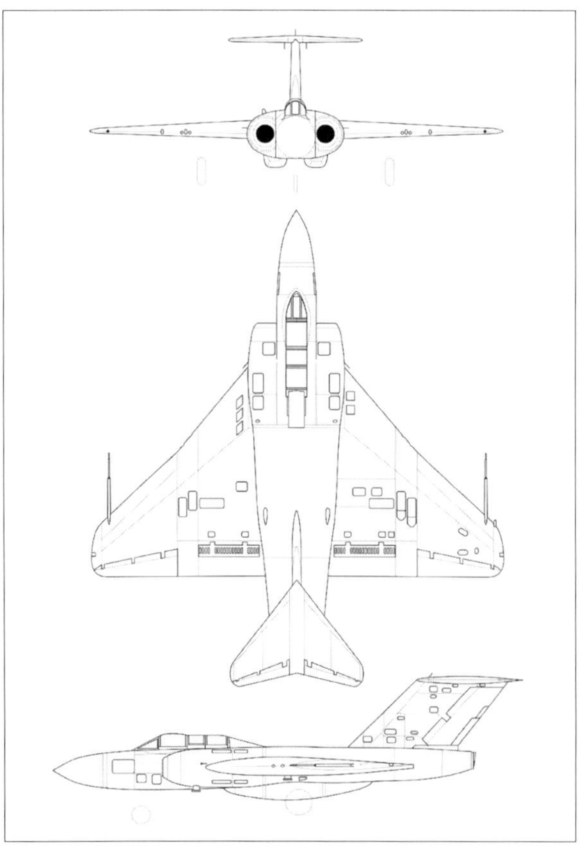

Three view drawing of the Gloster Javelin FAW.9. (*Kaboldy*)

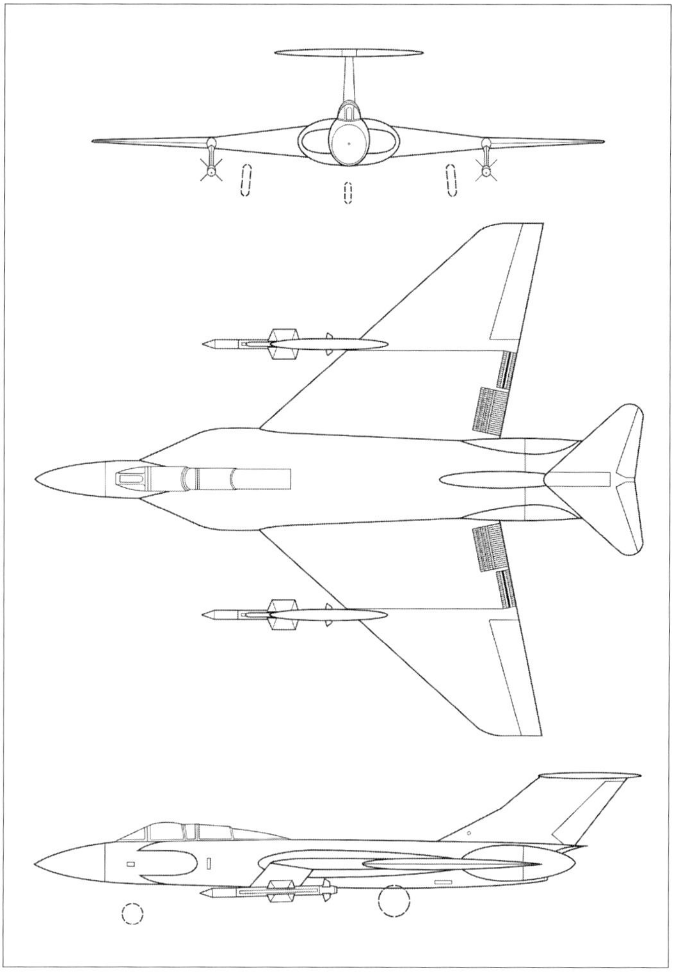

The Gloster P.376 supersonic Javelin. Powered by Olympus engines, it was expected to be capable of Mach 1.8 at altitude and would be armed with Vickers Read Dean missiles. A mock-up was built and 18 pre-production aircraft were ordered for the RAF, but the project met with cancellation in July 1956.

more sophisticated VTOL proposal which was substantially different from the P.505 and this is discussed in a later chapter.

In 1952, Gloster's design office began to consider a higher performance Javelin with a supersonic capability, provided by an improved wing design and more powerful engines. By the following year, this was receiving Air Ministry support as Specification F.153D. The thin wing Javelin would continue to utilise the same fuselage and in addition to all-weather interception it would be capable of undertaking ground attack missions. It was also briefly considered by the Air Staff in 1953 as a future tactical nuclear strike aircraft (should a suitable weapon become available) and this would also require an in-flight refuelling capability.

The design work would eventually produce the P.376. A thin wing delta, with a leading edge sweep of about 48° and an area of 1,235 ft^2 (114.73 m^2), it was still reminiscent of the Javelin, but essentially a new, much larger aircraft. Powered by two afterburning Olympus OI.21R turbojets each rated at 28,200 lb (125.5 kN) thrust. The stretched fuselage now complied with area rule and maximum speed was expected to be approximately Mach 1.8 at 36,000 ft (10,972 kph), with a ceiling of about 60,000 ft (18,288 m).

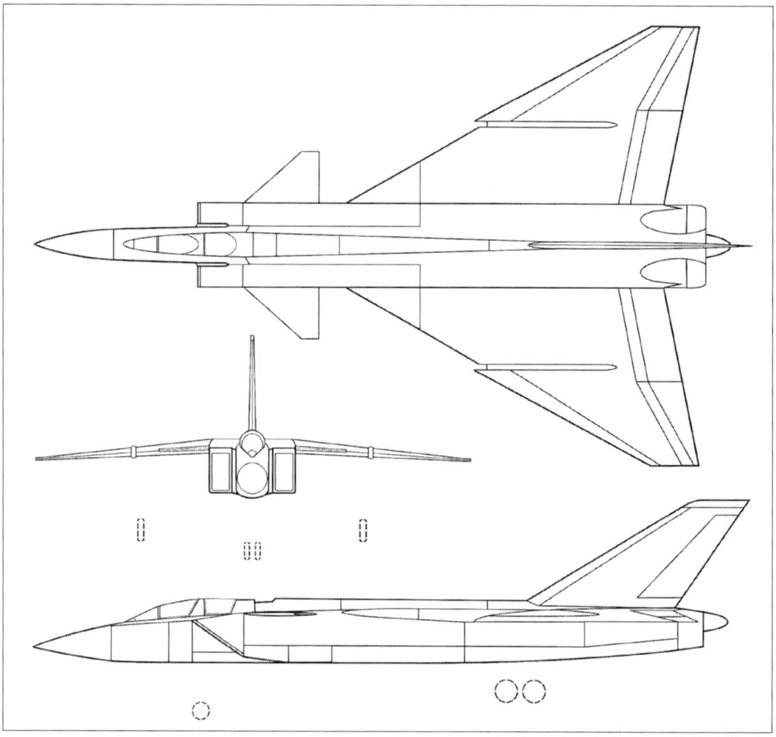

This drawing shows a possible 1970s development of the Avro-Canada CF-105 Arrow fighter with performance in the same class as the MiG-31 Foxhound, or perhaps even better. The CF-105 was a superb design that would have suited the RAF very well as an advanced interceptor. In basic form, it was superior in almost every respect to the Gloster P.376. Adaptable for various roles such as reconnaissance and nuclear strike, it might have remained in RAF service for several decades.

Interception armament was two Blue Jay (Firestreak) and/or two Vickers Red Dean air-to-air missiles. The RAF planned to replace half the existing Javelins with this aircraft and work began on a pre-production batch. However, there was considerable official interest in the Canadian Avro Arrow CF-105, which was a very impressive machine and one of the best fighter aircraft from that period.

The acquisition of military aircraft for the RAF was firmly in the hands of politicians and in this case, there would have been concern about funding the purchase, dollar exchange rates and the impact on British jobs. There seems little doubt that an Anglicised CF-105 Arrow would have been a good way to proceed, even if the aircraft required alteration to accept British avionics, weapons and replacement engines. But the politicians were sold on the idea that missiles were the way forward, so the Arrow was soon ruled out and then the advanced Javelin was scrapped. In turn so were future designs like the Fairey Delta III and for still unclear political reasons, perhaps connected to pressure from the Americans, The Canadian government abandoned the superb Arrow and then destroyed the completed pre-production aircraft in what appears to have been a moment of total madness.

It is also worth mentioning that a few Javelins, mostly FAW.1s, were adapted to serve as test platforms for new and modified engines, such as the afterburning Rolls-Royce RA.24R Avon and the Napier Gyron Junior turbojet.

The underside of Javelin FAW.8 (XH966) showing its four Firestreak missiles.

Javelin XA620 in flight.

In Service with the RAF

Nineteen RAF squadrons operated Javelins in the UK and overseas. They were often deployed to trouble spots such as Cyprus where Turkish, Egyptian and Soviet aircraft undertaking reconnaissance missions would be routinely intercepted and escorted away from UK controlled airspace. In 1963, RAF Javelins belonging to 60 Squadron based at Singapore were assigned to patrol the Malaya–Indonesia border during regional tensions. There were no official combat confrontations, but on one occasion in 1964, an Indonesian Air Force C-130 Hercules crashed as a result of trying to avoid a fast approaching Javelin. Perhaps this was the case, but a number of former RAF personnel suggested that the Javelin shot it down and for political reasons, there was a cover-up.

In late 1965, Javelin FAW.9Rs were deployed to Zambia after Rhodesia illegally declared independence from the UK, but there were no engagements with the Rhodesians. In the UK, Javelins were being replaced by the English Electric Lightning, although they continued to operate in West Germany, Cyprus and Singapore. The last deployment of any note was in 1967, when 60 Squadron were moved to Hong Kong as a result of unrest triggered by China's Cultural Revolution. In 1968, the last Javelin was retired from RAF service. Regrettably, there were many serious accidents with all versions of the Javelin throughout its service period with a number of crew members losing their lives. The main problem appears to have involved engine faults, frequently resulting in fires and occasionally explosions. This would sometimes happen during start-up using isopropyl nitrate starter cartridges, but also during flight. Records also show many undercarriage failures. That said, various sources suggest that crews generally found the aircraft fairly easy to fly, despite the recognition of various shortcomings. Clearly, the Javelin was not a great British military jet aircraft like the Hunter or Canberra, but probably adequate for duties at that time.

DH.108 Swallow

In 1943, the Brabazon Committee was formed to consider requirements for civil air transportation once the war had ended. This resulted in approaches being made to a number of aircraft contractors for submissions and one company who responded was de Havilland who had studied the Committee's Type 1V requirement for a jet powered 100-seat airliner. This resulted in proposals for a scaled up Vampire fighter, a tailless flying wing using four Ghost turbojets and a more conventional concept that would eventually become the DH.106 Comet. However, such a project would take the designers and engineers into uncharted territory and it was recognised that a small demonstrator was required to establish the viability of various swept wing configurations.

During October 1945, the company's chief designer Ronald Bishop (1903-1989) finally selected an experimental tailless proposal known as DH.108, which was based on a Vampire with a single swept tail fin. Drawing on generally proven engineering and a good number of readily available components would mean that the development time and cost of the project could be minimalised. In addition to Ronald Bishop, much of the DH.108's design can be credited to John Carver Meadows Frost (1915–1979), who is now remembered for his work on the Avrocar project in Canada.

In early 1946, the DH.108 received the official (Experimental) references E.1/45 and E.11/45, from the Air Ministry and approval for full development of Britain's first swept wing aircraft. Two similar, but slightly different versions would be built to provide data for the proposed jet airliner, plus future jet fighters like the DH.110 Sea Vixen. One of the de Havilland aircraft would be used to evaluate the performance of the swept wing at relatively low speeds, while the other would have a transonic capability.

Both of the DH.108 aircraft started life as fuselages for Vampire F.1 jet fighters that were taken directly from the production line. Propulsion for the first DH.108 was a single de Havilland Goblin 2 turbojet engine, producing 3,000 lb (13.4 kN) static thrust. It was also fitted with a new wing having a 43° sweep and fixed leading edge slats. Utilising quite a lot of wood in its construction, the new wing had a span of 39 ft (11.88 m) and an area of 328 ft^2 (30.4 $m^{2)}$, which was 15 per cent greater than the Vampire. Control of roll and pitch was undertaken by elevons outboard of the trailing edge split flaps and containers were fitted to the wingtips that carried small anti-spin parachutes for emergency use.

A single vertical fin replaced the twin tail boom fitted to the Vampire and this resulted in a sleeker more elegant looking aircraft that resembled something of a cross between the Vampire and wartime Messerschmitt Me 163B rocket interceptor. This was hardly surprising as German aeronautical developments had initially influenced the design.

Having been completed in what would now be regarded as an astonishingly short period of time the aircraft was assigned the official serial TG283 and named Swallow by MoS officials, although this was never formally adopted.

TG283 made its first flight on 15 May 1946, with test pilot Geoffrey Raoul de Havilland Jr., OBE (1910–1946) at the controls (son of the original Geoffrey de Havilland). The brief flight was relatively uneventful and de Havilland reported the DH.108 handled well although the aircraft was restricted to a maximum speed of 280 mph (450 kph).

Underside view of DH.108 TG283 in flight.

While the DH.108 was not in the strictest sense a classified project, some of the aircraft's technology was considered sensitive and details of flight trials were treated with some secrecy. There were also runway repair problems at Hatfield, so it was an easy decision to re-locate testing to RAF Woodbridge in Suffolk. At that time, Woodbridge was being used for classified RAF experimental work and its lengthy, well-maintained runway made this an especially suitable location. But somewhat surprisingly, the base was closed in March 1948 and passed to the USAF several years later.

The secrecy surrounding the DH.108 continued until the beginning of June 1946, when Parliamentary Secretary of the MoS Arthur Woodburn (1890-1978) visited de Havilland at Hatfield and disclosed the aircraft's existence. The DH.108 had now returned to the facility, where minor modifications were made, although it was becoming apparent that a tailless design based on prevailing technology was less than ideal for an airliner. Meanwhile, work continued on construction of the second prototype designed for high-speed flight, which was fitted with a slightly more powerful Goblin 3 engine rated at 3,350 lb (14.9 kN) static thrust.

The first DH.108 had an overall length of 25.83 ft (7.874 m), but this was marginally reduced to 24.5 ft (7.467 m) on the second aircraft and there was a slight increase of leading edge sweep to 45°. Automatic leading edge slats were fitted that could be locked by the pilot, a more streamlined cockpit canopy was fitted and improvements were made to the flight controls.

The second DH.108 received the serial TG306 and was built to explore flight at much higher speeds and perhaps supersede the existing air speed record of 616 mph (991 kph). TG306 first flew during June 1946 and appeared at the Society of British Aircraft Constructors (SBAC) September 1946 show at Radlett (which moved to Farnborough in 1948).

The clean compact de Havilland DH.108 tailless experimental aircraft, based on the Vampire jet fighter and drawing on wartime German aeronautical research. This photograph shows the second prototype TG306.

As well as being a static exhibit, it was flown by Geoffrey de Havilland during the show's final event and clearly impressed the visitors. A couple of weeks later on 27 September 1946, Geoffrey de Havilland took off from Hatfield, in the second DH.108. He had now logged 13 hours in the aircraft and intended to push it towards its limits during preparations for an attempt on the air speed record, which had already been unofficially broken in this aircraft. The emergency anti-spin parachute containers had been removed and the aircraft's metallic finish had been polished to a bright shine. However, things went disastrously wrong above the Thames estuary, when de Havilland encountered pitch oscillations at Mach 0.9. As a consequence, the main spar fractured, the wings came off and the fuselage was torn apart.

Wreckage showered down into the muddy waters of Egypt Bay near Gravesend, Kent and de Havilland was killed. Recovery of debris proved especially difficult and Geoffrey de Havilland's body could not be located, although it finally washed ashore at Whitstable on 7 October 1946.

This tragic accident would hold up high-speed flight testing for another year, during which time it was decided that the problems that had caused the accident could be effectively dealt with. So during July 1947, a decision was taken to replace the second DH.108 with a similar aircraft, albeit with modifications and improvements. This third DH.108 was based on a production Vampire F.5 fighter and it received the official serial VW120. It was slightly more streamlined than TG306 with a pointed nose, giving it an overall length of 26.79 ft (8.165 m). A sleeker, more aerodynamic cockpit canopy was fitted, the pilot's ejector seat was lowered, which reduced visibility and the cockpit remained unpressurised.

With engine performance steadily, although slowly improving, this aircraft was fitted with the latest Goblin 4 turbojet, producing 3,750 lb (16.68 kN) of static thrust. As a final major

Pieces of wreckage embedded in the mud at Egypt Bay near Gravesend, Kent, where Geoffrey de Havilland lost his life in the second DH.108.

upgrade, the third Swallow was fitted with power-assisted elevons to address the problem of pitch oscillations. Replacing Geoffrey de Havilland as the company's chief test pilot was wartime night fighter ace John Cunningham (1917–2002), who made his first flight in the new Swallow on 24 July 1947. The following year, on 12 April 1948, this aircraft piloted by de Havilland test pilot John Derry (1921–1952), set a new World air speed record of 605.23 mph (974 kph), on a 62 mile (100 km) closed circuit, later earning him the prestigious Segrave Memorial Trophy. Flying this aircraft, Derry would also become the first British pilot to exceed the speed of sound, which took place on the morning of 6 September 1948 above Windsor, although this did not qualify for an officially verified record.

For some weeks the third DH.108 had been tested at gradually increasing speed and on this occasion Derry decided that conditions were good enough to push the aircraft a little further. Rapidly descending from about 40,000 ft (12,000 m), the aircraft nudged past Mach 1 just before Derry pulled out of the descent at 30,000 ft (9,000 m). Although there was no serious instability, Derry later reported that the controls became heavy and unresponsive, despite the power boost system. But once he dropped down below Mach 0.96, everything returned to normal and Derry continued his flight to the de Havilland facility at Hatfield.

RAE test pilot Captain Eric 'Winkle' Brown also flew this DH.108 and was far from impressed with it, later describing the aircraft as a death trap. During a dive he reached Mach 0.88, encountering severe oscillations and almost lost control, before gently pulled back on the stick and throttle, which stabilised the aircraft. He later remarked about the cramped conditions of the cockpit and the lack of clearance above his head. Brown was quite a small man, whereas Geoffrey de Havilland Jr was tall and Brown believed that he might easily have smashed his head against the canopy and lost consciousness, leading to the accident at Egypt Bay. Trials with the DH.108 continued and it appeared at the 1949 Farnborough Air Show, taking third place in the SBAC's Challenge Trophy Air Race.

Unfortunately, the third DH.108 was lost on 15 February 1950 and its pilot Squadron Leader Stuart Muller-Rowland (1921–1950) was killed. He had been undertaking dives at high transonic speeds above Buckinghamshire when the aircraft broke up. Wreckage came down in the Little Brickhill area, with parts found near Bow Brickhill Church and as far away as Husborne Crawley. The local fire service was mobilised, along with the police, who were instructed to cordon off the area as some aspects of the aircraft remained classified.

Witnesses reported hearing an explosion, which may have been a sonic boom, with the cause of the accident later being determined as an oxygen system failure, resulting in the pilot losing consciousness.

The first DH.108 was still flying, but on 1 May 1950, it crashed at Hartley Wintney, Hampshire during stalling trials, killing the pilot, Squadron Leader George, Eric Genders (1920–1950). The three DH.108 Swallow aircraft completed a total of 480 flights, which provided invaluable data, despite all being lost in fatal accidents.

Many observers have claimed the aircraft were jinxed, cursed or the design was fatally flawed, but I am inclined to believe this is not an entirely fair observation. At that time, the DH.108 represented the cutting edge of aeronautical research and these aircraft were often flown at their performance limits.

Much of the research undertaken in the immediate post-war era meant actually going out and trying an idea to see if it worked. Both the Americans and Russians lost a number of research aircraft during this period, simply as a result of pushing the envelope that little bit further.

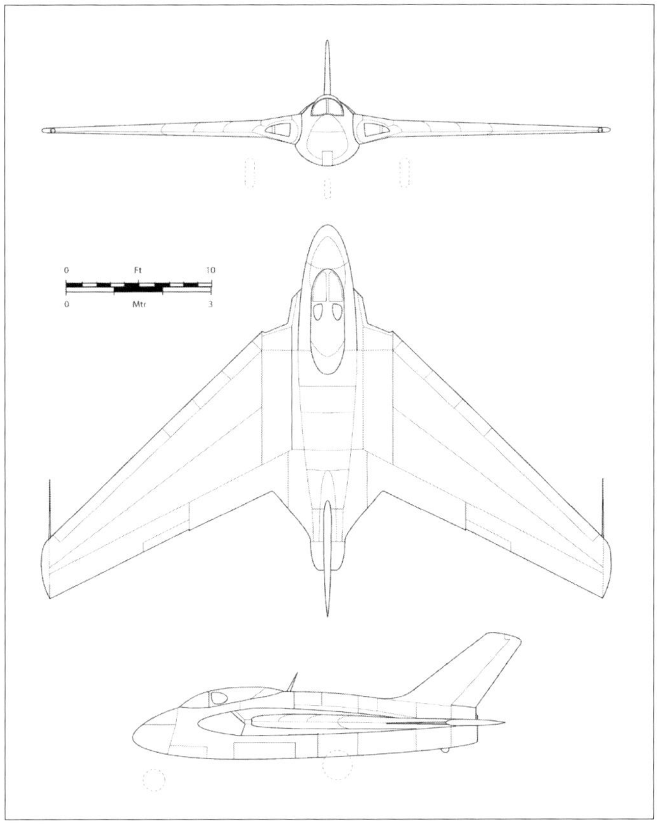

The third and most advanced DH.108, equipped with a Goblin 4 turbojet, producing 3,750 lb (16.68 kN) of static thrust and using power-assisted elevons to help control pitch oscillation problems. (*Chris Gibson*)

Configured for high speed flight, de Havilland's third DH.108 flown by John Derry set a World air speed record of 605.23 mph (974kph), on a 62-mile (100km) closed circuit during April 1948.

As a footnote, the DH.108 trials would inspire the British film director David Lean to make a fictional movie called *The Sound Barrier*, which was released in 1952. Starring Ralph Richardson and Ann Todd, it was very successful at the time, but is now largely forgotten. The film featured a new jet fighter called the Prometheus that was flown in an attempt to break the sound barrier. Prometheus was actually a Nene powered Supermarine Swift Type 535 prototype (VV119).

Westland PJD.144

In the immediate post-war years, the Royal Navy began to consider its future needs for a more advanced carrier-borne twin jet fighter with the ability to operate at night. It would need to be capable of achieving a maximum speed of 500 knots (927 kph), have a gross weight of no more than 30,000 lb (13,608 kg). A maximum wingspan of 55 ft (16.8 m) was recommended and folded, the span could be no greater than 18 ft (5.5 m).

The total, permissible length was 43 ft (13.1 m). Assisted take-off was anticipated and the armament would comprise of two or ideally four 30 mm cannon. This requirement (OR.246) led to Specification N.40/46 being issued to a number of aircraft contractors and one of the companies that responded was Westland, who undertook a detailed study, which resulted in an initial proposal designated PJD.129, followed by three differing variations. These were PJD.142, PJD.143 and PJD.144, with the designs completed in late 1947.

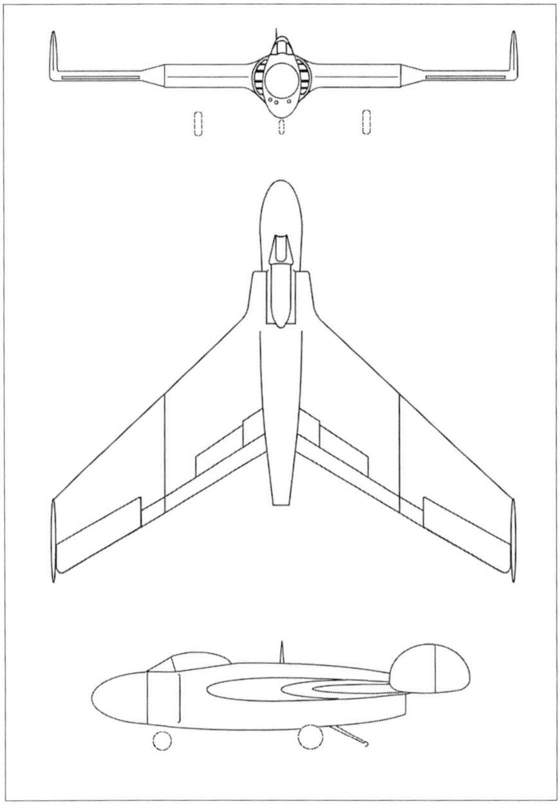

The tailless Westland PJD.144 carrier based warplane designed in response to Specification N.40/46 during the late 1940s.

The version preferred by Westland was the PJD.144, which was similar in overall appearance to the initial PJD.129 proposal. It was a completely tailless design, with vertical wingtip fins and rudders and this proposal utilised two turbojets in a stacked configuration along similar lines to the later English Electric Lightning. Air inlets for the engines were positioned on each side of cockpit, with a split central duct feeding both turbojets. The PJD.129/144 concept has been compared with the Junkers EF.128, which was a German proposal produced for the 1945 Emergency Fighter Competition. To what extent the designers at Westland were influenced by captured research material is hard to say, as much of the documentation for the EF.128 project fell into Soviet hands. But it seems clear that the Westland fuselage had more in common with aircraft like the de Havilland Vampire and the similarities to the German design are rather superficial. The main differences between the PJD.129 and the PJD.144 were alterations to the wings and fins. The leading edge wing sweep was reduced from 45° to 38°, made possible by changes to the wing's outer chord and the fin size was slightly increased. PJD.142 was broadly similar to this aircraft, but lacked the vertical wingtip fins and utilised a single upright tailfin. PJD.143 was the most conventional of these studies, with an upright fin and horizontal tail surfaces. It was also decided to alter the engine layout and have the turbojets side-by-side.

Initially, Westland designed these concepts around two unspecified turbojet engines in the Rolls-Royce Nene class with a static thrust of about 5,000 lb (22.24 kN), although the RAE decided that the newly prototyped and more advanced Rolls-Royce axial-flow Avon (then known as the Axial Jet—AJ65) was the preferred choice. 950 (UK) gallons (4,319 litres) of fuel were carried internally. Estimated maximum speed at altitude was about 630 mph (1013 kph) and general dimensions and weights complied with the N.40/46 specification. Armament appears to have been the same type for all variants and in this case, three 30 mm cannon would have been carried.

A fully retractable tricycle undercarriage was proposed for all models and the aircraft would have been equipped with arrestor landing gear. A radar dish for airborne interception was housed in the aircraft's nose and this system would have been operated by a second crew member, who was seated directly behind the pilot and facing rearward.

On 15 December 1947, a Design Study Conference was chaired by the Director-General of Technical Development (Air) for the MoS, Stewart Scott-Hall (1905–1961) to assess all the submissions for N.40/46. The Westland proposals were an early casualty and it was decided that performance projections for this aircraft were unsatisfactory and there were general concerns about the tailless design.

Delegates concluded that in addition to lacking adequate performance, the Westland proposal might suffer from tip stalling and the anticipated high-approach speed was unsatisfactory. The Conference also decided that Westland had not fully considered their options for an aircraft with a tail and fitting one would negate any drag reduction advantages of the tailless design. The selection process continued during the following year, with the de Havilland DH.110 finally being chosen as the best available design. This led to a contract being issued in October 1948 for the construction of a DH.110 prototype to meet Specification N.40/46 and for evaluation as a new RAF night fighter under Specification F.4/48.

Hawker Siddeley Tailless Post-War Fighter Proposals

One of the more unusual fighter designs to emerge from Hawker's design office at Kingston during 1949 was the tailless two-man P.1077 jet fighter, possibly intended to meet the RAF's Specification F.4/48 for a new night fighter. It is almost as if the designers had taken a look at the Westland PJD.144 proposal and then set about upgrading it.

The wingspan was 58 ft (17.67 m), the length was 55 ft (16.76 m) and it was to be powered by two stacked Rolls-Royce Avon turbojets equipped with afterburners. Air inlets for the engines would be positioned around the fuselage about mid-wing and the P.1077 would carry 1,000 gallons (4,546 litres) of fuel. Specific performance figures are unknown, but this design was probably intended to be capable of high transonic speed at altitude, with a ceiling in the region of 50,000 ft (15,240 m). The aircraft carried a crew of two and would be equipped with air intercept radar. The fully retractable undercarriage was a bicycle configuration with twin nose wheels and four larger main wheels. In addition, outrigger stabilising wheels were considered necessary. A radar dish would be carried inside the nose of the aircraft and two large vertical fins and rudders were positioned at the centre of each wing. Proposed armament was four 30 mm cannon in a ventral pack and it seems probable that underwing stores would have been considered. Needless to say, this interesting design never progressed beyond the drawing board.

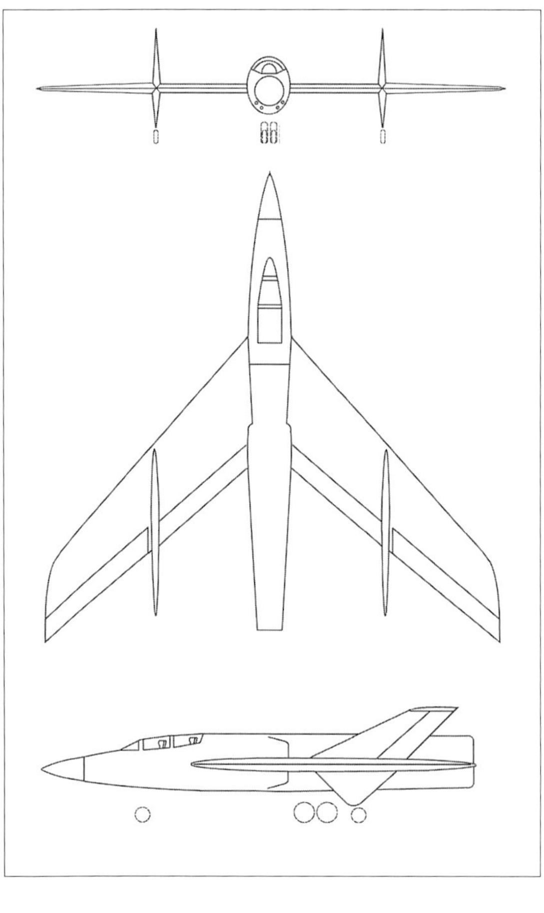

Hawker P.1077 tailless two-man jet design, produced by the Kingston Design Office in 1949.

Hawker Hunter Delta and Related Designs

In the immediate aftermath of the Second World War there was an urgent need to introduce new, higher performance British military aircraft using jet engine technology, but a reluctance to spend large amounts of money on development. Specification F.43/46 (OR.228) was issued to contractors, showing what was needed in the way of new fighters and this would eventually lead to the twin-engined, all-weather Javelin and Sea Vixen.

However Sir Sydney Camm (1893–1966) who headed Hawkers Design Office had conceived a single-engined jet fighter with the company reference P.1052 for this specification. He was sure it could be developed to meet the RAF's requirement for a daylight interceptor and requested that his company fund development of two prototypes. The first prototype P.1052 flew in 1948, but failed to secure official support. P.1052 was largely based on the Sea Hawk but given a new wing with a leading edge sweep of 35°.

Camm then redesigned the second prototype, making improvements to the tail and fuselage, with a single rear exhaust for the Rolls-Royce Nene RN2 turbojet rated at 5,000 lb (22.24 kN) thrust. This aircraft was re-designated P.1081 and it performed fairly well, despite some engine problems. However, the aircraft would eventually crash during a high speed trial flight on 3 April 1951 near Lewes, East Sussex, killing Hawker's chief test pilot Sqn Ldr Trevor Wade (1920–1951).

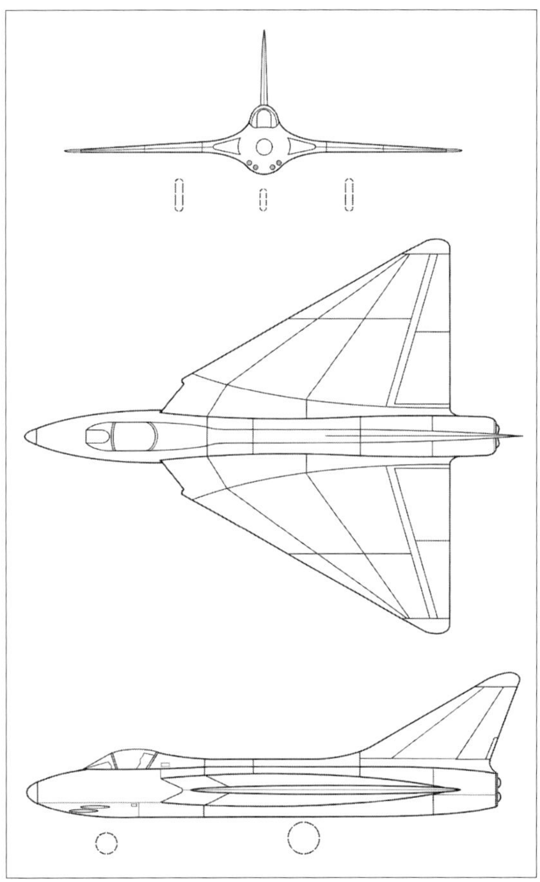

Hawker Delta Hunter P.1091 design from the early 1950s.

Sir Sydney Camm was one of Britain's leading aeronautical engineers and designed a string of famous British warplanes built by Hawker.

Although the RAF were interested in the Hawker fighter, the Air Ministry remained somewhat lukewarm, but Camm continued to refine the concept, producing a third prototype with the company reference P.1067. This would be powered by the new, higher performance Rolls-Royce AJ65 Avon axial flow turbojet or the Metrovick F.9 9, which would become the Armstrong-Siddeley Sapphire.

Armament for the re-designed single seat fighter would be four 30 mm cannon and there was finally sufficient official confidence in this proposal to issue a new specification for P.1067 with the reference F.3/48. Camm continued to refine the design and construction of a P.1067 prototype (serial No. WB188) began in 1950. It was now recognisable as the elegant Hunter and a contract was soon issued for 400 aircraft, with half being powered by Avon engines and the other half by Sapphires. This was considered important, as the engines were cutting edge designs and it was felt essential to have safeguards against unforeseen technical issues that might become evident. Taxiing trials began at Boscombe Down in July 1951 and the first test flight was made by Hawker's senior pilot Neville Duke (1922–2007) on 20 July 1951. Soon after this, the Avon powered WB188 returned to Hawker's airfield at Dunsford where trials continued. While not designed to have a supersonic capability, Neville Duke managed to push the aircraft through the sound barrier in 1952.

A second P.1067 prototype using the Avon engine followed and then a third fitted with a Sapphire. The first Hunter F.1 rolled off the production line during the following year and the aircraft would prove to be very successful, undergoing numerous upgrades and selling to a number of overseas customers. Nevertheless, it was clear before WB188 flew that it was only a matter of time before the next generation of supersonic combat aircraft arrived, pushing the Hunter into second place.

As a result of rapid aviation advances, the designers at Hawker had continued to examine ways of boosting the Hunter's performance from the late 1940s onwards. Initially, this centred on engine upgrades with a proposed P.1083 prototype being powered by a single afterburning Rolls-Royce Avon RA.7R producing a maximum thrust of 9,500 lb (42,25 kN). Some aerodynamic changes were also made and a mock-up completed, but the project seems to have stalled after this.

However, the design was quickly adapted to take a more powerful afterburning de Havilland Gyron turbojet that was under development. Newly configured air inlets were required, the leading edge wing sweep was 50° and the aircraft would be equipped with radar. The company reference P.1090 was assigned to the project, but it was never built and the Gyron never progressed beyond the experimental stage, being cancelled in 1957 due to government cuts.

The next idea to be seriously considered by Sydney Camm's design team in 1951, was a delta wing version of the Hunter with the reference P.1091. While looking very much like a Hunter in profile, this proposal would be fitted with a large delta wing having a 60° leading edge sweep and a single tail fin. Wingspan is quoted as 33 ft (10 m), with a wing area of 510 ft² (47.4 m²) and a slightly shorter than usual overall length of 42 ft (12.8 m). Apparently the study was undertaken in collaboration with Avro who were the established UK leaders in the field of delta wing aerodynamics. Power would be provided by an afterburning Sapphire 4 turbojet providing a maximum thrust of 8,000 lb (35.58 kN) and allowing transonic performance. The aircraft would be armed with four 30 mm ADEN cannon. The exact benefit of this design is not entirely clear. Perhaps the aim was to allow the carriage of more fuel or underwing stores. Alternatively, the aircraft might have had improved take-off and landing capability. Whatever the intention, P.1091 progressed no further than the design stage. The P.1092 study was undertaken alongside

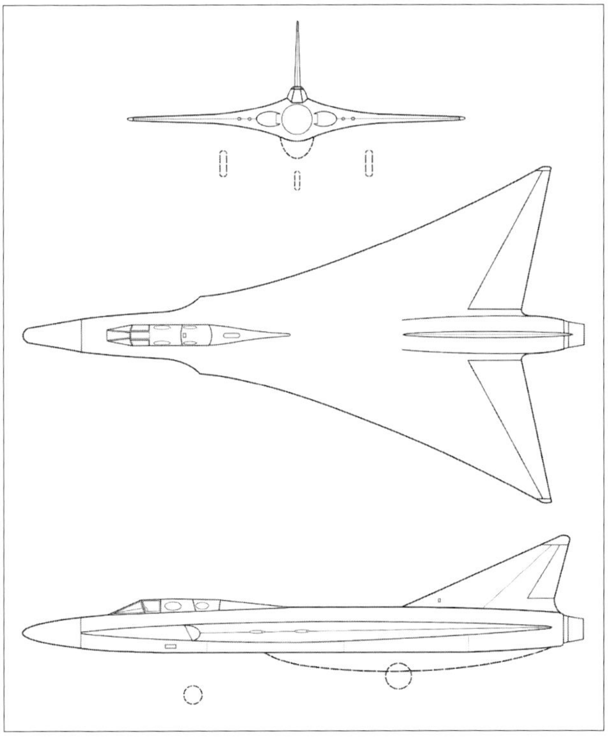

Hawker P.1092. This single engine, two seat delta winged supersonic interceptor progressed little further than an early 1950s design study. The nacelle beneath the rear fuselage section is thought to be an optional fuel tank.

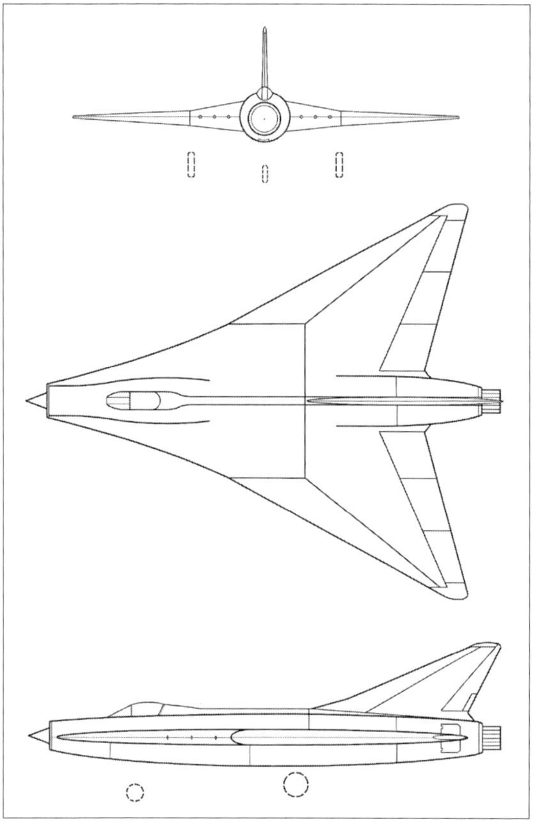

Hawker P.1093 single seat interceptor design, promising supersonic performance, bearing a resemblance to the MiG-21 from some angles.

P.1091 and had even less in common with the Hunter. It was a two-seat all-weather interceptor powered by a single afterburning Avon turbojet. The anticipated maximum speed was Mach 1.5 at 36,000 ft (10,972 m), with a ceiling of about 55,000 ft (16,764 m). Equipped with airborne radar and apparently requiring an extra ventral fuel tank, P.1092 would be armed with four 30 mm cannon carried in the wings.

This proposal would have been 55 ft (16.76 m) in length, with a wingspan of 35 ft (10.66 m) and a wing area of 580 ft^2 (53.88 m^2). Nothing came of the design, which failed to secure serious interest from the RAF. P.1093 which followed has more in common with P.1092 than is first evident. It could almost be described as a shortened version with a nose intake and a slightly larger wingspan. The wing now starts alongside the front of the fuselage, but it appears quite similar in both studies. In profile, P.1093 looks somewhat like the MiG-21 and as a single seater, the P.1093 would be powered by either an afterburning RA.14 Avon or an afterburning Gyron turbojet. Armament took the form of six 30 mm ADEN cannon carried in the wing and a radar system would be installed in the air intake shock cone. It has not been possible to locate any details of estimated performance, but it seems probable that the designers were aiming for a limited supersonic capability, with a ceiling of at least 50,000 ft (15,240 m). The wingspan was 41 ft (12.5 m), with a substantial wing area of 750 ft^2 (69.7 m^2) and a length of 49.66 ft (15.1 m). This study was completed in early 1952 and progressed no further. Many other studies attempted to improve the Hunter, with alterations to the aerodynamics, the installation of more powerful engines and the proposed use of air-to-air missiles as they became available. However, these projects and the overall history of the Hawker Hunter fall outside the general theme of this book and there are many other publications dealing with this British military classic.

Fairey FD.2, BAC 221, FD.3 and F.155

In 1943, Miles Aircraft were contracted to develop and build a supersonic research aircraft to meet UK Air Ministry Specification E.24/43. The one-man aircraft would be powered by a turbojet engine and hopefully capable of reaching 1,000 mph (1,600 kph) in level flight. The project was very ambitious, bearing in mind the early state of jet engine technology and the limited understanding of high speed flight. Miles designated their project M.52 and it was then classified as top secret. Work continued on the aircraft until 1946, when the Labour government run by Clement Attlee (1883-1967) brought M.52 to an abrupt halt. When the supersonic aircraft was disclosed to the public in September 1946, it was suggested that rising cost had been an issue, along with concerns about the danger of attempting to break the sound barrier, which was a popular term at that time. However, there is a weight of opinion that suggests the Americans applied pressure on the UK to cancel M.52, as they were working on a rocket-powered research aircraft called the Bell X-1. This was expected to take the supersonic prize and enter the history books. So the theory goes, Miles were then instructed by the UK government to pass all their M.52 research to Bell Aircraft in America and some of this was applied to the X-1, which went on to exceed the speed of sound in 1947. Despite all this, the British interest in supersonic flight continued and on 6 September 1948, de Havilland test pilot John Derry nudged his jet-powered DH.108 past the speed of sound over Windsor, creating an unofficial record. At around the same time, informal discussions were underway between the MoS and Fairey to develop a new research aircraft suitable for transonic and supersonic flight. The favoured design would utilise twin afterburning Avon turbojets, stacked one above the other, rather like the later Lightning fighter. The aircraft would also utilise an engine intake in the nose. It was hoped that this aircraft would be capable of attaining about Mach 1.35 in level flight, with a ceiling of around 60,000 ft (18,288 m). In October 1951, Professor Robert Lickley (1912–1998) who had been a senior project engineer with Hawker was recruited to become Fairey's technical director and their chief engineer. He then took direct control of the team working on the supersonic design. Most of the staff involved were based at the company's HQ in Hayes, Middlesex and as this was an RAE sponsored undertaking, the project was classified as top secret.

Swept wings now gave way to a 60° delta, with an astonishingly thin (4 per cent) thickness–chord ratio. By July 1949, the design proposed by Fairey had become a sleek dart shaped aircraft powered by a single afterburning Rolls-Royce Avon RA.14R, with air intakes at the wing roots. Refinement continued, until 1950 when Fairey received the official go-ahead to build two prototypes (to Air Ministry Specification ER.103), which were assigned the serials WG774 and WG777. With construction underway, revisions continued throughout the following year. The biggest alterations made, were to improve undercarriage retraction, which also meant the adoption of a tilting cockpit section which moved by 10° and enhance the pilot's view during operations like landing and taxiing. A similar system would later be chosen for Concorde. It was expected that the first prototype would fly before the end of 1953, but work on the aircraft continued into the following year, with the name Fairey Delta 2 (usually just FD.2) being adopted.

This picture is understood to show the FD.2 (WG774) at Boscombe Down just prior to its first test flight on 6 October 1954. One year later, it had achieved Mach 1.1, without using the afterburner.

On 6 October 1954, Fairey test pilot Peter Twiss (1921–2011) made the first flight in WG774. Testing proceeded fairly well, until the fourteenth flight on 17 November 1954, when WG774 experienced engine problems and Twiss was forced to make an emergency high-speed glide-landing, with the undercarriage only partly deployed. This resulted in considerable damage, although WG774 was not a write-off and Twiss was shaken up but not injured. Subsequently, the FD.2 was partly re-built and test flights resumed in August 1955. The aircraft was now regularly exceeding Mach 1 and this would lead to many complaints and claims for damage caused by sonic booms across southern England. Nevertheless, it was clear that FD.2 could easily reach 1,000 mph (1,600 kph) and it was decided to make an attempt on the existing world air speed record created by USAF pilot General Horace A. 'Dude' Hanes (1916–2002) in a North American F-100C Super Sabre on 20 August 1955. He achieved an average speed of 822 mph (1322 kph) while flying across the Mojave Desert in California.

Apparently, there was some resistance within Britain's MoS to undertaking this speed attempt with the FD.2, because at that time officialdom was being encouraged to accept that manned high speed flight (with a military connection, which I will come to later) had a limited future and guided weapons were the next big step forward. However, Fairey Aviation was finally granted permission on condition that they funded the undertaking. Another complication was finding suitable equipment to monitor the flight and this presented various technical challenges. It was also decided to undertake flights as soon as possible and without publicity, as there were fears that the Americans or Russians might snatch the record first. Trials were conducted throughout early 1956, but there were many problems and 10 March 1956 was set as the final date for these flights. The first run failed to meet strict control regulations, but on the second attempt, Peter Twiss broke the World Air Speed Record, pushing it up to 1,132 mph (1,821 kph), which was

On 17 November 1954, FD.2 (WG774) suffered engine failure due to a fuel problem on its 14th flight. Fairey's chief test pilot Peter Twiss managed to make a fast emergency landing without the full undercarriage deploying and despite considerable damage, WG774 was fully re-built within 8 months.

300 mph (482 kph) faster than Hanes previous record and making FD.2, the first aircraft to exceed 1,000 mph (1,600 kph) in level flight. The record would stand until 12 December 1957 when USAF Major Adrian E. Drew (1920–1985) set a new record of 1,207 mph (1,942 kph) in a McDonnell F-101A Voodoo fighter above Edwards AFB, California.

Following the FD.2s record-breaking flight, testing resumed, often at supersonic speeds above the UK. However, protests continued and the MoS decided that these test flights had to stop, or be undertaken overseas. Subsequently, Fairey, supported by the MoS arrange to continue testing at Cazaux Air Base, Bordeaux, France, although there was a significant trade-off, which involved sharing technical information about the aircraft with Dassault. This would prove invaluable to the French aircraft manufacturer, who rapidly moved forward with development of the Mirage fighter. Tests in France were then re-located to Norway and when completed, the first FD.2 was passed over to the RAE. The second FD.2 prototype (WG777) had been flying since February 1956 at RAF Boscombe Down and was formally accepted by the RAE for high speed research on 14 April 1956. Later that same year, both prototypes made an appearance at the Farnborough Air Show. By now, the RAE were investigating ideas for a suitable wing to be used on a supersonic airliner (eventually Concorde) and the ogee or ogival delta with its gradually inward curved leading edge was most favoured as early research showed it would perform well at all speeds.

While low speed trials would be handled by an aircraft specially built for the purpose (the Handley Page HP.115), it was felt necessary to have something equipped with an ogee wing that was capable of supersonic flight. In 1958, the RAE opened a dialogue with Fairey about the possibility of converting one of the FD.2s into a research aircraft suitable for development of the supersonic transport aircraft (SST). Fairey proposed a number of modifications that included stretching the fuselage and re-positioning the air inlets. Unfortunately, the project was held up by complicated industry changes when Fairey was taken over by Westland in 1960 and operations were moved to Bristol as part of the overall British Aircraft Corporation (BAC) restructuring. When work finally resumed, it was suggested that the fuselage would be extended forward by 6 ft (1.82 m), longer landing gear would be used, the air inlets for the engine would be under the wing and a new stabilisation system would be installed. Once the details were agreed a contract was issued and modifications to WG774 began at Bristol's Filton facility in April 1961. The conversion was largely completed three months later and the aircraft was renamed BAC 221.

WG774 undergoing ground tests, having been significantly modified and re-designated as the BAC.221. (*BAE Systems*)

BAC.221 (WG774) preparing for take-off.

Now powered by a Rolls-Royce Avon RA.28, the BAC 221 was capable of Mach 1.6 and one significant benefit from the re-design, was increased fuel capacity. BAC 221 made its first flight in May 1964 and continued to be used for research work until 1973. The BAC.221 (WG774) and second FD.2 (WG777) are now both museum exhibits, having worked as invaluable research tools throughout their lives.

I will just mention the Concorde SST, which is sometimes said to have been considered for development as a military aircraft. I have tried to track down any documentation that might support this, but nothing can be found and the design of Concorde does not lend itself to conversion into a supersonic bomber.

Yes, the Concorde stood a good chance of outrunning fighter interception with its impressive supercruise capability and high ceiling, having once been flow to an altitude of 68,000 ft (20,726 m) during a test flight in 1973. Yes, it might have been used to move a modest number of troops and equipment in an emergency where suitable landing arrangements existed and time was of the essence. It might have been possible to adapt a Concorde for some reconnaissance operations, but it was designed from the outset as a high speed airliner and I felt it was out of place in this book, which deals primarily with military and research aircraft.

As for the FD.2 being just a research aircraft intended to explore transonic and supersonic flight, there is rather more to the story. From an early stage in the project, Fairey viewed the aircraft as a potential fighter. They envisaged a follow-on prototype that would be similar in appearance, but larger in size called the ER.103B. It would be powered by either a version of the Rolls-Royce Avon or de Havilland Gyron turbojet and fitted with underwing fuel tanks to improve endurance. This would quickly give way to ER.103C, which was a proposed Mach 2+ interceptor, fitted with a Ferranti radar system, carrying air-to-air missiles and optionally equipped with additional liquid fuelled rocket propulsion. While it was obvious to the French that the FD.2 had great potential as a supersonic fighter, the British gave the idea a lukewarm reception. However, in 1955, the MoS issued Specification F.155 to a number of UK aircraft contractors, requesting submissions for a supersonic interceptor capable of defending the UK against Soviet high altitude supersonic bombers.

Fairey Aviation quickly responded to F.155 with a modified single engine delta, then moved to a much larger two seat aircraft that was somewhat similar in size and appearance to the Canadian Avro CF-105 Arrow. Given the designation FD.3, this proposal would be powered by two afterburning Rolls-Royce RB.122 turbojets, providing a Mach 2+ capability and a ceiling of around 60,000 ft (18,288 m). Two de Havilland Spectre Junior rocket motors were also considered as an addition to boost interception performance. The all-weather FD.3 would utilise an advanced radar system and carry two or possibly four air-to-air missiles. F.155 stipulated that the winner of the contest would be expected to have the first operational aircraft ready by 1962.

Of the main designs submitted to meet F.155 by Fairey, Saunders Roe, Hawker, Armstrong Whitworth and Vickers-Armstrong, the FD.3 and the Armstrong Whitworth AW.169 were the winners. The RAF also remained very interested in obtaining the Avro CF-105 Arrow and had been considering this advanced fighter as the Javelin replacement since F.153D was issued. There is little doubt that an adapted version of the Arrow could have entered service a year before the FD.3 or AW.169 and it was an outstanding design, with potential for development into a series of warplanes suitable for various roles.

By 1956, the FD.3 had been officially selected as the UK's future supersonic air defence fighter and it seemed as if the project would now move to the construction of a mock-up, followed by a prototype. However, there was a dramatic turn of events in 1957, when a White Paper on Defence was published which favoured guided weapons and sought to make huge reductions in military funding. At a stroke, the government cancelled most of the advanced UK military aircraft projects such as FD.3, the Saunders Roe mixed propulsion fighter and the Avro 730 bomber. The only real survivor was the English Electric Lightning, which was at a very advanced stage of development and regarded as worth retaining, although a few other aircraft projects under consideration like the P.17A (future TSR.2) bypassed these cuts.

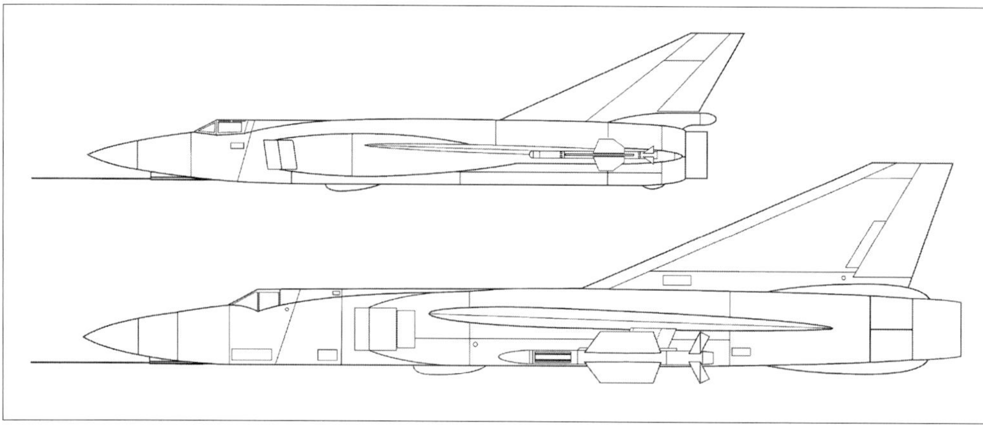

These are two different Fairey designs for interceptors proposed in the 1950s. The upper drawing shows the side view of a fighter directly based on the FD.2 research aircraft. The lower drawing (approximately to scale) shows the more substantial FD.3 long-range supersonic combat aircraft, armed with Red Hebe missiles (developed from the Red Dean). Although appearing to be sound designs that suited the RAF and would have proved successful in overseas markets, neither progressed beyond wind tunnel models.

A Fairey Delta III concept carrying two Red Hebe missiles (developed from Red Dean).

Hawker Looks Towards Hypersonic Flight

The FD.2 programme had been keenly observed by the aviation industry and it generated special interest at Hawker, with Sydney Camm recognising the need for even faster research aircraft. In late 1958, Camm and his senior designers Ralph Hooper and John Fozard visited the RAE to discuss the situation and make a number of suggestions for an FD.2 follow-on. Fairey had already considered the addition of underwing Napier ramjets for the FD.2 in an attempt to boost maximum speed and proposed the potentially faster ER.103D which would have a new engine, new air inlets and a 70° delta. Unfortunately, both these ideas were dismissed by the RAE. Now Camm felt that his company was better placed to develop and build something more advanced and this seems to have won favour with the RAE, although they expressed concern that the government was no longer interested in expensive, military linked aviation projects and funding would be difficult.

Nevertheless, Fozard was very enthusiastic about the possibility of developing a machine capable of setting a new world record and he envisaged it being powered by a combination turbojet and ramjet system (called RP.20) devised by Robin Jamison and his chief assistant John Lane at Bristol Aero Engines. While the RAE remained lukewarm about the chances of taking these ideas much further, Camm approved studies for a handful of different designs that would be capable of exploring the Mach 3–4.5 regime and the overall project was designated P.1134.

Somewhat surprisingly, Camm also managed to talk Jamison into incorporating the Rolls-Royce RB.146 (an afterburning development of the Avon) into his mixed propulsion system on the grounds of good reliability. By spring 1959, Fozard had produced an initial proposal for the P.1134/1, using a single afterburning RB.146 and ramjet units on either side. The aircraft was

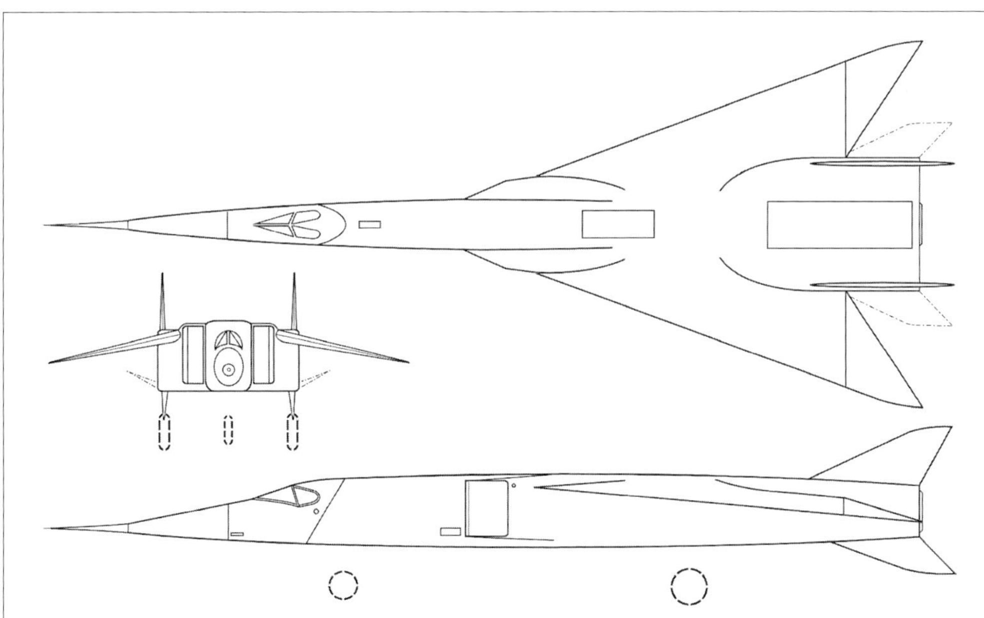

Hawker P.1134/1, the first design in a series of high speed, mixed propulsion research aircraft with an estimated top speed in the region of Mach 3.5.

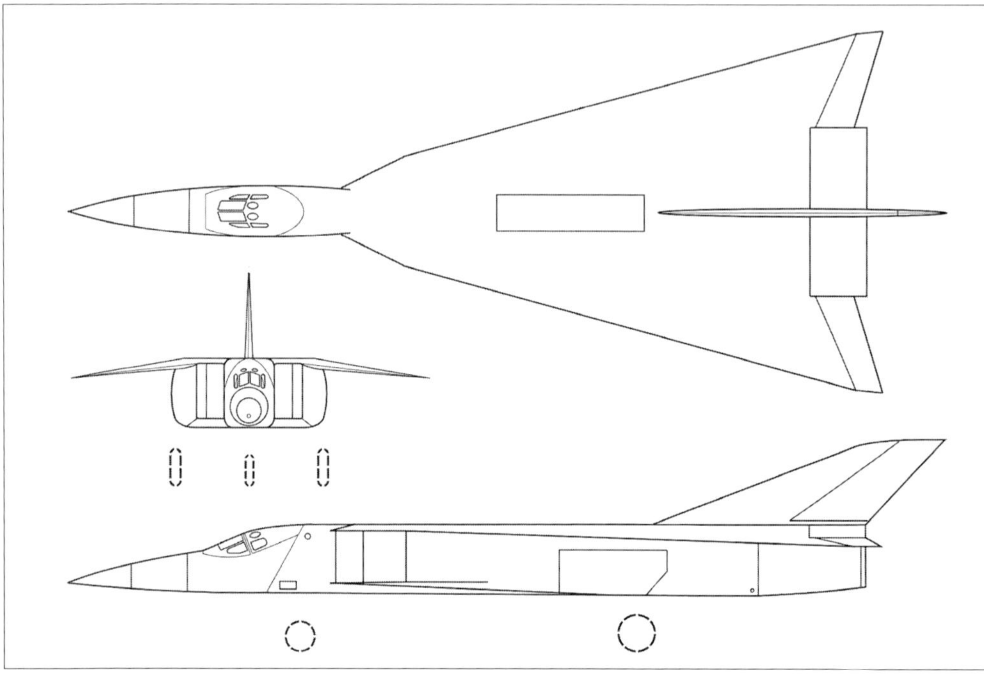

P.1134/4, was the final proposal in this design series. This mixed propulsion delta research aircraft designed by John Fozard would have an estimated capability of Mach 4+ at high altitude.

60 ft (18.28 m) long, with a leading edge sweep of 70°, a 10° anhedral angle, a relatively small wingspan measuring 25 ft (7.62 m) and ventral fins that folded downwards by 120° during flight. Estimated weight was 30,000 lb (13,607 kg) and much of this single seat aircraft would be built from stainless steel, considered the most suitable heat resistant material available.

Various refinements were apparent with P.1134/2 and the slightly larger P.1134/3. Both designs had re-positioned air intakes, canards and dispensed with the ventral fins. Estimated maximum speed for these designs was in the region of Mach 3.5–4 at high altitude.

P.1134/4 was the final proposal in this group, apparently completed in April 1959 at the request of the RAE, who had expressed interest in an aircraft capable of being flown at speeds beyond Mach 4. An even greater leading edge sweep of 75° was applied, plus a single tailfin and a revised cockpit canopy to meet high temperature considerations. Nevertheless, it was becoming clear that there were significant technical issues with the RP.20 propulsion system and manned flight at high supersonic speeds would take this project into very expensive unexplored territory. So the RAE made their excuses and cut funding for any further studies or research, with the project coming to an end, although Ralph Hooper completed a few more designs, including a Mach 3 four engined delta interceptor, before moving on to work on the Harrier.

Boulton Paul Deltas

In the immediate post-war scramble to make full use of captured German aviation research, the delta wing was given high priority and one company to benefit from this was Boulton Paul Aircraft Ltd, who wasted no time producing preliminary plans for an experimental jet aircraft in association with the RAE. This was given the company reference P.111. They were then issued with Air Ministry Specification E.27/46 and contracted to begin construction. Boulton Paul's chief designer Dr Seymour Redshaw (1906–1995) was largely responsible for this project and work began in 1947 at the company's Pendeford site. The P.111 featured a compact, slightly tubby fuselage housing a Rolls-Royce Nene 3 RN.2 turbojet, fed from an oval shaped nose intake. The cockpit was positioned well forward providing the pilot with reasonably good visibility and there was a Martin Baker ejector seat fitted for emergency use.

The 45° thin delta wing was slightly cropped, but could be fitted with small, interchangeable, pointed fibreglass extension pieces giving an overall span of 33.5 ft (10.24 m) and a wing area of 290 ft^2 (26.94 m^2). With a straight trailing edge, this provided a perfect delta shape. An extra section could also be fitted to the top of the 45° tailfin when requited and this tended to be left in place during most trial flights. Elevons and a tail rudder provided flight control, with a 7 ft (2.1 m) anti-spin parachute carried in a nacelle attached to the rear fuselage.

By the time the P.111 was completed, it had been issued with the official serial VT935 and soon began ground tests and taxiing trials. But Pendeford was a pre-war aerodrome without concrete runways and as a consequence, the P.111 was partly dismantled and transported by road to the RAE at Boscombe Down. The first flight was made by Squadron Leader Bob Smyth on 10 October 1950, with later trials being undertaken by Boulton Paul's chief test pilot Alexander E. 'Ben' Gunn (1923–1999). He was critical of the power controls, describing them as over-sensitive and noted a substantial trim change during raising or lowering the undercarriage.

Boulton Paul P.111, in original unpainted form.

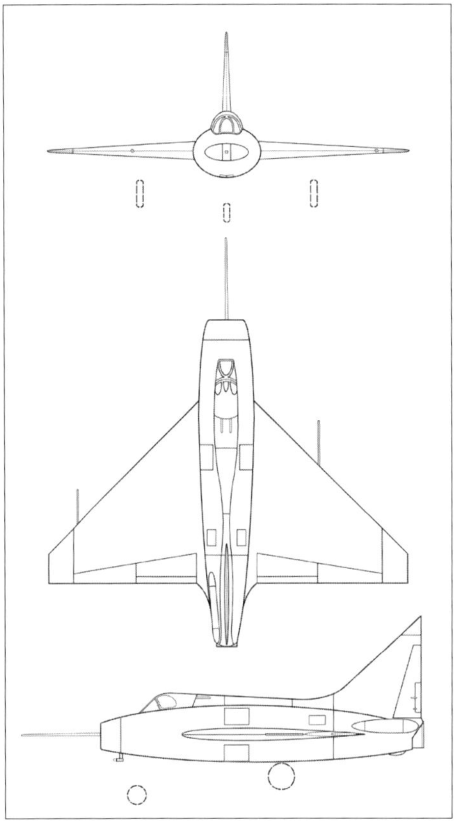

The Boulton Paul P.111 after repair work to address damage during a crash landing and a series of upgrades to fix various design shortcomings. Subsequently, the aircraft was re-designated P.111A.

Gunn also expressed concern about the need to maintain an engine speed of 7,000 RPM to keep the generators functional during landings and having no air brakes.

Following a hard landing due to an undercarriage problem, the P.111 underwent repairs and it was decided to make a series of upgrades based on Gunn's list of shortcomings. Among the changes made were modifications to the controls, the installation of four air brakes, strengthening of the anti-spin parachute to allow its use to assist braking on landing, alterations to the undercarriage doors and a new windshield. A long probe housing a pitot head was fitted in the nose and a yellow paint finish was applied to the aircraft's previously unpainted metal skin.

As a consequence of these changes, the aircraft was re-named as the P.111A. Test flights continued at Boscombe Down and three different wingtips were tested. This allowed aspect ratios of 2.3, 3.0 and 3.8 to be compared under similar conditions. The aircraft was then moved to RAE Bedford, flying on many occasions, until it was finally retired from service in 1958. P.111 was then passed to the Cranfield College of Aeronautics for static training purposes and finally presented to the Midland Air Museum at Coventry in 1975.

Boulton Paul were also responsible for a second jet powered research aircraft, which closely followed the P.111 and was fairly similar in appearance and overall design. Built to Air Ministry Specification E.27/49 for the RAE, it was given the company designation P.120 and received the official serial VT951. Powered by the same type of turbojet, the delta wing was virtually the same, aside from fixed wingtips that could be rotated to adjust trim and short, outboard wing

Boulton Paul P.120 (VT 951) in its "black" paint scheme, on a test flight from RAE Boscombe Down in August 1952.

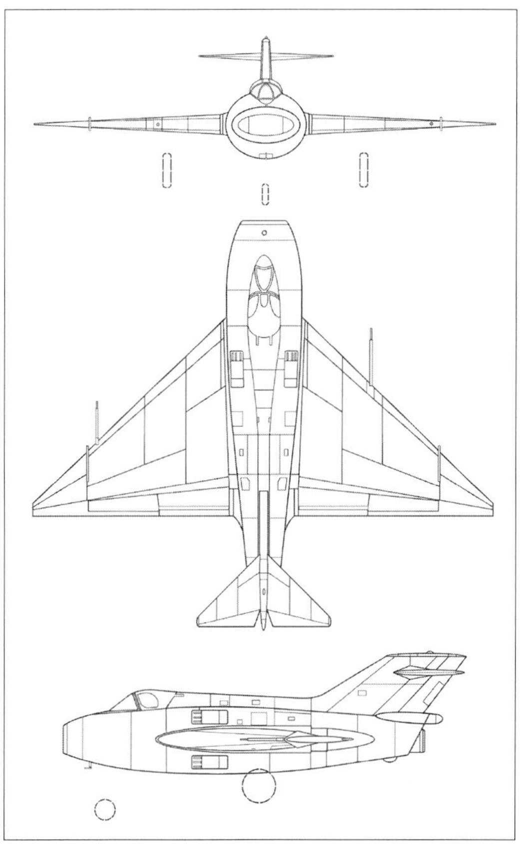

General arrangement of the Boulton Paul P.120.

fences. More significant changes were made to the tailfin, with the addition of horizontal control surfaces to generally improve stability. Ben Gunn made the first test flight on 6 August 1952 at Boscombe Down and although there were some relatively minor initial issues relating to the tailplane, the aircraft flew well and was scheduled to appear at the Farnborough Air Show during the following month. Now painted in a black finish, the P.120 continued to undertake test flights and on 29 August 1952, Gunn encountered extreme flutter at an altitude of 5,000 ft (1,524 m) above Salisbury Plain. This was followed by the detachment of the port elevon, making the aircraft almost impossible to handle. For the next half an hour, Gunn struggled with the controls, while calmly discussing the situation with engineers via the radio. It was finally agreed that he stood no chance of making a landing at Boscombe Down and he would have to abandon the aircraft.

With the P.120 barrel rolling at about 2,000 ft (609 m) altitude above Grateley, near Andover, Gunn ejected downwards, becoming the first pilot to do so from a delta winged aircraft. He landed in a wood relatively unscathed, but the P.120 was completely destroyed on impact. At the enquiry into the accident, it was determined that the tab control mechanism had been unable to withstand the force loads, causing a fracture and loss of the elevon. P.120 had made 20 flights, lasting a total of just over 11 hours and after the crash, it was proposed that P.111 might be re-built to P.120 specifications, although the idea was soon dropped. Sadly, P.120 was the last aircraft to be developed and built by Boulton Paul Aircraft, who became part of the Dowty Group in 1961.

Handley Page HP.115

From the early 1950s onwards, there were a number of studies into the viability of building supersonic transports (SSTs). However, the technical challenges and cost of development were very obvious, while the commercial practicality of SSTs were generally considered an unrealistic aspiration for the near term future. Nevertheless, there were expectations that the next generation of strategic bombers would have supersonic performance and the know-how was already available to move forward. So the UK MoS eventually decided that it was reasonable to sponsor several modest studies into the feasibility of supersonic airliners. The need for powerful new, reliable engines that were capable of sustained supercruise and economic to operate was obvious, but the aerodynamics would undoubtedly generate even bigger design challenges.

The wing would obviously need to provide adequate lift and good handling at low speeds, while also functioning properly above the speed of sound.

In 1956, The Supersonic Transport Aircraft Committee (STAC) was established at RAE Farnborough and chaired by Sir Morien Morgan (1912–1978) who was the RAE deputy director. Committee members included aircraft and jet engine manufacturers, along with representatives from the airlines and government. This formalised the idea of exploring development of an SST and it became apparent that a large dart shaped aircraft with a delta wing was the preferred choice if a string of complex design issues could be properly addressed.

Dietrich Küchemann and his mathematician Johanna Weber (1910–2014) who worked for Handley Page had been studying the production of large vortices above delta wings at low speeds which generated increased lift. They believed that a suitable SST wing should run alongside much of the fuselage, with a leading edge sweep of at least 65°. Nevertheless, there would be issues with the need for a high angle of attack during take-off and landing and a long forward landing strut was required.

The HP.115 research aircraft during a test flight in the early 1960s. This aircraft was retired in 1974 and became a museum exhibit.

In flight above the English countryside, the HP.115 was specifically developed to test low speed handling characteristics of a slender delta design, under consideration for a future supersonic airliner.

This research was put to STAC, who decided that funding would be sought for further wind tunnel testing of models and hopefully the adaption of a Fairey FD.2 research aircraft to take such a wing for supersonic flight trials. In addition, another aircraft was needed to explore low speed handling and STAC decided this should be a simple low cost glider that could be towed to an altitude of about 30,000 ft (9,144 m) by a Canberra light bomber before release. Slingsby Sailplanes were contracted to design this glider which received the company reference T.48. However, when the project was reviewed, STAC realised that a powered version would have many advantages and cost a good deal less to operate. As a consequence, Handley Page received a contract to build this low cost delta wing demonstrator which was given the company designation HP.115. The delta wing had a 75° leading edge sweep, the tricycle undercarriage was fixed in position and a single, low-powered Bristol Siddeley Viper BSV.9 turbojet would be accommodated in a dorsal nacelle above the rear of the fuselage. Initial designs under the direction of George King, it became progressively less elegant as every effort was made to keep the aircraft as simple and inexpensive as possible.

Safety concerns (should there be a crash landing) were then raised by the RAE about the long pitot tube, which was directly in-line with the pilot and this led to a more bulbous forward section for the cockpit, allowing the rod to be relocated. Many components were simply spare parts for other aircraft, like undercarriage units designed for Jet Provosts, cockpit components made for the Percival Prentice and assorted parts intended for the Hawker Sea Hawk, Gloster Meteor, Vickers Viking and Miles Aerovan. This is actually not unusual when putting together an experimental aircraft.

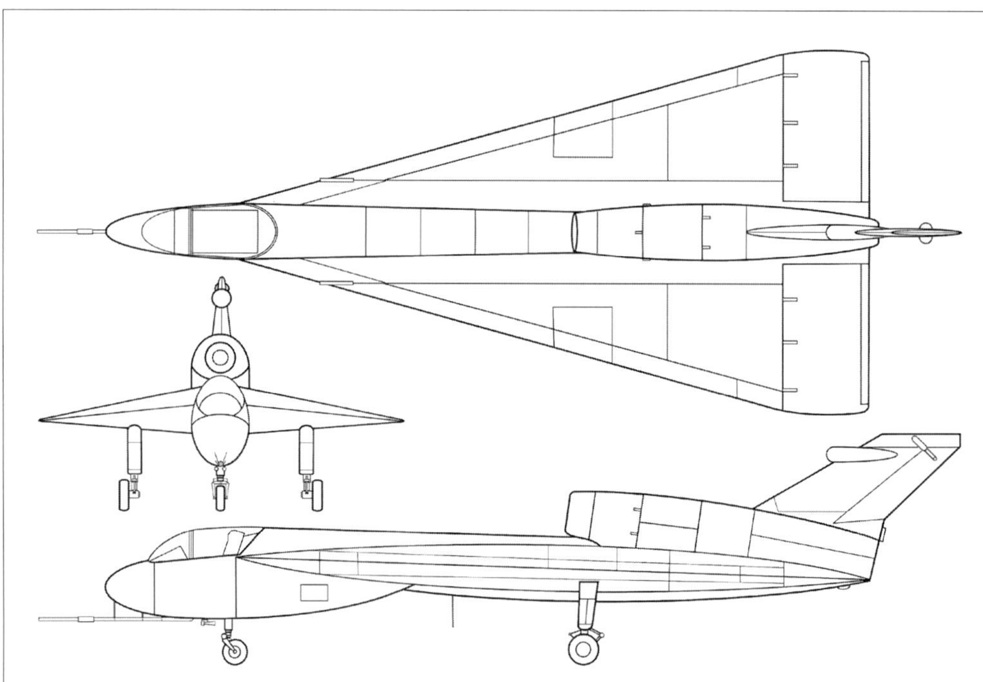

General arrangement of the HP.115 research aircraft.

Assembly began at Handley Page's Cricklewood factory in May 1961 and HP.115 was assigned the official serial XP841. Three months late, the aircraft was completed and transported by road to the RAE's Bedford facility where the Viper turbojet was installed. Finally, the RAE's senior test pilot Wing Commander Jack Henderson (1931–1990) made the first flight on 17 August 1961.

The aircraft was flown extensively in support of the UK's SST project, which received the name Concorde when France became a joint partner in November 1962. From this period onwards, French engineers and scientists from Sud Aviation were involved with the HP.115 trials and NASA was also given access to the programme. This would eventually lead to astronaut Neil Armstrong being allowed to fly the HP.115 after he returned from the Moon.

During test flights, the HP.115 demonstrated an ability to remain in the air at very low speeds, recorded on one occasion as 69 mph (111 kph). In 1964, smoke generators were installed above the forward inboard wing section, which provided useful air flow visualisation. Trials continued until after the first Concorde flight, with the somewhat inadequate Viper 9 turbojet requiring replacement, having operated at high thrust for most of its life. The only serious mishap took place in November 1964, when the port undercarriage wheel hit an obstruction during take-off, causing considerable damage. The aircraft was being flown by Jack Henderson, who decided to make an emergency landing rather than eject and he was able to save the aircraft, which was soon repaired. Test flights continued until 1974, when HP.115 was formally retired. It was then put on display at RAF Colerne, moved to the RAF Museum at Cosford and finally re-located to the Fleet Air Arm Museum, alongside Concorde 002 and the BAC 221.

Battlefield Fighters

During 1970, the UK Air Staff decided that a new all-weather close support aircraft would be needed by the mid-1980s to take the place of Harriers and Jaguars. This was considered absolutely essential in the event of a major war in Europe, with NATO facing large numbers of invading Soviet tanks. As a consequence, (Air Staff Target) AST.396 was created with BAC Warton and Hawker Siddeley at Brough being contracted to undertake studies and provide proposals for various new aircraft to fill the requirement. Numerous designs would emerge, often looking like slightly downsized Jaguars or relatives of the Hawk. Perhaps one of the most interesting ideas came from Hawker Siddeley Aviation in 1973, who proposed a delta wing aircraft, in part developed from the Harrier. This would use an uprated Pegasus engine fitted with an afterburning single rear exhaust outlet and two forward positioned plenum chamber burning swivelling outlets. While not a VTOL capable aircraft, it was expected to have good STOL performance from improvised airstrips and stretches of motorway or German autobahns. Given the reference HS.1193, the compact, single seat aircraft was designed as a missile launch platform with exceptional manoeuvrability. In one configuration it would carry six advanced AAMs to take on low flying aircraft.

With a limited supersonic capability, HS.1193 had estimated dimensions of about 45 ft (13.7 m) in length a wingspan of about 24 ft (7.3 m) and a height of about 16.5 ft (5 m). The undercarriage appears to have been similar to a Harrier, with stabilising wheels carried in the wings, although the available drawings are not entirely clear about these details. While the delta wing's leading edge was an ogival shape, the sweep roughly translates to about 60°. This aircraft and indeed other proposals for AST.396 never progressed much further than the concept stage, but a few of the design features would re-surfaced in new proposals around a decade later.

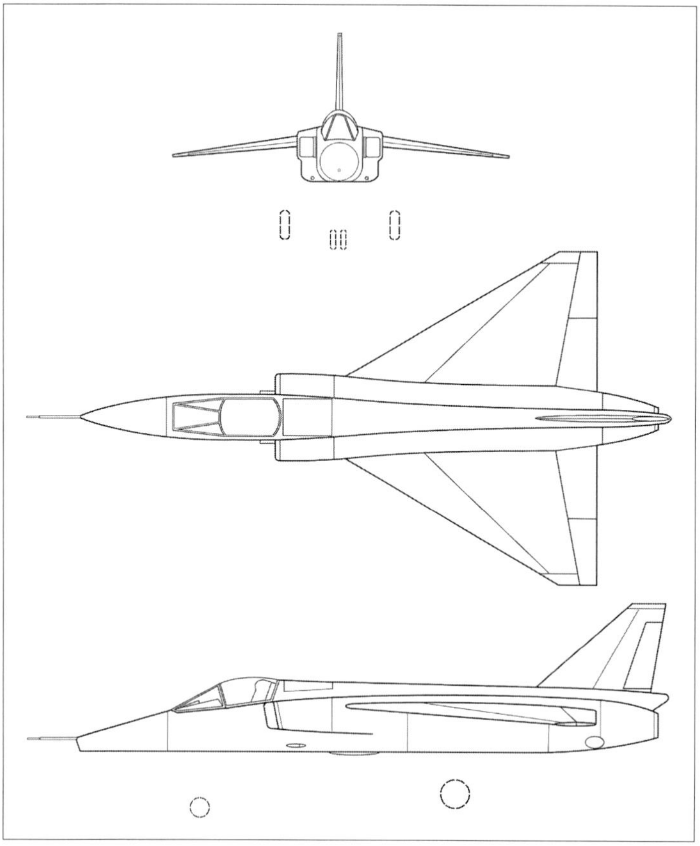

Developed as a Warton study for a compact delta winged strike and close support aircraft with STOL performance, this version of the BAC P.72 bore a passing resemblance to the larger Jaguar.

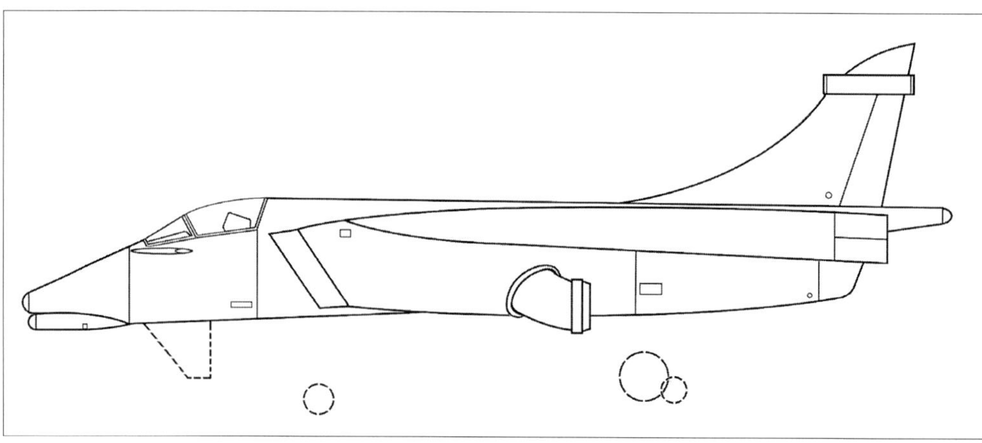

The Hawker-Siddeley Kingston HS.1193 battlefield fighter, dating from 1973. Highly agile, armed with six SRAM AAMs and powered by a modified Pegasus engine using forward outlets with plenum chamber burning and a single afterburning outlet at the rear. Small forward canard wings and a single fin mounted below the cockpit would provide exceptional directional control. The wing was an ogival delta with large elevons for control and a tail rudder. This aircraft was expected to have modest supersonic performance and the rear exhaust would be capable of vectoring. While VTOL may have been considered, it seems more likely this was intended to be an STOL, high agility fighter, perhaps also capable of undertaking some ground attack missions.

Artist's visualisation of the BAe P.1233-1 close support aircraft, utilising a canard layout and driven by a rear mounted contra-prop pusher arrangement. (*BAE Systems*)

In late 1987, British Aerospace unveiled the design of its Small Agile Battlefield Aircraft (SABA) which was given the company reference P.1233-1. It had been secretly undergoing development for around two years and was described as being primarily intended for air-to-air combat with attack helicopters, while also having the ability to shoot down cruise missiles, engage low-level jet fighters (in favourable circumstances) and undertake ground attack missions. Two initial BAe SABA, single-seat concepts had been chosen for further development and one was a compact twin boom aircraft with the company designation P.1238, that used a pusher propfan. But but the sleeker P.1233-1 was the more favoured design. This had a wingspan of 36 ft (10.97m, a length of 31.33 ft (9.54 m) and an estimated maximum take-off weight of about 11,000 lb (4,989 kg). Propulsion would be provided by a development of the Lycoming T55 turboshaft engine, producing about 4,500 hp (3,355 kw) and driving a rear mounted multi-blade propfan.

The aircraft's compact size and small air intake would considerably reduce its radar cross section and it was also decided to use helicopter style armoured flat panels for the cockpit to reduce glint and lower the visual signature. The aircraft would be capable of operating from an 800 ft (250 m) dirt strip and would have a maximum speed of about 450 mph (724 kph), which was considered less important than very high agility. The P.1233-1 would in theory be able to turn through 180° in around five seconds at 300 mph (480 kph) and engage something like a

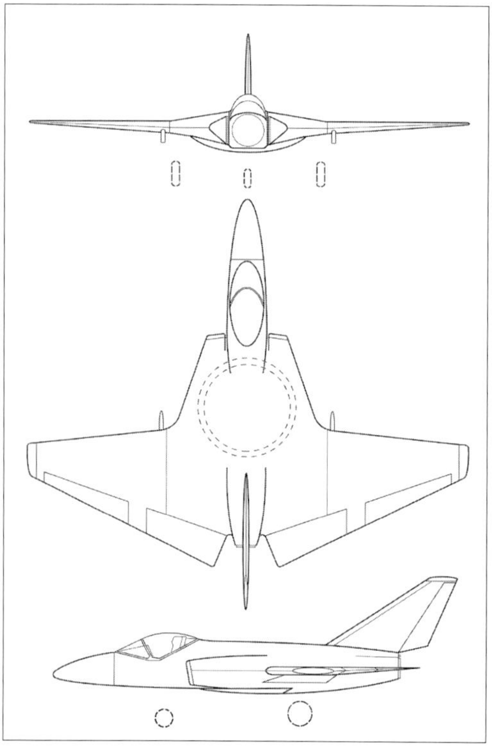

The BAe P.1234-1 was an unusual design for a close support aircraft, with various features like a gun turret controlled by a sight built into the pilot's helmet. There were three different concepts produced for this particular study.

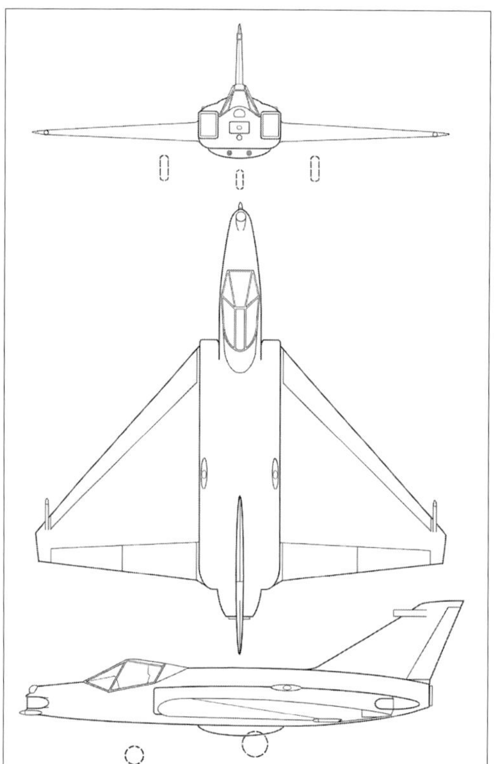

The BAe P.1234-3 was a compact delta winged ground attack aircraft, using a combination of high performance air-to-surface missiles and a machine gun. Part of a substantial 1987 study, it progressed little further than the design phase.

multi-role fighter in the F-16/MiG-29 class head on with air-to-air missiles before it could escape from attack. Expected to have a four hour loiter capability, the P.1233-1 would carry six underwing AIM-132 air-to-air missiles and an internal 25 mm cannon with 150 rounds. Other armaments would be available as required and the aircraft would be equipped with a laser seeker/designator.

The initial thinking behind the SABA project was to provide the US Army with an advanced and more capable, all-weather, single-seat replacement for the A-10A Thunderbolt II. SABA was based on careful analysis of US Army requirements for the future, with service entry in the 1990s and informal discussions with the Army and USAF were underway by the time SABA was disclosed to the aviation press. This was to be a joint development between British Aerospace and McDonnell Douglas, with the potential sale of 1,000 aircraft and BAe were considering funding the construction of a P.1233-1 prototype. Soon after these announcements, BAe disclosed several further SABA designs using turbofan propulsion. BAe's thinking behind this was to provide alternatives using proven technology as the propulsion technology was relatively new and there could be unforeseen issues combining it with a new type of canard airframe.

Two of the proposals appear in this book as they are tailless jets. The P.1234-1 utilised what has been described as a blended body wing and it was powered by a single Rolls-Royce Adour RT-172-871 low bypass ratio turbofan, providing 5,715 lb (25.4 kN) static thrust. It also features a rotatable turret holding a 25 mm cannon on the underside which would be helmet controlled, plus two ASRAAMs for self-defence. Overall dimensions for this aircraft were similar to the canard design, although the wing area was somewhat greater. Nevertheless, it was considered quite stealthy and was expected to be hard to visually detect at low level.

The P.1234-2 proposal utilised the same forward fuselage section, cockpit and undercarriage. It had straight wings, tailplanes and upright tailfins with the objective of enhancing low level manoeuvrability. It was another compact design like the P.1233-1 and powered by an Avco Lycoming ALF.502 turbofan, originally developed for use in the Northrop YA-9 ground attack prototype, which lost out to the A-10 Thunderbolt II in 1972. Armament was a fixed forward firing 25 mm cannon and there were six underwing hardpoints.

The next in this series was the tailless delta winged P.1234-3, with an advanced hypervelocity missile capability. The aircraft would carry 12 missiles internally, which would be launched from two tubes in the fuselage underside. The missiles would be controlled by three sensors positioned in the nose and on each side of the fuselage. In addition, there would be a fixed 12.7 mm machine gun for use against ground targets. Propulsion would be very similar to that of the P.1234-1, which was an Adour RT-172-871 turbofan providing almost identical performance and the P.1234-3 would have an impressive instantaneous turn rate of about 40°/sec.

Despite this being a series of very interesting proposals with some unique features, BAe and McDonnell failed to generate sufficient interest with the US military or NATO partners to proceed further with the project. It is hard to understand exactly why SABA was unsuccessful. More than 30 years has passed since SABA designs emerged, but the A-10A remains in US service. While there have been recent attempts to replace it with the exceptionally expensive and rather unsuitable F-35, the A-10 will continue to receive upgrades and is expected to remain in service until 2040.

Martin Baker Delta Interceptor
Crew: 1
Wingspan: 36 ft (10.97 m)
Wing area: 360 ft^2 (33.44 m$^{2)}$
Sweep (leading edge): 60°
Length: 39.5 ft (12 m)
Height: 14 ft (4.26 m)
Weight: 8,710 lb (3,950 kg)
Powerplant: 1 × Rolls-Royce AJ65 Avon turbojet rated at 6.500 lb (28.9 kN) static thrust. Twin turbojets and turbojet/rocket engine version were considered.
Maximum speed: 640 mph (1,030 kph) ground level. estimated
Rate of climb: 6 min to 45,000 ft (13,716 m)
Service Ceiling: 50,000 ft (15,240 m)
Range: N/A
Armament: 2 × 20 mm Hispano Cannon in Wing sections. 200 RPG

Gloster P.275
Crew: 1
Wingspan: 45.5 ft (13.9 m)
Wing area: 750 ft^2 (69.7 m$^{2)}$
Sweep (inner leading edge): 60°
Length: 48 ft (14.6 m)
Height: 16 ft (4.87 m) estimated
Gross weight: 18,500 lb (8,391 kg)
Powerplant: 1 × turbojet with afterburner (possibly a future version of the Armstrong Siddeley Sapphire) producing 12,000 lb (53.37 kN) static thrust
Maximum speed: 668 mph (1,075 kph) at sea level
Rate of climb: N/A
Service ceiling 55,000 ft (16,764 m)
Range: N/A
Endurance 2 hrs
Armament: 4 × 30 mm ADEN Cannon

Hill Transformable Delta
Crew: 1
Wingspan: fully open 42 ft (12.8 m). Swept: 24 ft (7.3 m)
Wing area: fully open 157 ft^2 (14.5 m^2) swept: 268 ft^2 (24.8 m^2)
Length: 47 ft (14.3 m)
Height: N/A
Gross weight: 13,000 lb (5,896 kg)
Powerplant: 1 × Rolls-Royce Avon turbojet, providing 6,500 lb (28.9 kN) thrust. With afterburner: 10,400 lb (46.2 kN) thrust
Maximum speed: Mach 1.29 at 36,000 ft (10,972 m)
Ceiling: N/A

Gloster Javelin FAW.Mk 1
Crew: 2
Length: 56.25 ft (17.15 m)
Wingspan: 52 ft (15.84 m)
Wing area: 927 ft^2 (86.12 m^2)
Sweep (leading edge): Initial 39.5°, followed by 33.8° to the wingtips
Height: 16 ft (4.8 m)
Empty weight: 24,000 lb (10,886 kg)
Loaded weight: 31,580 lb (14,325 kg)
Powerplant: 2 × (non-afterburning) Armstrong Siddeley Sapphire ASSa.6 102/103s turbojet engines, each developing 8,000 lb (35.58 kN) of static thrust
Maximum speed: 709 mph (1,141 kph) at sea level
Range: 951 miles (1,530 km)
Ceiling: 52,000 ft (15,849 m)
Armament: 4 × 30 mm ADEN cannon
Avionics: AI.17 radar

Gloster Javelin FAW Mk 9
Crew: 2
Length: 56.75 ft (17.29 m)
Wingspan: 52 ft (15.84 m)
Wing area: 927 ft^2 (86.12 m^2)
Sweep (leading edge): Initial 39.5°, followed by 33.8° to the wingtips
Height: 16 ft (4.87 m)
Empty weight: 24,000 lb (10,886 kg)
Maximum take-off weight: 43,165 lb (19,580 kg)
Powerplant: 2 × afterburning Armstrong Siddeley Sapphire ASSa 7LR Mk 209/210s turbojets, each rated at a maximum thrust of 12,300 lb (54 kN)
Maximum speed: 710 mph (1,140 kph) at sea level
Range: 954 miles (1,530 km)
Service ceiling: 52,800 ft (15,865 m)
Armament: 4 × 30 mm cannon. Up to four de Havilland Firestreak air-to-air missiles
Avionics: Westinghouse AN/APQ-43 radar

Gloster P.376
Crew: 2
Length: 72 ft (21.94 m)
Wingspan: 60 ft (18.28 m)
Wing area: 1,235 ft^2 (114.73 m^2)
Sweep (leading edge): 48° approximate
Height: 16 ft (4.87 m)
Empty weight: N/A
All up weight: 60,300 lb (27,351 kg)
Powerplant: 2 × afterburning Olympus OI21R turbojets each rated at 28,200 lb (125.5 kN) thrust
Maximum speed: Mach 1.8 at 36,000 ft (10,972kph)
Range: N/A
Service ceiling: 60,000 ft (18,288 m) approximate

Armament: 2 (or possibly 4) Red Dean air-to-air missiles
Avionics: Possibly a version of the Ferranti AI.23 radar

De Havilland 1st DH.108 (TG283)
Crew: 1
Wingspan: 39 ft (11.88 m)
Length: 25.83 ft (7.9 m)
Height: N/A
Gross weight: 8,800 lb (3,991 kg)
Powerplant: 1 × de Havilland Goblin II turbojet rated at 3,100 lb (13.8 kN) static thrust
Maximum speed: 280 mph (450 kph)
Ceiling: N/A
Range: 730 miles (1174 km)

De Havilland De Havilland 3rd DH.108 (VW120)
Crew: 1
Wingspan: 39 ft (11.89 m)
Wing area: 327.86 ft² (30.47 m²)
Wing Loading: 133 kg/m² (27 lb/ft²)
Length: 26.83 ft (8.17 m)
Height: 14 ft (4.27 m)
Gross weight: 8,940 lb (4,064 kg)
Powerplant: 1 × de Havilland Goblin 4 turbojet rated at 3,738 lb (16.67 kN) static thrust
Thrust/weight: 0.42
Maximum speed: 677 mph (1,090 kph)
Ceiling: 40,000 ft (12,192 m)

Westland PJD.144
Crew: 1
Wingspan: 55 ft (16.8 m)
Wing area: 745 ft² (69.2 m²)
Length: 43.5 ft (13.3 m)
Gross weight: 27,260 lb (12,365 kg)
Powerplant: 2 × Rolls-Royce AJ65 Avon turbojets, each provided 6,500 lb (28.9 kN) static thrust
Maximum speed: 632 mph (1017 kph) at sea level
Ceiling: 50,000ft+ (15,240m+) estimated
Armament: 3 × 30 mm ADEN cannon

Hawker P.1077
Crew: 2
Wingspan: 58 ft (17.6 m)
Wing area: 750 ft² (69.67 m²)
Length: 55 ft (16.7 m)
Powerplant: 2 × Rolls-Royce AJ65 Avon turbojets, each provided 6,500 lb (28.9 kN) static thrust. Afterburners considered, details unknown
Maximum speed: 650–700 mph (1,000–1,100 kph) estimated
Ceiling: 50,000ft+ (15,240m+) estimated
Armament: 4 × 30 mm ADEN cannon

Hawker P.1091 Delta Hunter
Crew: 1
Wingspan: 33 ft (10 m)
Sweep (leading edge): 60°
Wing area: 510 ft² (47.3 m²)
Length: 42 ft (12.8 m)
Empty weight: N/A
Gross weight: N/A
Powerplant: 1 × Armstrong-Siddeley Sapphire 4 turbojet with afterburner, provided 8,000 lb (35.5 kN) static thrust
Maximum speed: Mach 0.98 estimated
Ceiling: 50,000ft+ (15,240m+) estimated
Range: N/A
Armament: 4 × 30 mm ADEN cannon

Hawker P.1092
Crew: 2
Wingspan: 35 ft (10.6 m)
Sweep (leading edge): 60°
Wing area: 580 ft² (53.8 m²)
Length: 55 ft (16.7 m)
Empty weight: N/A
Gross weight: N/A
Powerplant: 1 × unspecified Avon turbojet with afterburner. No details
Maximum speed: Mach 1.5 estimated
Ceiling: 55,000 ft (16,764 m)
Armament: 4 × 30 mm ADEN cannon

Hawker P.1093
Crew: 1
Wingspan: 41 ft (12.50 m)
Sweep (leading edge): 60°
Wing area: 750 ft² (69.6 m²)
Length: 49.6 ft (15 m)
Empty weight: N/A
Gross weight: N/A
Powerplant: 1 × Avon RA.14 turbojet, provided 9.500 lb (42.25 kN) static thrust. Equipped with afterburner, but full thrust not specified
Maximum speed: Mach 1.5 estimated
Ceiling: 55,000 ft (16,764 m)
Range: N/A
Armament: 6 × 30 mm ADEN cannon

Fairey FD.2 (ER103A)
Crew: 1
Wingspan: 26.83 ft (8.18 m)
Sweep (leading edge): 60°
Wing area: 360 ft² (33.44 m²)
Length: 51.58 ft (15.74 m)
Height: 11 ft (3.35 m)
Empty weight: 11,000 lb (4,990 kg)

Gross weight: 13,884 lb (6,298 kg)
Powerplant: 1 × Rolls-Royce Avon RA.14R turbojet providing 9,486 lb (42.2 kN) static thrust and 14,477 lb (64.4 kN) with afterburner
Maximum speed: 1,300 mph (2,092 kph)
Ceiling 55–60,000 ft (16,764–18,288 m)
Range: 830 miles (1,336 km)
Rate of climb: 2.5m to 45,000 ft (13,716 m)

Fairey ER103B
Crew: 1
Length: 54.33 ft (16.5 m)
Wing Span: 28 ft (8.5 m)
Height 12.33 ft (3.75 m)
All-up weight: 20,650 lb (9,366 kg)
Engine: 1 × de Havilland Gyron (or RR RB.122) turbojet rated at 20,000 lb (89 kN) static thrust.
Maximum speed: Mach 2.72 at 45,000 ft (13,716 m), Mach 2.49 at 55,000 ft (16,764 m)
Ceiling 60–65,000 ft (18,288 m–19,812 m)
Rate of climb: 2.5 m to 45,000 ft (13,716 m)

Fairey ER103C
Crew: 1
Wing Span: 37.58 ft (11.4 m)
Wing area: 600 ft² (55.7 m²)
Sweep (leading edge): 60°
Length: 58.33 ft (17.77 m)
Height 14.16 ft (4.28 m)
Gross weight: 30,100 lb (13,653 kg)
Engine: 1 × de Havilland Gyron turbojet rated at 20,000 lb (89 kN) static thrust, presumably with afterburner (unspecified) and 2 × de Havilland Spectre Junior rocket engines, each rated at 5,000 lb (22.24 kN)
Maximum speed: Mach 2.54 at 45,000 ft (13,716 m) Mach 2.25 at 60,000 ft (18,288 m)
Ceiling 60–65,000 ft (18,288 m–19,812 m). 90,000 ft (27,432 m) using rocket power
Rate of climb: 1.9 m to 45,000 ft (13,716 m)
Range: N/A
Armament: 2 × Blue Jay Mk.4 air-to-air missiles
Avionics: Ferranti radar

Fairey Delta III
Crew: 2
Length: 74.3 ft (17.1 m)
Wingspan: 46.8 ft (14.2 m)
Wing area: 1,100 ft² (102 m²)
Sweep (leading edge): 60°
Height: N/A
Gross weight: RD AAMs: 50,460 lb (22,888 kg), BJ AAMs: 48,000 lb (21,772 kg)
Powerplant: 2 × Rolls-Royce RB.122 turbojets each providing 17,000 lb (75.6 kN) thrust and 2 × de Havilland Spectre Junior rocket engines each rated at 5,000 lb (22.24 kN)
Maximum speed: Mach 2.27
Ceiling: 70,000 ft (21,336 m)
Range: N/A
Armament: 2 × Red Dean or 2 × Blue Jay Mk.4 air-to-air missiles

Hawker P.1134/1
Crew: 1
Wingspan: 25 ft (7.62 m)
Wing area: N/A
Sweep (leading edge): 70°
Length: 60 ft (18.28 m)
Height: N/A
Empty weight: 30,000 lb (13,607 kg)
Powerplant: 1 × Rolls-Royce RB.146 turbojet producing 12,690 lb (56.44 kN) static thrust and 17,110 lb (76.10 kN) with afterburner, plus 2 Bristol ramjets
Maximum speed: Mach 3+
Ceiling: 65,000 ft+
Range: N/A

Hawker P.1134/4
Crew: 1
Wingspan: 25 ft (7.62 m)
Sweep (leading edge): 75°
Wing area: 570 ft² (52.95 m²)
Length: 63.5 ft (19.35 m)
Height: N/A
Empty weight: 30,000 lb (13,607 kg)
Gross weight: N/A
Powerplant: 1 × Rolls-Royce RB.146 turbojet producing 12,690 lb (56.44 kN) static thrust and 17,110 lb (76.10 kN) with afterburner, plus 2 Bristol ramjets
Maximum speed: Mach 4.5+
Ceiling: 90,000 ft+ (27,432 m+)
Range: N/A

Boulton Paul P.111A
Crew: 1
Wingspan: 25.66 ft (7.82 m), 29.75 ft (9.07 m) and 33.5 ft (10.21 m) With detachable wingtips
Wing area (with detachable wingtips): 269 ft² (24.99 m²), 284 ft² (26.38 m²) and 290 ft² (26.94 m²)
Sweep (Leading edge): 45°
Length: 26.08 ft (7.95 m) without nose probe
Height: 12.5 ft (3.81 m)
Empty weight: 7,517 lb (3,410 kg)
Loaded weight: 10,127 lb (4,595 kg)
Powerplant: 1 × Rolls-Royce Nene R3N2 turbojet, 5,100 lb (22.69 kN) static thrust

Maximum speed: 649 mph (1,045 kph) at sea level
Ceiling: 35,000 ft (10,670 m)
Rate of climb: 9,400 ft/min (48m/s)

Boulton Paul P.120
Crew: 1
Wingspan: 33.45 ft (10.20 m)
Wing area: 290.13 ft^2 (26.96 m^2)
Length: 29.62 ft (9.03 m)
Height: 9.54 ft (2.91 m)
Empty weight: 10,656 lb (4,844 kg)
Loaded weight: 12,580 lb (5,718 kg)
Powerplant: 1 × Rolls-Royce Nene RN.2, 5,100 lb (22.7 kN) static thrust
Maximum speed: 600 mph (956kph)
Ceiling: 35,000 ft (10,670 m)

Handley Page HP.115
Crew: 1
Wingspan: 20 ft (6.1 m)
Wing area: 432 ft^2 (40.1 m^2)
Sweep (leading edge): 75°
Length: 50.33 ft (15.33 m)
Height: 12.75 ft (3.9 m)
Empty weight: 3,680 lb (1,669 kg)
Loaded weight: 5,050 lb (2,290 kg)
Powerplant: 1 × Armstrong Siddeley Viper ASV.9 turbojet, providing 1,900 lb (8.455 kN) of static thrust
Maximum speed: 248 mph (399 kph)
Ceiling: 10,000 ft (3,048 m)
Maximum Range: 300 miles (482 km)
Endurance: 40 minutes

BAC P.72 Delta
Crew: 1
Wingspan: 24 ft (7.31 m)
Wing area: 320 ft^2 (29.73 m^2)
Length: 42.2 ft (12.86 m)
Maximum take-off weight: N/A
Powerplant: 1 × Turbofan engine
Maximum speed: 650 mph (1,046 kph) estimated
Ceiling: 45,000 ft (13,716 m) estimated
Range: N/A
Armament: 2 × 30 mm cannon, various underwing stores, possibly 2 × AAMs

BAe SABA P.1234-1
Crew: 1
Wingspan: 36 ft (10.97 m)
Wing area: 387 ft^2 (36 m^2)
Length: 31.5 ft (9.6 m)
Maximum take-off weight: 11,000 lb (4,989 kg)
Powerplant: 1 × Rolls-Royce Adour RT-172-871 low bypass ratio turbofan, providing 5,715 lb (25.4 kN) static thrust
Maximum speed: 500 mph (800 kph) estimated
Ceiling: 40,000 ft (12.192 m) estimated
Range: N/A
Armament: A rotatable turret holding a 25 mm cannon on the underside, controlled using the pilot's helmet and two ASRAAMs for self defence

BAe SABA P.1234-3
Crew: 1
Wingspan: 30 ft (9.1 m)
Sweep (leading edge): 48°
Wing area: 331 ft^2 (30.75 m^2)
Length: 31.25 ft (9.5 m)
Maximum take-off weight: 12,747 lb (5,781 kg)
Powerplant: 1 × Rolls-Royce Adour RT-172-871 low bypass ratio turbofan, providing 5,715 lb (25.4 kN) static thrust
Maximum speed: 500 mph (800 kph) estimated
Ceiling: 40,000 ft (12.192 m) estimated
Range: N/A
Armament: 12 Guided hypervelocity missiles in ventral unit. 1 × 12.7 mm machine gun for ground attack.

4

Pushing the Design Envelope

The 1950s and early 1960s saw a number of aviation and space projects that were right on the fringes of what was technically possible, with a few belonging to the wishful thinking and slightly mad category. Some were based on complex unproven ideas that would have cost a fortune to investigate further, or they employed dangerous approaches that would never win acceptance, even if they could be made to work. One long standing aim to achieve boundary layer reduction would run into insoluble problems that remain perplexing. Another hopeful project from this period was the superb looking variable geometry Swallow bomber, which promised things it could never deliver, although in this particular case, the key design feature would be utilised in several American military aircraft. Atomic propulsion was yet another area of considerable post-war interest that suggested much, but remains unacceptably dangerous. That said, in 2018, the Russians announced development of a nuclear powered and nuclear armed cruise missile with unlimited range known as 9M730 Burevestnik (Petral). One prototype is understood to have been lost in a serious accident which killed several technicians and scientists during 2019.

Atomic power aside, the post-war British designers also had ideas for high-supersonic and hypersonic aircraft that must have seemed feasible at the time. But even today, this technology remains cutting edge and largely beyond realisation. Other ideas for manned British spacecraft can be found in a later chapter and most were simply pie-in-the-sky proposals that were unaffordable and belonged in the centre of the *Eagle* comic.

Handley Page Boundary Layer Research

The project described in this section was an ambitious post-war attempt to develop the aerodynamic capability known as Boundary Layer Control (BLC). The objective was a significant reduction in drag by ensuring laminar flow in the boundary layer surrounding the aircraft. Drag has been—and still is—a major concern for aircraft designers and BLC underwent a revival of interest during the 1950s when scientists believed there was a realistic possibility of overcoming all the known technical issues and developing a practical system. This would hopefully allow the construction of more advanced transporter/airliners with greater ranges and significantly lower operating costs. Furthermore, it was probable that new military aircraft could be developed for various long endurance operations.

Boundary Layer Theory (BLT) can be traced back to the beginning of the twentieth century and it is generally attributed to the German scientist Ludwig Prandtl (1875–1953). Many sources also acknowledge concurrent theoretical research undertaken in England by Frederick William Lanchester (1868–1946) and it is quite common to find references to the Lanchester–Prandtl Theory. However, it was some years before anyone carried out full-scale experiments to explore this area and looked for ways of using BLC as an aerodynamic improvement. This would be undertaken in 1936 by the Swiss scientist Dr Werner Pfenninger (1913-2003) at the Institute for Aerodynamics in Zurich. His research was followed in 1939 by work at NACA, Langley, which involved some elementary BLC tests using suction slots, but the research programme ended after America joined the war, with attention switching to the perfection of laminar flow aerofoils. At about the same time, Miles Aircraft in Britain carried out similar tests and scientists in Germany experimented with BLC, using a modified Me 109. Dr Gustav Lachmann who headed Handley Page's design office was also very interested in this area of research and had co-invented the leading edge slot with Frederick Handley Page.

However, Lachmann was a German citizen by birth and when the Second World War started, MI5 decided he was a security threat. So Lachmann was detained and initially sent to Quebec, Canada, before being moved to the Isle of Man. Fortunately, Handley Page were able to put some pressure on the authorities, who finally allowed Lachmann to continue working for them at Lingfield Prison.

Dr Gustav Lachmann who spent most of his working life with Handley Page and was responsible for a number of important aerodynamic innovations.

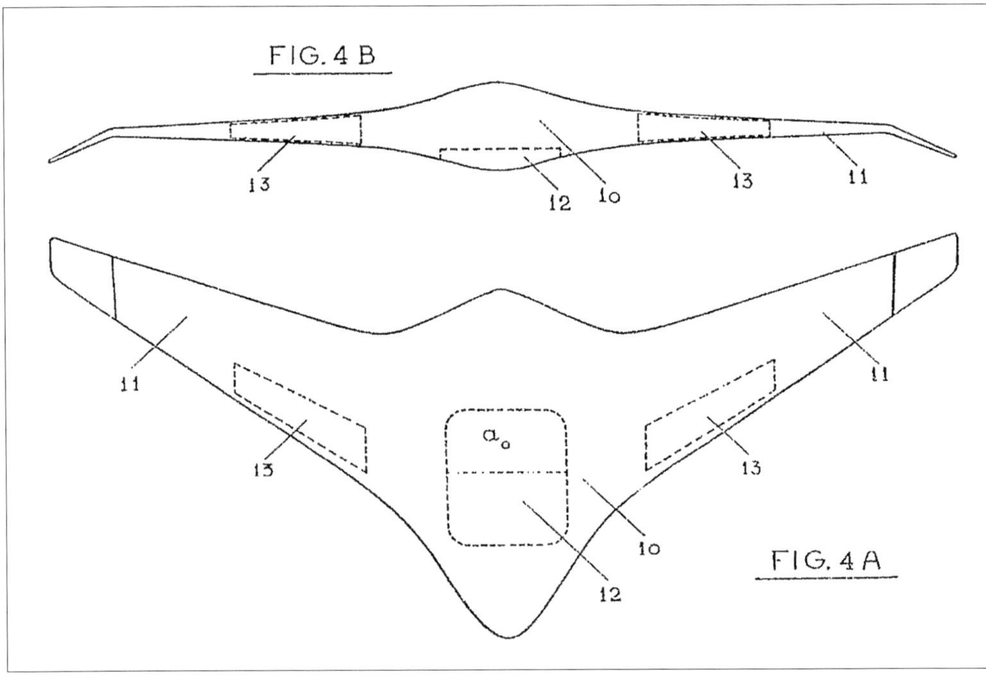

A 1944 flying wing design by Gustav Lachmann, which would feature boundary layer control.

During this time, he developed ideas for BLC and produced a very advanced looking flying wing aircraft design that was patented in 1944. Once the war ended, Lachmann returned to work at Handley Page, applied for British citizenship and would remain with the company as their chief aerodynamicist until he retired. After considerable involvement with development of Handley Page's H.80 (Victor) jet bomber, Lachmann and Lee undertook BLC research at Radlett, which was mostly funded by the MoS.

Initially, they experimented with wind tunnel models and then moved on to airborne trials using the prototype D.H 113 Vampire fighter. Meanwhile, the RAE at Farnborough was using the A.W.52 flying wing for BLC trials, although results proved disappointing and this project was abandoned in 1953. Like much aviation research during this period, the details were considered to have military implications and frequently classified as secret. That said, Dr Lachmann outlined much of his project to the Royal Aeronautical Society on 11 November 1954.

By 1956, Lachmann was starting to consider the application of BLC to relatively conventional airliners like the de Havilland Comet and this evolved into a design much closer to the Boeing 707. Nevertheless, Lachmann and Lee finally concluded that the flying wing remained the best candidate for a long-range transport aircraft utilising boundary layer reduction methods. By 1958, both the RAE and NACA had generally lost interest in BLC, although work in the US continued at Northrop under the direction of Dr Werner Pfenninger, who had been recruited by Jack Northrop in the late 1940s. Some limited research was also undertaken by the US Navy, which tested various BLC methods with a modified Cessna 170 and a Grumman Panther jet fighter, while the USAF sponsored tests conducted at Edwards AFB, using an adapted F-84 fighter. This ongoing American research was just enough to keep the Handley Page programme alive and received a boost when Northrop was preparing to assemble three X-21A research aircraft for BLC trials. The aircraft had started life as Douglas WB-66Ds, although only two X-21Bs would actually be completed. As a consequence, Handley Page managed to maintain official support for the BLC project and a new flying wing aircraft utilising this system was designed by Lachmann and Lee. It was assigned the company reference HP.117 and the initial, rather loose set of proposals was completed in April 1959.

The HP.117 was initially planned to have a wingspan of 125 ft (38 m), with a leading edge sweep of 44° at mid-chord. As an airliner, it was expected to accommodate 200 to 300 passengers, depending on the internal layout. Propulsion would be provided by four to six turbofans, with Rolls Royce RB.163 Spey engines as the prime choice. However, there were discussions at one stage about using turboprops in a pusher configuration, although this was finally ruled out, after the idea was considered unsatisfactory. There have also been suggestions that a version of the HP.117 may have been considered as a long endurance RAF launch platform for Skybolt nuclear tipped missiles.

Chris Gibson notes in his excellent book *Vulcan's Hammer*, that a version of the HP.117 carrying eight Skybolt missiles would have had a gross weight of about 354,000 lb (160,544 kg) and a patrol endurance of 12 hours. He goes on to suggest that the missiles could have been carried within the cargo bay and launched by rearward ejection.

In 1960, a model of the HP.117 appeared on display at the Farnborough Air Show and re-appeared the following year at Le Bourget. The media showed considerable interest in the HP.117

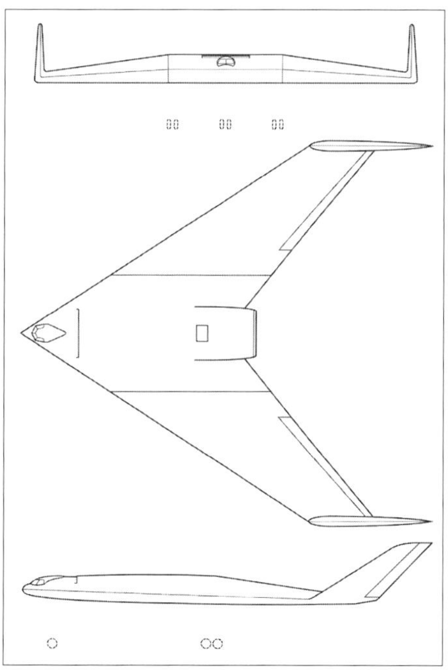

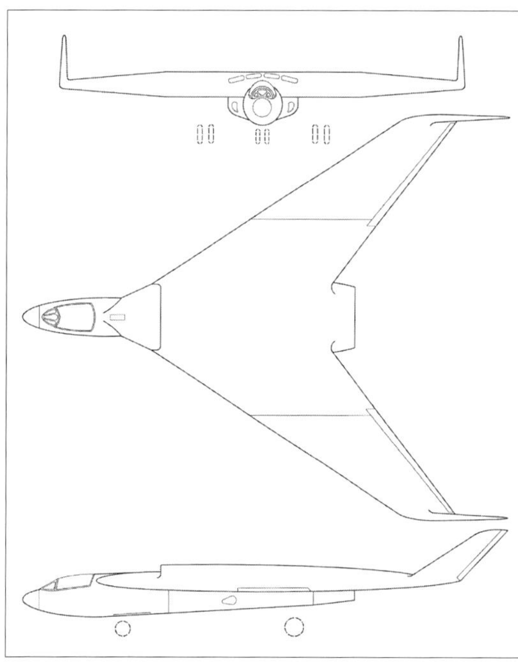

Left: This was the last configuration of the HP.117 produced in 1961. Slightly larger, with the ability to carry 300 passengers, it would be powered by six jet enginess and have intercontinental range.

Right: The HP.119 was essentially, a scaled down version of the HP.117, primarily intended to demonstrate the advantages of boundary layer control and allow further research into this area.

and Handley Page were keen to suggest that their research programme could lead to transatlantic fares reduced by as much as 30 per cent, making long distance travel a reality for many ordinary people. Refinement of the HP.117 continued, with an increased wingspan, adjusted undercarriage height and different wingtip fins, with the gross weight now set at 330,000 lb (149,685 kg) and an estimated range of 5,000 miles (8,000 km).

At the same time, a highly modified Folland Midge wing with a 45° sweep was mounted in an upright position on the dorsal section of an Avro Lancaster (PA474), which belonged to the College of Aeronautics at Cranfield. While Lachmann was keen to begin these aerodynamic trials, the first flight was considerably delayed and did not take place until 2 October 1962. Nevertheless, progress with the BLC project remained sluggish and Lachmann met with representatives of the Air Ministry. He proposed converting a Victor bomber for use as a test bed and if it performed well with the BLC system installed, this would be followed by the construction of two scale size demonstrators based on the HP.117, which would be designated HP.119. However, money was tight and things did not go as Lachmann hoped, with no promise of financial support for adapting a Victor, or the construction of prototypes.

Despite considerable reluctance to spend more government money on this Handley Page research project, the Air Ministry agreed in 1963 to follow the research undertaken at Cranfield with trials of a test wing fitted to a Hawker Siddeley HS.125 transport jet.

By now, the HP.117 project had led to a considerably different design for a very substantial military transporter designated HP.135. This was shown in model form at various trade events, but failed to attract the interest required for further development. The HS.125 project never progressed beyond this point and in 1965, Lachmann retired. A year later he was dead and so was the HP.117 project. Work on boundary layer control was at a standstill in Britain and the X-21A trials in America concluded at about the same time. Northrop showed that boundary layer reduction could be made to work, but many of the previously identified problems remained unresolved. In the 1980s, there was a brief revival of US interest with trials involving an F-111 and F-14 being undertaken at Dryden. These were followed by supersonic experiments with the F-16XL. However, at the present time an application of this technology remain elusive.

Wallis's Swallows

Sir Barnes Wallis CBE, FRS, RDI, FRAeS (1887–1979) is now best remembered as the scientist who devised the bouncing bomb that was used in May 1943 by the RAF to attack the Möhne, Sorpe, and Eder dams in the Ruhr. Operation Chastise (more widely known as the Dambusters Raid), eventually earned Barnes Wallis international fame and made him one of the relatively few British aircraft designers to be portrayed in a feature film (*The Dambusters* 1954). The bouncing bomb project was essentially a one-off undertaking and when it was completed, Wallis returned to designing massive ground-penetrating bombs, such as the Tallboy (12,000 lb—5.44 metric tons) and the even bigger Grand Slam (22,000 lb—9.9 metric tons), which were used with considerable success against special targets such as rocket launching facilities and massively hardened U-Boat pens.

Towards the end of the Second World War, Barnes Wallis began to take an interest in the possibility of supersonic flight and envisaged a tailless aircraft with adjustable wings, a concept generally attributed to Geoffrey Hill who had already experimented with the idea. The concept seemed very attractive to Wallis and in 1946, he wrote a technical paper entitled, 'The Application of the aerodynamic properties of three dimensional bodies to the stabilisation and control of aerodynes.' This was followed by work on the design of a flying model that would provide useful data on the use of laminar flow techniques. Starting with small hand launched models Wallis progressed to larger versions, propelled from a trolley on rails at 100 mph (160 kph). These models had slender, smooth ovoid bodies with aft mounted variable sweep wings and a highly swept tail fin.

Vickers had been awarded a contract worth half a million pounds for supersonic tests related to the M.52 project, but this was abandoned and it became possible to re-allocate part of the money to Wallis's project. Given the name Wild Goose, it would allow the construction of sophisticated new models. Some would be used for wind tunnel research, while twelve larger vehicles would be built for flight trials. These were issued with serials XA197-202 and XA947-952. The completed models were slender with the wings mounted towards the rear and a single upright tailfin was fitted. There was also provision to fit a small rocket motor as the project progressed. In late 1949, these trials began at Predannack Aerodrome near the Lizard in Cornwall and considerable secrecy surrounded the project, which was regarded as pure military research. The Wild Goose models were flown initially as gliders and controlled using rather basic radio equipment. This presented many challenges to Wallis's team, as separate operators were required for pitch and roll.

The models remained fairly stable in flight with the team soon graduating to powered tests using rocket propulsion. Meanwhile, The National Physical Laboratory at Teddington, Middlesex were conducting wind tunnel tests on Wild Goose models and there was official interest in using this research to develop a new surface-to-air missile. The first really successful flight of a Wild Goose test vehicle took place in April 1952, although the model was written off in crash soon afterwards. The programme would continue until late 1954, when it was realised that anticipated laminar flow was unattainable.

However, much of this research was now being supported by a classified weapons system called Green Lizard, which would comprise of a compact missile fired from a launch tube. Early designs began soon after the end of the Second World War, with several patent applications being made in 1949 and held unpublished until 1956. The design was considered as a surface-to-surface and surface-to-air missile, eventually becoming a turbojet-powered AA missile that was equipped with flip-out swept wings. It would be based around the British Isles to protect against Soviet bombers and when used, it would dispense 100 sub-munitions in the path of attacking bombers. Work on this project was abandoned in the early 1950s, but some design features can be seen on current air launched weapons.

In 1951, Wallis had begun to consider ideas for a manned variable geometry aircraft that would perform well across wide a range of different speeds and he hoped that the next stage in his programme would be the construction of a small demonstrator. George Cornwall (1897–1960) was the chief designer for Heston Aircraft and his company was heavily involved in the Wild Goose project, as the main sub-contractor. Wallis had drawn up proposals for a small manned variable geometry aircraft and Cornwall was asked to finalise the design. A contract was then issued to Heston Aircraft, leading to the construction of a prototype, which received the designation JC.9.

The one-man JC.9 was 46.5 ft (14.1 m) in length, with a maximum wingspan of 38 ft (11.58 m) and a height of 8.33 ft (2.5 m). It was fitted with a retractable tricycle undercarriage and appears to have intended for use as a glider, with the possibility of installing a turbojet later.

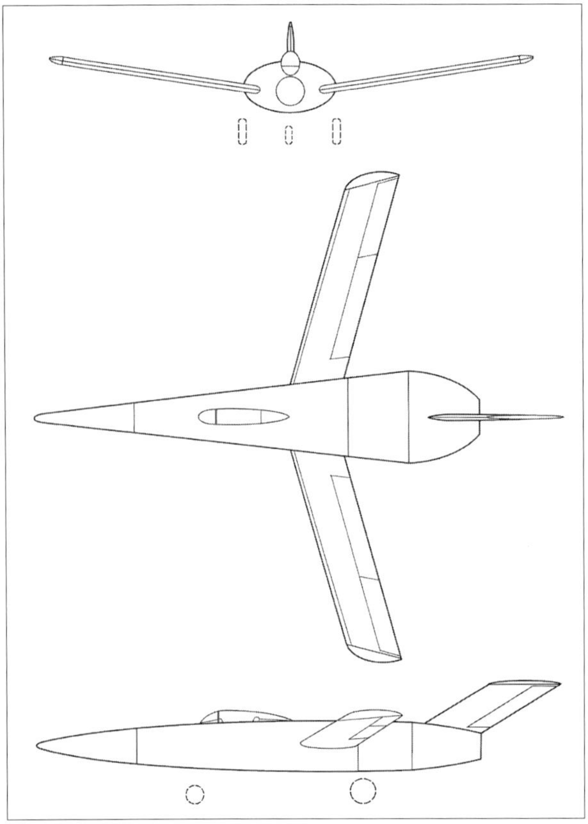

The one-man Heston JC-9, which was built in sections and transported to Weybridge for use during the Swallow programme. However, the JC-9 was never re-assembled and remained in a hangar until the project ended. It was then scrapped.

In appearance, the JC.9 was quite unusual having a bulbous rear fuselage, which tapered towards the nose, and a single swept, vertical tailfin. It was built in sections and transported to Weybridge for final assembly, where it remained uncompleted in a hangar for some time, until JC.9 was finally scrapped. Exactly why this happened remains unknown, although somewhat strangely, it has been suggested that Barnes Wallis was encouraged to have this particular aircraft built, despite being strongly opposed to the manned tests of new prototypes and he delayed the aircraft's construction until it was no longer required. Nevertheless, before the Wild Goose trials concluded in 1954, Wallis had started to work on the design of a manned high performance variable geometry tailless aircraft that could fly intercontinental distances. This was at the same time as the RAF was considering new ideas for a future high flying supersonic reconnaissance bomber, which resulted in OR.330 being issued.

Vickers were not approached to submit a design for this aircraft, but Wallis obtained a copy of OR.330 and adapted his variable geometry concept to meet this need. He envisaged a sleek arrow shaped tailless aircraft with a flattened profile and variable geometry wings pivoted towards the rear of the fuselage, using a form of knuckle joint. Engines in pods would be mounted towards the wing tips, which would swivel and also be adjustable in pitch. This would allow the propulsive system to take over from conventional control surfaces. Position of the engines was also important for minimising centre of gravity (c.g) problems as the wing angle altered.

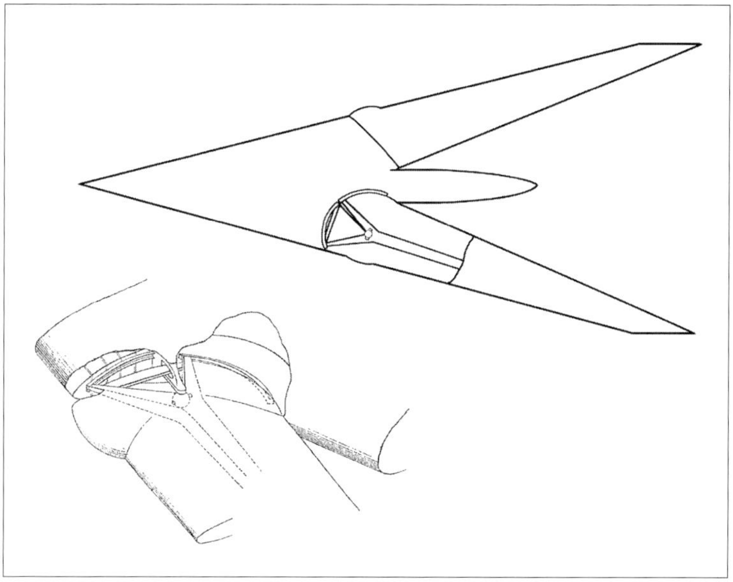

This drawing from a 1964 UK Patent (GB950400) shows the internal system of rotary adjustment for the Swallow's wings.

Models of Wallis's new design called Swallow, were initially tested in the Vickers Armstrong wind tunnel and construction was approved of 10 flying models, each having full wingspans of 30 ft (9.1 m) with wingtip fins and elevons. These models were issued with the serials XK831-835 and XK850-854, with tests beginning at Predannack Aerodrome in 1955 and continuing until the late 1950s. On one occasion, a model powered by two rocket motors reached a speed of Mach 2.5, while fully developed models with dummy engine pods underwent supersonic tests in the wind tunnel at RAE Bedford.

Although the Swallow was not chosen for OR.330, official interest in Wallis's project was considerable. Vickers continued to receive financial support for the Swallow trials and serious discussions about building two different manned research aircraft took place in 1957. The initial proposal was for a small one-man demonstrator with an approximate weight of 10,000 lb (4,535 kg), which gave way to a similar but larger aircraft with a gross weight of 25,000 lb (11,339 kg). This aircraft would have a similar airframe to later production versions, with a conventional forward cockpit that accommodated a pilot and could be adapted for a second crew member.

The Research Swallow had a proposed length of 68.75 ft (20.95 m) with the wings fully swept, a wingspan of 75 ft (22.86 m) with the wings fully forward and a wingspan of 30.75 ft (9.37 m) fully swept. One noticeable difference between the manned aircraft and earlier models was the extension of the fuselage rearwards to house additional equipment, fuel or in later versions, a military payload.

Height of the aircraft is unclear, although it is known that a substantial ground clearance was considered necessary for take-offs and landings. The undercarriage was to be a multi-wheel tricycle design, with take-off speed calculated at 155 mph (250 kph) and landings made at 130 mph (209 kph). At low speed the Research Swallow would have an aspect ratio of 10.7 and this would alter to 1.88 fully swept. Wingtip stabilising fins were also proposed. Empty, the aircraft would weigh 14,500 lb (6,577 kg) and the additional fuel weight would be 9,000 lb (4,082 kg).

Barnes Wallace prepares a model of his flying wing for a lecture.

Four Bristol turbojet engines with afterburners would be housed in wing pods measuring 34 inches (863 mm) in diameter and 24 ft (7.3 m) in length. Wallis intended to do away with conventional control surfaces during flight and the engine nacelles would tilt and rotate as needed.

Suggested maximum speed was Mach 1.6, with a cruise altitude of 35–40,000 ft (10,668–12,192 m) and a ceiling of about 50,000 ft (15,240 m). Developed into a military aircraft, the Swallow would have the same overall dimensions as the Research prototype. Two different variants were proposed for the RAF and the Royal Navy. The first was a high/low level bomber or naval strike aircraft and the second was a high performance fighter.

As a strike aircraft, the Swallow would have a maximum performance of Mach 2 at a typical altitude of 36,000 ft (10,972 m). In the low level role, it would have a maximum speed of Mach 0.95 at an altitude of 500 ft (152 m). The service ceiling would be 80,000 ft (24,382 m). At low speed, the main cockpit section would rise upwards to facilitate an improved view for the crew.

Gross weight was estimated at 30,000 lb (13,607 kg) and the initially considered payload was probably a single rearward ejected free-fall nuclear bomb in the Red Beard (15 kiloton yield) class. It is hard to see this aircraft being considered for the delivery of conventional ordnance, but it might have been suitable for adaptation to a reconnaissance role. The estimated range for the bomber is believed to have been about 5,000 miles (8,000 km). This variant would be capable of operating from an improvised tactical airstrip such as a good stretch of straight adequately wide roadway, or the deck of an aircraft carrier, although it would require some structural strengthening and modifications for the latter.

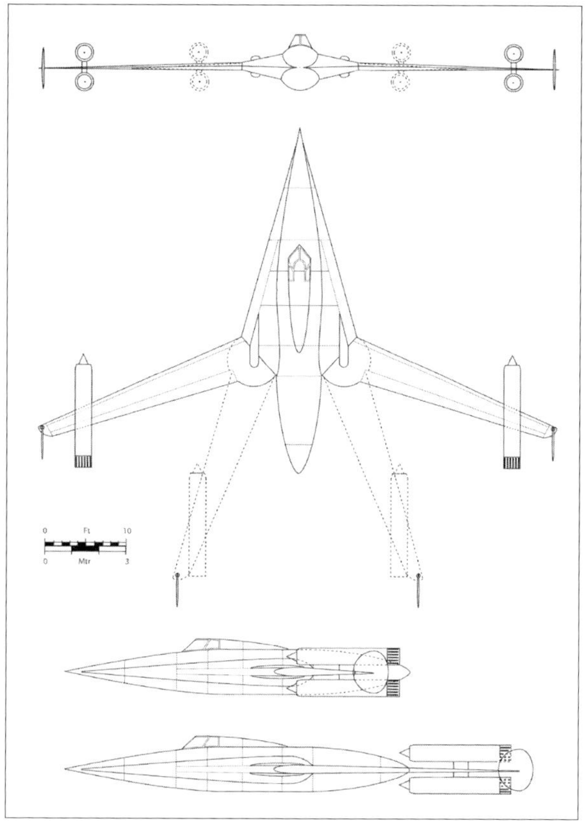

General layout of the 25,000 lbs (11,339kg) Swallow Research Aircraft. (*Chris Gibson*)

The most likely choice of propulsion for the Strike-Swallow was four afterburning Bristol Siddeley BE.38 turbojet engines. The BE.38 was a proposed high-performance variant of the Orpheus engine, but it was never completed. The fighter version of the Swallow was similar in many respects, but the maximum speed quoted was Mach 2.5 and a realistic range might have been approximately 1,500 miles (2,414 km), although some documentation suggests substantially more allowing for economic cruise. Armament is unknown, but it seems probable that two or four air-to-air missiles would be carried externally.

Several larger variable geometry versions of the Swallow were proposed that included a bomber with an overall length (at full 80° wing sweep) of approximately 130 ft (39.6 m) and a wingspan (with the wings fully extended) of about 130 ft (39.6 m), making it quite close in size to the Rockwell B-1B variable geometry bomber. This version of the Swallow would probably have carried a crew of 4–5 and possessed a maximum speed of about Mach 2. The payload would have been one or possibly two nuclear weapons ejected rearward from the extended tail section.

As a supersonic military transport aircraft, Wallis proposed a version of the Swallow with an overall length (at full wing sweep) of 160 ft (48.76 m) a fully extended wingspan of 174 ft (53 m) and a fully swept wingspan of 71.5 ft (21.8 m). It would have exactly the same aspect ratios as the smaller designs. The aircraft would utilise a multi-wheeled tricycle undercarriage layout, with a substantial ground clearance of about 20 ft (6 m), considered necessary during take-off and landing.

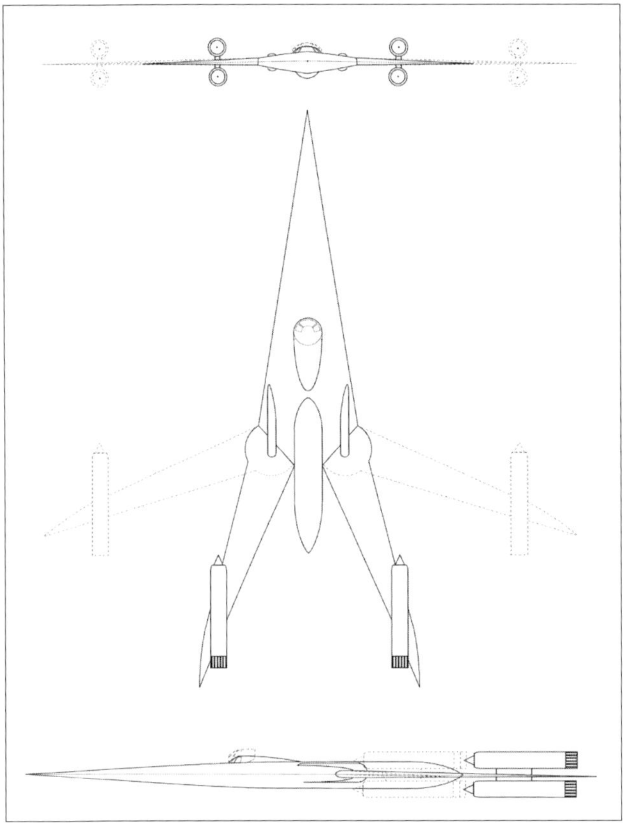

This version of the variable-geometry Vickers Armstrong Swallow was configured as a nuclear strike aircraft. Roughly comparable in size to the Rockwell B-1B and manned by a crew of 4-5, it would have possessed a maximum speed of Mach 2. (*Chris Gibson*)

Its gross weight was set at 150,000 lb (68,038 kg), with a maximum speed of Mach 2.5 and a cruise altitude of 67,000 ft (20,421 m). Operation range would be 4,600 miles (7,400 km) and the payload capability would be 25,000 lb (11,339 kg). Powered by four engines in wing-mounted nacelles, the size of each unit would suggest that Wallis was considering a choice of several different afterburning turbojets. While this aircraft was envisaged for military use, Wallis also considered the idea of a slightly smaller commercial supercruise airliner, capable of carrying 60 passengers to Australia without any re-fuelling stops. A further variant of the airliner would use eight turbojets mounted in individual wing pods and various ideas were studied for cockpit layouts, which included a rising capsule that would allow improved visibility at low speeds. Nevertheless, it was now recognised that development of the Swallow would take at least 10 years to complete.

Unfortunately, 1957 was the year of the infamous Duncan Sandys White Paper, which suggested that the era of manned military aircraft was drawing to a close and as a direct consequence, many advanced programmes were terminated. Further official funding for the Swallow was cut, but Wallis was allowed to approach the American run Mutual Weapons Development Programme (MWDP) Office in Paris for help. This led to a US team visiting Weybridge and a small delegation led by Wallis visiting NASA at Langley. All the Swallow research data was then passed to the Americans and although a six-month joint US–UK development programme was discussed with MWDP staff, much of the research was undertaken at Langley.

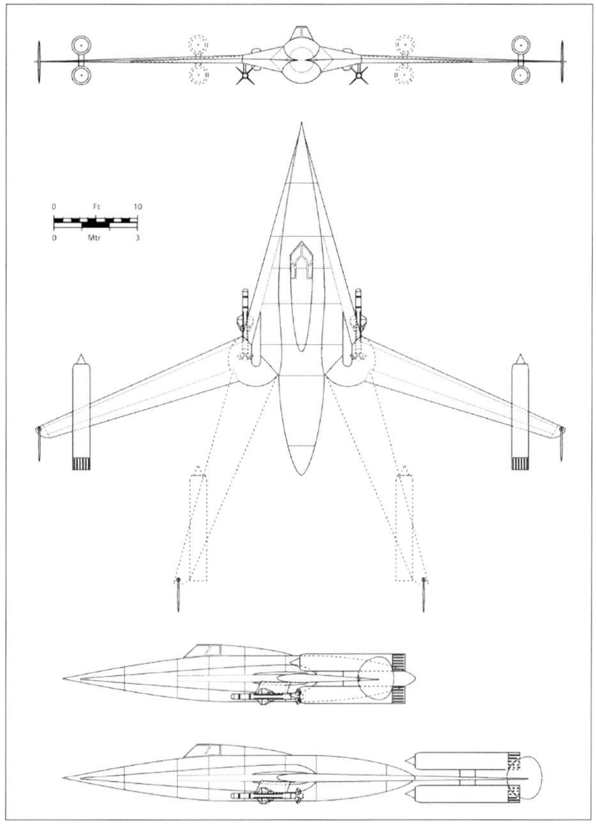

A proposal for a Vickers-Armstrong supersonic Swallow fighter equipped with two external air-to-air missiles. (*Chris Gibson*)

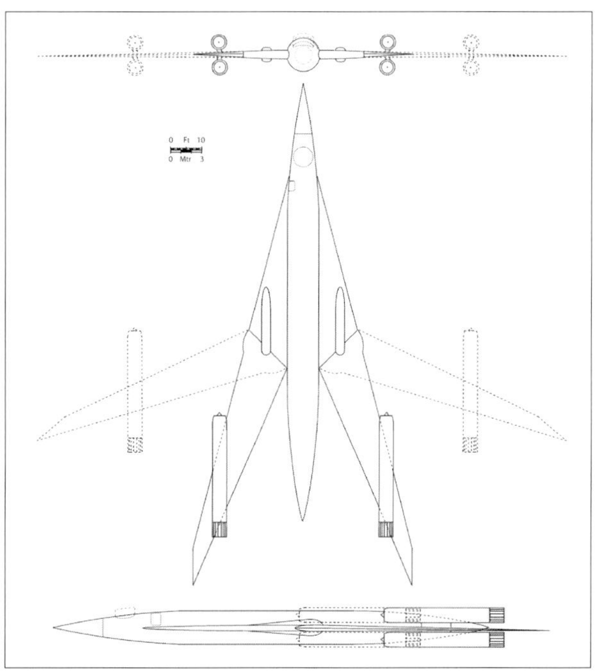

A number of Swallow variants were considered, including this proposal for a long-range airliner or military transport aircraft with a Mach 2.5 capability. Cruising at an altitude of 67,000 ft (20,421 m), this design would have an un-refuelled range of about 4,600 miles (7,400 km). (*Chris Gibson.*)

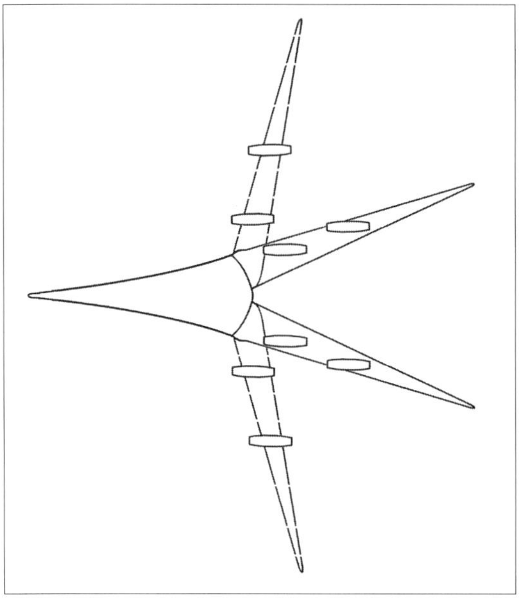

Left: This UK Patent drawing (Ref: GB885033) shows one of the early proposals for an eight engined variant of the Barnes Wallis Swallow.

Middle: One of the scale models based on the Swallow bomber design undergoing tests at the Langley Research Center during 1959. This was a joint US/UK research project sponsored by the American Mutual Weapons Development Program. (*NASA*)

Bottom: A large model of the proposed Swallow bomber undergoing wind tunnel testing at Langley in 1959 with the wings set fully forward. (*NASA*)

One of several different Vickers Swallow models being wind tunnel tested at NASA Langley, in Virginia, USA. Unfortunately, these trials revealed pitch-up and drag issues, although the variable geometry system was refined and would later be adopted by several US and UK aircraft. (*NASA*)

The most detailed examination of the Swallow was Test 159, undertaken over a period of months in Langley's 16 ft (4.87 m) Transonic Wind Tunnel. By June 1959, NASA was reporting significant lift/drag ratio and pitch-up problems with the Swallow (Langley Ref: 010), but they recognised that Wallis's variable geometry design was a considerable improvement on previous ideas and thought it might be suitable for a less ambitious tailed design.

Wallis's Swallow was effectively dead, although a good deal of the research undertaken during the Swallow programme was used to perfect the variable sweep wings used for the F-14, F-111 and B-1. The Swallow was a superb looking design that still appears futuristic today. There has been ongoing speculation as to whether this impressive concept could have been developed into an operational military aircraft if sufficient funding had been available. In reality, this exotic design would undoubtedly continue to present major engineering challenges if anyone attempted to re-boot the project today.

UK Atomic Powered Bomber Projects

The post-war period saw considerable interest in the possibilities offered by nuclear power. Science magazines constanty predicted atomic-powered ships, submarines, planes and even automobiles. Trips around the Solar System would be undertaken by atomic-powered spaceships and as I recall reading during my days as a schoolboy in the 1950s, most of Britain's electricity would be generated with atomic power by the 1980s and it would be virtually free for everyone!

It was certainly clear that atomic power would be beneficial if applied to submarines and warships, but could something similar be applied to military aircraft? The idea had initially been considered by American scientists during the Second World War and some regarded it as silver bullet technology. Others were much more reserved, but during 1946 the USAAF provided sufficient funding for the Nuclear Energy for the Propulsion of Aircraft (NEPA) project. This involved two different proposed systems. The first was the direct air cycle concept, assigned to General Electric. It was relatively uncomplicated, with the front section of a turbine feeding air into the core of a small nuclear reactor where it was heated and fed back into the rear section of the turbine producing thrust. The second more complex indirect air cycle method was explored by Pratt & Whitney. In this system, the air would pass through a network of pipes containing a molten liquid metal that was heated by the reactor. In theory, this would be smaller and require less radiation shielding, but Pratt & Whitney apparently gave up on the idea quite quickly, considering it too scientifically challenging. Nevertheless, the prospect of supersonic bombers with almost unlimited range carrying atomic weapons, was obviously very attractive and by September 1951, General Electric were ready to start testing some first generation hardware. Subsequently, the USAF awarded Convair a contract under (MX-1589) to adapt two B-36 bombers into flying nuclear test beds. They would carry a direct air cycle system with a reactor using a 143 lb (65 kg) core of uranium oxide fuel elements. Four custom-built GE J-53 turbojets would be connected by a manifold system to the front and rear of the reactor, with compressed air passing through the reactor's hot core and then out through the engine's rear stages. The weight of this test system was expected to be around 128,000 lb (58,000 kg) and 60,000 lb (27,000 kg) of the mass was lead shielding. The first B-36, renamed as the NB-36H Nuclear Test Aircraft (NTA) would be used specifically to evaluate reactor shielding and the second called the X-6, would have a fully operational engine system and fly on nuclear power.

The NB-36H was flown over West Texas and Southern New Mexico on 47 occasions between 1955 and 1957 although the technical issues mounted up. However, the X-6 was never completed and all aspects of the nuclear aircraft program (that we know about), including the advanced WS-125 concept were scrapped in 1961 by the Kennedy Administration. The reason this project endured for so long was probably due to similar research taking place in the Soviet Union and the Pentagon's concerns that they might gain a significant lead with new military technology. The CIA had been aware of Soviet nuclear propulsion research taking place since the early 1950s but either their information was flawed, or they intentionally misled many politicians with claims that the Russians were gaining a lead, perhaps to secure extra funding? The CIA knew about the Myasishchev M-50 supersonic bomber project, which began in 1952 and led to a prototype. When test flights of the NB-36H ended, the CIA leaked details of the M-50 to *Aviation Week* magazine, suggesting it was a Soviet atomic powered bomber. This turned out to be completely untrue, but the US response was to continue development of a nuclear powered bomber.

During this period, the British took a considerable interest in the idea of an atomic powered warplane and decided to study the idea of building their own. General information is surprisingly thin on the ground, but the Atomic Energy Research Establishment (AERE) near Harwell, Oxfordshire were already working on the design of small nuclear reactors, suitable for use in aircraft. Some records describe the development of a liquid metal heated jet engine and there were detailed studies undertaken on shielding, involving de Havilland and Hawker Siddeley. It is also understood that Rolls-Royce, Saunders Roe and Avro took a close interest in nuclear aircraft propulsion and were involved with research taking place at Harwell.

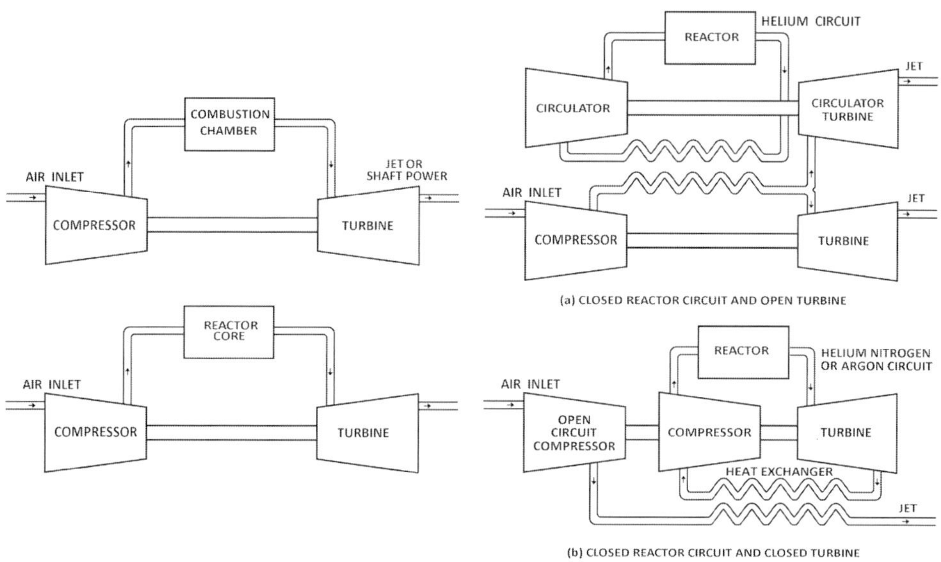

Fig. 1. **OPEN CYCLE NUCLEAR GAS TURBINE** *Fig. 2.* **CLOSED CYCLE NUCLEAR GAS TURBINE**

Two outlines of the principle nuclear aircraft propulsion systems. The drawings are closely based on original de Havilland schematics.

Intriguingly, an article about a hypothetical atomic bomber appeared in the October 1954 issue of the *Royal Air Force Flying Review*, written by Kenneth William Gatland (1924–1997). At that time, Gatland was working directly under Sydney Camm as a designer for Hawker Aircraft, with an expert's grasp of cutting edge aviation developments. He clearly had considerable knowledge of nuclear power and could only have put pen to paper on the topic with official approval. Gatland suggests that work might have already been undertaken on nuclear aircraft propulsion and he talked about developments in America. However, the interesting part of all this, are some detailed illustrations by J. W. Wood, which must have been made from Gatland's suggestions. What we see is a large aircraft, clearly based on the Avro Vulcan, with a much longer, fairly slender fuselage ahead of the wing section. The aircraft had a Javelin tail and was powered by four turbojets connected to a central nuclear reactor.

Gatland suggest a weight of 142–166 metric tons and the crew of 3–4 would be placed at the front of the aircraft in a pressurised cockpit that was heavily shielded from the reactor. The range of this aircraft was presumably substantial and its performance perhaps a little better than the Vulcan B.2, although probably not supersonic. For weapons, Gatland's atomic bomber carries two underwing air-to-surface guided missiles, presumably equipped with nuclear warheads. These missiles look rather like Folland Gnat fighters, but are presumably intended to be rocket powered, with a range of about 100 miles (160 km). While this was no more than an artist's illustration backed by sound technical advice, it is hard to dismiss the probability that Gatland knew of early plans for an Avro nuclear bomber, which perhaps evolved into the Avro 774 LEWS (Long Endurance Weapons System) that still remains something of a mystery design.

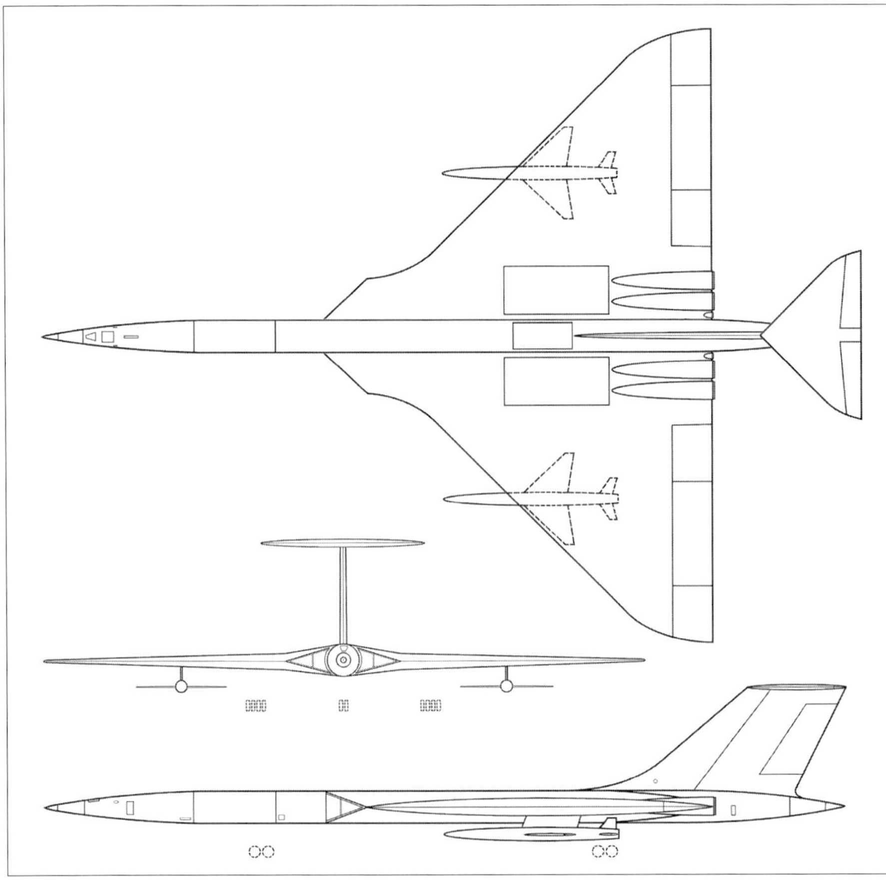

This 3-view drawing is based on two original illustrations by J. W. Wood that accompanied an article on atomic bombers, written by Kenneth W. Gatland for the October 1954 issue of RAF *Flying Review*. Looking rather like an Avro Vulcan on steroids, it would be powered by four turbojets using the nuclear open cycle method, probably assisted by supplementary rocket propulsion for take-off. The bomber was expected to have an almost unlimited range and be armed with two underwing nuclear tipped missiles. While this is no more than a speculative design, it is known that Avro examined nuclear propulsion possibilities and Gatland may have drawn on his industry contacts at a time when military aircraft using atomic power were being seriously considered by the UK authorities.

About a year after this article was published, Hawker Siddeley established a new division near Gerrards Cross, Buckinghamshire, to develop nuclear power systems. Soon, it was being reported that an experimental uranium reactor was undergoing construction on the 70 acre (28.32 hectares) site. Following this, much of the company's work appears to have concerned the licensed manufacture of small, water-cooled Argonaut class reactors, originally developed by the US Argonne National Laboratory and first tested in February 1957. One particular 10 kW Argonaut reactor called Jason began running at Hawker Siddeley's site from February 1959 and the company then sold it in 1962 to the Ministry of Defence (MoD) for training use by the Royal Naval College in Greenwich, London. Whether or not the Hawker Siddeley Nuclear Power (HSNP) Company was only really interested in nuclear naval applications is unclear, but there were certainly strong links to other parts of the UK military.

The difficulty I had researching this division of Hawker Siddeley would seem to suggest that many aspects of nuclear engineering remain sensitive. However, it has been possible to discover some details about the HSNP chief executive Edward P. Hawthorne (1920–). He worked for the RAE during the Second World War and from 1945 to 1954 was employed by turbine manufacturer C. H. Parsons as a design engineer. After this he joined A. V. Roe and then became attached to the Atomic Energy Establishment at Harwell, acting on behalf of Hawker Siddeley. Perhaps somewhat surprisingly, Hawthorne gave a lecture to the Graduates and Students Section of the Royal Aeronautical Society in October 1956 about the future application of atomic power to aircraft. Having briefly outlined the technology and shielding requirements, Hawthorne suggested that a closed cycle system with a heat exchanger using liquid sodium would be suitable for an aircraft of substantial size with an empty weight in excess of 100 metric tons. He also claimed that it would be capable of Mach 2.5 at 60,000 ft (18,288 m) with global range. A payload of 10,000 lb (4,535 kg) could be carried, which coincidentally was the requirement for the first operational UK nuclear fission bomb. This detail and his acceptance that an accident might have catastrophic consequences, suggests that Hawthorne's principle interest was nuclear power for a long range warplane and he largely confirmed this at the end of the lecture. Hawthorne showed an illustration of a hypothetical nuclear aircraft with a conventional high-speed fuselage, a central location for the reactor and the turbojets in wingtip nacelles. The design appears to have been based on an earlier Hawker concept for a Mach 3 interceptor, but it looked quite similar to the highly classified, supersonic, hydrogen powered, Lockheed CL-400 Suntan. This was under development in the US at that time,

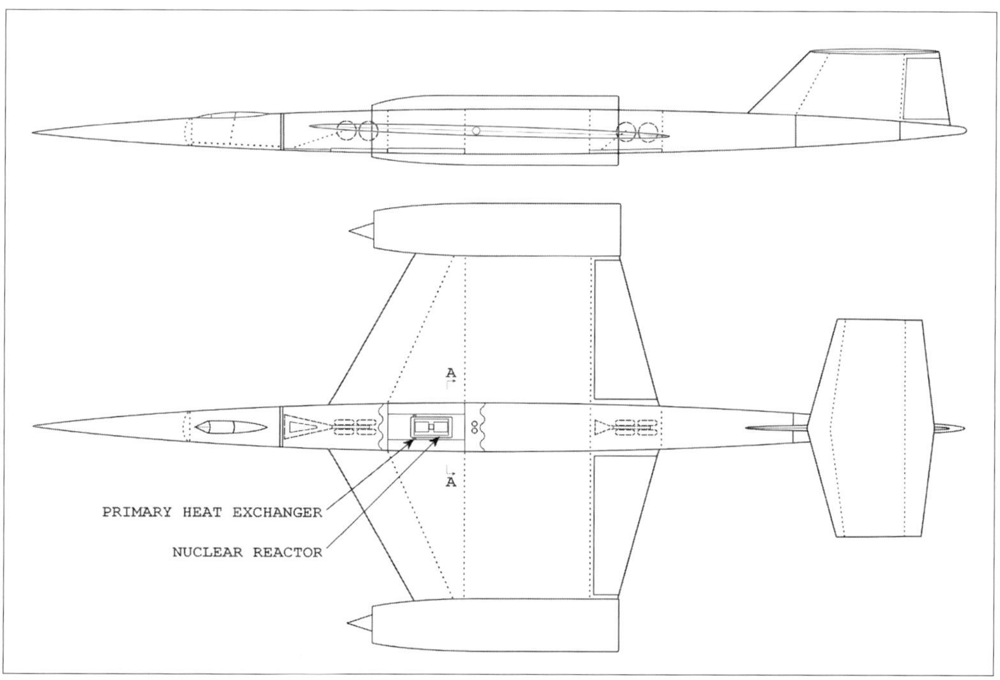

Hawker "Hawthorne" nuclear powered bomber proposal from 1956. The drawing is a fully restored copy of the original, made by the author to improve clarity.

as a replacement for the U-2 spy plane, but met with cancellation due to technical problems. Suntan had a projected length of almost 165 ft (50.2 m) and Hawthorne's design would almost certainly have been larger.

The elementary drawing of another atomic aircraft concept was found in the UK National Archives. It shows an unusual delta shaped design. The central reactor appears to be part of a liquid metal closed cycle system, apparently designed at the AERE Harwell. This would have undoubtedly involved engineers like Hawthorne and representatives from other aviation companies. The aircraft design has 32 turbojets in upright positions, located in three separate sections, theoretically facilitating VTOL operations. Because of the design complexity, it is hard to imagine so many small engines being connected to the reactor and they would undoubtedly just run on aviation fuel.

Twelve turbojets would be used for level flight and air for these engines would most likely be drawn in through slots in the leading edge of the craft. However, in its existing form, this design would have many complex issues concerning inlet and exhaust positions. What the design does suggest is input from Dr A. A. Griffith at Rolls-Royce, who was a leading VTOL proponent, favouring banks of compact upright turbojets to facilitate vertical take-off and landing (VTOL). As with many other unusual aviation ideas from this period, nothing came of this fairly substantial nuclear powered flying triangle, described as a tactical bomber.

Some interest (mostly American) in the possibility of using nuclear energy to power flying boats persisted and Saunders Roe undertook studies with Pratt & Whitney for open and closed cycle power systems for a version of the Princess flying boat. Nothing came of this, but there was what appears to be one final attempt to revive interest in nuclear aircraft.

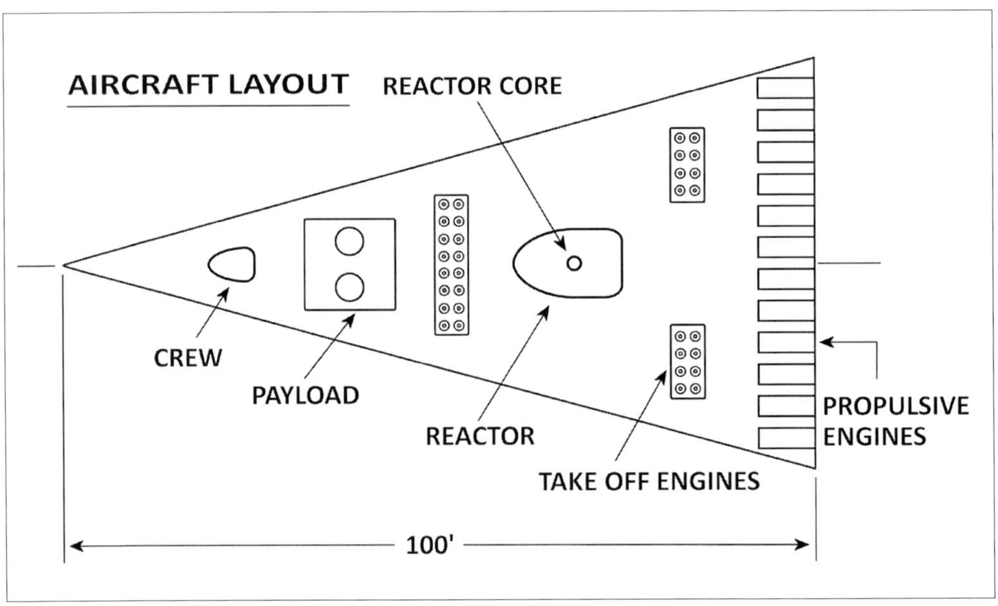

A nuclear powered VTOL aircraft, utilising 32 lift engines and probably intended for a military role. It may have been partly developed by A. A. Griffith at Rolls-Royce, as the engines layout is a typical feature of his design work.

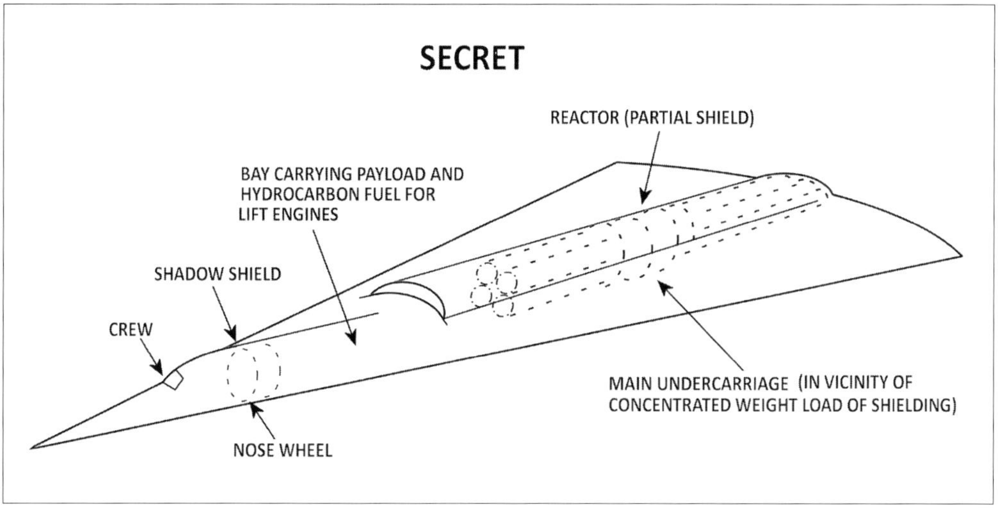

The design of a four engine nuclear powered supersonic bomber, possibly attributable to Hawker Siddeley in the 1950s. It appears that this aircraft was expected to have a VTOL capability, but details are not shown on the drawing.

De Havilland NP-3/4

In 1961, Professor Alexander Duncan Baxter (1908–1988) presented a lecture to members of the Royal Aeronautical Society's Swindon Branch, which outlined his vision of future aircraft utilising nuclear propulsion. As an engineering consultant for the de Havilland Engine Company in North London (where the author's father was a senior manager during the Second World War) and former professor of aircraft propulsion at Cranfield College of Aeronautics, Baxter was one of the UK's leading authorities on this subject. He unveiled proposals for two nuclear powered aircraft in the Concorde+ class that were a six engined, open-cycle concept with the reference NP.3 and an eight-engined closed-cycle design knows as NP.4. Although the two designs differed in overall appearance, both were intended to have intercontinental range and the ability to cruise at Mach 2.2, with a ceiling in the region of 60,000 ft (18,288 m). Knowing the serious hazards posed by radiation, it is hard to imagine that Baxter anticipated any aircraft with a large centrally positioned nuclear reactor as suitable for anything aside from a military role. The intention to use NP.3 and NP.4 as human transporters seems inconceivable. However, as an advanced next generation V-bomber, carrying several nuclear tipped standoff missiles, the idea starts to appear more credible.

It would eventually emerge that during the late 1950s, Sud-Aviation took a close look at developing a sleek canard shaped aircraft with an all-up weight of about 135 metric tonnes that would be powered by a nuclear reactor in the tail section. Connected to two substantial turbojets, this would provide sustained supersonic performance over a global range.

Given the name Super-Caravelle and presented as a passanger carrying aircraft, it seems probable that in reality this was cover for a black project proposal intended for military use. Whether or not this design was linked to de Havilland in any way remains unknown. However, widespread public resistance to nuclear technology started to take shape during the 1950s and amongst other things, it would prevent several aviation and space projects from progressing any further.

Looking back, it seems possible that much of Britains nuclear aircraft propulsion research was shared between scientists and engineers working for the major aviation contractors. It is also evident that aside from the possibility of adapting some flying boats for nuclear propulsion, most of the aircraft considered for this technology were deltas.

While there was considerable enthusiasm for nuclear powered aircraft during the 1950s, the technology was crude, dangerous and scientists were generally out of their depth. Things finally came to a head during October 1957 when there was a major (INS Level 5) nuclear accident at Windscale (now Sellafield) in Cumbria. The No. 1 graphite moderated reactor caught fire, unleashing a huge cloud of radioactive material into the atmosphere and it was three days before the situation could be brought under control. As a direct consequence, Prime Minister Macmillan ordered an immediate press black-out and the details would remain classified as top secret for the next thirty years. The government also decided that these secret documents should indicate staff errors, which helps to confirm an increasing belief that classified material eventually released under The Freedom of Information Act 2000 (UK) is often forward sanitised (for various reasons) and the truth is never properly revealed. That aside, the fire at Windscale currently ranks (after Chernobyl, Fukushima, Kyshtym and Three Mile Island) as the fifth worst nuclear accident in history and this clearly added to concerns about putting more money into dangerous proposals like atomic powered aircraft. The UK government was primarily concerned with production of plutonium for weapons and after the near catastrophic accident, both reactors at Windscale were permanently shut down, with plutonium production being switched to Calder Hall.

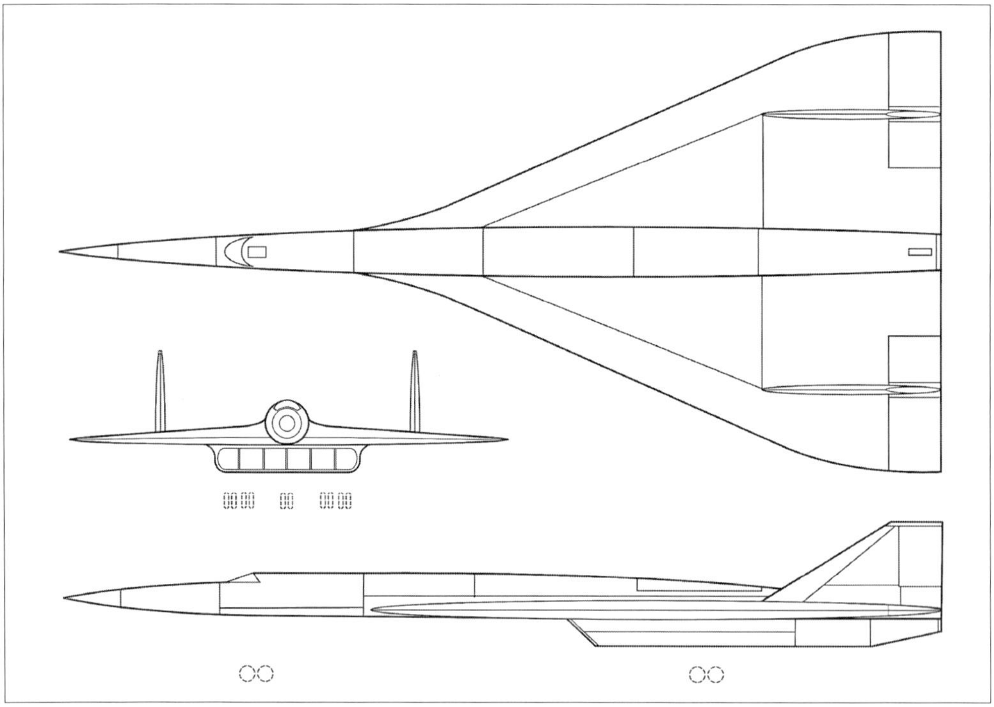

This de Havilland nuclear powered proposal is one of several produced by Professor A. D. Baxter in 1961. The six-engined, open-cycle NP.3 would have an anticipated Mach 2.2 capability at 50,000 ft (15,240 m) and appears to be intended primarily for a military role.

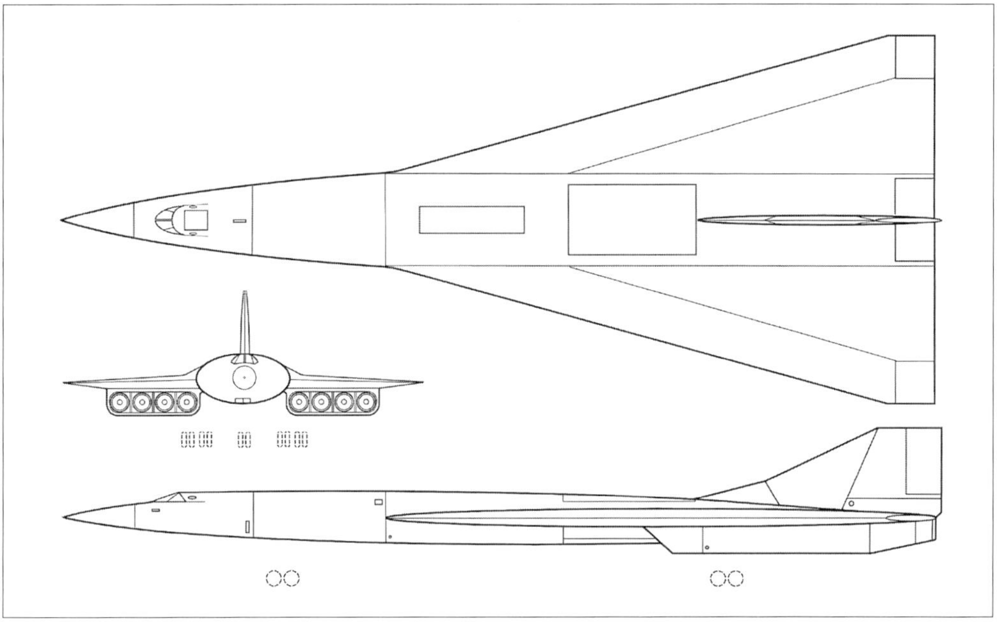

The de Havilland NP-4 proposal, powered by eight engines using the closed cycle nuclear propulsion system. The design emerged at the same time as the NP-3 and also appears to have been intended for military use.

The Windscale accident sent large ripples through the UK establishment and there was already considerable public opposition to what was widely perceived as very dirty and dangerous technology. Atomic power had been presented to the world as a revolutionary gift that would solve many of humanities problems, but it was not properly understood, hazardous, costly and even today feared by many. Perhaps nuclear powered aircraft will be re-considered in the future, but you can be fairly sure that if this happens, the technology will be very different to earlier ideas, now regarded as unworkable.

Advanced English Electric Designs

The English Electric Company came into existence shortly after the end of the First World War. Their main business was the manufacture of industrial electrical components such as motors, transformers and switchgear, while another part of the company built locomotives and diesel engines. However, Dick, Kerr & Company and the Phoenix Dynamo Manufacturing Company (which were absorbed into the English Electric Company in 1918), had both manufactured aircraft during the First World War and continued to maintain some relatively modest interests in aviation. The situation began to change in 1935, when English Electric started producing airframes in conjunction with Handley Page and things went much further during the Second World War. Before long, the company was assembling substantial numbers of the Handley Page Hampden, Halifax and de Havilland Mosquito aircraft under licence. By the end of the Second World War, English Electric had branched out into many different military areas, manufacturing aircraft engines, components for submarines, tanks and various other pieces of military equipment.

Soon after the Second World War ended, English Electric began licensed construction of the de Havilland Vampire jet fighter at their Preston works and had gained considerable experience with the latest aviation technology. Subsequently, the design office, headed by William Edward 'Teddy' Petter (1908–1968) was given the task of responding to an Air Staff Requirement B.3/46 for a jet-powered replacement for the Mosquito. This would lead to the very successful Canberra, which undertook numerous roles over a long service life and sold to many overseas customers. Petter then moved on to design the supersonic P.1 research aircraft, which was taken over by the new chief designer Sir Frederick Page (1917–2005), who eventually developed it into the P.1B Lightning fighter. Surprisingly, this remains the only indigenous supersonic combat aircraft to enter UK service.

At the same time, English Electric developed ideas for an advanced supersonic replacement for the Canberra and this project was initially handled by two of the company's top engineers, Raymond Creasey (1922–1976) and Bernard 'Ollie' Heath (1925–2014). In 1956, the Air Staff issued a requirement (GOR.339) for a supersonic strike aircraft able to deliver nuclear or conventional weapons. It was initially designated as the P.17A and English Electric were eventually contracted to fully develop the project in association with Vickers Armstrong. The aircraft was now called the TSR.2 and work continued after English Electric became part of the British Aircraft Corporation (BAC) in 1960. However, four years earlier, English Electric had started investigating the next generation of manned military aircraft to follow designs like the P.17A. They were considering the possibility that hypersonic performance would be a realistic goal, as engine technology rapidly advanced and new construction materials became available. Little was understood about flight at this speed and some of their aspirations were completely unrealistic. To begin with there were proposals for huge Mach 5 transports and manned two stage spaceplane systems, but as the studies proceeded, it became clear that a more realistic performance ceiling was about Mach 4.

By the time that English Electric became part of BAC, the overall study had been given the company reference P.42 and it tended to primarily focus on substantial delta winged aircraft, with a leading edge sweep of 70°, powered by various experimental engines ranging from turbofans to turboramjets, sometimes running on exotic fuels. Proposed future roles for the fully developed aircraft ranged from high performance strike, to high altitude reconnaissance and satellite launching craft. Much of the P.42 study at BAC Warton was undertaken with Rolls-Royce and Bristol Siddeley Engines, who put forward proposals for propulsion systems that would work in a complementary way to the BAC designed airframes. The first notable P.42 study carried the project reference EAG.3273 (EAG is just a drawing reference used by The English Electric Company). EAG.3273 was to be a sleek 70° delta with large underwing podded ramjets built by Bristol Siddeley that could be replaced with alternatives fairly easily. But because ramjets only function at significant speed, the EAG.3273 was also equipped with two retractable and adapted Rolls-Royce RB.162 turbojets to facilitate take-off, landings and certain emergencies if they arose.

This proposed one-man research aircraft was to have an overall length of 75 ft (22.8 m) and a wingspan of 45 ft (13.7 m). Suggested weight would have been around 50,000 lb (22,679 kg), with fold down wingtips designed to generate a degree of compression lift at very high speed. It is not entirely clear what maximum speed and altitude were anticipated from this design, but it was certainly in excess of Mach 4, perhaps with a ceiling of 90,000 ft (17,000 m). Another interesting concept was the slightly smaller, one-man EAG.3277, which dispensed with the engine pods and enclosed a very substantial ramjet within the fuselage. Two Rolls-Royce RB.162 jet engines would provide power at low speeds. This resulted in a rather unattractive looking aircraft, with a large air intake below the nose. The wing design appears similar to the EAG.3273, with the same degree of leading edge sweep and drop down wingtips. It appears that the P.42 design team anticipated this proposal would be briefly capable of hypersonic speed.

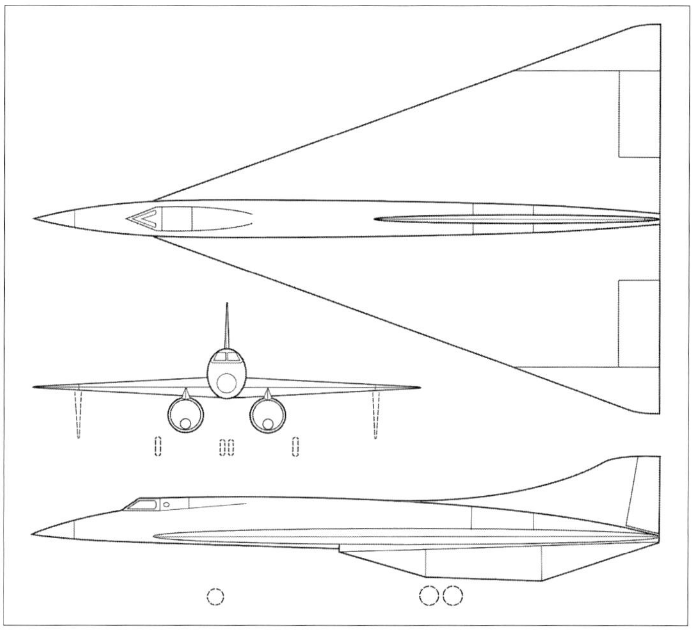

EAG.3273, was an early design in the BAC P.42 series of concepts for a high-speed delta research aircraft It would have been powered by two underwing ramjets and two retractable turbofans for low speed flight.

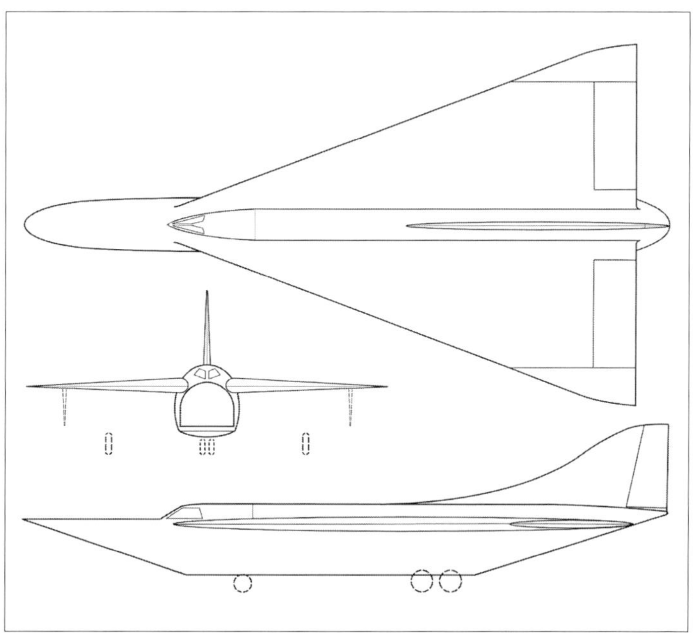

This rather unattractive design with the reference EAG.3277 featured a 70-degree sweep and was to be powered by two turbojets and a BSEL ramjet.

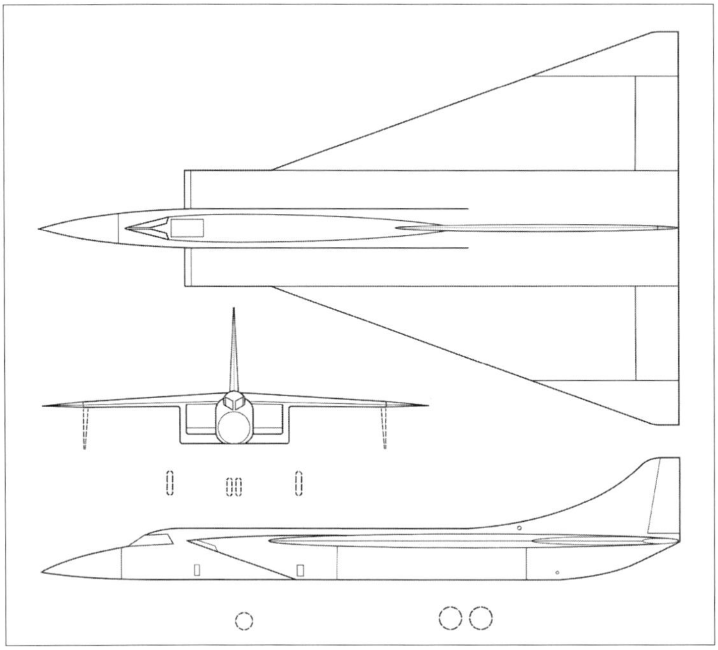

Powered by RR Spey engines, the EAG.3280 design was expected to be capable of reaching Mach 4.5 and possibly adapted for use as a satellite launch vehicle.

As the P.42 study continued, many different concepts were explored. EAG.3280 was reasonably conventional in appearance, powered by two uprated Rolls-Royce RB.168 Spey low bypass turbofan engines with afterburners. Theoretically, this would allow a maximum speed at altitude of around Mach 4.5. It was also suggested that this design could be used as a launch vehicle for a rocket carrying a small satellite into orbit. To do this, a change of propulsion was considered necessary and Rolls-Royce proposed an unspecified two engine turborocket system that was almost certainly still on the drawing board or at a very early stage of development. This seems to have led directly to EAG.3281, which was a proposed two-man delta test vehicle for this propulsion system with a long fuselage, a large air intake beneath the nose and twin upright fins.

Moving on, the Warton design team now considered various ideas for building the propulsion system into a military aircraft and looked at some rather unlikely ideas such as EAG.3299, which would be runway-launched by a massive solid fuel booster supported by a trolley that would be released after 10 seconds at about 200 mph (322 kph). The booster would then continue to burn until the aircraft reached Mach 2.5 and it would detach as the two underwing ramjets took over. Presumably, the thinking behind this design had something to do with range and fuel conservation? On completion of its flight, the EAG,3299 would extend the two RB.162 turbojets it carried and make a normal landing on its retractable undercarriage. Whether or not it could operate in the same manner as the original EAG.3273, making runway take-offs using the two turbojets is unknown. It is also unclear if this particular idea was the initial plan for a hypersonic strike or reconnaissance aircraft or simply another suggestion for a research prototype. Nevertheless, it would have been an impressive sight in operation.

Further studies progressed on to the use of liquid hydrogen for fuel and as the Americans discovered with their top secret Mach 2.5 Suntan spy plane, this is a useful fuel, but it takes up a great deal of storage space and introduces a number of ground handling issues. Nevertheless,

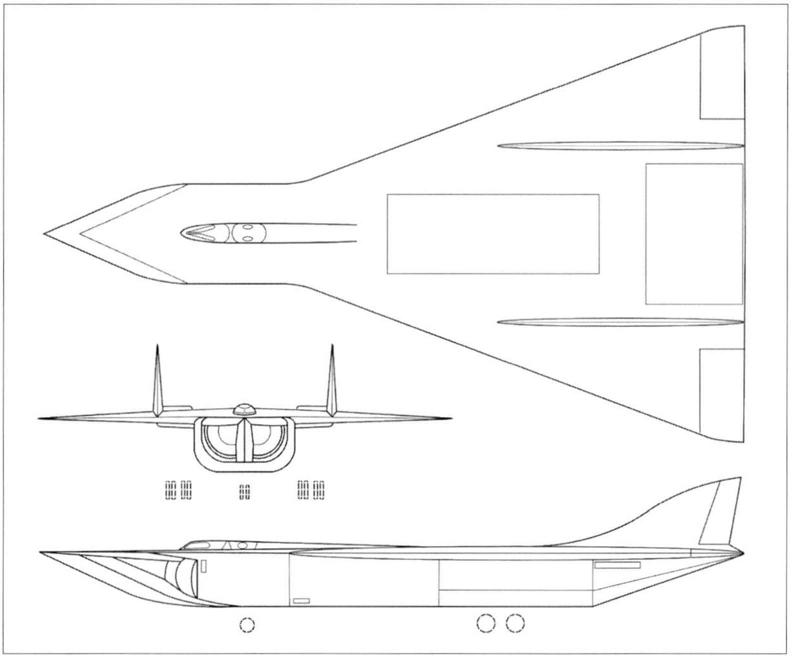

EAG.3281 would have been a large two-man delta wing aircraft, powered by a pair of turboramjets.

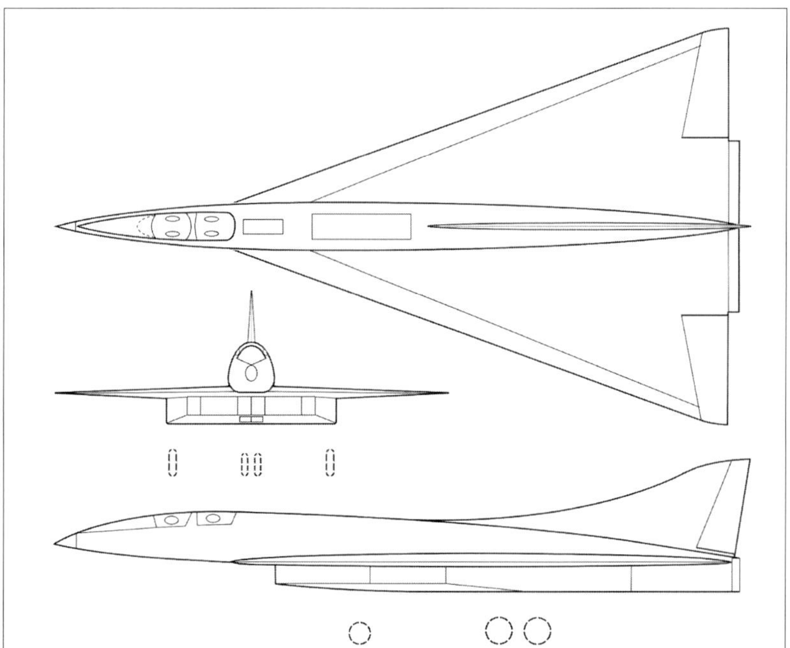

This proposal with the reference EAG. 3282/3, was a considerable refinement from its immediate predecessor (EAG.3282/2) having the wing wing position lowered and changes made to positioning of the two turboramjet engines and rear fuselage. This would be a become a new series of two-seat, high performance deltas intended for use as strike aircraft.

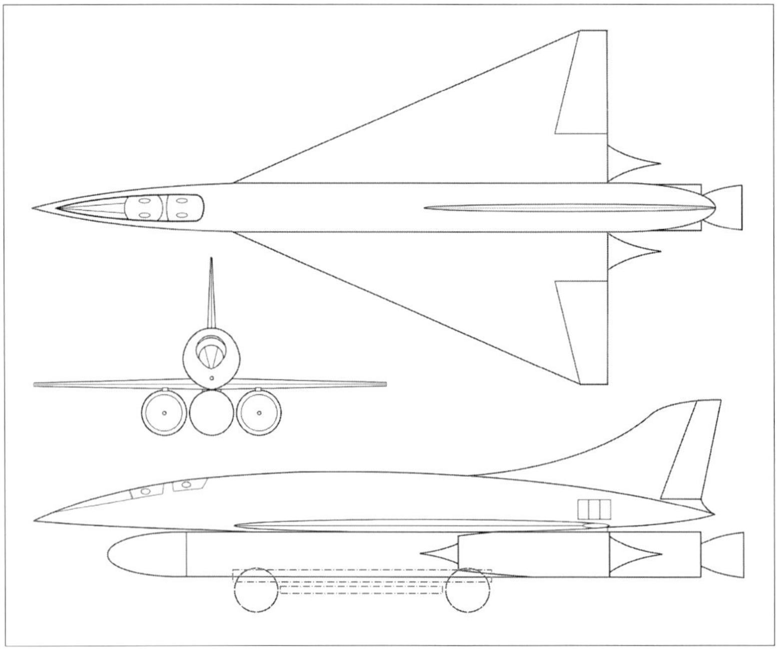

An unusual and probably somewhat impractical trolley launched ramjet aircraft. EAG.3299 would have used a very substantial rocket booster for launch and to achieve ramjet ignition. Such an arrangement would also require a suitable airfield for operations.

EAG.4416 was one proposal with three very large underslung pods containing hydrogen-fuelled Rolls-Royce Flashjet engines, which were a proposed form of turboramjet. This aircraft was of substantial size and featured large fold-down wingtips to generate compression lift. Nevertheless, there were undoubtedly concerns about the reliability of the flashjets, which would have been considered expensive experimental technology at that time and probably a step too far. Perhaps for this reason EAG.4424, while similar in many respects to EAG.4416 was designed with six turbojets and afterburners in a ventral pack.

As the P.42 studies continued into the early 1960s, it was effectively split into two somewhat differing areas of interest. There was the high performance next generation of military aircraft and a number of very ambitious ideas for satellite launching and manned orbital spacecraft systems. This second group will be discussed in a later chapter.

The engineers and designers at Warton working on ideas for advanced military aircraft were now focusing their attention on consolidating the best of their previous ideas into workable proposals for a TSR.2 follow-on. This led to the EAG.4426 strike/reconnaissance aircraft and a very similar looking, but smaller version of this design with the company reference EAG.4427 which was intended for naval carrier operations. It was specifically designed with a folding nose section and shorter wingspan for hangar deck storage and would require strengthening in parts of the airframe for deck landings using arrestor gear.

EAG.4426 would have been an impressive military aircraft, assuming the technical, political and cost issues had not got in the way. Knowing how things went after the 1957 UK defence cuts initiated by Duncan Sandys and what happened to the TSR.2, which had almost reached production when it was scrapped in 1965, this advanced design would have been on difficult ground from the outset. So, assuming those behind the P.42 project anticipated the EAG.4426 in service by the 1990s, it is hard to see EAG.4426 delivering the flexibility or value for money

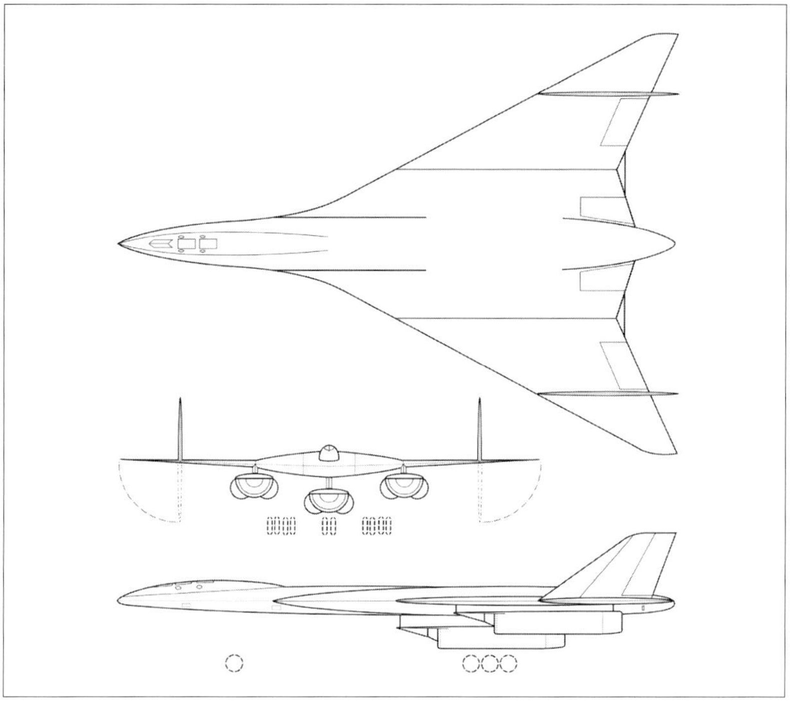

Using podded Roll Royce experimental flashjet engines running on liquid hydrogen the proposed EAG.4416 would have been substantial in size.

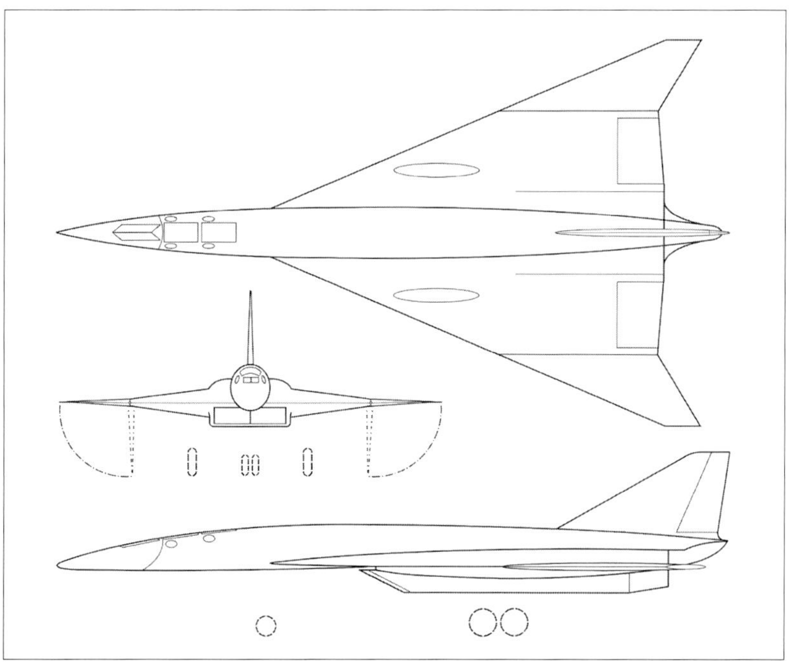

BAC EAG.4426 considered as a possible high performance follow-on to the TSR.2.

provided by the Tornado in a non-nuclear role and the sophistication of the EAG.4426 would have made every aircraft very expensive and demanding to maintain. On the other hand, in the nuclear strike role and as a reconnaissance aircraft, it probably would have been outstanding.

One other P.42 design I want to mention in this section, is the EAG.4441. A double delta design of substantial size, this aircraft was specifically intended for reconnaissance flights, with a Mach 5 capability and powered by two Bristol-Siddeley BS1011/2 combination engines. It is certainly tempting to describe this as an early British version of the supposed top secret USAF 'Aurora' spy plane, which may or may not have been built and tested. Whatever the truth about Aurora, this UK concept was very advanced and extremely ambitious for a time, when aircraft were expected to rapidly progress from ideas to hardware, without the assistance of supercomputers, massive test facilities or gigantic budgets. The lengthy P.42 project finally ended in 1964 and although none of the concepts progressed any further, it seems likely that lessons were learned in terms of what might be achievable in the future. Unfortunately, these very ambitious designs were mostly unrealistic and at best belonged to the next century.

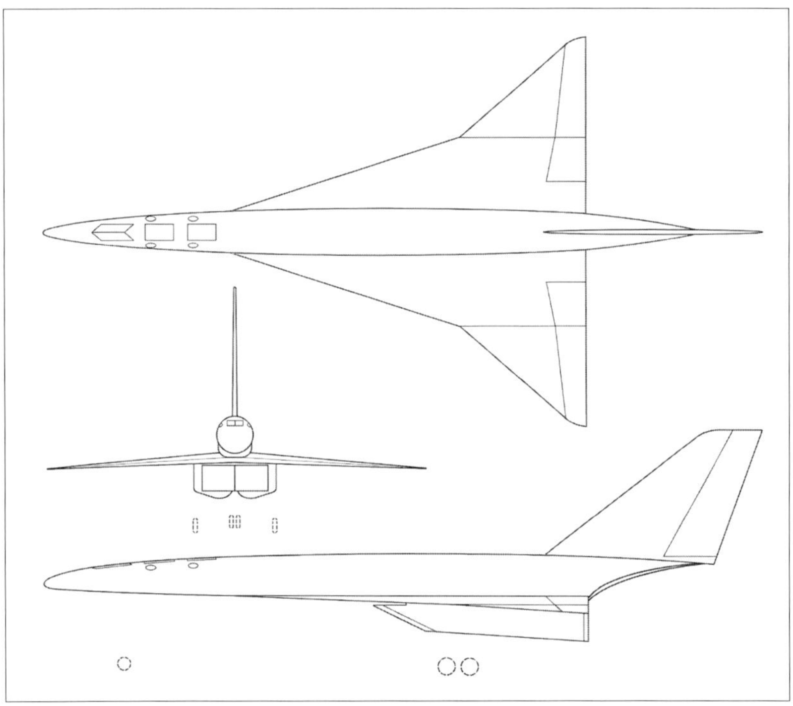

A proposal for a twin engined, high altitude Mach 5 reconnaissance aircraft with the reference EAG.4441.

Handley Page H.P.117
Crew: 4-8
Passengers: 200–300 depending on internal layout
Wingspan (initial): 125 ft (38 m); final: 148.8 ft (45.3 m)
Sweep (leading edge): 57°
Wing area (initial): 5,820 ft² (540 m²)
Length (initial): 101 ft (30.78 m); final: 144.5 ft (44 m)
Height: 21.5 ft (6.55 m)
Empty weight: 150,000 lb (68,038 kg); approximately
Gross weight: 330,000 lb (149,685 kg); revised to 305,000 lb (138,345 kg)
Powerplant (1961): 6 × Rolls Royce RB.163 Spey turbofans, drawing half their air from the suction and half by a combination of ram intake and a removal of the boundary layer behind the flight deck which would otherwise form a turbulent wedge. Auxiliary intakes would be used for take-off
Cruise speed: 592 mph (954 kph)
Ceiling: 45,000 ft (13,716 m); revised: ceiling: 55,000 ft (16,764 m)
Range: 5,000 miles (8,000 km)

HP.119
Crew: 2
Wingspan 44.66 ft (13.6 m); later: 47.25 ft (14.4 m)
Length: 58.4 ft (17.8 m)
Height: 12.75 ft (3.88 m)
Sweep (leading edge): 50°
Gross weight: 30,000 lb (13,607 kg)
Powerplant: 3 × Bristol Siddeley Viper BSV.20 turbojets, each rated at 3,000 lb (13.3 kN) static thrust. Two engines for propulsion, with the third used to draw off air from the boundary layer
Range: 6,700 miles (10,000 km) at 527 mph (848 kph) at 40,000 ft (12,192 m)

Heston JC.9 Research Aircraft
Crew: 1
Wingspan: 38 ft (11.58 m)
Length: 46.5 ft (14 m)
Height: 8.33 ft (2.5 m)
Powerplant: unknown
Performance: unknown

Vickers Swallow 1958 Research Proposal
Crew: 1 (possibly 2)
Wingspan (fully forward): 75 ft (22.86 m)
Wingspan (fully swept): 30.75 ft (9.37 m)
Aspect ratio (low speed): 10.7 (16.7 wing only)
Aspect ratio (swept): 1.88)
Length: 68.75 ft (20.95 m)
Height: N/A
Empty weight: 14,500 lb (6,577 kg)
Gross weight: 25,000 lb (11,339 kg)
Fuel weight: 9,000 lb (4,082 kg).
Payload capacity: 1,500 lb (680 kg)
Powerplant: 4 × Bristol afterburning turbojets
Engine pod dimensions: 2.83 ft × 24 ft (863 mm × 609 mm)
Maximum speed: Mach 1.6
Take-off speed: 155 mph (250 kph)
Landing speed: 130 mph (209 kph)
Cruise Altitude: 35–40,000 ft (10,668–12,192 m)
Ceiling: 50,000 ft (15,240 m)
Range: N/A
Armament: none

Vickers Swallow High/Low Level Bomber/Naval Strike
Crew: 1–2
Wingspan (fully forward): 75 ft (22.86 m)
Wingspan (fully swept): 30.75 ft (9.37 m)
Aspect ratio (low speed): 10.7 (16.7 wing only)
Aspect ratio (swept): 1.88)
Overall length: 68.75 ft (20.95 m)
Height: N/A
Empty weight: 16,100 lb (7,302 kg)
Gross weight: 30,000 lb (13,607 kg)
Fuel weight: 12,250 lb (5,556 kg)
Powerplant: 4 × Bristol afterburning turbojets
Engine Pod Dimensions: 2.83 ft × 24 ft (863 mm × 609 mm)
Maximum speed (high level): Mach 2
Maximum speed (low level): Mach .95
Take-off speed: 172 mph (276 kph)
Landing speed: 130 mph (209 kph)
Cruise altitude: 36,000 ft (10,972 m)
Ceiling: 80,000 ft (24,382 m).
Range: N/A
Payload capacity: 1,500 lb–2,000 lb (680 kg–907 kg)
Armament: single tactical nuclear weapon

Vickers Swallow Fighter
Crew: 1
Wingspan (fully forward): 75 ft (22.86 m)
Wingspan (fully swept): 30.75 ft (9.37 m)
Aspect ratio (low speed): 10.7 (16.7 wing only)
Aspect ratio (swept): 1.88)
Height: N/A
Overall length: 68.75 ft (20.95 m)
Empty weight: 15,250 lb (6,917 kg)
Gross weight: 30,000 lb (13,607 kg)
Fuel weight: 13,220 lb (5,996 kg)
Payload capacity: 1,530 lb (680 kg)
Powerplant: 4 × Bristol afterburning Orpheus turbojets
Maximum speed: Mach 2.5
Take-off speed: 172 mph (276 kph)
Landing speed: 130 mph (209 kph)
Cruise altitude: 40,000 ft (12,192 m)

Ceiling: 80,000 ft (24.384 m)
Improvised tactical airstrip take-off distance: 3,000 ft (914 m) loaded
Range: 1,500 miles (2,414 km) estimated
Armament: AAMs

Vickers Swallow Military Transport/Long Range Bomber Versions
Crew: 4-5?
Wingspan open: 174 ft (53 m)
Wingspan folded: 71.5 ft (21.79 m)
Aspect ratio (low speed): 10.7 (16.7 wing only)
Aspect ratio (swept): 1.88
Overall length (swept): 160 ft (48.76 m)
Height: unknown
Gross weight: 150,000 lb (68,038 kg)
Landing weight: 95,750 lb (43,431 kg)
Fuel weight: 58,750 lb (26,648 kg)
Powerplant: 4 × afterburning turbojets, each producing 12,850 lb (57 kN) static thrust
Engine pod dimensions: 3.33 ft × 30 ft (1 m × 9 m)
Payload capacity: 25,000 lb (11,339 kg)
Maximum speed: Mach 2.5
Take-off speed: 164 mph (263 kph)
Landing speed: 131 mph (210 kph)
Cruise altitude: 67,000 ft (20,421 m)
Ceiling: N/A
Range: 4,600 miles (7,400 km)
Armament: One, possibly two free fall nuclear weapons

De Havilland NP-3
Crew: 4?
Wingspan: N/A
Length: N/A
Gross weight: N/A
Powerplant: 6 engined, open-cycle nuclear propulsion system
Maximum speed: Mach 2.2–2.5
Ceiling: 60,000 ft (18,288 m)
Armament: Nuclear bombs or stand-off missiles

De Havilland NP-4
Crew: 4?
Wingspan: N/A
Length: N/A
Gross weight: N/A
Powerplant: 8 engined, closed-cycle nuclear propulsion system
Maximum speed: Mach 2.2–2.5
Ceiling: 60,000 ft (18,288 m)
Armament: Nuclear bombs or stand-off missiles

BAC EAG.3273 Research Aircraft
Crew: 1
Wingspan: 45 ft (13.7 m)
Sweep (leading edge): 70°
Length: 75 ft (22.8 m)
Height: N/A
Powerplant: 2 × BSEL ramjets. 2 × Rolls-Royce RB.162 turbojets
Weights: loaded 50,000 lb (22,679 kg)
Maximum speed: Mach 4.5
Ceiling: 90,000 ft (27,432 m) estimated
Range: N/A
Armament: none

BAC EAG.4426 Interdictor/Strike
Crew: 2
Wingspan: 46 ft (14 m)
Sweep (leading edge): 70°
Length: 87 ft (26.5 m)
Height: N/A
Powerplant: 2 × Rolls-Royce Type C afterburning turbojets. Sea level static thrust of 27,000 lb (120 kN)
Weights: loaded 90,000 lb (40,823 kg) estimated
Maximum speed: Mach 4.5 (clean)
Ceiling: 90,000 ft (27,432 m) zoom climb: 120,000 ft (36,576 m)
Range (internal fuel): 1,000 miles (1,609 km)
Armament: 2 × BAC Tychon air-to-surface missiles with conventional or nuclear warheads carried semi-recessed over wing. 2 × Anti-radiation missiles carried over wing, or 1 × glide bomb carried below fuselage centreline. C. Gibson has suggested this might have been a kinetic energy weapon. Some internal carriage was considered, possibly being suitable for AAMs or reconnaissance equipment

BAC EAG.4441 Reconnaissance Aircraft
Crew: 2
Wingspan: 65.5 ft (19 m)
Sweep (leading edge): 70°
Length: 148.5 ft (45.3 m)
Height: N/A
Powerplant: 2 × Bristol-Siddeley BA.1011/2 engines
Weights: loaded N/A
Maximum speed: Mach 5
Ceiling: 100,000 ft+ (30,480 m+)
Range: N/A
Armament: none

5

Rocket Powered Interceptors

Once more, German aviation research and development, mostly conducted during the Second World War would have a profound effect on the thinking of American and British designers. The Allies were already aware of what might be possible using rocket propulsion, but it was still something of a shock when the enemy's high performance rocket fighters were first encountered in combat during 1944.

The application of rocket propulsion to an aircraft had initially been demonstrated by Alexander Lippisch during 1928. He designed a small sailplane called the Ente (Duck) and it was adapted to take two solid fuel rockets. The initial flight was made by Lippisch's test pilot Fritz Stamer (1897–1969) who completed a successful circuit of the Wasserkuppe landing field. However, on the second flight, one of the rockets exploded setting the Ente on fire. Stamer managed to make an emergency landing and escaped unharmed, but the aircraft was destroyed. Nevertheless, the idea proved workable and it led to the construction and testing of Fritz von Opel's RAK.3 rocket powered aircraft, which flew at Rebstock Airport near Frankfurt-am-Main in 1929.

German engineers remained at the forefront of experimentation and the next important development came about in 1935, when Hellmuth Walter (1900–1980) switched his attention from work on advanced submarine propulsion to aircraft rocket engines running on highly concentrated hydrogen peroxide and a suitable catalyst. As a consequence, he soon established the Hellmuth Walter Kommanditgesellschaft (HWK) company in Kiel.

At around the same time, future German space pioneer (and director of Peenemünde rocket centre) Dr Wernher von Braun (1912–1977) had become very interested in the application of rocket propulsion to aircraft. He was kicking around several ideas for piloted rocket interceptors and also developed a proof-of-concept, liquid fuel engine running on oxygen and alcohol. After a series of static trials, he approached the well-known aircraft manufacturer Ernst Heinkel (1888–1958), who took an immediate interest in the idea. Heinkel provided an He-112 monoplane, which was adapted to carry one of von Braun's engines in its tail. The modified He 112 was first flown at Kummersdorf in June 1937 by Flugkapitan Erich Warsitz (1906–1983), although it subsequently sustained damage after several accidents and Heinkel immediately provided a replacement aircraft. Warsitz then made a very hard landing when the rocket engine failed and this aircraft was also a write-off. It seems that a third He-112 was then supplied by Heinkel, which was tested with another von Braun rocket engine and an alternative prototype unit provided by Walter. After a number of flights, von Braun accepted the superior reliability and performance of the more controllable Walter engine and as a direct consequence, Ernst Heinkel authorised the secret construction of He-176 V1 (Versuchs–Experimental, or Version One), which was a small, one-man demonstrator, powered by an improved Walter HWK R1 liquid fuel rocket engine, capable of delivering 1,323 lb (5.88 kN) thrust for 50 seconds.

When the aircraft was completed, it was moved to the large wind tunnel at Göttingen for testing and then transported to Peenemünde, where secret flight trials could be undertaken. Once minor adjustments were completed, the He-176 V1 took to the air in mid-1939, piloted by Erich Warsitz. The aircraft performed quite well, but a demonstration to the German leadership failed to impress them and the project was officially terminated by the Reichsluftfahrtsministerium (RLM—Air Ministry) on 12 September 1939.

Heinkel had intended to build a more advanced V2 version of the He-176, but this never happened and V1 was eventually dismantled and placed in storage. Meanwhile, von Braun completed the design for a vertical take-off (VTO) rocket powered interceptor, which he submitted to the RLM, while continuing to undertake further development of his liquid fuel engine, thought to have been tested by Dr Helmut von Zborowski (1905–1969) at the BMW Bramo facility in Berlin-Spandau. The estimated performance was impressive with the rate of climb calculated at 50 seconds to 25,000 ft (7,620 m) and the engine would be fitted with a secondary cruise chamber allowing a speed of 430 mph (692 kph) to be maintained at altitudes up to 35,000 ft (10,668 m). Once the fuel was exhausted, the interceptor would return to base, making a glide-landing on a retractable skid.

Although the Heinkel He-176 V1 had been cancelled by the RLM, Ernst Heinkel expressed a strong interest in developing von Braun's proposals and Dr Motzfeld carried out a full evaluation for the company. He concluding that von Braun's concept was sound but the aircraft needed to

The Heinkel He-176V1 rocketplane, which was secretly built at Marienehe under the direction of Hans Regner in the late 1930s.

attain higher altitudes and show improvements in endurance to keep ahead of expected foreign developments. Nevertheless, these proposals were rejected by the RLM in 1941, as there was no official requirement at that time for a VTO interceptor and Alexander Lippisch had been busily working on the Messerschmitt Me 163 powered by a more advanced Walter rocket engine and this was now on order for the Luftwaffe. Nevertheless, von Braun continued to develop his plans and exchange ideas with his colleague Dr Erich Bachem (1906–1960) who was technical director of Gerhard Fieseler Werke and responsible for development of the Fi-103 (V-1) flying bomb at Peenemünde. Bachem initially designed a rather basic looking twin jet engine interceptor based on a Bf-109 airframe that would be strapped to a modified A5 rocket and launched to high altitude. This was given the designation Fi-166, but it never progressed beyond the concept stage. Bachem soon dropped the idea and produced a second proposal for a Fi-166 VTO interceptor that was closer to one of von Braun's later designs and powered by a single Walter rocket engine. However, this also failed to secure any RLM support.

Although the He 176 had not been a great success, it indirectly led to a separate RLM-sponsored rocketplane programme called Projekt X, which was undertaken by Dr Alexander Lippisch and his team at the German Research Institute for Soaring Flight (Deutsche Forschungsanstalt fur Segelflug—DFS). By 1938, Lippisch's engineers began construction of a mainly wooden small tailless glider with the reference DFS 194. This would form the basis of a more advanced rocketplane. Project X was classified as top secret, requiring special security and work space at the DFS was limited, so The RLM decided to move the entire operation to Messerschmitt at Augsburg. This was completed in early 1939 and while Lippisch had intended to fit a piston engine driving a pusher propeller for flight trials, but the RLM decided that it was time to press ahead and install the rocket engine. With the DFS 194 ready for this next phase in early 1940, the aircraft was transported to Peenemünde–Karlshagen, where the Walter RI-203 rocket engine was fitted. Once powered flights began, the construction of two Me 163As was approved and work started at Augsburg, although progress was slow because there were restrictions on how many skilled personnel could be spared from the Messerschmitt production lines.

By mid-1941, these Me 163A prototypes (V1 and V4) had been completed and were moved to Peenemünde–Karlshagen for installation of their Walter HWK RII-203b rocket engines and flight testing. The fuel used by the RII-203b was a mixture of very corrosive HT peroxide (T-Stoff) and a calcium permanganate liquid catalyst (Z-Stoff), which converted the hydrogen peroxide into a hot steam. Even when these chemicals were carefully handled by highly trained operatives, there was the chance of a serious explosion. However, it was clear that this small rocketplane had great potential as a high performance interceptor and Lippisch was already working on a more sophisticated, armed version of the aircraft.

Rocket-propelled flights of the fully fuelled Me 163A V4 began in Autumn 1941, with test pilot Heinrich 'Heini' Dittmar (1911–1960) at the controls. He was towed into the air behind a Bf 110C and released at an altitude of 13,124 ft (4,000 m). Then Dittmar ignited the Walter rocket engine and accelerated to an astonishing speed of 624 mph (1,004 kph), before running into severe stability problems and throttling back. He had broken all existing air speed records by a huge margin, although the achievement had to remain secret.

As a consequence, the RLM were so impressed, they immediately ordered the newly designed Me 163B into production. Assembly of the Me 163B began on 1 December 1941, although there were ongoing modifications and upgrades to the aircraft and the new and more advanced Walter HWK 109-509A rocket engine. While the scientists at Walter had replaced the temperamental Z

Me 163A (KE-SW) Werk Nr 1630000001. The first prototype Me 163A assigned the reference V4 which made its initial test flight at Lechfeld in spring 1941. (*Deutsches Bundesarchiv – German Federal Archive*)

Stoff catalyst with a mixture of methyl alcohol, hydrazine hydrate and water called C-Stoff, there were still significant issues with the more advanced engine, which would not be ready until late July 1943. The Me 163B differed considerably from the Me 163A and it was designed to carry more fuel, which improved the maximum speed, ceiling and range. Armament consisted of two 30 mm MK 108 cannon. Lippisch had never got on well with Willy Messerschmitt and left the company in 1943 to become director of the Vienna Aviation Research Institute. Most of his staff went with him. Production of the rocket fighter continued at Messerschmitt, with many components now being produced at dispersed sites due to intensified Allied bombing. The Me 163B had also received the name Komet (Comet), although the aircraft would often be referred to by test pilots as The Powered Egg and sometimes The Devil's Sledge.

With the first Me 163B aircraft ready for delivery to the Luftwaffe, a new fighter staffel (squadron) known as I/JG 400 had been formed by May 1944 to fly these aircraft from Brandis Airfield near Leipzig. This location was chosen as their specific duty would be to protect the nearby Leuna synthetic fuel plant, which was vital to the Nazi war effort. After a handful of fleeting encounters with Allied aircraft, the first operational mission took place at the end of July and Me 163B pilots scored several kills by the beginning of August 1944.
However, there were problems with the guns jamming, difficulty making sufficiently accurate attacks on bombers at high speed and major concerns about handling the very dangerous rocket fuel. Nevertheless, the Allies were astonished by the performance of this small interceptor with its fantastic rate of climb and amazing speed, although soon recognised it was vulnerable to attack while gliding back to base.

Work continued on improving the rocket fighter and two Me 163Bs (V6 and V18) underwent modifications to accept the more powerful two-chamber Walter HWK 109-509C rocket engine. This was expected to power the improved Me 163C that began development after Lippisch and his team left Messerschmitt. Three Me 163C prototypes were completed by Messerschmitt and had been test flown by 1945.

An Me 163B interceptor during take-off. Like the earlier Me 163A, it had a two-wheel dolly that was dropped after leaving the ground and the aircraft would make a glide landing, touching down on a deployable skid and tail wheel. This saved weight and avoided the need for a complicated undercarriage.

An Me 163B caught by the gun-camera of a USAAF P-51 Mustang fighter just before it was shot down.

The Me 163D was a further development of the design and following the construction of a wooden mock-up, the company received immediate RLM approval to proceed with production of a prototype. The Me 163D V1 was completed by spring 1944 and gliding tests followed almost immediately. The Me 163D V1 was essentially a slightly larger version of the Me 163B, with a similar cockpit arrangement, a fully retractable tricycle undercarriage, the improved two chamber Walter rocket engine and larger fuel tanks. However, the RLM were still not entirely satisfied with the Me 163D V1 and voiced concerns that Messerschmitt resources had become too stretched to continue with the project. As a consequence, development was passed to Heinrich Hertel's design office at Junkers. The project was now re-named Ju 248 and Hertel's engineers made a series of immediate improvements. This included a new pressurised and armoured cockpit, a modified dorsal section, easier engine maintenance, larger flaps and automatic wing slots. The Walter HWK 109-509C rocket engine was retained, but allowances were made to accommodate the more advanced BMW 708 rocket engine when available. This was expected to provide considerably better performance and the fuel it used was S Stoff (mostly nitric acid) and R Stoff (57 percent monoxylidene oxide and 43 percent trimethylamine). At the end of 1944, the RLM decided to approve full production of the Ju 248, although accepted a complaint about the designation from Willy Messerschmitt and re-named it as the Me 263. Towards the end of the war, one prototype Me 263 V1 had been built and airframes for the V2 and V3 were almost complete.

When hostilities ceased, the Soviet military secured the Junkers plant and everything of interest including the V1, with vast amounts of useful equipment being shipped back to Russia. A number of Me 163Bs were also secured and taken to the Gromov Flight Research Institute for evaluation. However, there was no facility within the Soviet Union or captured territories able to produce the quantities of HT peroxide required to power Walter rocket engines. So trials were restricted to glide-flights, using a Tupolev Tu-2 bomber to tow an Me 163B into the air.

At the same time, Mikoyan–Guervich OKB were assigned to undertake development of the captured Me 263 into a point defence rocket interceptor. This led to an improved version of the aircraft called the MiG 1-270 (Zh). It was superior in many ways and was equipped with thin straight wings. Two slightly different prototypes were built during 1946, with assistance from several German engineers, although the first aircraft was only ever intended for glide-trials and it was eventually written off in a landing accident. The second 1-270 was ready for testing at the beginning of 1947 and it was equipped with a two-chamber GRD-2M-3V rocket engine designed by Leonid Dushkin (1910-1990) and Valentin Glushko (1908-1989). It probably utilised some German engineering techniques, but was mainly based on an earlier Russian design and fuelled with nitric acid and kerosene, providing a maximum thrust of about 3,190 lb (14.2 kN). Powered flights began in early 1947, but this second prototype was badly damaged during a hard landing and a decision was then made to abandon further attempts to develop rocket powered interceptors as there was considerable progress being made with turbojet propulsion and effective surface-to-air missiles.

In total, about 365 Me 163Bs were produced during the Second World War and this relatively new technology made a substantial impression on the Western allies, who believed it might open the door to a number of new possibilities such as fighters able to intercept enemy bombers at very high altitudes and supersonic speed. Subsequently, the British took a considerable interest in rocket-powered aircraft and in addition to the Messerschmitt Me 163B, they secured a good deal of documentation for Eric Bachem's Ba 349A manned VTO rocket interceptor, although there is nothing to show that any of these aircraft were returned to the UK. However, the Ba 349A will be discussed in the next chapter.

As the war drew to a close, Royal Navy/RAE test pilot Captain Eric Brown was assigned to evaluate advanced German aviation and associated technology. Brown spoke fluent German and interviewed a number of leading scientists and designers, which included Dr Wernher von Braun, Kurt Tank, Ernst Heinkel, the Horten Brothers and on one occasion, he spoke with former Nazi chief Hermann Göring. During this same period, Brown flew the Me 262 jet fighter, The Heinkel He 162 jet fighter, the Arado Ar 234 jet bomber and an Me 163B Komet that was found intact at the Husum Airfield in northern Germany, where Jagdgeschwader 400 had operated. Assisted by German technicians and pilots, Brown made three glide-flights in a Komet, finally deciding to undertake an (unofficial) powered fight on 10 June 1945. He was astonished by the performance of the aircraft, but also fully aware of just how dangerous the propulsive system was. During the same period, about 24 Me 163B Komets were shipped back to the UK (mostly from Husum Airfield), although the RAE at Farnborough had taken delivery of its first complete Me 163B Komet several weeks earlier. Most of the technical evaluation was carried out by the RAE's Experimental Flying Department in secret as rocket propulsion, especially in combination with jet power was considered a potentially significant step forward in fighter propulsion.

Little is known about the initial history of this particular Me 163B, but it was soon assigned the UK serial VF241 and partly repainted to show RAF colours. The rocket engine is known to have been removed and the space filled with test equipment and ballast, allowing glide-trials to study the aircraft's handling.

Wing Commander 'Roly' Falk was assigned the task of flight testing VF241. He was a very experienced pilot, perhaps a little eccentric, often wearing a business suit while flying and is best remembered for his later contribution to the Avro Vulcan trials. Falk made the first glide-flight of the Me 163B in July 1945, but there were technical problems with the aircraft's hydraulic system. This held up testing for the remainder of the year and a decision was taken by the MoS (on Brown's advice) that powered flights in this aircraft were too dangerous, so plans to fly the Komet under rocket power in Britain were abandoned. The Americans had also been contemplating powered trials, but decided to stick with glide-flights on the grounds of safety and there were the Russians, who had several examples of the Me 163B but lacked the ability to produce adequate quantities of suitable fuel for the engines. That said, it is known that Dushkin built and tested several experimental versions of the Walter 109-509C fitted with an upper cruise chamber, but this did not go much further as the Russians gave maximum priority to the development of gas turbines.

British Glide-flights with VF241 resumed during February 1946, using a Spitfire IX as the tow aircraft. The flights were undertaken from Wisley Airfield in Surrey, which was owned by Vickers-Armstrong, but is now derelict and still awaits possible housing re-development. Later flights were made at RAF Wittering, although it is not entirely clear why this more distant location was chosen. Many of these flights were undertaken by the senior RAE test pilot Captain Eric Brown. One of the purposes of these trials was to gain experience with skid landing techniques as the RAE was developing proposals for an experimental swept wing supersonic aircraft designed by the German engineer Hans Multhopp (1913-1972) and aerodynamicist Martin Winter who had been Multhopp's assistant at Focke Wulf during the war. It was hoped that the Multhopp-Winter aircraft would reach at least Mach 1.26 and climb to an altitude of 60,000 ft (18,288 m). This alternative to the proposed Miles M.52 experimental aircraft also carried the pilot in a prone position and utilised a landing skid system to minimise weight.

On 15 November 1947, VF241's hydraulic landing skid failed as Brown touched down and the Komet was badly damaged. Brown was slightly injured, but the aircraft was a complete write-off. At about the same time, the Multhopp-Winter supersonic project was cancelled and VF241 would be one of the last captured German aircraft that was test flown by RAE personnel. That aside, the Me 163B rocketplane had quite an impact on British officialdom, not to mention the designers and engineers. So much so, that the DH.108 experimental jet programme (discussed in a previous chapter) was strongly influenced by the Me 163. It was now accepted that rocket

Several Me 163B Komets were secured by the British during 1945 and the best example (shown here) was provided to the RAE for testing and evaluation, having been given the UK reference VF241. The engine was replaced with ballast and VF241 was partly re-painted with RAF markings.

propulsion technology was extremely dangerous and there were issues with things like endurance and suitable armament for this type of aircraft, but these were thought to be problems that could be addressed in due course. Britain's senior air staff simply wanted an interceptor capable of countering the perceived threat from future high-flying Soviet bombers. Eventually the jet engine might have the capability, but this technology requiring substantial funding to develop it further. It was clearly going to be at least another decade before jet engines became reliable and started to deliver the kind of performance needed to provide adequate rates of climb and sustained supersonic flight.

At the end of the Second World War, Hellmuth Walter was detained by a British T-Force unit and his factory was raided and secured by a specialist team of Royal Marines. Having seized a substantial amount of hardware and research material, Walter and a number of his colleagues were taken to the UK, where they were debriefed and encouraged to work for Vickers, although mostly on submarine propulsion, which did not really lead anywhere. He was then allowed to return to Germany in 1948 and two years later, accepted a job offer in America.

One of the first commercial UK organisations to undertake detailed studies of German rocket engine technology was the de Havilland Engine Company, under the direct control of engineering director Frank Bernard Halford (1894–1955). The company was assisted by the MoS, who provided various Walter rocket engines and a series of trials commenced in early 1947, testing Walter 109-501 units (designed to assist aircraft with take-off). The MoS was also responsible for setting up the Guided Projectile Establishment at Westcott, Buckinghamshire and one of the first projects undertaken at this research facility was the development of a compact HT peroxide / kerosene fuelled 'hot' engine. Based on the Walter HWK R1-203, it produced 800 lb

(3.55 kN) thrust and was used to power the Vickers Transonic Research Vehicle during flight trials in 1948. This scale-sized, unmanned demonstrator was smaller version of the proposed M.52 supersonic research aircraft that met with cancellation. However, the Vickers test vehicle briefly attained 930 mph (1,497 kph) in level flight at an altitude of 36,000 ft (10,972 m), which was impressive for that time. With overall development of rocket engines progressing well, de Havilland were soon working hard on a full-sized successor to the Walter 109-509 engine and this would become the Spectre DSpe.l, with rig testing beginning in 1952.

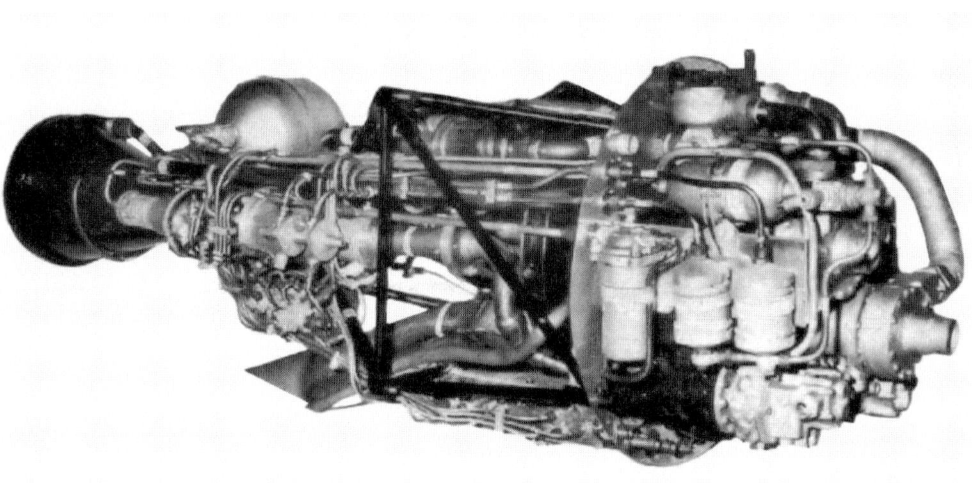

The Armstrong Siddeley Screamer rocket engine, which was designed to run on methanol and liquid oxygen (LOX). It was eventually cancelled in favour of the rival Spectre design, as the RAF were less enthusiastic about using LOX.

The de Havilland Spectre rocket engine, which used a combination of kerosene and high test peroxide (HTP). The engine's variable output provided a maximum thrust of 8,000 lb (35.5 kN). It was chosen for the SR.53 and flight tested to supersonic speed before the entire project was cancelled.

Armstrong Siddeley were another company who saw great potential in rocket propulsion and wasted little time after the Second World War ended setting up a rocket division at Ansty, near Coventry, under the control of chief engineer S. Allen. Their first major project was the development of a liquid oxygen/methanol rocket engine called the Snarler, which initally ran at 2,000 lb (8.9 kN) thrust during ground trials and was then flight tested on the Hawker P.1072 prototype. This engine would eventually give way to the more advanced Screamer, which ran on a mixture of liquid oxygen and kerosene and would eventually achieve 4,000 lb (17.7 kN) thrust when first tested in March 1954., with this figure steadily rising to 8,000 lb (35.5 kN).

With the expectation of sufficiently powerful and reliable rocket engines becoming available in the near future, a decision was taken by the Air Staff in early 1951 to issue an operational requirement (OR.301) for a rocket powered interceptor that could be put into production by the mid-1950s. Of primary importance, was a very high rate of climb to counter the perceived future threat posed by advanced long-range Soviet nuclear bombers that might be capable of sustaining supersonic speed at extreme altitude. In an all-out war, these British rocket powered interceptors would tackle this specific threat, while RAF Hunters and Swifts concentrated on taking out any slower Tu-4s. That aside, it was generally accepted that in a substantial aircraft attack on major UK targets, there was no way of telling which enemy bombers carried nuclear weapons and some of them would get through.

Discussions under the direct control of MoS Director of Aircraft R&D Arthur Woodward-Nutt (1902–1980) were soon underway with several aircraft companies and the MoS finally issued a tender specification (F.124T) for development proposals.

Chosen manufacturers included Hawker, Avro, Shorts, Blackburn, Boulton Paul, Bristol, Fairey and they were joined by Saunders Roe who had not been initially listed, but applied to participate. F.124T initially called for a fighter totally powered by rocket propulsion with an exceptional rate of climb, a ceiling of at least 60,000 ft (18,288 m) and ideally supersonic performance at high altitude for an acceptable duration. The pilot would be guided to the target by ground radar and the aircraft would be armed with unguided air-to-air rockets, although these would hopefully be replaced with guided missiles when available.

Some of the manufacturer's proposals were eliminated fairly quickly, for various technical, performance and manufacturing issues. This included the application of unproven technology, unsatisfactory constructional ideas, or an assessment of the company's ability to manufacture the aircraft. Clearly, some firms were stretched by existing contracts, lacked suitable premises, had insufficient staff, dated research facilities and finally, there were cost issues.

In addition, there would be the need for future upgrades to the design when more sophisticated weapons, a suitable radar system, improved communications and possibly changes or modifications to the propulsion system were needed. As discussions progressed it became apparent that any aircraft meeting the requirements of F.124T would never be officially considered as much more than a proof-of-concept demonstrator and the stepping stone to a more sophisticated design. Some of the initial submissions from companies like Bristol and Blackburn were quite conventional in appearance, with swept wings, tailplanes and simply lacking engine air inlets, while Bristol proposed an aircraft (the Type 178) that looked very much like the US Lockheed F-104 Starfighter! Nevertheless, most of the favoured designs were deltas. Hawker submitted an especially pleasing tailless delta concept with the reference P.1089. Spectre powered, the aircraft was compact with a length of 37.5 ft (11.5 m) a wingspan of 24.25 ft (7.4 m), having an area of 336 ft^2 (31.2 m^2).

As specified, the armament was air-to-air rockets. P.1089's cockpit also provided the pilot with good visibility and the aircraft was fitted with a fully retractable tricycle undercarriage. Estimates for performance are somewhat unclear, but looking at the fully fuelled weight, the clean aerodynamics and spec for similar designs, it would be supersonic and expected to reach 60,000 ft (18,288 m) in at least 2 minutes.

Another fairly elegant design that looked ahead of its time was produced by Fairey Aviation. A cranked delta design, using the Screamer engine, with supersonic performance, this was given the name Scheme A and it had some resemblance to the FD.2, which has already been described. In turn there was a slightly more conventional alternative design submitted with swept wings and a tailplane called Scheme B. This was a lighter, more compact aircraft, using the same rocket engine, but with a slightly superior rate of climb, calculated at 2.19 minutes to 60,000 ft (18,288 m). As the Scheme A design was the larger and heavier aircraft, it presumably carried more fuel, so it seems reasonable to deduce that it was expected to have better endurance. This additional weight is also probably the reason why Fairey's Scheme A interceptor was to be equipped with six solid fuel boosters beneath the rear fuselage to assist take-off.

Both proposals were described as being armed with air-to-air rocket packs, but drawings show each aircraft carrying two Blue Jay missiles. Scheme A was to be equipped with a tricycle undercarriage and although not shown in available drawings, this was probably the case with Scheme B.

Another submission for F.124T that generated considerable interest came from Short Brothers. They suggested the PD.7, a rocket-powered interceptor with an appearance that in some ways looked like a smaller Gloster Javelin. Designed by David Keith-Lucas, it was built around a delta wing with a span of 30 ft (9.14 m) and a leading edge sweep of 60°. The tailplane was a scaled down version of this, with a span of 10 ft (3 m). The overall length of the PD.7 was 39.75 ft in (12.11 m) and it was powered by the Armstrong Siddeley Screamer rocket engine providing the anticipated 8,000 lb (35.5 kN) thrust. PD.7 would be equipped with a tricycle undercarriage, the pressurised cockpit was positioned well forward to provide the pilot with good visibility and the aircraft was to be armed with two air-to-air rocket packs. Aside from space for the pilot and engine, most of the aircraft's interior was taken up by fuel tanks. Looking at the drawings of PD.7 it is hard to ignore the aircraft's rather hefty wing design. This undoubtedly limited performance and it was estimated that the rate of climb would be 3.72 minutes to 60,000 ft (18,288 m) and speeds below Mach 1 during patrol and combat. In view of this, Keith-Lucas pointed out to Woodward-Nutt in correspondence that a purely rocket-powered fighter was a bad idea and in the case of the PD.7 performance could be substantially improved by the use of two supplementary turbojets. This would have several benefits; the rate of climb could be improved to less than two minutes and the aircraft could have a total patrol time extended by about 8.5 minutes. The PD.7 would be able to make safer powered landings and ferrying the aircraft to diferent locations around the UK would present no problems using jet power. As a consequence, Keith-Lucas proposed a revised aircraft with the company designation PD.701. It had much the same appearance and dimensions as the PD.7, but two Bristol BE.22 4,700 lb (20.9 kN) thrust turbojets would supplement the Screamer rocket engine. A re-structuring of the airframe for air inlets, the jet engines and exhaust systems would obviously add weight, but according to Keith-Lucas, the aircraft would actually have ended up with a lower gross weight due to an alteration in fuel requirements.

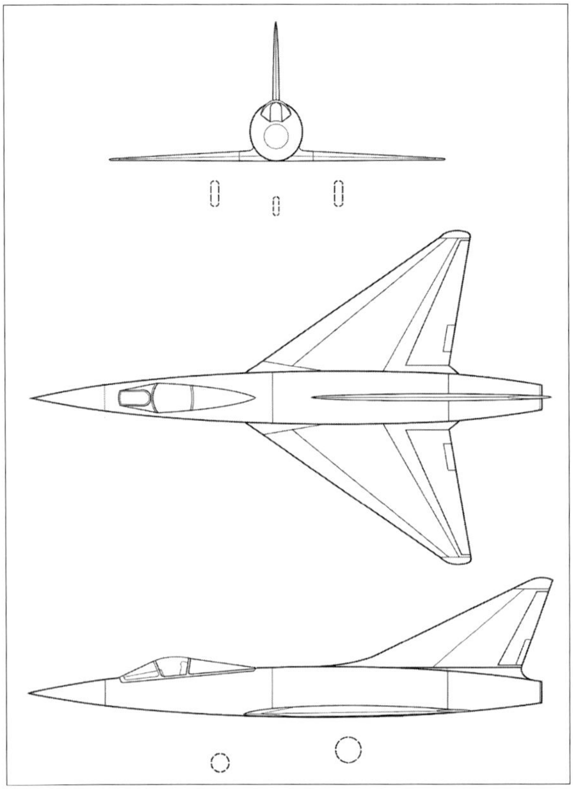

Hawker's initial proposals for a purely rocket powered interceptor, the P.1089. The clean appearance and wing design of this concept suggests that it was intended to achieve supersonic speed. But the P.1089 progressed little further than the drawing board.

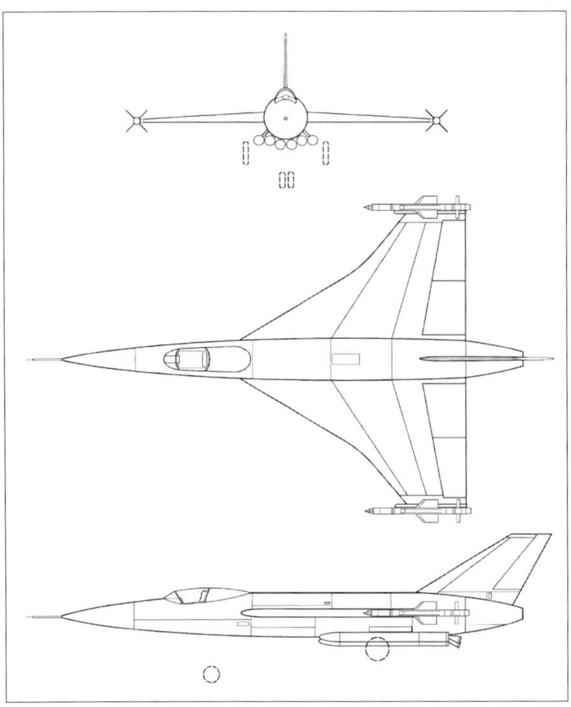

Fairey's Scheme A rocket powered interceptor to meet Specification F.124T.

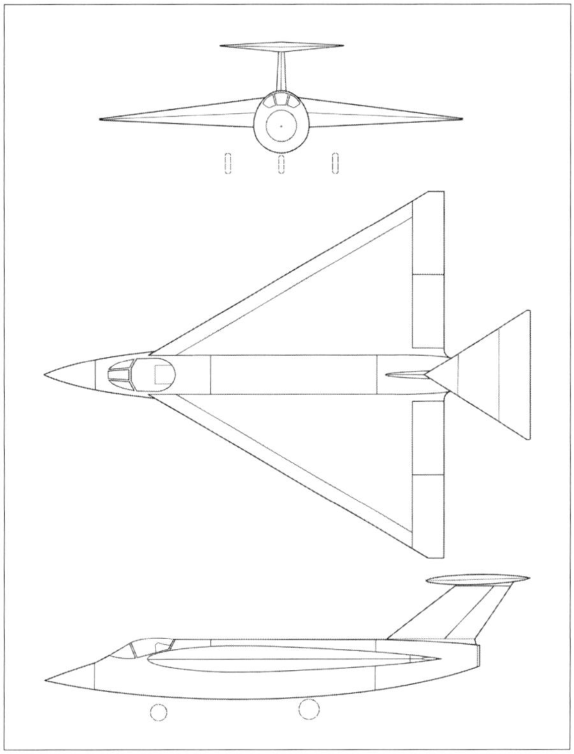

Shorts PD.7 rocket powered interceptor.

Although Saunders Roe were not initially considered for the rocket fighter competition, they made representations to the MoS and were accepted to submit proposals. The chief designer at Saunders Roe was Maurice Brennan (1913–1986) and while the company was best known for flying boats, he had been overseeing considerable research into the idea of constructing a rocket-powered aircraft capable of operating at an altitude of 100,000 ft (30,000 m). Brennan's initial proposal to the MoS was for a reasonable conventional swept wing aircraft powered by a Spectre engine with compact dimensions of 37 ft (11.2 m) in length, with a wingspan of 26 ft (7.9 m). Given the company reference P.154, it had a good rate of climb, optimistically calculated at 1.87 min to 60,000 ft (18,288 m), and supersonic performance. Nevertheless, Brennan would also point out that reliance on just rocket propulsion presented major problems and the aircraft should have a secondary turbojet, which if nothing else would make the return to base less dangerous.

The other significant proposal came from Avro, who submitted a rocket-powered interceptor with the company reference 720. This was a delta wing aircraft that drew on the experience already gained by Avro's designers and engineers working on the Vulcan and the Avro 707 series. Under the overall control of Avro's chief designer Stuart Duncan Davies (1906–1995), the 720 was developed as a compact, daylight rocket interceptor capable of meeting the MoS's requirements. Propulsion was flexible with Avro allowing for installation of either a Spectre or Screamer 8,000 lb (36 kN) thrust rocket engine. The thin delta wing would have a span of 28.25 ft (8.6 m), with an area of 385 ft^2 (35.8 m^2) and an initial sweep of 51°. Overall length was expected to be about 48 ft (14.6 m), but all these figures were variable estimates, subject to change. Some parts of the airframe would comprise of a bonded metal honeycomb sandwich and there would be stainless steel used for the aircraft's skin, with the pressurised cockpit positioned well forward to allow the pilot good visibility.

A tricycle undercarriage supported the 720 and the intended armament was 48 2-inch (50.8 mm) air-to-air rockets. At this stage, there were no plans to equip the aircraft with radar, but this would change as the project developed. Avro estimated the 720's rate of climb at 1.96 min to 60,000 ft (18,288 m), with a maximum speed about Mach 1.8. However, like those at Shorts and Saunders Roe, the problems created by a purely rocket-driven interceptor were clearly apparent to Avro's designers and they were raised at the time of the submission, with a recommendation that mixed propulsion should be adopted. A number of semi-formal meetings followed, with the MoS accepting that mixed propulsion was the way forward and this resulted in requests to modify or replace the existing designs.

The submissions which followed were carefully studied and a Tender Design Conference was arranged by the MoS at Thames House on 18 July 1952, chaired by MoS Director-General of Technical Development Stewart Scott-Hall. This resulted in the Saunders Roe design, now using the company reference SR.53 being selected as their first choice, closely followed by the Avro 720. It was normal practice to issue contracts to both leading competitors when funding permitted as a safeguard against one of them running into serious technical issues. Subsequently, Specification F138D was issued to Saunders Roe for full development of their mixed propulsion SR.53 and a similar Specification F137D was issued to Avro for the 720. Three SR.53 prototypes would be completed by Saunders Roe for just under £900,000 and two 720s would be built by Avro for no more than £500,000. (Money rates for that period) There would also be the need to provide airframes for stress testing and mock-ups, plus the separate cost of engine development. The first flights were expected to take place in 1956 and official serials were issued to both companies for the prototypes, which were XD143, XD151 and XD153 for Saunders Roe and XD696 and XD701 for Avro.

Wind tunnel testing of Avro scale models continued, with assistance from RAE Bedford who used their 3 ft × 3 ft (.91m × .91 m) tunnel to study a 1:30 scale, steel model with a 60° leading edge sweep at speeds up to Mach 2. Some instability was recorded at Mach 0.99 and there were suggestions to make minor modifications to the wing's leading edge, in the form of notches. The revised version of the 720 remained reasonably similar to the original design and would be fitted with an Armstrong-Siddeley Viper turbojet producing 1,750 lb (7.8 kN) of thrust and using a ventral air inlet beneath the cockpit. Another obvious modification was the provision to carry two de Havilland Firestreak air-to-air missiles on pylons beneath the wing.

It is understood that some of the airframe intended for stress testing started to be assembled in 1953 and used for a full metal mock-up of the 720, which was completed at Manchester in 1954. The few pictures showing this were released without a great deal of accompanying information and it led to the belief that this was the prototype due to its 'almost finished' appearance, which included full markings and the serial XD696 on the aircraft's rear fuselage. Avro is also known to have considered an improved version of the aircraft fitted with the superior afterburning de Havilland PS.50 Gyron Junior turbojet and carrying airborne radar. The fuselage would be adapted to take advantage of the more aerodynamic area rule configuration and a V-shaped cockpit windshield would be fitted which was somewhat similar to that chosen for the American Convair F-102 interceptor.

This company picture of the Avro 720 was originally thought to show the first prototype aircraft nearing completion at Manchester and it is marked with the official serial (XD696) assigned to this aircraft. However, it is now understood to be a largely completed metal skinned mock-up. (*Avro/Bill Rose*).

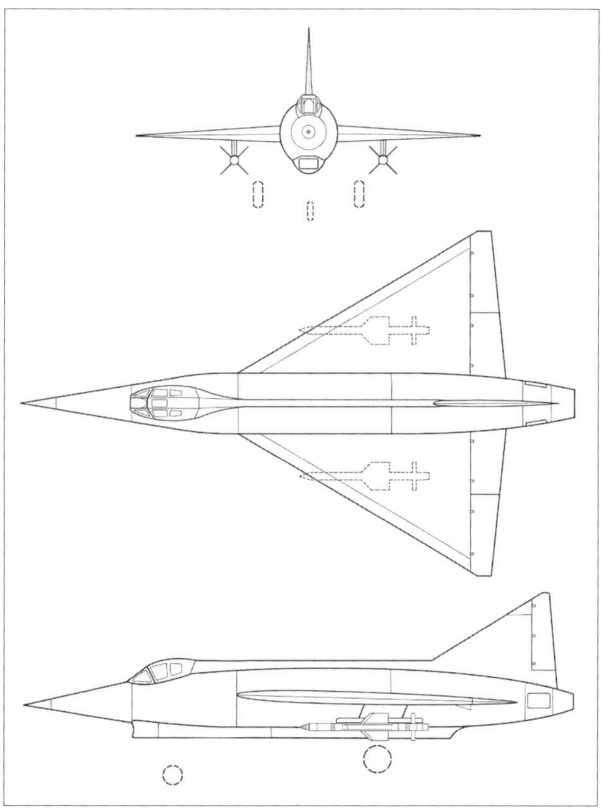

General view of the mixed propulsion 720 armed with two underwing Blue Jay (Firestreak) infrared homing air-to-air missiles.

Yet another drawing board proposal was a turbojet only version of the aircraft with the designation 726. This compact fighter would be powered by a choice of several possible afterburning jet engines, all providing supersonic performance. Avro's 726 was intended to undertake interception or escort duties and it would be armed with two 30 mm ADEN cannon or two air-to-air missiles. This was followed by the 727, which was a similar version for NATO use and the 728, which was essentially a 720 adapted for naval use with appropriate landing gear and structural strengthening.

The more favoured Saunders Roe SR.53 also began the process of further refinement, while wind testing of models continued to provide positive results and a mock-up of the aircraft was completed for official inspection by October 1953. This was followed by construction of the first SR.53 prototype (XD145) beginning in early 1954 at the Saunders-Roe factory on the Isle of Wight. The SR.53 was a compact single-seat aircraft with a clean design and the clipped delta wing had a span of 25 ft (7.62 m) and an area of 274 ft^2 (25.5 m^2). Overall length of the aircraft was 45 ft (13.7 m) and it was propelled by the de Havilland Spectre rocket engine, supplemented by a relatively low-powered Armstrong Siddeley Viper 8 turbojet. This was initially placed below the rocket engine, but that proved unsatisfactory and it was moved to the top. The aircraft's empty weight was calculated at 7,400 lb (3,356 kg) and fully loaded, about 18,400 lb (8,346 kg).

The SR.53 used a conventional tricycle undercarriage and the forward-positioned, pressurised cockpit was well placed to provide the pilot with good visibility. In the initial design, Brennan envisaged the entire cockpit being jettisoned in an emergency and making a parachute landing, but the complexity of this proposal soon gave way to simply fitting a Martin Baker Mk 3 ejector seat. While the SR.53 carried no radar, Brennan was fully aware that it would be very difficult to fly missions without it. However, suitable airborne units were too big to fit into the aircraft and it was clear that a larger aircraft would be needed.

Armament was initially a rocket pack, but this would be replaced by air-to-air missiles and for trial purposes, dummies were attached to wingtip pylons. Estimated performance was a maximum speed of approximately Mach 2.2 at high altitude, with a ceiling of 67,000 ft (20,421 m) and a rate of climb given as standstill to 50,000 ft (15,240 m) in 2m 12 sec.

This aircraft was especially important for survival of the company and it was rather optimistically suggested by company representatives that the first prototype would be ready for its maiden test flight during mid-1954, with production aircraft entering service by 1957.

Soon, the MoS would start to show concern about the project's slow progress and Saunders Roe must have been concerned when they were advised by the MoS in early 1954 of cost cutting measures which reduced the number of SR.53 prototypes on order from 3 to 2.

Somewhat perplexingly, it has proven difficult to find very much official paperwork on the Avro 720 from this period, up to the aircraft's official cancellation in April 1955. But it might be possible that by 1954, the MoS had secretly decided to drop the Screamer and the 720 when the time was right.

While Avro continued to work on the 720 project at a slower pace than Saunders Roe, the MoS may have simply decided to allow this project to continue as a means of maintaining some pressure on Saunders Roe to complete the more favoured aircraft on time. Progress was becoming important, because the RAF were still expected to see flight trials of both aircraft before making a final choice, but it appears that their interest in these fighters was starting to tail off due to continual delays and this was probably causing concern for the MoS. Clearly Saunders Roe were in trouble with development of the SR.53 and in the rush to secure a lucrative government contract, there had been falure to allow for unexpected challenges with the aircraft's advanced design. These included very complex fuel storage issues and big problems with the Spectre engine. While this was obviously de Havilland's responsibility and a reliable, safe rocket engine was crucial to the project, the development of the Spectre had run into serious problems, which reached crisis level when a prototype engine exploded during a ground test. The schedule was simply impossible to adhere to and holding down the cost of this project had also become a major concern. As a consequence, the first overdue test flight in early 1955 was cancelled and because ongoing technical issues had slowed the project right down, it was not until 28 June 1956 that the first prototype (XD145) was moved from Cowes to The Aeroplane and Armament Experimental Establishment at RAF Boscombe Down for final assembly.

A further six months would pass before the Spectre rocket engine and Armstrong Siddeley Viper 8 turbojet were installed. In April 1957, the Spectre rocket engine was tested and this was followed by taxiing trials using the Viper. Finally, the SR.53 took to the air on 16 May 1957, with RAF test pilot Squadron Leader John Stanley Booth DFC (1919–1958) at the controls.

There were no significant problems and Booth reported that the aircraft was pleasant to fly and handled well. The second prototype (XD151) was completed by August of that year and made its first flight on 6 December 1957. Test flights continued, with occasional issues concerning the rocket engine and buffeting, but the trials went fairly well and it was decided that the next stage would involve one of the aircraft being used for air launched missile trials. However, on 5 June 1958, XD145 piloted by Booth crashed during an aborted take-off from the Boscombe Down runway. Exactly what happened would never be properly determined, but the rocket engine malfunctioned in some way, the turbojet lacked adequate power for take-off on its own and Booth is thought to have attempted to reduce the aircraft's speed by releasing the tail parachute. This failed to make any difference and the SR.53 ran off the runway, collided with a concrete approach light and there was a large explosion, which threw Booth from the aircraft while still in the ejector seat, instantly killing him. Trials with XD151 continued, after Lt Cdr Peter 'Sheepy' Lamb (1923–2000) became the chief test pilot for the project. Generally, the flight testing was a

The single-seat Saunders Roe SR.53 (XD145) prototype mixed propulsion interceptor during a test flight. (*SARO Archives*)

success, with the SR.53 achieving supersonic speed several times and on one occasion it climbed to 55,000 ft (16,764 m). When these flights concluded, the SR.53 was transported to the RAF Museum storage facility at Henlow. It remained there for another ten years until it was passed to the Brize Norton Aviation Society, where it was restored to display condition and finally handed over to the RAF Museum at Cosford on 30 November 1981.

SR.53 Special Projects

During the SR.53's development, there were proposals to adapt an existing aircraft or build a new version for classified military and general research purposes. One secret proposal involved a purely rocket powered SR.53 that would be carried beneath an adapted Avro Vulcan bomber and air-launched. The aircraft would then undertake some kind of undisclosed military mission. Following release, the SR.53 would accelerate to supersonic speed, covering a distance of about 100 miles (160 km) very rapidly. Once the operation was completed, the pilot would then glide to a safe landing site or eject. This was obviously not a reconnaissance mission and it may have involved the near-suicidal delivery of a nuclear weapon to a well-protected target. However, during the 1950s, atomic bombs were still fairly substantial in size, so perhaps this concept was based on hopes of future weapon miniaturisation? But even if such an idea had been taken seriously, there would be many technical issues to solve, like the release of a large bomb at supersonic speed. Undoubtedly, a better idea would have been an unmanned, guided version of the SR.53 containing the nuclear device. So is it possible that this rather strange proposal laid some groundwork for the later Blue Steel missile?

Another very ambitious plan called for a special version of the SR.53 capable of reaching the edge of space like the North American X-15. This will be discussed in a following chapter.

The Next Generation

From a very early point in the SR.53 project, Saunders Roe designers and the RAF were fully aware that this aircraft was little more than a proof-of-concept stepping stone to a more advanced design. The SR.53 needed a more powerful turbojet and an improved rocket engine. An advanced airborne radar was essential to intercept high flying bombers, endurance had to be better and the aircraft needed the ability to carry additional, or more advanced weapons. Ideally, an operational aircraft would also have an in-flight refuelling capability and could be easily adaptable for reconnaissance missions. With all this in mind, Brennan made a semi-official approach to the MoS, setting out his ideas for a suitable successor to the SR.53 and assigned a separate design team to begin work on this proposal in 1953.

Brennan was particularly concerned about the need for airborne radar, which was missing from the SR.53 and the Avro 720. Guidance from the ground and reliance on the pilot's vision was unacceptable for any new supersonic combat aircraft given the crucial task of defending the UK against a nuclear air attack. This led him to contact the Royal Radar Establishment (RRE), who introduced him to the AI.23 airborne system, which they had developed and was now being manufactured by Ferranti in Scotland. The system was too big and heavy for the SR.53, but would be an excellent choice for his proposed follow-on interceptor.

Just as important, was the need for better performance, which meant a larger turbojet and afterburner, an improved rocket engine and bigger fuel tanks. When combined with other features like airborne radar, it was clear that the aircraft would be quite substantial in size. After carefully reviewing the initial proposals for the new Saunders Roe interceptor, the MoS decided to fully support development, issuing Specification F.177D to the company, which would soon include OR.337 and naval requirement NR/A.47 for a version adapted for aircraft carrier deployment.

Saunders Roe had already chosen the designation SR.54 for this aircraft, but decided to alter it to SR.177, so it could be linked directly with the official specification. The SR.177 was expected to have a supersonic cruise capability above 30,000 ft (9,114 m), a ceiling of at least 75,000 ft (22,860 m) and it was initially hoped that their next-generation interceptor would become operational with the RAF during 1957, although this was clearly unrealistic.

Aerodynamic testing of scale models was underway and RAE Bedford studied the use of blown flaps at low speeds in their No. 2 Wind Tunnel, using a ¼ scale wing section. This indicated that a useful reduction of speed during take-off and landing could be anticipated for a full sized aircraft, which was welcomed as an essential feature of the aircraft. Work was now underway to complete a mock-up of the SR.177 at Cowes and preparations were being made to start work on pre-production aircraft once the official go-ahead had been received.

With the preliminaries proceeding well and the first SR.53 being prepared for testing at Boscombe Down, the MoS placed an initial order with Saunders Roe on 4 September 1956 for nine SR.177s. These aircraft were issued with the serials XL905–XL907, which would be regarded as prototypes and serials XL920–XL925, for pre-production aircraft. Furthermore, there was now interest in the aircraft from NATO partners and especially the West Germans, who wanted to replace their F-84 and F-86 fighters with a more capable supersonic interceptor.

Some artwork showing the proposed SR.177K, which was intended for use by the Luftwaffe.

A largely wooden mock-up of the SR.177 under construction at Cowes. (*Saunders Roe*)

As anticipated, the SR.177 was somewhat heavier than the SR.53, with an expected empty weight of 14,533 lb. (6,592 kg) and an absolute maximum take-off weight of 28,174 lb (12,780 kg). The aircraft retained broadly similar aerodynamics to the SR.53, although larger in size, having a wingspan of 30.25 ft (9.22 m) when carrying air-to-air missiles on wingtip rails and a wing area of 327 ft^2 (30.4 m^2). Length was expected to be 50 ft (15.2 m) and the height 14 ft (4.26 m). At the front of the deeper fuselage beneath the cockpit, was the air inlet for the afterburning de Havilland PS.50 Gyron Junior turbojet. This was expected to provide a maximum thrust of 14,000 lb (62 kN), which represented an increase of almost eight times the SR.53s turbojet performance.

The very rapid boost to high altitude would be provided by a single de Havilland Spectre 5A rocket engine, providing 10,000 lb (44 kN) thrust. This would allow the aircraft to reach 60,000 ft (18,000 m) in just over 2 minutes from brake release and to briefly sustain altitudes of about 80,000 ft (24,000 m). Maximum speed achieved was in excess of Mach 2, with an expectation of supercruise. The armament as an interceptor was to be two Red Top (Blue Jay Mark 4) missiles, with possibly two more on underwing pylons.

In addition to this version, Brennan's designers developed a modified aircraft for the Royal Navy, with structural and undercarriage strengthening, arrestor gear, an in-flight refuelling capability and the provision to carry extra underwing stores. A third variant for possible RN use, but favoured by West Germany's Luftwaffe would have been fitted with the slightly more powerful Rolls-Royce RA-24R Avon turbojet rated at 14,430 lb (64.18 kN) with afterburner. Two more turbojet-only options were considered, which were specifically intended for ground attack and photo-reconnaissance missions.

Aircraft for the RAF would be designated SR.177R, versions for the RN would be SR.177N and the Luftwaffe model would be the SR.177K. A further order was now issued for 27 SR.177 interceptors, which would be distributed amongst the RAE, RAF and RN.

Because Saunders Roe would be stretched in terms of manufacturing capability with further orders that would amount to several hundred aircraft, the MoS were looking for help from other contractors. The most favoured companies were Armstrong Whitworth and possibly Marshalls of Cambridge. In the case of West German orders for the SR.117K, it was planned to pass initial assembly work to Heinkel, and then licence them to begin manufacturing.

Finally, it is worth mentioning that in 1955, Saunders Roe submitted a proposal for a more advanced version of the SR.177 to the MoS. This was in response to Specification F.155T (with OR.329), that requested an interceptor capable of dealing with Soviet enhanced high altitude bombers. Given the company reference SR.187, this Saunders Roe design was an even bigger version of the SR.177, powered by two afterburning de Havilland PS.52 turbojets (developed from the Gyron) and four Spectre 5 rocket engines below the tailfin. SR.187 was to have a length of 83.5 ft (26.36 m), a wingspan of 51.6 ft (15.7 m), a wing area of 870 ft^2 (80.82 m^2) and a gross weight of about 97,000 lb (43,998 kg). This two-man aircraft was expected to have a maximum speed of about Mach 2.5 and a zoom climb ceiling of at least 75,000 ft (22,860 m). From brakes off, it would reach 60,000 ft (18,288 m) at a range of 80 miles (130 km) in 6 minutes. SR.187 would be equipped with the latest radar system and armed with two or four missiles. One unusual feature was the sliding nose section to improve the pilot's view when landing as the cockpit was flush with the fuselage during flight. Nothing came of this complex design, or the best alternative contenders for F.155T, which were the Fairey FD.3 and an outsider, which was the superb Avro Canada CF-105 Arrow in modified form.

The future had been looking bright for Saunders Roe, but then things took a dramatic turn when a controversial White Paper was produced by Minister for Defence Duncan Sandys on 5 April 1957. This savagely cut back on many advanced projects, including the Saunders Roe SR.177.

An ultimate 1950s proposed development of the Saunders Roe mixed propulsion interceptor. This was the missile armed Mach 2.5 SR.187, which probably progressed little further than a basic concept.

With the stroke of a pen, many British defence contractors were left reeling and the only fighter to survive these draconian cuts was the English Electric Lightning. West Germany remained interested in taking the SR.177K, but with the existing UK orders cancelled, it was no longer viable for the company to be involved with this aircraft as there was insufficient financial support. One year later, the first SR.53 made its initial flight at Boscombe Down, but this dead-end project formally ended in 1960. As a consequence of the White Paper, Saunders Roe were pushed to the edge of collapse, with more that a 1,000 employees being made redundant and the company then moving into hovercraft development and the manufacture of aircraft parts.

Fairey F.124T (Scheme A) Rocket Powered
Crew: 1
Wingspan: 27.5 ft (8.4 m)
Wing area: 387 ft² (36 m²)
Wing sweep (leading edge): 60° inner, 40° outer (estimated)
Length: 52.67 ft (16.1 m)
Height: 10.25 ft (3.1 m)
Empty weight: 8,517 lb (3,863 kg)
Gross weight: 20,307 lb (9,210 kg)
Powerplant: 1 × Screamer rocket engine, producing 8,000 lb (35.6 kN) thrust
6 × solid fuel Rocket boosters for take-off
Maximum speed: supersonic
Ceiling 60,000ft+ (18,288m+)
Rate of climb: 2.2 minutes to 60,000 ft (18,288 m)
Range: N/A
Armament: 44 × air-to-air rockets or 2 × Blue Jay missiles

Hawker P.1089 Rocket Interceptor
Crew: 1
Wingspan: 24.25 ft (7.4 m)
Wing area: 336 ft² (31.2 m²)
Length: 37.75 ft (11.5 m)
Gross weight: 16,000 lb (7,257 kg)
Powerplant: 1 × Spectre rocket engine producing 8,000 lb (35.65 kN) thrust
Maximum speed: supersonic
Ceiling: 60,000ft+ (18,288m+) estimated
Armament: 53 × air-to-air rockets

Short PD.7 Rocket Interceptor
Crew: 1
Wingspan: 30 ft (9.14 m)
Wing area: 430 ft² (39.9 m²)
Wing sweep (leading edge): 60°
Length: 39.75 ft in (12.11 m)
Height: 10.75 ft (3.27 m)
Aspect ratio: 2.14
Empty weight: 8,355 lb (3,789 kg)
Loaded weight: 19,934 lb (9,041 kg)
Powerplant: 1 × Armstrong Siddeley Screamer rocket engine Methanol/water & liquid oxygen with an anticipated 8,000 lb (35.6 kN) thrust
Maximum speed: Mach 0.95 (kph) (Originally hoped for higher than Mach 1)
Rate of climb: 60,000 ft (18,288 m) in 3.72 minutes
Ceiling: 60,000ft+ (18,288m+)
Endurance: 15 minutes (with 10 minutes cruise) estimated
Armament: Rocket pack or possibly 2 × 30 mm ADEN cannon

Short PD.701 Mixed Propulsion
As PD.7, but with the addition of: 2 × Bristol BE.22 Saturn afterburning turbojets, each with an expected static thrust of 4,700 lb (20.9 kN). The BE.22 engine was under development, until the MoS requirement lapsed in 1952 and the project was abandoned; these turbojets would run at almost full RPM during an intercept mission
Total Patrol Time: 18.2 minutes
Rate of climb to 60,000 ft (18,288m+): 1.95 m
Estimated ferry range (using turbojets): 1,200 miles (2,200 km)

Avro 720 Initial Rocket Only
Crew: 1
Wingspan 28.25 ft (8.6 m)
Wing area: 385 ft² (35.7 m²)
Wing sweep (leading edge): 60°
Wing section: RAE 101
Length: 48 ft (14.6 m)
Height: 12 ft (3.65 m)
Empty weight: 6,714 lb (3,045 kg)
Loaded weight: 14,988 lb (6,802 kg)
Landing weight: 6,145 lb (2787 kg)
Powerplant: 1 × Screamer or Spectre rocket engine, rated at 8,000 lb (35.6kn) thrust
Maximum speed: Mach 2
Ceiling: 60,000 ft (18,288 m)
Rate of Climb: 1.96 minutes to 60,000 ft (18,288 m)
Armament 48 2 in rockets

Avro 720 Mixed Propulsion
Crew: 1
Wingspan: 27.3 ft (8.3 m)
Wing area: 360 ft^2 (33.44 m^2)
Wing sweep (leading edge): 60°
Length: 43.13 ft (13.1 m)
Empty weight: 7,812 lb (3,543 kg)
Loaded weight: 17,575 lb (7,972 kg)
Powerplant: 1 × Armstrong Siddeley Screamer liquid-fuelled rocket engine, providing 8,000 lb (35.6 kN) thrust 1 × Armstrong Siddeley Viper 101/ASV 8 turbojet providing 1,640 lb (7.3 kN) thrust
Maximum speed: Mach 2.0
Ceiling: 60,000 ft (18,288 m)
Time to altitude: 1 minute 50 seconds to 40,000 ft (12,200 m)
Armament: 2 × Blue Jay (Firestreak) infrared homing air-to-air missiles

Avro 726 Turbojet Only
Crew: 1
Wingspan: 27.3 ft (8.3 m)
Wing area: 385 ft^2 (35.76 m^2)
Wing sweep (leading edge): 60°
Length: 39.25 ft (12 m)
Empty weight: N/A
Loaded weight: 14,330 lb (6,500 kg) escort configuration
Powerplant: 1 × Armstrong Siddeley P.151 turbojet providing 8,000 lb (36.5 kN) thrust and 10,500 lb (46.7 kN) with afterburner; other engines considered
Maximum speed: Mach 1.5
Ceiling: 55,000 ft (16,764 m)
Armament: 2 × 30 mm ADEN cannon and/or 2 × Blue Jay (Firestreak) infrared homing air-to-air missiles
Avionics: spiral scan Ekco A.I radar 18 in (457 mm) dish or Ferranti radar with 24 in (609 mm) dish

Saunders Roe P.154
Crew: 1
Wingspan 26 ft (7.9 m)
Wing area: 272 ft^2 (25.2 m^2)
Length: 37 ft (11.2 m)
Loaded weight: 14,237 lb (6,458 kg)
Powerplant: 1 × de Havilland Spectre thrust: 8,000 lb (35.6 kN)
Time to 60,000 ft (18,288 m): 1.87 minutes
Maximum speed Mach 2 estimated
Rate of climb: 1.87 minutes to 60,000 ft (18,288 m) estimated
Armament 64 2in rockets

Saunders Roe SR.53
Crew: 1
Wingspan: 25.08 ft (7.65 m) without dummy missiles.
Wing area: 274 ft^2 (25.45 m^2)
Wing sweep (leading edge): 42°
Airfoil: RAE 102
Length: 45 ft (13.7 m)
Height: 10.8 ft (3.29 m)
Empty weight: 7,400 lb (3,356 kg)
Loaded weight: 18,400 lb (8,346 kg)
Powerplant: 1 × de Havilland Spectre rocket engine producing 8,000 lb (35.6 kN) thrust and 1 × Armstrong Siddeley Viper 8 turbojet rated at 1,640 lb (7.3 kN) static thrust
Maximum speed: Mach 2.1
Ceiling: 60,000 ft+ (18,288 m+)
Rate of Climb from standstill to 50,000 ft (15,240 m): 2.2 minutes
Endurance at Full Power: 7 minutes
Armament: 2 × (Dummy) Blue Jay (Firestreak) air-to-air missiles.

Saunders Roe SR.177
Crew: 1
Wingspan: 27.15 ft (8.27 m) without missiles. SR.117N: 30.44 ft (9.28 m)
Wing area: 327 ft^2 (30.37 m^2)
Wing sweep (leading edge): 40°
Length: 50.5 ft (15.4 m)
Height: 14 ft (4.26 m)
Empty weight: 14,533 lb (6,592 kg)
Loaded weight: 25,786 lb (11,696 kg)
Maximum take-off weight: 28,174 lb (12,780 kg)
Powerplant: 1 × de Havilland Spectre 5A liquid-fuelled rocket engine, producing 10,000 lb (44 kN) thrust. RAF version: 1 × de Havilland PS.50 Gyron Junior turbojet with afterburner, producing 14,000 lb (62 kN) thrust. Royal Navy & West German version: 1 × Rolls-Royce RA-24R Avon turbojet rated at 11,250 lb (kN) static and 14,430 (kN) with afterburner
Maximum speed: Mach 2.35
Ceiling: 70,000 ft+ (21,336 m+)
Rate of climb from standstill to 60,000 ft (18,288 m): 2.2 minutes
Endurance at Full Power: 7 minutes
Armament: 2 × Hawker Siddeley Red Top (Firestreak Mark 4) missiles, underwing hardpoints for additional stores
Avionics: AI.23 airborne interception radar

Proposed SR.177 Versions:
SR.117R RAF
SR.117N RN
SR.117K West Germany

6

VTO/VTOL/STOL Projects

Many of the German's impressive wartime aviation developments would influence aircraft designers for years to come. One area directly connected to the previous chapter was for all intents and purposes, a last ditch request by the Reichsluftfahrtsministerium (RLM—German Air Ministry) for new types of low-cost, high performance interceptors capable of slowing Allied bomber raids and dealing with the anticipated arrival of high-altitude Boeing B-29s. The RLM's requirement was known as the Emergency Fighter Programme of July 1944. A number of companies responded with proposals using various forms of propulsion including turbojet, pulsejet, ramjet and rocket. All designs received serious consideration and a number of suggestions went forward for development. However, generating the most interest were simple designs that met RLM needs and offered good production lead times with the lowest possible cost. These were the compact, one-man, daylight, rocket powered interceptors such as the Heinkel P.1077 'Julia', the Junkers EF 127 'Walli,' and later, the Arado E.381, which was a small aircraft launched 'parasite' fighter with some similarities to the Japanese Yokosuka MXY-7 Ohka rocket propelled suicide aircraft. Guided missiles like Wasserfall were also in development, but the technology was complex, expensive and would remain unreliable for perhaps another decade. So the proposed lower cost rocketplanes stood a better chance of success than any of the anti-aircraft guided weapons in development. The astonishingly fast Me 163 had demonstrated, that manned rocket interceptors worked, even if they were fraught with dangers for ground crews and the pilots. While impressive jet propelled warplanes were starting to replace propeller driven types, they were expensive to build and the engines remained unreliable, partly due to wartime shortages of special materials.

Manned rocket interceptors that could be constructed from cheap components by semi-skilled workers in small, dispersed workshops were obviously a way forward, even if they smacked of desperation.

In the case of the torpedo-shaped Heinkel P.1077, this was the RLM's favoured rocket interceptor for development. In service it would be transported by road to an improvised launch site, positioned fairly quickly, fuelled-up and launched from a rail assembly. Once the mission was completed, the P.1077 would make a glide-landing on to a grass recovery area.

The Heinkel P.1077 "Julia" rocket powered interceptor, which was the RLM's first choice for this type of aircraft in the 1944 Emergency Fighter Programme. This retouched photograph may show a completed mock-up of the aircraft.

Alternatively, there was the Junkers EF.127, which appears to have been designed to take-off from a runway or a suitable stretch of autobahn using a jettisonable trolley assisted by solid fuel rocket boosters. That said, it seems likely that some form of upright rail launch was considered. Like the P.1077, this aircraft would be equipped with a basic retractable skid system to facilitate landing.

The Arado E.381 was something of a scaled down version of the initial Heinkel P.1077, with the pilot in a prone position. It would be carried into combat beneath an adapted Arado Ar 234C jet bomber, released at altitude and flown under the power of its Walter rocket engine. After mission completion, the small aircraft would glide back to base and land on a retractable skid.

Despite not being approached to develop a rocket powered interceptor, Dr Eric Bachem still submitted a proposal to the RLM. This drew heavily on Bachem's earlier work developing the Fi-166 concept and various ideas he discussed with his friend von Braun, who provided him with considerable advice and assistance.

Bachem had left Fieseler in early 1942 to set up Bachem Werke, which was a small company manufacturing spare parts and components for fighter aircraft. However, Bachem wanted to expand into producing a simple VTO rocket interceptor known as the BA-20, which he spent considerable time developing. Initially, the RLM was less than enthusiastic about another proposal for a rocket interceptor, but Bachem somehow secured the support of SS Reichsführer Heinrich Himmler and convinced him that the aircraft was essential for future air defence. As a consequence, Himmler ordered the construction of 150 interceptors, which would be paid for from SS funds and this was rapidly followed by an additional order from the Luftwaffe for another 50 aircraft. Nobody apart from Hitler would dream of arguing with Himmler and full development began immediately at Bachem Werke. As a consequence, work on the Heinkel

Dr Erich Bachem (1906–1960) at Kassel-Waldau in 1938. He became Technical Director of Gerhard Fieseler Werke at Peenemünde and was responsible for developing the Fi-103 (V-1) flying bomb. After setting up his own production company for aircraft spare parts and components, he developed the Ba 349A Natter manned rocket interceptor. (*Archiv der Gerhard-Fieseler-Stiftung*)

P.1077 and Junkers EF 127 projects slowed right down. Heinkel diverted most of their engineers to other tasks and only two unpowered prototype rocket interceptors were completed by the end of the war. In the case of Junkers, they appear to have simply abandoned the EF 127.

Arado continued to work on their E.381 parasite fighter, undertaking wind tunnel tests, building several airframes and a wooden mock-up which was briefly suspended below an Arado Ar 234C jet bomber, although this is as far as project went before the war ended.

However, there was a price to be paid for securing contracts to develop and build the BA-20 interceptor. Bachem would have to deliver what he promised in terms of its capability, the price was non-negotiable and there would be no acceptable excuses for serious development or production delays. In December 1944, Himmler passed control of the project to Waffen SS Obergruppenführer Hans Kammler (1901-1945), who enjoyed a fearsome reputation for getting results whatever the consequences. Bachem had calculated that each complete aircraft would take about 1,000 man-hours of labour to complete using relatively unskilled workers operating in small dispersed workshops, but the time allowed appears to have been cut to 600 man-hours before too long probably as an indication of growing pressure from the SS.

The design accepted for development was smaller and lighter than the initial BA-20, receiving the new designation Ba 349A and the name Natter (Adder). The airframe would mainly be built from wood and once completed it was fitted out with internal components and the Walter rocket engine. Then, it would undergo a brief test before being transported by road to a suitable launch site in the vicinity of a strategic target.

Solid fuel boosters would be attached to assist the vertical launch from a simple metal framework. The boosters would be jettisoned once the aircraft gained sufficient altitude, with the take-off being largely automated, using radio guidance to the target. It was thought that a relatively inexperienced pilot could fly the aircraft, which was in reality little more than a manned missile. Once in flight, the Ba 349A would climb at an impressive rate, expected to be about 30,000 ft (9,144 m) per minute. The maximum calculated speed was 560 mph (900 kph), with a ceiling of 52,000 ft (15,849 m) and an expected range of about 37 miles (59 km).

The plan was to arc over enemy aircraft and as the interceptor came within range, the pilot would attack by firing a salvo of 24 Föhn (Storm) 73 mm unguided air-to-air rockets, or alternatively 33 R4M 55 mm folding fin rockets, contained in the nose section. The Ba 249A would now dive as its fuel was exhausted and the pilot would finally level out at about 10,000 ft (3,048 m) altitude, and bale-out. At the same time, the tail section would separate and the engine section would descend by parachute for recovery and re-use, providing it remained undamaged, although the early tests were not especially encouraging. Altogether, the entire interception mission would be completed in a few minutes.

Bachem's vertically launched Ba 349A was 18.75 ft (5.7 m) in length, with a wingspan of 11.83 ft (3.60 m) and fully fuelled it weighed 4,800 lb (2,200 kg). Power was provided by a Walter HWK 109-509A rocket engine of 3,750 lb (16.6 kN) thrust, chosen for all the other Emergency Fighter Programme proposals. This was supplemented by four strap-on Schmidding 553 solid fuel boosters, each providing an additional 1,000 lb (4.4 kN) thrust. Initially, wind tunnel trials of Ba 349A models were undertaken at Braunschweig, up to Mach .95. Once completed and judged satisfactory, work began on the construction of several pre-production airframes at Bachem's factory at Waldsee in the Black Forest. Progress was rapid and the first glide-flight took place on 3 November 1944 at Neuberg on the Danube, with the initial prototype being towed behind a Heinkel He-111 to an altitude of about 10,000 ft (3,048 m) and released. To maintain balance, the engine was replaced by ballast and the test pilot Flugkapitan Erich Klöckner (1913-2003) reported that the aircraft handled well and the escape procedure was satisfactory. Klöckner made a further three test flights and Flugkapitan Hans Zübert (1919-1999) made the fifth and final glide-flight on 14 February 1945, reporting that the prototype Natter handled surprisingly well.

Meanwhile, unmanned rocket launches were underway at the Ochsenkopf military training site, with the first of 11 tests commencing on 22 December 1944, using the additional solid fuel booster rockets. Not all were satisfactory, but the pressure from the SS to have the aircraft in operation was increasing, with growing concerns about the imminent deployment of high-altitude USAAF B-29 bombers to Europe. Finally, the first manned, powered flight was undertaken on 1 March 1945. Unfortunately, Bachem's test pilot Lothar Siebert (1922–1945) was killed when a serious technical problem arose. Despite this setback, it is claimed (but unconfirmed) that three further manned test launches took place, which all proved successful.

Finally in April 1945, the first batch of ten Ba 349A Natters were deployed to a site at Kircheim on Teck to intercept Allied daylight bombers. This was apparently given the code name Operation Krokus. The first three Ba 349As were fuelled-up and armed, while the pilots waited for orders to launch, but the US 10th Armoured Division were approaching the site and the ground crews were forced to destroy the aircraft, thus preventing them from falling into enemy hands. At the end of the war, an improved version of the interceptor called the Ba 349B was entering production. The aircraft provided a greater rate of climb, higher top speed of 630 mph (1,013 kph) and extended endurance. It was also proposed that two recoverable 30 mm MK 108 cannon might be fitted to supplement the 24 Foehn 73 mm unguided air-to-air rockets. Yet a further proposal was the Ba 349C, intended for rail launch from the back of a suitable vehicle or possibly the deck of a ship, but this never progressed beyond a study.

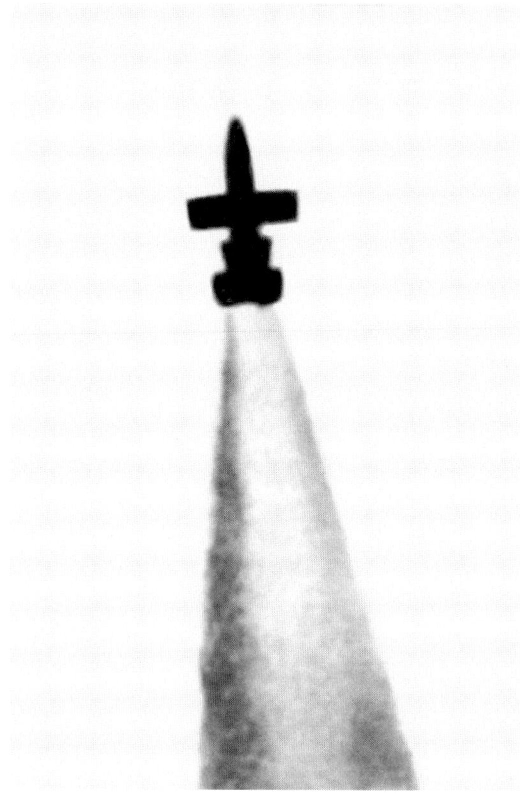

Left: An unmanned Natter prototype is prepared for launch at Ochsenkopf. The exact date is unknown.

Right: This launch of a Natter is thought to show one of the unmanned aircraft lifting off with booster assistance.

Most of the factory aircraft were destroyed at the end of the war, but four examples of the Ba 349A were secured by US forces at Sankt Leonhard im Pitztal, Austria and one sample aircraft which had been transported to a new production site in Thuringia fell into Soviet hands.

French troops occupied Waldsee on 25 April 1945 and took over the Bachem-Werk. It is not clear if they were aware of exactly what the facility had been used for at that time. Nobody was entirely sure what happened to Eric Bachem when the war ended, but it has been suggested that the Americans tried to track him down so he could be sent to the US under Operation Overcast. In fact, Bachem managed to escape to Sweden and from there, Argentina. In 1952, he returned to West Germany and became technical director of an engineering company. It appears that he never passed on any information about his work for Fieseler or development of the rocket interceptor directly to the Allies. That aside, a good deal of technical data about the Natter was secured and shared among Western Allies although no known example of Bachem's interceptor was ever transported to the UK. However, many British engineers and designers took great interest in aircraft like the Me 163B, the Bachem Ba 349A and various exotic design proposals like the VTOL Focke-Wulf Triebflügel (Thrust Wing) fighter. It seemed obvious that a vertically launched jet or rocket powered fighter that could operate from an improvised site or perhaps a ship might be the next big step forward. Combined with supersonic speed it looked like the perfect solution to air defence needs. At the same time, the helicopter was coming of age and this also hinted at the possibility of flat riser combat/transport aircraft that were able to take-off and land without the need for a runway, perhaps by swivelling propellers or jet engines to provide lift.

One of the first British companies to start design work on a VTO interceptor was Fairey Aviation. Soon after the conclusion of the war in Europe, they began to receive an approved share of captured German aviation research material. In addition to this, the well-known German flying wing designer Reimar Horten (1915–1994) was brought to England and assigned to work for Fairey. However, there were problems with this arrangement and hostility from the company staff, which eventually led to Horten being returned to Germany. Despite bad relations, the British engineers were very interested in Germany's flying wing and delta research and the company's chief designer Herbert Eugene Chaplin (1896–1979) was undoubtedly influenced by the documentation in his possession and discussions with Horten, which encouraged him to produce an initial proposal in 1946 for a twin jet-engined flying wing VTO concept. Although this would have been a research aircraft if built, it was presented in documentation as a shipboard fighter.

The single-seat aircraft would be launched from a mounting positioned on the side of an aircraft carrier, but could also be flown from a suitable land site or air base. Once the mission was completed, it would make a conventional horizontal landing. This proposal was initially filed as a UK patent application (733770) in June 1946, although it would be some years before the documents were disclosed. The patent probably shows what was initially called the Fairey Type K design. The fuselage was relatively short and stubby, somewhat reminiscent of the Saab J 29, which had been partly based on wartime German research and development. The Type K was a tailless swept wing jet fighter, powered by two side-by-side Rolls-Royce AJ65s (the proposed Avon), with air drawn from two nose inlets. Maximum thrust was estimated at 6,500 lb (28.9 kN) per engine which would have been inadequate for VTO with the take-off weight estimated at 13,500 lb (6,123 kg). While there are vague suggestions in some original documentation that sufficient jet engine thrust was available for VTO, it's also the case that Chaplin started this project anticipating rocket assisted take-off and was fully aware that turbojets were in an early stage of development and needed to improve much further before they could be used for a vertical launch.

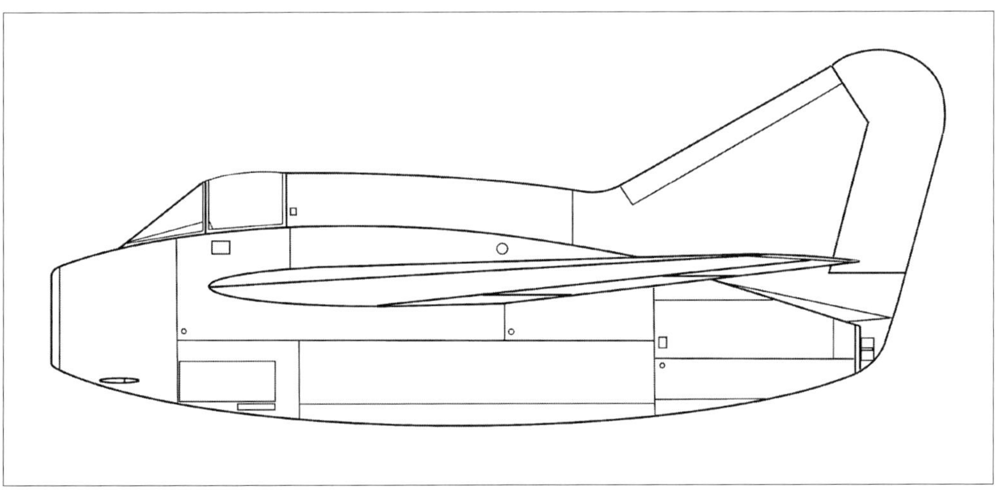

An early Chaplin design for a VTO fighter based on the Type K proposal.

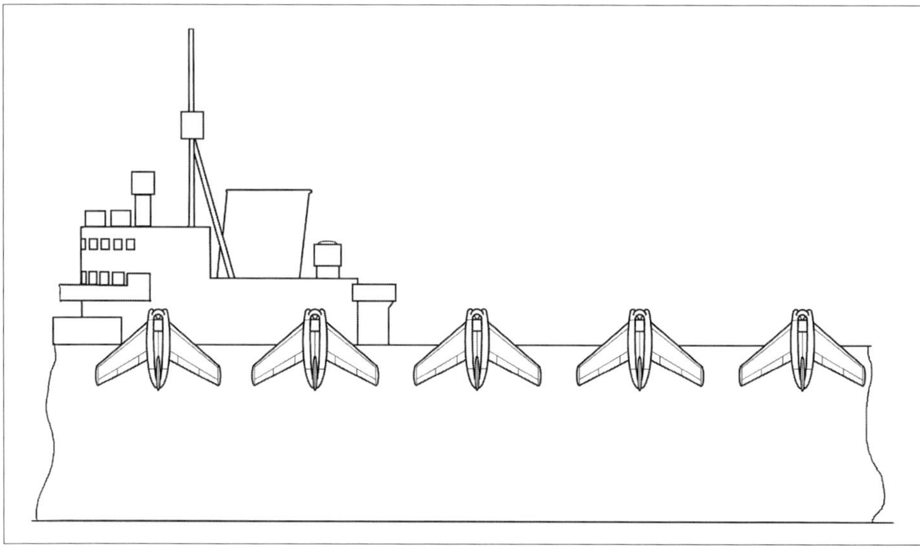

Herbert Chaplin's VTO flying wing fighters mounted on the sides of a carrier and ready for launch. (*Herbert Chaplin/Restoration Bill Rose*)

Once airborne, the Type K had an estimated maximum speed of 650 mph (1,046 kph) at sea level. Armament was expected to be two 30 mm cannon. Some drawings show this tailless, swept wing twin jet fighter suspended over the side of an aircraft carrier for vertical launch. Chaplin made the entire cockpit swivel forward by 90° when the aircraft was in an upright position for VTO, so the pilot would remain sitting upright during launch. There is nothing in the available documents to explain how the aircraft lands back on the carrier and it does not appear to use a conventional undercarriage, but might have been fitted with one. However, a second UK Patent (761230) applied for in May 1952 shows a similar aircraft in slightly more detail, now equipped with a rather complicated retractable skid undercarriage and it was suggested that a large landing mat arrangement could be used at the stern of a ship to capture a returning aircraft. A complicated retractable undercarriage arrangement is also described that would allow the aircraft to take-off and land in an upright position and this kind of system would also allow take-off and landings in a conventional horizontal manner. An aircraft with this capability may have been intended for naval use and possibly called the Type N and Chaplin also suggested the construction of a sub-scale experimental glider based on his initial designs with a maximum weight of about 5,420 lb (2,376 kg).

The MoS was approached to fund continuing development of the Type K proposal in mid-1946 and although they expressed a general interest in the concept, it failed to generate a great deal of enthusiasm for development. Chaplin then undertook a substantial revision of the aircraft, replacing the swept wing with a clipped delta, including a new design of cockpit, some revision of the tail fin and a different propulsion system. This aircraft called the Type R would now be fitted with a single Rolls-Royce Derwent V, which was a downsized version of the Rolls-Royce Nene, producing 3,500 lb (15.56 kN) of thrust. With a gross weight of about 6,800 lb (3,084 kg), there was no possibility of VTO using this turbojet and it was suggested that four rocket engines would be positioned on each side of the Nene's exhaust outlet. Most of the initial artwork fails to show this, perhaps for security reasons, as the project was considered top secret.

Early artwork showing a future ship-launched VTO fighter based on the Type R. (*Fairey*)

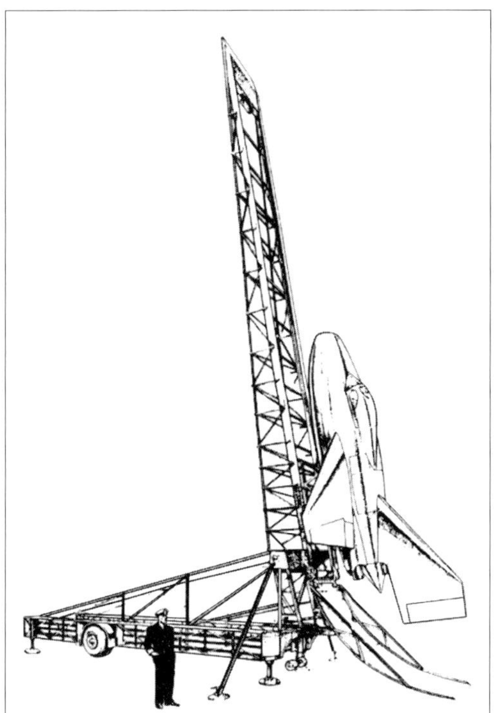

A drawing of the Fairey Type R on a launch ramp, prepared for VTO. (*Fairey*)

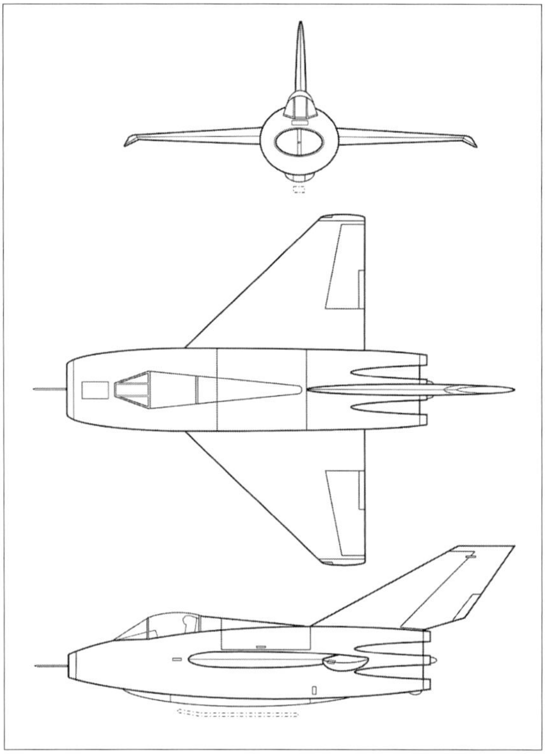

The original design for the Fairey Type R, vertical launched one-man aircraft, utilising a retractable landing skid.

The Type R proposal was submitted to the MoS in early 1947 and they liked the idea of using this design for delta wing research, as opposed to VTO development. So Specification E.10/47 was issued and Fairey were contracted to construct three prototypes. The aircraft continued to evolve with a slightly more powerful Rolls-Royce Derwent 8 jet engine being selected. Other changes included a modest revision to the overall dimensions and the addition of a tailplane section to correct pitching problems. Serials were assigned to these aircraft and the first completed would be VX350, followed by VX364 and VX375.

Because this aircraft was now required for aerodynamic testing, it would be equipped with a conventional tricycle undercarriage and the rear fuselage sections intended to accommodate rocket propulsion units for VTO were faired in. Work on the first prototype VX350 was underway by April 1948 and assembly began in August 1948 at the company's Heaton Chapel facility, Greater Manchester, with the aircraft receiving the new name Fairey Delta One (FD.1) While Chaplin's ideas for a VTO interceptor maintained limited interest within the MoS, they finally decided to fund trials of small VTO rocket powered test models, which were based on the Fairey Type R and built at Heston. These remote-controlled vehicles were normally referred to as the Fairey-Heston VTOs (or sometimes Fairey-Heston Deltas).

The compact radio controlled model had a 7 ft (2.13 m) wingspan and a 48° leading edge. Propulsion was provided by an RAE developed and Fairey manufactured liquid fuel Beta-1 rocket engine that utilised two 900 lb (4 kN) thrust chambers. It was fuelled with a mixture of HT peroxide and methanol hydrazine that would normally be exhausted within one minute. In addition, two jettisonable solid fuel rocket boosters were fitted to assist the launch;

A Fairey-Heston pilotless test vehicle undergoing pre-flight checks in a workshop at Woomera, Australia.

One of the Fairey-Heston rocket powered VTO models is test launched at Woomera, Australia.

each provided an additional 600 lb (2.66 kN) of thrust. The model was equipped with elevons and a tail rudder, with an autopilot controlling pitch and yaw and a telemetry link to the control centre. The first flight test of a Fairey-Heston VTO took place from a ship anchored in Cardigan Bay during 1949. However, two accidents and poor weather would result in the operation being transferred to Woomera, Australia, where trials continued until 1953. By this time, the idea of a rocket assisted VTO interceptor had largely been abandoned, although useful data was obtained for missile development.

Fairey FD.1

Running in parallel to Fairey–Heston's model programme was development and construction of the FD.1, which proceeded without too many problems. Once the first FD.1 (VX350) prototype had been largely completed in early 1950 at the company's Chapel Stockport factory, it was taken by road to Fairey-Heston's test facility at Manchester's Ringway Airport for final assembly. Starting on 12 May 1950, VX350 made several high-speed taxi runs along the 4,200 ft (1,280 m) main

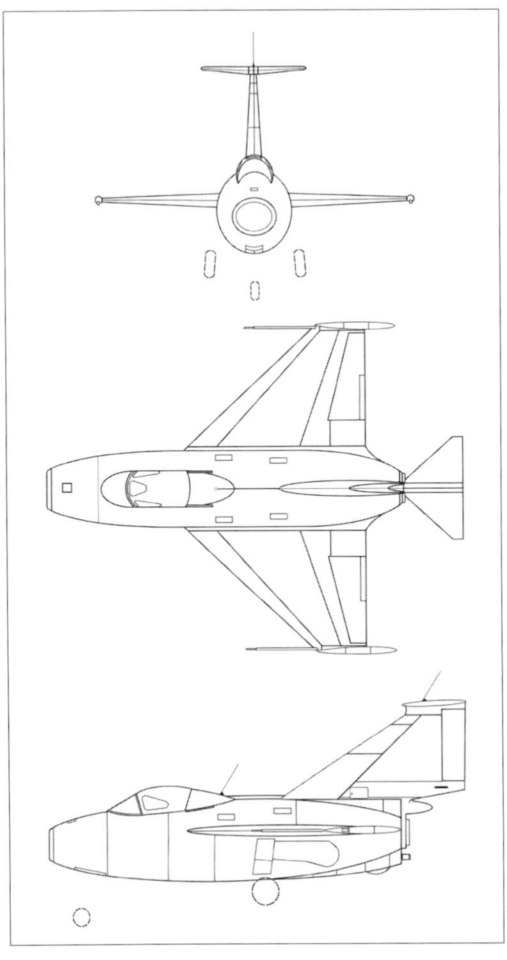

3-view drawing of the FD.1 in its final revised form.

The Fairey FD.1 suffers some damage during a landing accident in September 1951.

runway, undertaken by Fairey's chief test pilot Group Captain R. Gordon Slade (1912–1981) and his deputy Peter Twiss. The aircraft was then partially dismantled and transported by road to the Aeroplane and Armament Experimental Establishment (AAEE) at RAF Boscombe Down. Further taxi runs followed and the maiden flight was finally undertaken on 12 March 1951, by Gordon Slade. What soon became obvious were issues with the triangular shaped, horizontal control surface on top of the tail-fin which was intended to stop serious pitching as the aircraft gathered speed. Further flights would point to stability problems that were characterized as 'dangerous,' with the maximum speed limited to a rather pedestrian 345 mph (555 kph).

The aircraft was generally considered difficult to fly and there were fuel supply problems which needed to be resolved. After a landing accident in September 1951, the FD.1 underwent repair and further modifications, including the removal of the leading edge slats, changes to the tail housings originally intended for additional rocket engines and elimination of the wingtip anti-spin parachutes. Trials resumed during May 1953, but the usefulness of the aircraft remained in question and official enthusiasm for a basic VTO interceptor had declined considerably. As the two remaining prototype airframes approached completion, it was decided to scrap them. FD.1 continued to fly, but on 6 February 1956, there was a fairly serious crash-landing at Boscombe Down and the aircraft was almost written off. Some work was done to repair the damage, but FD.1 (VX350) was finally taken to the Shoeburyness Weapons Range in October 1956 and used for target practice. What remained of the aircraft was finally sold off as scrap. In retrospect, it seems that there was little to like about the FD.1 and the amount of useful data provided by it was somewhat limited.

Avro VTOL Tailsitters

The Avro VTOL tailsitter research programme was on a significantly higher level than the Fairey VTO interceptor had beent. It was a classified study undertaken in the early 1950s and essentially an alternative to the associated Project Y semi-disc shaped VTOL interceptor developed in Canada by the company's subsidiary.

Propeller-driven VTOL tailsitting aircraft had been envisaged in the 1930s, with Austrian engineer Otto Heinrich Muck (1892-1956) patenting a design prior to the Second World War. In 1939, the American inventor Lloyd Hugo Leonard also produced several very advanced looking tailsitter concepts. He hoped to attract the interest of the US Army Air Corps and the US Navy for further development, but Leonard's plans were rejected as too unusual. Then during the Second World War, the VTO Bachem Natter was developed in Germany and advanced VTOL tailsitters such as the Focke-Wulf Triebflügel were at the design stage.

After the cessation of hostilities, research into this type of aircraft was soon underway in America and Britain, with Avro being one of the larger UK companies to take a serious interest. They began a detailed study, which was assigned the company reference P.724 and the first proposal completed in early 1953 was for a rather unattractive looking tailsitter powered by a single afterburning turbojet and flown from a less than satisfactory prone position. This was a daylight interceptor guided to its target by ground control, that had no provision for an on-board radar system. Armament is not specified, but it is possible that air-to-air rockets were considered, perhaps later replaced by two heat-seeking missiles carried on wingtip launch rails. At rest, the aircraft would stand in an upright position, supported on the ground by a shock absorbing leg carried in the single tailfin and two further legs with shock absorbers that retracted

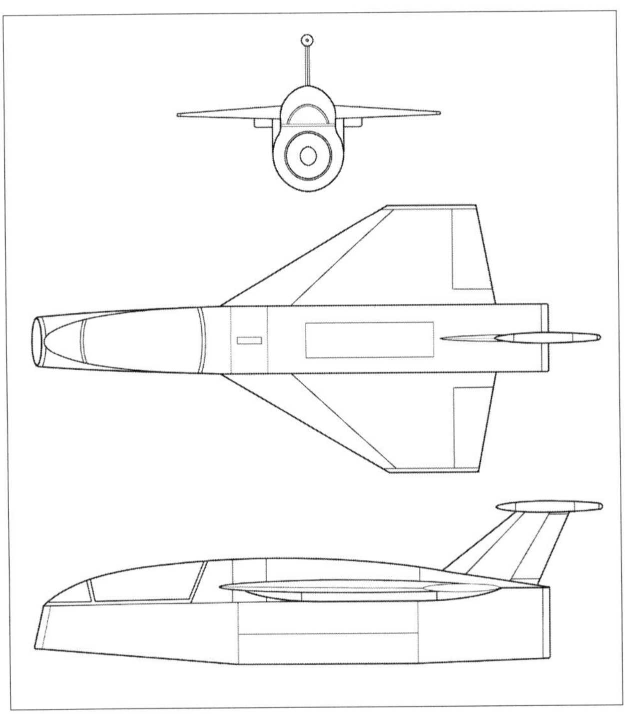

Version 1 of the rather unattractive Avro P.724 VTOL interceptor shown in this drawing was abandoned when it was realised that a single engine provided insufficient power for reliable VTOL operations.

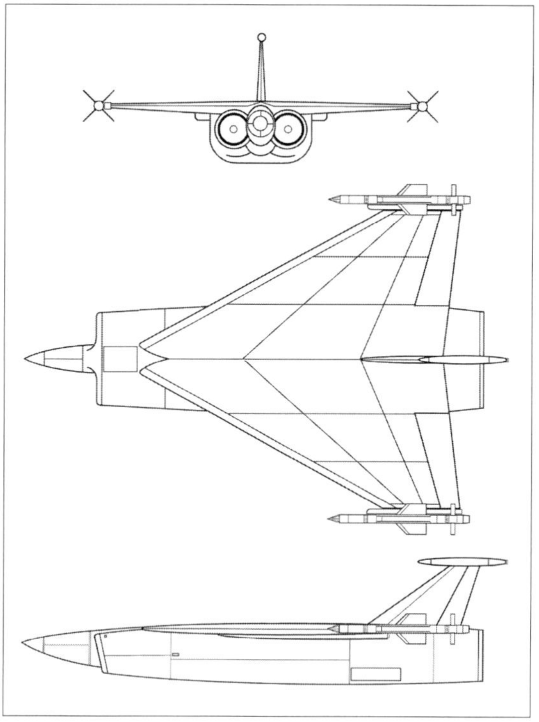

Avro's twin engined Version 2 of the P.724 VTOL interceptor is believed to have reached the stage of models being wind tunnel tested. It was regarded as an alternative to the Project Y VTOL fighter project being undertaken by the company's Canadian subsidiary.

into fairings along the wing roots. Propulsion was to be provided by a single, very sophisticated Rolls-Royce RB.106 axial flow turbojet engine, fed from a nose intake. This engine was still in the experimental stage, but promised a new standard of performance. It was expected to have an anticipated static thrust of 15,000 lb (66 kN), rising to 21,800 lb (97 kN) with the afterburner, which formed an integral feature of the design.

At low speed, the P.724 would be controlled using vanes to direct the exhaust stream and compressor bled air channelled to the wingtips. In normal flight, elevons and a rudder would be used. The Avro P.724 had an overall length of 32.5 ft (9.9 m) and a wingspan of 16 ft (4.87 m). The aircraft's exact take-off weight is unclear, but it was expected to be in the region of 18,000–20,000 lb (8,164–9,071 kg).

Mach 2 performance at altitude was anticipated, with a ceiling of about 60,000 ft (18,288 m). Take-off and landing could only be undertaken in an upright position and this would burn rather a lot of fuel, so endurance would be limited, perhaps no better than the rocket powered or mixed propulsion interceptors under investigation at around the same time. However, the real problem with the P.724 was the thrust-to-weight ratio which had little spare capacity for variations in operating conditions or any allowance for the possibility of carrying alternative weapons or additional equipment. It is possible that jettisonable rocket boosters were considered, but the Avro designers soon realised that their concept was seriously flawed and could not continue in its existing form.

Subsequently, the Avro design team working on this project undertook a major revision of the P.724, effectively scrapping the original proposal. While the same company reference was retained, the new design was totally different, using two side-by-side afterburning RB.106

engines with air intakes on either side of the pressurised cockpit. As with the first proposal, the pilot would fly the aircraft from a prone position and there was no mention of how they might escape in an emergency, unless the whole cockpit section was designed to detach. Visibility for the pilot is hard to determine and the suggestion that this interceptor would be able to carry a radar dish in the nose seems impossible.

The aircraft could be described as a clipped delta with a 60° leading edge and a single tailfin with a nacelle to accommodate a dampened undercarriage strut. The undercarriage arrangement was largely the same as planned for the earlier single-engine design, comprising of the tailfin strut and two fully retractable shock absorbing legs carried in nacelles below the wing roots. Overall length of the revised P.724, was 37 ft (11.2 m), with a wingspan of 24 ft (7.3 m). Take-off weight was expected to be about 24,500 lb (11,113 kg), which included 8,000 lb (3,628 kg) of fuel carried in the wings and central tanks. With two high performance engines, this overcame any initial concerns about VTOL performance. Armament would comprise of two Blue Jay (later called Firestreak) heat-seeking air-to-air missiles mounted on wing tip launch rails.

Avro believed that the twin-engined P.724 would be capable of Mach 2.5, with a service ceiling of 60,000 ft+ (18,288 m+). By June 1953, several P.724 models had been tested in Avro UK's wind tunnel although this project never progressed as far as the exotic Project Y interceptor, developed at Avro-Canada.

The P.724 was certainly less complex than the Project Y designs and perhaps Avro just wanted to have an alternative concept under consideration if there was an unexpected surge of UK/NATO interest in VTOL tailsitters. This never came about and the Avro P.724 was moved onto the back burner and eventually forgotten about. The promising RB.106 also met with eventual cancellation in 1957, but it seems possible that some of the technology found its way into the Orenda Iroquois engine developed for the Avro-Canada CF-105 Arrow.

Rolls-Royce VTOL Engine Development

In the late 1940s, Rolls-Royce was looking at practical ways to facilitate VTOL by using jet power, under the leadership of their chief scientist Dr Alan Arnold Griffith. He had first considered the idea of using a jet engine for vertical lift during the Second World War and could now see an obvious way forward.

The company had been developing an expendable, very compact axial flow turbojet known as the RB.82 'Soar' for missile propulsion and Griffith thought this design could be modified to become an engine suitable for VTOL use by fitting new bearings and making several alterations to ensure reliable oil flow in an upright position. Development work moved rapidly to testing and the newly named RB.108 turbojet used an eight stage compressor driven by a two stage turbine supported by three bearings. The engine had an overall length of 46.5 in (118 cm), a weight of 269 lb (122 kg) and a maximum thrust of 2,130 lb (9.47 kN).

At the same time, Rolls-Royce began design work on a manned test platform known as the Thrust Measuring Rig (TMR), to explore VTOL and hover capabilities. The TMR was powered by two Rolls-Royce Nene turbojets, ducting their exhausts downwards at the platform's centre. Stabilisation of the TMR was provided by a reaction control system using (what were called) puffers, fed with air bled from the compressor stages of the engines.

This example of a Rolls-Royce RB.108 turbojet engine can be found at the RAF Museum, Cosford. (*Nimbus227*)

Construction was soon approved and assembly of the first of two rigs with the reference XA314, was completed by spring 1953. The pilot sat on top of a tubular steel framework enclosing two jet engines, and this was supported by legs. As a consequence of the TMR's unusual appearance, it soon received the name Flying Bedstead, which was adopted by everyone involved in the project. The first trial flight was undertaken on 3 July 1953 at Hucknall Aerodrome, Nottinghamshire, although this was little more than a small lift upwards. A second lift-off was attempted three days later by test pilot Wing-Commander Harvey Hayworth (1910-1959), but there were obvious problems and it was realised that a substantial gantry was needed to safely tether the rig during further tests. The gantry was completed quite quickly and testing resumed on 19 August 1953, but it would be almost a year before the first completely free flight was considered safe to undertake and this was made by the company's chief test pilot Ronald Thomas Shepherd OBE (1896–1955). However, the TMR was an extremely demanding machine to control, with the engines suffering from throttle lag aside from many other tricky considerations like height control. The power-to-weight ratio was only just adequate to allow lift-off, with the engines providing a maximum thrust of about 8,100 lb (36 kN), with approximately 8 per cent of this being lost to the puffers.

When fully loaded with 1,385 lb (628 kg) of fuel, the rig weighed 7,500 lb (3,401 kg), so there was quite a narrow performance margin, reduced a little further by exhaust gases being recirculated through the engines. This was a problem that would plague the development of many VTOL designs. Furthermore, all the TMR's fuel would be exhausted within 11 minutes. Trials continued until the TMR was moved to RAE Farnborough in late 1954, where a series on modifications were made and further testing undertaken. Then in June 1956, it was relocated once more to RAE Bedford, where development of the automatic stabilisation system took place.

The Rolls-Royce Thrust Measuring Rig (TMR), better known to most people as the Flying Bedstead. It was first tested on 3 July 1953 at Hucknall Aerodrome, Nottinghamshire by the company's chief test pilot Ronald Thomas Shepherd OBE.

In July 1956, XJ314 began further testing and finally crashed on 16 September 1957, whilst being piloted by RAE test pilot Wing Commander Stan Hubbard (1921–2015). On 29 November 1957, the second TMR, (XK416), was largely destroyed during a test flight at Hucknall Aerodrome, resulting in the death of Wing Commander Henry Larsen (1916–1957), who was piloting the aircraft for the first time. Some of the parts from this rig were used to rebuild the XJ314, but it was taken out of service and currently resides at the London Science Museum.

So, to briefly sum up on the Rolls-Royce RB.108 and TMR, these two different pieces of technology would rapidly advance the development of VTOL flat risers, which would be demonstrated by another British experimental project that incorporated all aspects of the RAE's research work, namely the Short SC.1.

Short SC.1

In September 1953, the MoS issued a number of aircraft contractors with a tender request (ER.143T) for a VTOL research aircraft. It is unclear exactly who responded, but there were plans put forward by Percival Aircraft of Luton (later Hunting Aircraft) for a design called P.94. The MoS rejected this, on the ground of Percival lacking sufficient experience to develop and build the aircraft. Avro also submitted a proposal, which appears to have suggested making major modifications to the delta wing Avro 707B (VX790) already in service with the RAE at Boscombe Down. Alternatively, Avro may have offered to build a new broadly similar aircraft as a VTOL test-bed. The Avro VTOL aircraft would have been equipped with six RB.108 engines mounted vertically in the centre of the fuselage with exhaust diverters on the two rear turbojets to facilitate forward flight. The cockpit canopy would also be replaced with new sections to aid the pilot's visibility and the aircraft would have been fitted with a robust, fixed position tricycle undercarriage, raising the aircraft to about twice its normal height from the ground. No further information is available about this design, but it was rejected by the MoS for unknown reasons.

Shorts also submitted a proposal with the company reference PD.11 that was conceived by David Keith-Lucas's design team in Belfast. It was judged by the MoS to be the best concept and Shorts were issued with a contract to build two aircraft on 15 October 1954. These prototype test vehicles would represent a substantial step forward from the relatively crude TMR. They would be equipped with advanced technology such as a fly-by-wire system and able to clearly demonstrate the aircraft's behaviour and handling during transition from vertical lift to horizontal flight. Various anticipated issues would be highlighted and it would hopefully allow rapid advances in automated control of transition. The PD.11 reference was now changed to SC.1 and official serials XG900 and XG905 were issued.

The design of this aircraft would quickly evolve in some areas, mainly evident in the cockpit which was equipped with controls somewhat similar to a helicopter. The initial canopy also resembled a soap bubble type of enclosure rather like a Bell 47 helicopter, which provided excellent visibility for the pilot. However, this was soon modified to a more conformal shape, with a metal lower fuselage section reaching around the nose. The aircraft's overall length (excluding the

A scale model of the proposed adaptation of an Avro 707 to the role of a VTOL testbed. This can be found on display in the excellent Avro Heritage Museum at Manchester.

boom) was 25.5 ft (7.77 m), with a wingspan of 23.5 ft (7.16 m), a wing area of 211.5 ft^2 (19.65 m^2) and a leading edge sweep of 54°. It was a very compact tailless delta with four RB.108 lift engines designed to swivel that were positioned vertically in the centre of the airframe. A fifth horizontal RB.108 turbojet in the rear of the fuselage would provide the propulsion for normal flight and all engines were connected to an air bleed system providing reaction control at the front, rear and wingtips. In horizontal flight, the four vertical turbojets used for lift would be shut down, with compressor air from the horizontal engine being used to restart them when needed.

Most of the aircraft was built from aluminium alloy, apart from some sections of the engine bays made from titanium and a few parts made from steel alloy. SC.1 was never intended for high speed flight, so the tricycle undercarriage was fixed in position to reduce weight and mechanical complexity. Maximum VTO take-off weight was 7,800 lb (3,538 kg), with the four lift engines providing 8,520 lb (37.9 kN) thrust. The single RB.108 turbojet used for level flight provided 2,130 lb (9.47 kN) thrust and the maximum speed available was a modest 246 mph (395 kph), although the SC.1 was never intended to be anything much more than a VTOL test-bed. The first SC.1 (XG900) was completed at Short's Belfast factory in November 1956, although it lacked the lift engines and was only fitted with a single horizontal RB.108. Taxiing trials began at Belfast during December 1956 and the aircraft was then transported (partly by sea) to Boscombe Down, where the first conventional flight was made on 2 April 1957 by company test pilot Tom Brooke-Smith. SC.1 is said to have proved more difficult to handle than anticipated. The second SC.1 (XG905) was ready for testing in May 1958, by which time the project had become public knowledge. Four Roll-Royce RB.108 lift engines were installed in this aircraft and hovering tests were soon underway at Belfast.

With the aircraft tethered to a substantial gantry, the first piloted jet lift was completed on 26 May 1958. These tests continued without any major problems and the first untethered hover took place on 25 October 1958. By the following year, XG905 had undergone a number of engineering modifications and was moved to RAE Bedford. The main concern for the VTOL lift system was ingestion of hot exhaust gas and debris, although the high rate of fuel consumption (when running all five engines) and the pilot's workload were also serious issues. In the case of XG900, once initial trials at Boscombe Down had been completed, it was returned to Short's factory in Belfast for installation of the lift engines and various minor modifications. By the start of summer 1960, XG900 was ready to resume testing, with upgraded undercarriage shock absorbers and new automatic engine covers. Meanwhile, XG905 had completed its first successful transition on 6 April 1960 and would be demonstrated at the Farnborough air Show by Brooke-Smith. The following year, the SC.1 was flown across the Channel to appear at the Paris Air Show.

The first prototype was then moved to RAE Bedford, while the second SC.1 was returned to the workshops at Belfast, where it received a new auto-stabilisation system. Former RAE test pilot J. R. Green joined Shorts in August 1963 and one of his initial tasks was to evaluate the auto-stabilisation system fitted to XG905. On 2 October 1963, Green lost control of XG905 above the Belfast airfield and it plunged to the ground from a height of about 30 ft (9.1 m). Green was killed in the crash, although the SC.1 was found to be repairable and a decision was taken to keep the aircraft in service. Various improvements were made to the control systems with flights resuming in 1966. These trials continued until 1971, when the project came to an end. XG900 would eventually become part of the London Science Museum's aircraft collection and XG905 was presented to the Ulster Folk & Transport Museum, in Northern Ireland.

A modified two-seat version of this aircraft was proposed in late 1959, which received the company reference SC.8 (PD.43). This would have used five or six RB.108 lift engines to compensate for the additional weight, but it never progressed much further than the drawing board and was not considered necessary for research by the MoS/RAE. (Short Brothers SC.2-SC.7 designs were not VTOL aircraft.)

The Short SC.1 (2nd prototype XG905) flown by J. R. Green during hover trials at Sydenham in 1963.

The Short SC1 XG905 Sydenham after its re-build.

Advanced Belfast Fighter Designs

While the first SC.1 was still under construction, designers working for Short Brothers began to consider the possibility of utilising the same VTOL technology for future civil and military aircraft. This would initially lead to new fighter aircraft designs that might be ready to enter service by the late 1960s. The majority of these concepts used delta wings, which were right at the forefront of aviation development during the post-war period. The first concepts would be powered by at least four centrally located lift engines, with one or two turbojets for horizontal flight, using a similar general layout to the SC.1. The first application was an interdictor, fitted with relatively small wings to improve high-speed handling at low attitude. As an interceptor, this kind of aircraft might be used from a smaller warship, a merchant vessel or an improvised land site. VTOL was potentially a very useful feature, allowing combat aircraft to operate from locations only available to helicopters. Initial ideas for a single-seat VTOL strike-fighter produced in the late 1950s used a similar engine layout to the SC.1, but Shorts were aware of the need to carry more fuel, at least two underwing weapons and use a fully retractable undercarriage. This meant a larger heavier aircraft and consequently, the requirement for more powerful lift engines which Rolls-Royce were working on. They recognised the need to improve the RB.108 from an early stage and this would lead to the RB.162, providing double the power of the original engine and using a simplified overall design. While the initial VTOL fighter proposals were developments of the SC.1, Shorts were soon exploring a wide range of different ideas for VTOL combat aircraft. At the time of writing, there is limited documentation available, but different methods of lift were being considered, such as swivelling engines in wing mounted nacelles for VTOL and horizontal flight.

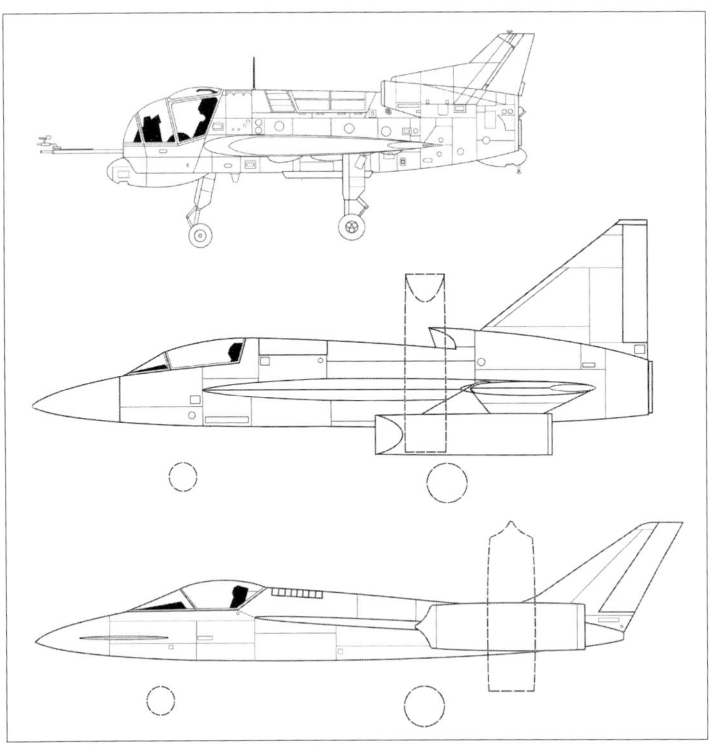

The upper drawing shows the Shorts experimental SC.1 delta winged VTOL aircraft, which is placed here for comparison purposes. Below this, is a Shorts proposal for a lightweight VTOL strike-fighter, developed from the SC.1 project and now utilising swivelling podded underwing engines for VTOL operations and level flight, plus two forward positioned downward exhausting turbojets to balance lift and an additional single turbojet in the rear fuselage. The lower drawing shows an even more advanced Short VTOL strike-fighter concept from this series, with a canard configuration and further alterations to the propulsion layout. The centre and lower designs may be part of the PD.25 study group, but this is unclear and the drawings are not precisely to scale.

Several designs thought to belong to a wide ranging study called PD.25 show ideas for strike fighters using jet engines in swivelling nacelles to provide VTOL and level flight. One proposal used two underwing jet engine nacelles that would be used for forward flight and when needed, swung into an upright position for VTOL operations. In addition to this, the aircraft would use two vertically mounted RB.162 turbojets that were installed behind the cockpit and used to balance lift during VTOL. Two further non-afterburning turbojets were located in the rear fuselage to boost horizontal performance. These would be fed from a dorsal air intake just ahead of the tailfin. However, regardless of assistance from Rolls Royce, the designers at Shorts would have experienced problems finding the ideal engines for this kind of proposal, as turbojet technology was relatively new and tended to suffer from weight, size and performance limitations.

A further development of the swivelling engine design utilised a thin, highly swept delta wing with nacelles containing turbojets at the tips. The type of engine they planned to use is unknown. No propulsion for forward flight would be carried in the fuselage, but there were two vertical RB.162 engines located behind the cockpit to balance lift during VTOL operations. This would be achieved when the wingtip engine exhausts were turned downward and a mostly automated air bleed system would provide the pilot with control during take-off and landing operations. A conventional tricycle undercarriage would be used to allow horizontal runway operations and although it was probably designed for subsonic strike, this version might have had brief supersonic performance. The cockpit was well positioned, affording the pilot good visibility and swept canard fins were attached close to the aircraft's nose. The wing was equipped with conventional control surfaces and there would be a single swept tailfin. Armament would probably be carried underwing and the aircraft would have a daylight photo-reconnaissance capability.

Short Brothers Consider the Wibault Engine

As this book is aimed specifically at flying wings, deltas and tailless designs, I will not be delving into the history of Britain's most successful V/STOL combat aircraft the Harrier. It would be inappropriate and I have already described the Harrier and some of its proposed clones in a previous book: *Vertical Take-off Fighter Aircraft,* published in 2013 by Classic Publications. However, I will mention that during the late 1950s, Shorts are known to have undertaken a delta-winged aircraft study which was designed around an early version of the engine which made the Harrier possible. This particular proposal was part of the broad P.25 V/STOL study. Many of the P.25 proposals remain sketchy, but PD.25/2 was an STOL strike fighter that would use the Bristol BE.52 engine, which was based on work undertaken by the French aeronautical engineer Michel Henri Wibault (1897–1963). In the early 1950s, Wibault approached the French government with his ideas for VTOL propulsion, but they were rejected. He then visited the MWDP Office in Paris where his research was swiftly forwarded to their senior aerodynamic consultant, Dr Theodore von Kármán (1881–1963), who immediately recognised the potential. The details were then passed to Sir Stanley Hooker (1907–1984) at Bristol Aero Engines in England and he arranged to meet Wibault without delay. Hooker was very impressed with the design and assigned engineers Gordon Lewis (1924–2010), Pierre Young (1926-1985), and Neville Quinn to examine Wibault's proposals in detail. They all recognised the engine's potential and noted that it could be significantly improved by a re-arrangement of system, using two forward positioned swivelling exhaust ducts that could channel some of the engine's airflow in a useful direction. This resulted in the construction of an experimental Orion-based engine called the BE.48, which was soon replaced by the BE.52. Wibault was invited to join Bristol as a technical consultant and at the start of 1957 Bristol-Siddeley Engines Ltd applied for a UK patent on behalf of Wibault and Lewis for the new engine. However, there was no suitable aircraft in development to make use of it. While the engine would eventually become the Pegasus turbofan that powered the Harrier, it now appears that Hawker Aircraft were not the only company with access to this new engine technology.

At some date, (probably during 1957), Shorts (who were deeply involved in V/STOL development), undertook a modest study that investigated the possibility of using the BE.52 to power a new V/STOL strike fighter. Shorts designers produced the PD.25/2 concept, which was a compact, tailless delta wing design, with a fairly substantial fuselage and a forward positioned cockpit. Two intakes, around either side of the lower cockpit section provided the engine with air and further back alomg the fuselage were the forward swivelling ducts. The main exhaust from the engine was positioned at the tail. This was because the early BE.52 engine design lacked the twin rear, vectoring 'hot' outlets that became a key feature of the evolving Pegasus turbofan. No estimates for performance are available, but maximum speed at altitude would have probably been in the region of 600 mph+ (965 kph+). It is also clear that the PD.25/2 would not have been capable of VTOL using the BE.52 engine, although STOL should have been very good, aided by the wing design.

The PD.25/2 would have carried stores underwing on pylons and the aircraft was supported on the ground by a tricycle undercarriage. It is not known if any wind tunnel testing of models was undertaken, as the project did not progress much further than a preliminary study. This may simply be because Sydney Camm convinced Hawker's board to fund the construction of a prototype aircraft using the next version of the Bristol engine and Shorts realised they were out of the running at that point. As a consequence, the PD.25/2 was filed away and largely forgotten about, although it may well have been a superior design to the initial unbuilt Hawker concept that would have used the same engine.

Another design in the PD.25 series, has the reference PD.25/4 and was a very different, more conventional looking single-seat aircraft that did not utilise the BE.52 engine. Instead, it was equipped with eight lift jets in two sections at the front and sides of the fuselage and a single more powerful afterburning turbojet for horizontal flight. A modest delta wing was chosen for this aircraft, with a conventional tail. It is quoted as having a maximum speed at sea level of Mach 0.98, a supersonic capability at altitude and a range of about 250 miles (400 km). The payload was also anticipated to be one ton, although PD.25/4 probably lacked sufficient capability for submission to the NBMR-3 competition of 1961. As far as is known at present, the design never progressed much further than wind tunnel testing of small models.

Many military VTOL designs were produced by Shorts, including a number of quite large naval strike aircraft generally powered by twin Avons for horizontal flight and banks of RB.108s for lift. The purpose of these aircraft fitted with small delta wings and delta tailfins appears to have been primarily tactical nuclear strike and Shorts gave them the reference PD.23. That said, they fall outside the general terms of this book.

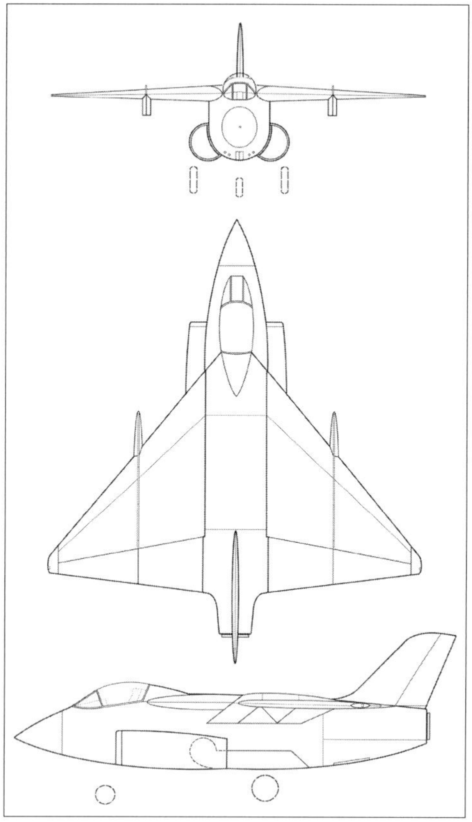

Shorts PD.25/2 STOL Strike fighter designed around the BE.52 engine.

Mirage Influences

Yet another series of VTOL designs to emerge from Shorts during 1960, resided within the PD.49 study. An early concept in this group was a supersonic twin delta strike fighter, using VTOL systems developed for the SC.1.

A cluster of four or six, vertically positioned lift engines provided the VTOL capability, with one, or possibly two additional turbojets used for level flight. Air for the main engines would be provided by inlets on the forward inner wing section. Short stubby outer wings were moved well back and there was a single tailfin. In common with the German VAK-191B, this formula would probably have made it very difficult to safely take-off and land horizontally in a normal manner.

The accepted system of compressor-bled air would have been used for the control system during VTOL and hover, with elevons and a rudder for normal flight. The forward positioned cockpit would afford the pilot good visibility and a tricycle undercarriage was standard equipment.

Possible armament carried by this aircraft, might have been two air-to-air missiles in the fighter role and alternatively, a modest load of free fall conventional bombs or air-to-surface missiles, with stores carried on underwing pylons. Airborne radar was proposed and the ability to carry photo-reconnaissance equipment.

At this point the design study becomes rather confusing as PD.49 appears to have evolved from a double delta into a pure delta wing fighter, very reminiscent of the French single-seat

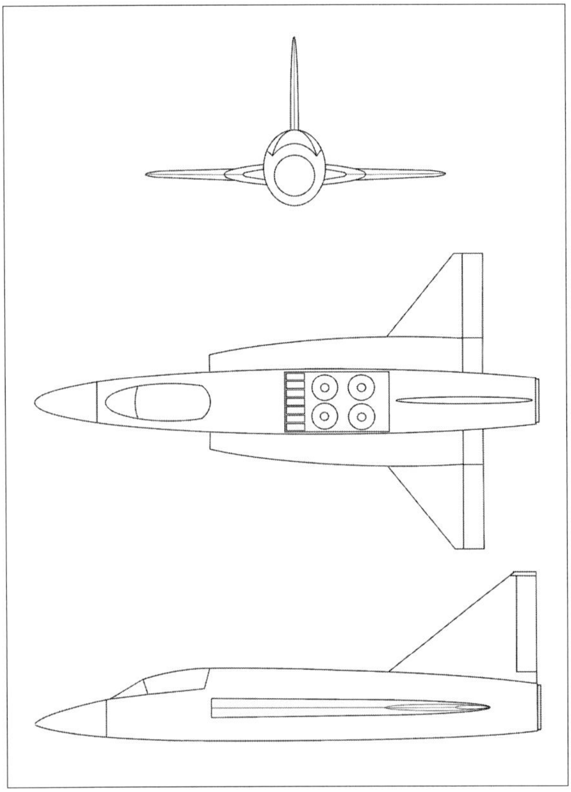

This design for a VTOL strike fighter had quite a lot in common with the Short SC.1, using four centrally located lift engines and is understood to be an early concept from the PD.49 study.

experimental VTOL Dassault Balzac V. This PD.49 proposal would use eight upright RB.162 turbojets, split into two groups for lift, plus an afterburning Rolls-Royce RB.168-IR turbofan for level flight that was under development. Supersonic performance was anticipated at altitude, with a vertical take-off weight of about 23,000 lb (10,433 kg). In the strike role, this version of the PD.49 would carry underwing Bullpup air-to-surface missiles or free-fall bombs. Another eventual option might have been an underwing WE.177 nuclear weapon with a balancing fuel tank on the opposite side. As an interceptor, it might have carried Firestreak missiles, air-to-air rockets or 30 mm ADEN cannons. The aircraft utilised an airborne radar system and was equipped with a tricycle undercarriage, also allowing conventional runway take-offs and landings.

Shorts chief engineer Frank H. Robertson was apparently responsible for this series of delta wing VTOL designs, which led to a further development using the PD.56 designation. Direct comparisons using the available drawings indicate that the PD.49 and PD.56 were virtually the same aircraft, with some alterations to the PD.56 that re-positioned the lift engines into four separate units. This seems to have been done to allow the carriage of an extra fuel tank or semi-recessed tactical nuclear weapon beneath the fuselage. In the strike role, this aircraft would have a combat radius of 250 miles (400 km) travelling partly at supersonic speed. The range could be further improved with a speed reduction. A ceiling in excess of 50,000 ft (15,240 m) was anticipated. The aircraft would be capable of interception, using Firestreak or Sidewinder missiles and have the ability to undertake daylight reconnaissance missions. Robertson apparently

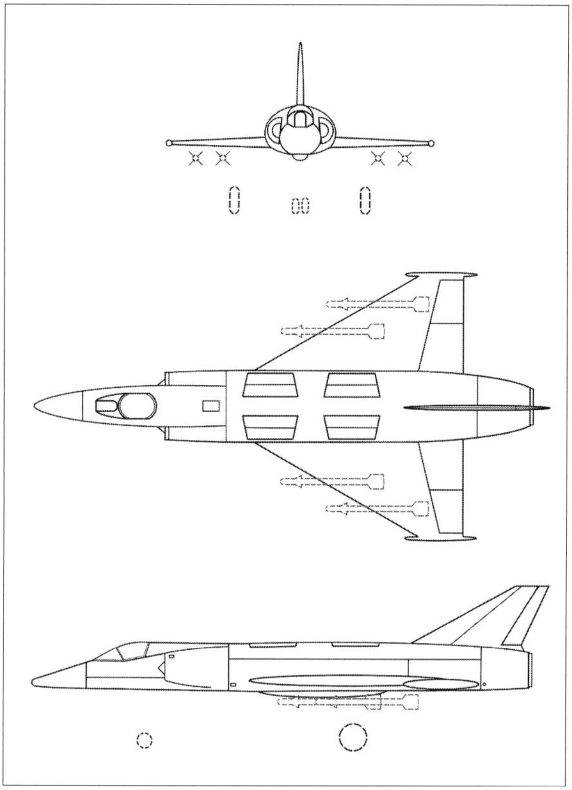

Shorts PD.56 strike-fighter configured as an interceptor, with four underwing AIM-9 Sidewinder missiles.

considered plans for a two-seat version of the aircraft and may have produced further variants. Some wind tunnel testing of these designs is know to have taken place using models.

In 1961, Short Brothers submitted plans for the PD.45, PD.49 and PD.56 to NATO for their NBMR-3, V/STOL strike aircraft competition. NBMR-3 closed on the 31 December 1961 and Shorts failed to generate significant interest with their designs, which were then filed away and largely forgotten about. However, the story does not completely end at this point as the next section will show.

The English Electric V/STOL Combat Aircraft Patent

Some time ago, I located a 1962 UK Patent Specification 993,731 for improvements to a V/STOL aircraft. It was applied for by English Electric Aviation (which became part of The British Aircraft Corporation—BAC, in 1958) and I concluded that it simply showed some useful upgrades to a company design produced in the past that might have some further commercial potential. The documentation showed relatively minor enhancements to the propulsion system of a V/STOL strike fighter and this had been undertaken by engineers Frank Gerrie Willox and Gerald David Walley. It appeared that English Electric had been considering ideas for V/STOL strike aircraft to compete with the French VTOL Mirage designs, the Shorts proposals for NBMR-3 and maybe a Rolls-Royce VTOL fighter concept. What I had overlooked was the fact that English Electric and

Shorts worked together at various times during the 1950s. So, it began to look as if the single-seat aircraft in this patent was a version of the Shorts PD.56 and the proposed improvements were specifically tailored to this design, but might be used on similar aircraft. Everything began to point towards English Electric being involved in the development of the PD.56 and the English Electric patent being linked to the project. Further confirmation came by simply making comparison overlays with the available drawings of the aircraft.

The English Electric design was presented in two slightly different forms for VTOL and STOL. In the case of the VTOL design, eight separate engines would be used for lift and these would probably be Rolls-Royce RB.162-31 turbojets, each producing 4,409 lb (19.61 kN) of thrust. They would all pivot on centrally placed mountings that could be moved hydraulically. This would allow the exhaust from these engines to be directed slightly forward or rearward, depending on lift, landing, hover, or transition requirements. During horizontal flight, the engines would be shut down and secured in-line with the fuselage. Sealing doors would cover the upper and lower engine ports. This modification appears to be the main difference between the English Electric design and the PD.56.

A single, centrally positioned jet engine would provide propulsion for normal flight and this would most likely be a version of the afterburning Rolls-Royce RB.168 turbofan. The VTOL version of the strike fighter would also be capable of STOL. For control during VTOL operations, air would be bled from the compressors of all lift engines, plus outlets at the front, tail and wingtips. In keeping with the Shorts PD.56 design, the aircraft would use a fully retractable tricycle undercarriage, which appears a little more robust in the English Electric patent. This would allow STOL and conventional horizontal runway take-offs and landings.

The second version of this design intended for STOL, would have fewer lift engines, which would also swivel. After turning through 90° they would be shut down and enclosed in flush containment units, improving the aircraft's aerodynamics during horizontal flight. In addition, air drawn from the lift engines or the main turbofan would be used to improve low speed capability with blown flaps. This second aircraft would have superior STOL performance to the VTOL design and appears able to carry more fuel, thus improving range. In horizontal flight, control would be exercised by a rudder and two full-span elevons.

Like the Shorts PD.56, this aircraft could be configured for strike, daylight photo-reconnaissance or interception. Missiles and other stores would be carried underwing and a ventral fairing used for extra fuel or probably the carriage of a tactical nuclear weapon. The aircraft would be capable of high subsonic speed at low level and supersonic speeds at altitude. However, the shape of the fuselage does not appear to conform to area rule and like the PD.56, high-speed flight might have been limited for this reason.

Because Rolls-Royce were involved with Shorts VTOL development programme, it is perhaps surprising that Dr Griffith's office were not shown as responsible for any of these particular propulsion modifications made by Willox and Walley. Anyway, until more information appears, this simply remains an interesting BAC patent showing an aircraft that seems almost identical to the Short PD.56. Perhaps these late additional features were retained by BAC on the off-chance that the PD.56 project would undergo a revival, or the technology could be used for another design? It would be interesting to know the full story!

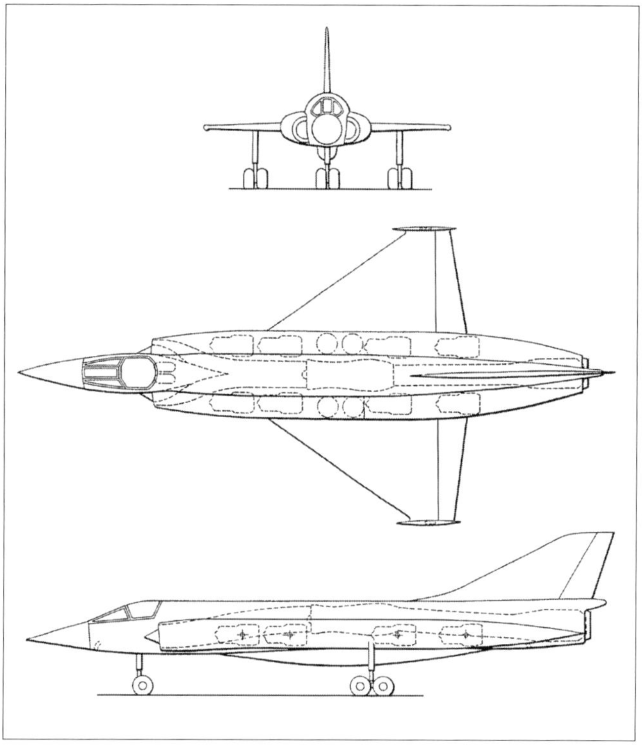

An English Electric/BAC design from a patent filed in 1962 for a strike-fighter with VTOL/STOL capability in roughly the same class as the Mirage IIIV and very similar to the Shorts PD.56.

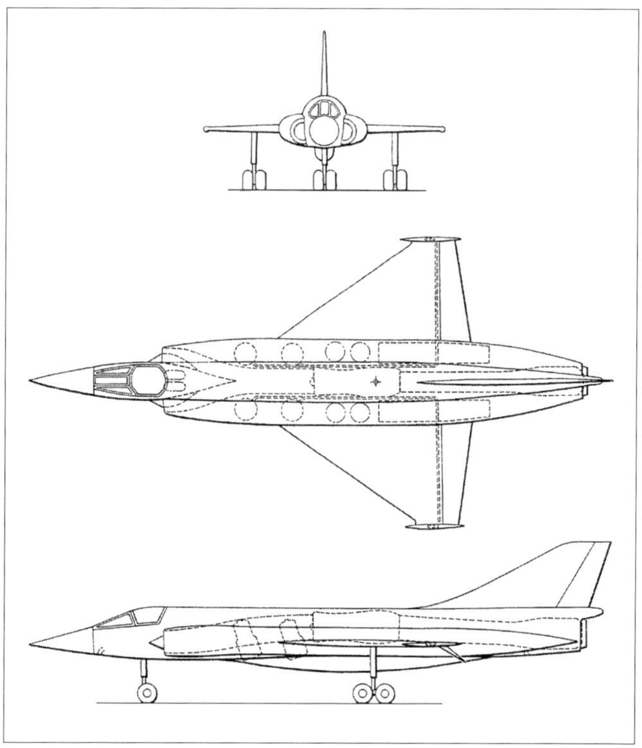

A second English Electric design from the 1962 STOL strike-fighter patent, using four forward positioned lift engines and blown flaps, allowing very short take-offs, but incapable of VTOL.

Short VTOL Lift Platforms

In the early 1950s, the UK Air Staff began to consider finding a more advanced replacement for the English Electric Canberra light bomber. This aircraft was one of the best in its category and versions were built for various alternative roles such as high altitude, daylight photo-reconnaissance. However, its days in service were already numbered and a more capable replacement would be needed by the late 1960s. The MoS began discussions with English Electric about the possibility of a new aircraft in 1956 and this led to a preliminary company study with the reference P.17A.

During March 1957 GOR.339 (General Operational Requirement 339) was issued to several aircraft contractors by the MoS, with a long list of demanding requirements for the Canberra replacement. These ranged from an all-weather capability and supersonic high/low performance, to short field take-off from poorly maintained sites or stretches of autobahns, the carriage of nuclear weapons, reconnaissance equipment and numerous other features and abilities.

Despite the massive defence cuts, introduced by UK Defence Minister Duncan Sandys on 4 April 1957, GOR.339 remained in place, with the completion date for submissions being 31 January 1958. The candidates then selected were (as expected) the English Electric P.17A and in close second place, the Vickers-Armstrong 571. As a consequence, the two companies were invited to work together under OR.343 and they soon reached an agreement, with the project being given an official go-ahead in January 1959 and now formally named as the TSR.2 (Tactical Strike & Reconnaissance 2). The long and torturous history of this project is well documented and does not belong here. However, Short Brothers were involved with early proposals to make the P.17A into a VTOL capable strike aircraft and their design office came up with some interesting ideas that were submitted in association with English Electric. They developed a manned VTOL lift platform that could carry the P.17A to a sufficient height and speed for release under its own power and then rendezvous in the sky once the aircraft returned from the mission. It would then dock with the VTOL platform and make a safe vertical landing. One suggestion, was to dispense with the P.17A's undercarriage and flaps, but this was quickly discounted as the aircraft would be unable to operate normally from a runway, or return somewhere else after initially using the VTOL platform.

Rather confusingly, this Shorts project had a company reference of PD.17D, which appears to have been nothing more than a coincidence, although it is has sometimes been quoted as P.17 or P.17D, which is incorrect. PD.17D was a flat bodied, triangular shaped craft with what might be described as rear mounted stubby wings fitted with stabilising fins. The approximate length of this vehicle was about 80 ft (24.3 m) with a width of 50 ft (15.2 m) and a height of around 14 ft (4.2 m). The leading edge sweep of the forward section of PD.17D was approximately 73.5° and on the ground, it would be supported by three fixed position dampened legs. Presumably, it was planned to attach wheel units for various requirements like movement on the ground, maintenance and storage. The weight of the platform has been quoted at 49,000 lb (22,226 kg) and it would need to lift a P.17A aircraft weighing about 66,000 lb (29,937 kg), with provision for slightly heavier loads and the ability to cope with the platform suffering from an engine failure in the field.

The lift requirements, meant that PD.17D would utilise 44 vertically positioned RB.108 turbojets, providing in excess of 93,720 lb (417 kN) thrust and 16 tilting RB.108 turbojets producing a further 34,080 lb (151 kN) thrust (some sources indicate that 56 RB.108 lift engines were initially considered). In addition, there were ten horizontally mounted RB.108 engines providing 21,300 lb (95 kN) of thrust (or the superior RB.145 turbojets) for forward flight. Maximum speed only needed to be sufficient for the launch operation and the altitude for aircraft release is unknown,

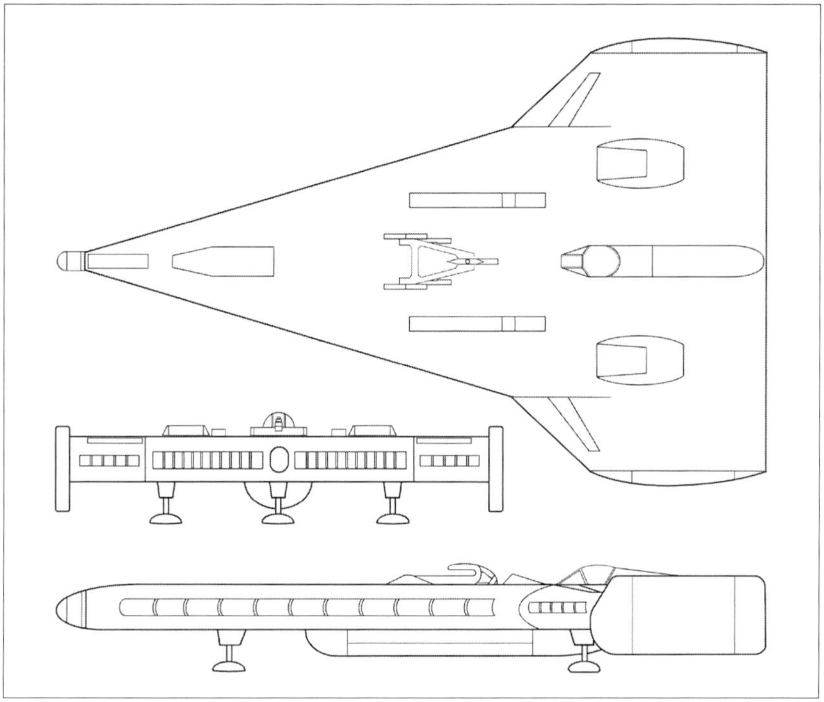

Shorts PD.17D (also occasionally and incorrectly referred to as the P.17D) VTOL lift and transportation platform.

Artwork showing the primary function of the Short PD.17D VTOL platform to lift an English Electric P.17A strike aircraft into normal flight from an improvised site. It was suggested that the PD.17D would be capable of recovering its aircraft in flight. Powered by a large number of Rolls-Royce turbojets, the PD.17D would be adaptable to transport, small numbers of personnel, fuel and ammunition, work as an in-flight refuelling tanker and operate from aircraft carriers and large merchant ships.

but would be modest. Also the PD.17D's range carrying an aircraft would be somewhat limited as the amount of fuel required for any kind of mission would be considerable.

The large number of engines would draw their air from intakes along the leading edge and/or through slats along the upper section of the PD.17D. Exactly what was decided on is somewhat unclear, as the re-ingestion of exhaust gases might have been a major problem for the designers to eliminate.

The cockpit for the PD.17D was located towards the rear of the aircraft, behind the locking connector that secured the combat aircraft to the platform. Shorts also suggested that the PD.17D might be used to rapidly transport fuel, supplies and perhaps small numbers of personnel (in a suitable accommodation unit) to difficult locations. P.17A and PD.17D were submitted to the MoS in January 1958 and while the P.17A was considered suitable for further development, the VTOL platform was discarded. It is also worth mentioning that Shorts suggested a jointly built, stretched version of the P.17A capable of VTOL, with the company reference PD.17/2 but this met with swift rejection.

Despite failing to sell the idea of a VTOL platform to the MoS, Shorts drew up plans for scaled down version of the PD.17D that could be used from improvised sites to lift small fighters into the air and possibly recover them in flight. Clearly intended for submission to NATO, the first of these was the PD.34 platform. It would be capable of carrying an adapted Folland Gnat that would deliver a single tactical nuclear weapon to an enemy target. A second fairly similar design with the reference PD.40 would perform the same function for a Fiat G.91 strike-fighter. The lift platform would utilise eight centrally located upright turbojets, possibly Rolls-Royce RB.162-31 turbojets, each producing 4,409 lb (19.61 kN) of thrust. These would also provide an air-bleed system for low-speed control during VTOL operations, with nozzles positioned at the front and each wing tip. For horizontal flight a further two turbojets (possibly RB.162-31s) would be buried in the fuselage of the platform with air intakes along the leading edge and exhausts at the rear on each side of the cockpit.

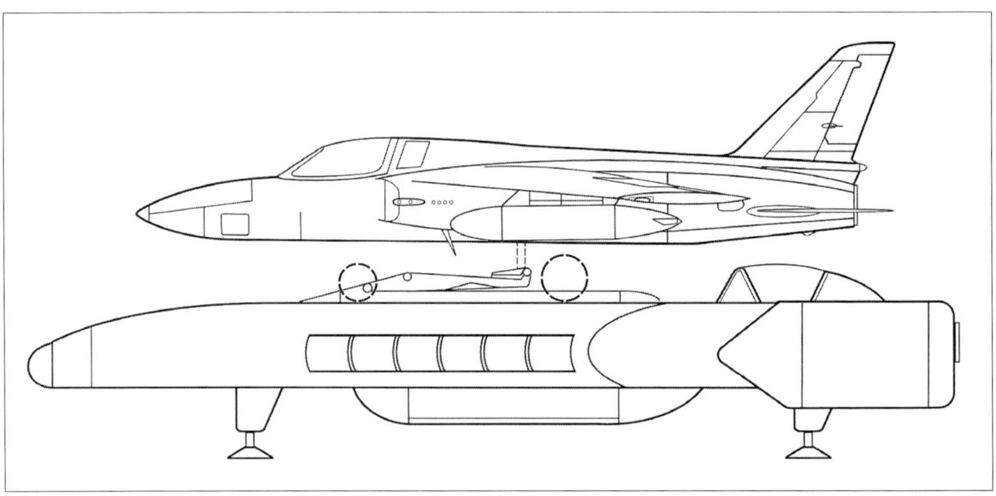

Shorts PD.34 with Folland Gnat light-fighter temporarily secured to the upper surface.

The Rolls-Royce Concepts

Dr A. A Griffith joined Rolls-Royce in 1939 after working for many years at RAE Farnborough and was regarded by many as the country's leading expert on gas turbine development. He designed an internal combustion jet engine some years before Frank Whittle wrote his thesis on a simpler centrifugal gas turbine at the RAF College. As things turned out, Whittle received the glory for his basic engine, but it would eventually give way to the more advanced axial flow design, which was originally proposed by Griffith and later developed in Britain and Germany. Griffith would go on to design the AJ65 axial turbojet, which led to the highly successful Avon. He also worked on development of the turbofan and many other engine designs until he retired from the company in 1960. During his time as chief scientist at Rolls-Royce, Griffith remained at the centre of British jet engine research and development. He was in constant contact with all the major aircraft constructors and everyone of any importance in an official government capacity, especially his former colleagues at the RAE. He was a tireless promoter of VTOL concepts and his compact RB.108 engine had opened a door to flatriser aircraft, capable of operating from a helicopter pad, an improvised site, the deck of a ship, or simply a normal runway. It is unclear when he began serious work on aircraft designs able to accommodate the RB.108 lift engine, but one of the earliest concepts on record, was a diamond shaped flying wing test-bed with twelve upright engines at its centre and wingtip nacelles, each accommodating four turbojets which would power the aircraft in horizontal flight. This study was patented by Rolls-Royce, with the work dating back to October 1954. While there is a mention of jet nozzle deflectors, most of the VTOL control appears to be undertaken by two dimensional tilting of the lift engines. This rather basic concept formed the basis of many increasing ambitious ideas for futuristic, highly swept VTOL aircraft with supersonic capabilities, using substantial banks of lift engines.

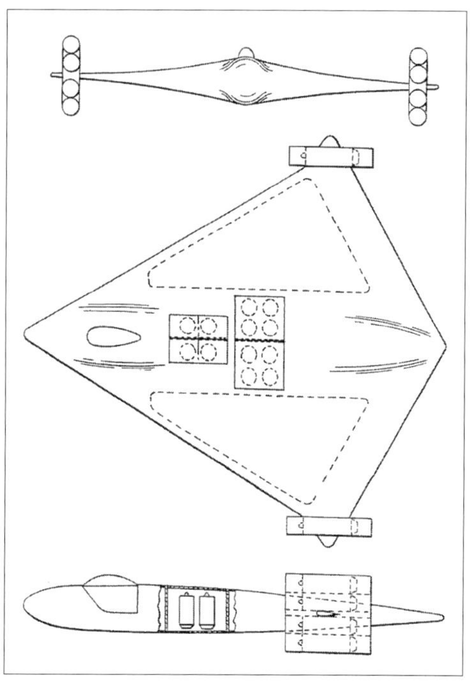

An early Griffith proposal for an experimental VTOL design showing the central positioning of lift engines, wingtip units for engines used in horizontal flight, large fuel tank areas and the forward located cockpit. This proposal never progressed much further than a concept and lacked a degree of refinement, but established many of the features that Griffith considered essential for this type of aircraft.

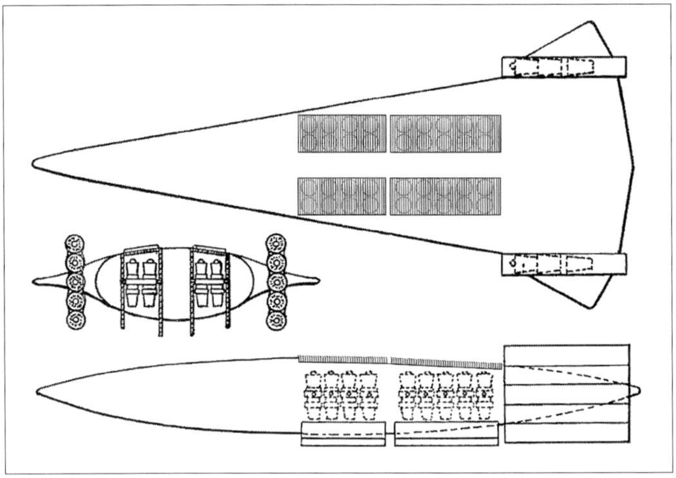

One of many VTOL aircraft proposals to emerge from the Rolls-Royce design office. This concept was jointly produced by Dr A. A Griffith and William Shaw in 1955 and it shows the swift evolution of the design. It would utilise 36 lift jets for VTOL operations, with a series of flaps along the upper fuselage to provide air for the lift engines at low speed, along with four sets of larger ventral doors for engine exhaust. Ten turbojets mounted in wingtip nacelles would be used for horizontal flight.

Griffith was deeply involved with the RAE's VTOL projects such as the Shorts built SC.1 and the Rolls-Royce Flying Bedstead, which both generated official interest in the future application of his compact RB.108 lift engine to more exotic designs. Griffith now worked on a number of low aspect ratio concepts and these quickly caught the imagination of the RAE and MoS in the same way as Wallace's stylish Vickers variable geometry supersonic Swallow had done. It must have seemed that a substantial leap forward in aircraft design and technology would soon be possible.

Griffith initially proposed several different options for VTOL airliners. These would carry 44–100 passengers at a cruising speed of Mach 2.3, allowing journeys from London to New York in 2 hours 10 minutes. Flights would be undertaken at an altitude of 70,000 ft (21,336 m), with propulsion provided by 10 turbojets in two wingtip nacelles at the rear of the aircraft. The VTOL capability would be provided by about 56 RB.108 vertically mounted turbojets within the outer sections of the dart shaped fuselage. Some of Griffith's designs show three to six additional RB.108s positioned at the front of the aircraft, while other proposals relied on air bled from the lift engines to provide forward balance and control.

The emphasis in available documents would suggest that civil applications were favoured for this new type of aircraft, but there are indications that the underlying consideration was the development of a VTOL supersonic bomber with the ability to deliver at least one nuclear weapon over a long range. This is undoubtedly the reason why many documents associated with this design work were originally classified as secret. And following what must have been a number of discussions between Dr Griffith and various members of the RAE and MoS, there was a decision taken to move forward with the construction of a manned, scale-sized supersonic VTOL prototype. In September 1955, the MoS issued ER161T, which requested proposals for two broadly similar prototypes having different aerodynamic properties. These were described in ER161T as Version A and Version B. It is not clear how many aircraft companies were approached, but Armstrong Whitworth provided a set of designs which were provisionally accepted, although not given the full go-ahead. Armstrong Whitworth allocated the company designation AW.171 to Version A and AW.172 to Version B. These aircraft differed due to wing design. AW.171 had a leading edge sweep of 83° and a wing thickness/chord ratio of 6 per cent. In the case of AW.172, this had a leading edge sweep of 76° and a wing thickness/chord ratio of 3 per cent. The weight specified in ER161T was 15,000 lb to 20,000 lb (6,800 kg to 9,070 kg) and Armstrong Whitworth proposed an all-up weight of about 16,000 lb (7,257 kg) for the AW.171. No weight details can be found for AW.172. Powered by two Bristol-Siddeley Orpheus turbojets, with a combined thrust of 9,700 lb (43 kN) this was expected to provide a maximum speed of Mach 2 at altitude.

Dr A. A. Griffith, one the Britain's lesser known, but nevertheless brilliant scientists, who was responsible for major advances in jet engine design.

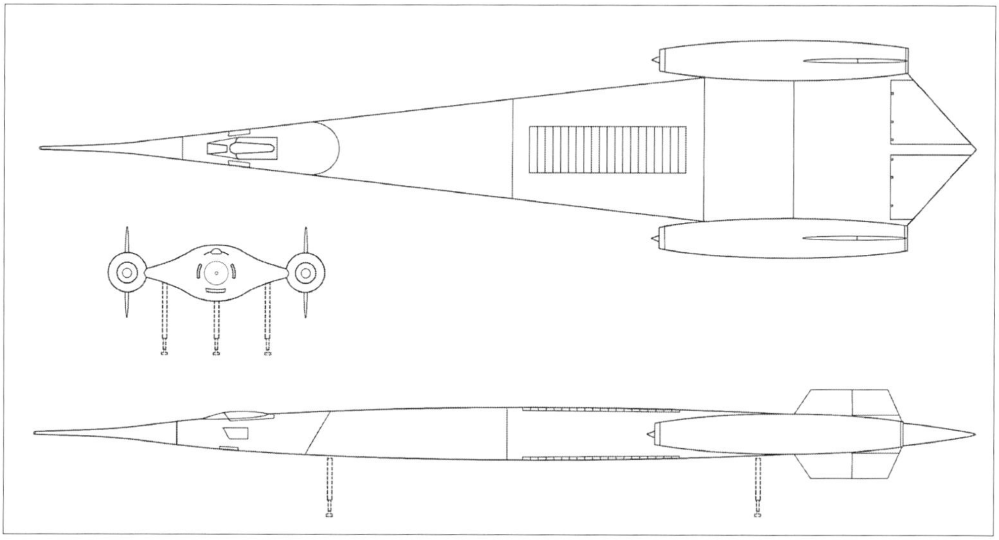

During 1955, Armstrong Whitworth produced this advanced design to meet the MoS ER161T specification for a supersonic research aircraft with a VTOL capability given the company reference AW.171. It was equipped with two Bristol Orpheus engines for horizontal flight and a central bank of ten Rolls-Royce RB.108 engines for VTOL operations. As far as is known, the AW 171 could not have been adapted for normal take-off from, or landing on a runway. The project didn't progress much further than wind tunnel testing with models, but it is understood that Dr A. A. Griffith was involved with this study and continued to develop the idea after the AW.171 was cancelled.

Overall length of the AW.171 was set at 70 ft (21.59 m), with a wingspan of 17.5 ft (5.36 m). Lift for VTOL would be provided by ten upright RB.108 engines at the centre of the fuselage with air bled from these engines to provide low speed control of the aircraft. The pilot was accommodated in a prone position in a pressurised cockpit at the forward area of the fuselage, with a minimal canopy that would eliminate additional drag. A glass panel in the cockpit floor would also provide the pilot with some downward visibility and in an emergency the entire cockpit section would detach from the rest of the aircraft and make a parachute descent. On the ground AW.171 was supported by three dampened and retractable landing legs and it is probable that they would be fitted with some kind of wheel attachment units for handling and maintenance purposes. Nevertheless, even if the legs had been replaced with struts using wheels

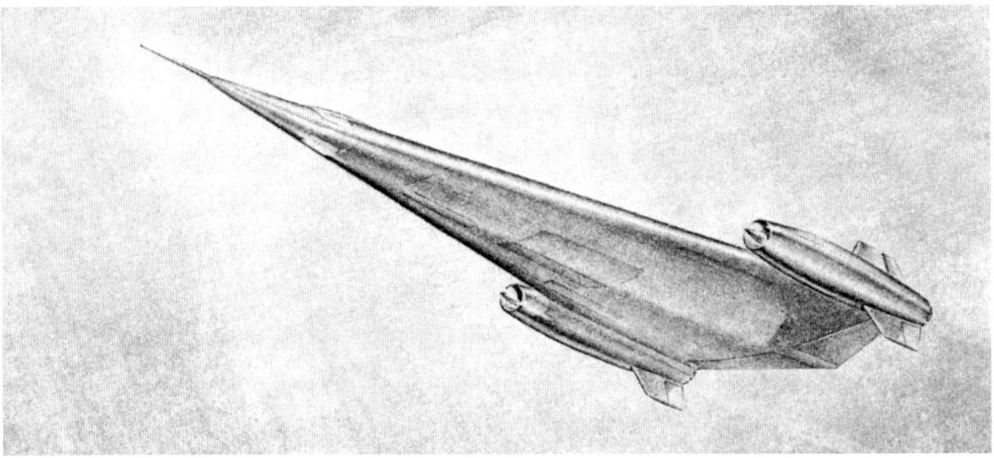

A brochure drawing for the AW.171 showing it undertaking a test flight. Note the closed central bay housing the lift jets and the downward observation panel for the pilot, lying prone in the cockpit area.

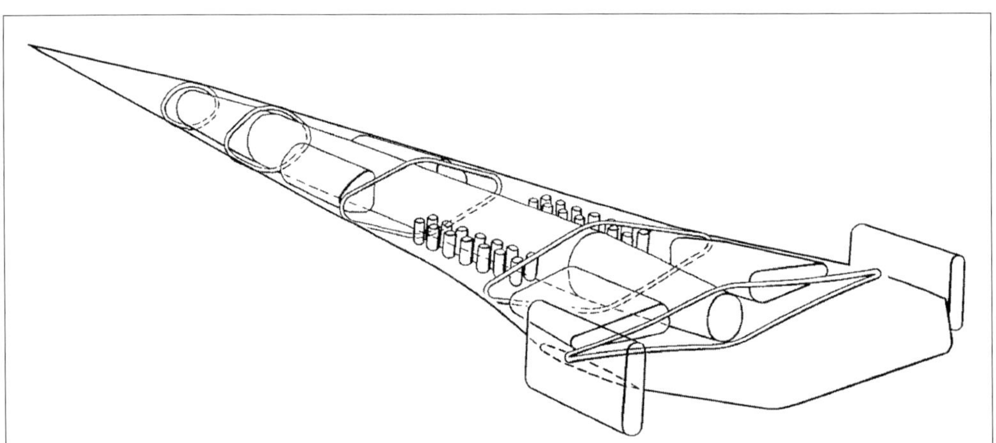

This illustration shows a Griffith concept for a broadly similar, but larger aircraft than the AW.171. Two banks of centrally located lift engines would be used for VTOL operations and wingtip nacelles, each carrying several turbojets to provide the power for horizontal supersonic flight. The design was the subject of a UK Patent (910795), which was applied for in 1960.

it is unlikely that conventional take-offs and especially landings would have been possible. That aside, the AW.171 became the favoured official design and there were wind tunnel tests of models conducted during late 1955 to early 1956. Unfortunately, this did not go quite so well as anticipated, with trials unable to confirm the aerodynamic qualities that were expected and as a consequence, the project was cancelled.

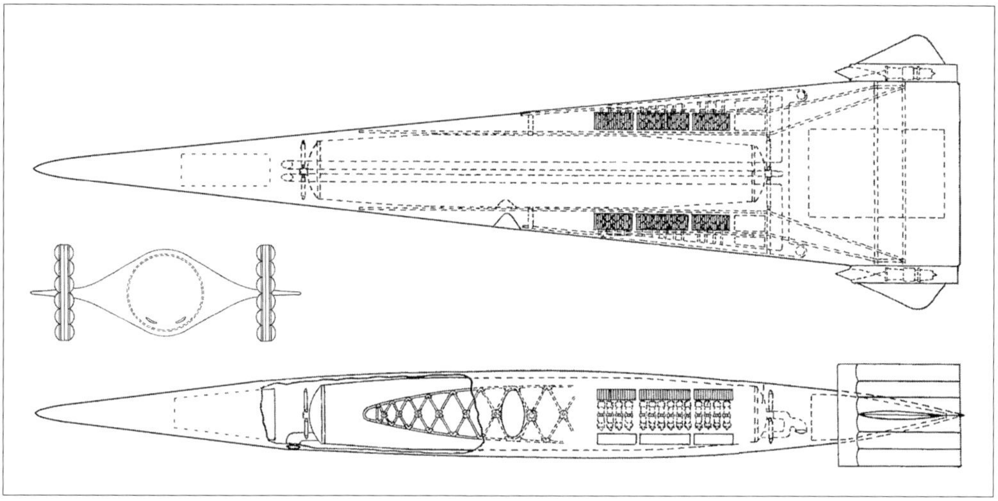

This drawing is closely based on a Rolls-Royce patent (GB821544) from 1956, that was not released until 1959. It shows the general layout of a supersonic VTOL aircraft designed by A. A. Griffith and Donald Eyre. A substantial number of jet engines would be used to provide lift and level flight, with allowances made for airframe expansion during sustained high-speed flight and air bleed from the lift engines for control and stabilisation during VTOL operations.

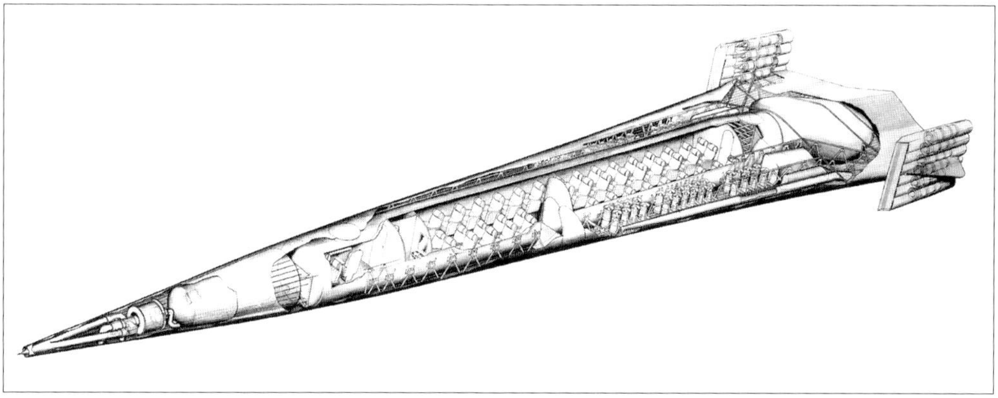

This Rolls-Royce design for a futuristic supersonic VTOL airliner would utilise 56 turbojets for lift and a further 12 turbojets for horizontal flight. A cruise speed Mach 2.3 at 70,000 ft (21,336 m) was anticipated with trans-Atlantic range. Air bled from lift engines would stabilise and control the aircraft during VTOL operations. Later, somewhat larger versions of this design are shown with 3-6 additional lift engines in the nose section of the aircraft. There does not appear to be any windows for passengers or crew, who would hope to rely on automated flight systems and see the outside world using CC TV even if the technology would have pushed the boundaries of what was possible in the 1950s. Although this design was proposed as a 44 seat commercial transport aircraft, much work was classified as secret. In a military role, this type of aircraft might well accommodate two free fall nuclear weapons, perhaps ejected rearward and there would be obvious uses as a supersonic VTOL transport for special forces, assuming this concept could have been developed and built at an affordable price.

However, there was a brief revival, with Rolls Royce submitting plans for what could be described as a scaled-up version of the AW.171 to STAC, which held its first official meeting at Farnborough on 5 November 1956. This proposal was for a VTOL supersonic airliner with intercontinental range. The aircraft would have a length of about 240 ft (73 m), a span of 58 ft (17.6 m) and an all-up-weight of 420,000 lb (190,508 kg). Capable of carrying 136 passengers, it would have a very substantial number of RB.108 lift engines and eight turbojets in wingtip nacelles for horizontal flight. Again, the concept was rejected, perhaps on the grounds of previous wind tunnel testing, the major technical challenges this design presented, or perhaps the cost.

Rolls-Royce VTOL Flying Wing

In 1956, Geoffrey Light Wilde (1917–2007) was appointed as the head of the advanced projects design office at Rolls-Royce in Derby. He was an outstanding engineer and is now best remembered for his initial work on the RB.211 engine. But back in 1956, Wilde's newly formed department began detailed studies of many different ideas for civil and military engine applications including a number of VTOL aircraft designs. Wilde was particularly interested in developing a VTOL flying wing, which would use a central cluster of thirty RB.108 lift turbojets, with four separate engines for horizontal flight.

Working with his senior designer John Coplin (1934–), they settled on a basic layout that would use louvered inlet and exhaust shutters to cover the lift engines in level flight and turbojets mounted on the trailing edge of the aircraft for horizontal flight. Wilde also envisaged a

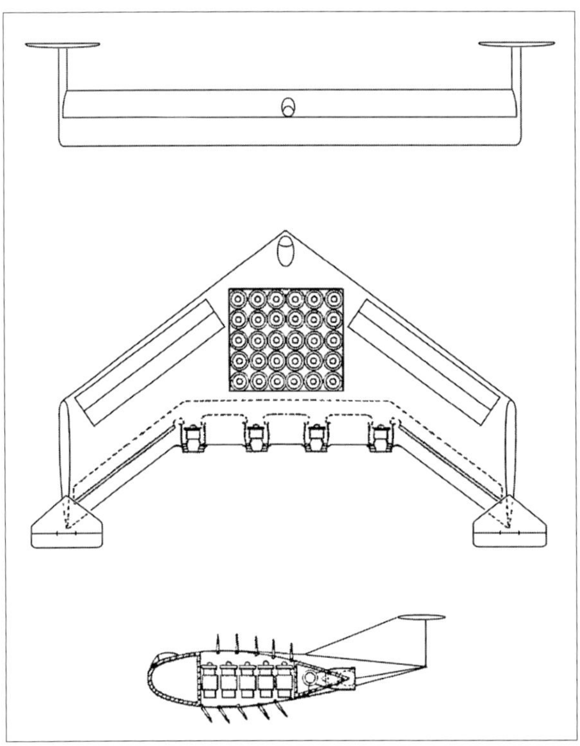

General arrangement of the Rolls-Royce VTOL flying wing designed in the late 1950s by Geoffrey Wilde and John Coplin.

boundary layer, drag reduction system with air being drawn through conduits from the wing and fed to the inlets of the rear-mounted engines. Proposed dimensions of this VTOL design are unknown, although the cluster of engines at the centre of gravity would result in a substantial wing thickness/chord ratio of as much as 20 per cent. Wilde hoped that the RAE might be encouraged to fund development of this aircraft as a research prototype, providing Rolls-Royce with an opportunity to promote new technology.

However, this complex paperwork study failed to progress any further, even though Rolls-Royce applied for a patent in 1959 naming Wilde and Coplin as the inventors. This was published in 1963 and it received the reference GB920875. That seems to have been the end of any interest in VTOL flying wings at Rolls-Royce. Professor Wilde retired from Rolls-Royce in 1978 and Professor John Coplin became the Director of Design and Technology, eventually leaving Rolls-Royce to become an aerospace consultant and chairman of Hiflux Ltd.

Dragons by Any Other Name!

In the mid-1950s, Hawker at Kingston-upon-Thames appear to have been taking an interest in Saab's development of a double delta wing fighter, which would become the J-35 Draken (Dragon). Hawker were looking at ways the impressive Saab design could be adapted to incorporate a VTOL capability. This soon led to a Hawker design given the company reference P.1126, powered in level flight by two Bristol-Siddeley Orpheus BOr 3 turbojets (of an unspecified precise variant), each providing 4,850 lb (21.57 kN) dry thrust. For VTOL operations, there would be two separate (swing down) units in the inner wing sections, each containing six Rolls-Royce RB.108-1A turbojets. These would provide a total thrust of 25,920 lb (115.29 kN).

During VTOL operations, large upper doors would remain open and the turbojets would be moved into an upright position with their exhausts facing downwards. The retractable undercarriage comprised of three shock-absorbing legs without wheels and P.1126 was never intended to operate from a runway; nor was it expected to have a supersonic capability. The proposed role would have been somewhat similar to the later Harrier, primarily as a ground attack aircraft. Available information suggests that the P.1126 study was completed in 1957, undoubtedly with advice and assistance from Rolls-Royce and possibly the RAE.

Yet again, the Saab Draken proved to be a very influential design and in 1961 Geoffrey Wilde disclosed proposals for a Rolls Royce double delta strike fighter he had been working on, that had VTOL capability. It would utilise four centrally located, upright mounted RB.162-86 turbojets for lift, each delivering at least 5,250 lb (23.3 kN) thrust and behind this a single RB.168-1A Mk 101 Spey turbofan for horizontal flight. This would have a rating of 11,100 lb (49.3 kN) thrust and it was suggested that this engine might at some later stage be equipped with an afterburner. In common with other VTOL designs, air would be bled from the lift engines to operate the low speed manoeuvring system. Wilde described this concept as a successor to the Shorts SC.1 and it was certainly more refined than the Hawker P.1126 and closer in appearance to the Saab Draken.

Wilde's design was expected to provide high subsonic performance at sea level and supersonic speed at altitude. He also anticipated carrying a military payload that would equal approximately 10 per cent of the aircraft's gross weight. Fitted with a tricycle undercarriage and a rear tail wheel for safety purposes, the double delta would have a good STOL runway capability and might have been developed just for this purpose, perhaps using fewer lift engines that would allow a welcome weight reduction.

As with the VTOL flying wing, the thinking behind this strike-fighter concept was undoubtedly to encourage designers working for major aircraft manufacturers to push ahead with new ideas and fully utilise Rolls-Royce propulsive systems and related engineering features. That said, there were major technical issues to overcome, such as power-to-weight ratios, fuel consumption, exhaust re-ingestion, dead weight in flight and the sheer engineering complexity, not to mention the huge cost and finding suitable customers. This must have discouraged the UK aircraft companies and Rolls-Royce certainly had no known intention of moving into the aircraft construction business. They were (and remain) a major UK engineering company primarily producing high-quality engines and related equipment for a range of applications from airliners to nuclear submarines. However, there may have been some interest shown from overseas.

In France, Sud Aviation, perhaps now best remembered for building the Caravelle airliner, were exploring the idea of developing a new delta wing military VTOL fighter for consideration as an alternative to the next version of the Dassault Mirage. Like many other major aircraft companies, Sud Aviation were a customer of Rolls-Royce. Their proposed VTOL fighter called the X-600, had begun as a delta winged design, using four centrally located Rolls-Royce lift engines and at this point, it seems possible that the British provided some technical assistance that changed the design of the fighter to resemble a slightly smaller, double delta VTOL version of the Saab Draken. For lift, this revised model now used six centrally located RB.162 turbojets (hidden by doors during normal flight), with a single afterburning Spey turbofan for horizontal propulsion, fed by half-cone air inlets on either side of the fuselage section alongside the cockpit.

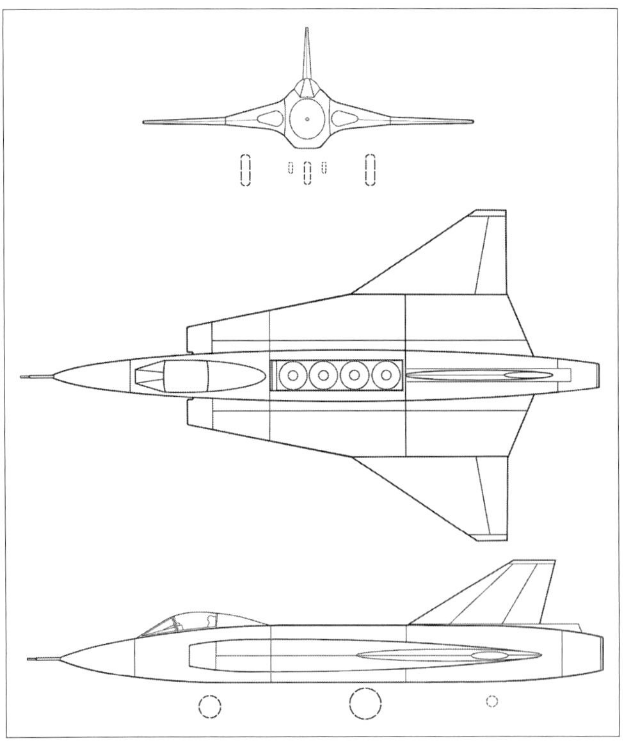

A VTOL design from Rolls-Royce, based on, or influenced by the Swedish Saab J 35 Draken and using four lift engines for VTOL. French manufacturer Sud Aviation produced plans for an aircraft called X-600 which was very similar to this Rolls-Royce concept, but used six vertically mounted lift jets.

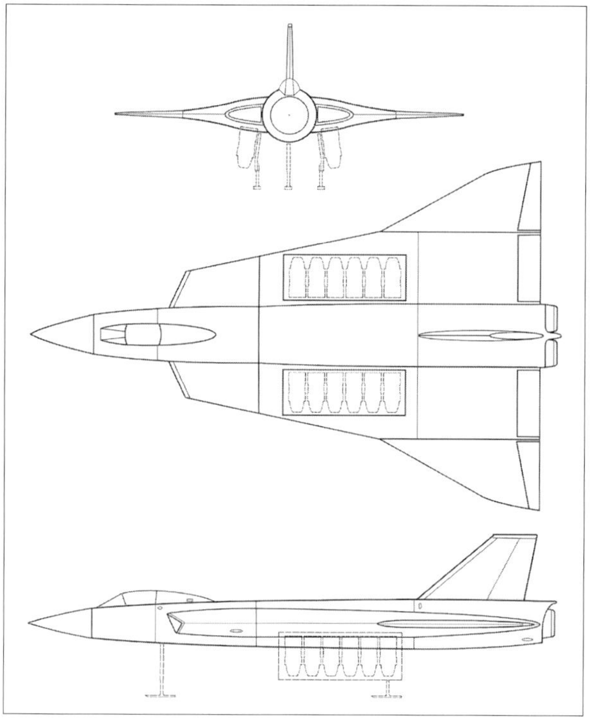

The Hawker P.1126 strike fighter, equipped with 12 extra engines mounted on two panels that would swing downwards into a vertical position to facilitate VTOL.

While there are obvious differences between this and the known Rolls Royce design, it is so similar that it is impossible to image that this aircraft did not emerge from at least some kind of informal cooperation. However, it appears there was little official interest in the X-600 and this design failed to progress much further than the drawing board.

Gloster Proposals

By the mid-1950s, it seemed that the Rolls-Royce lift engines had opened the doors to V/STOL flat-riser combat aircraft. New designs would be able to operate from improvised sites, or stretches of suitable roadway. This meant that in the event of a conflict, some warplanes could be dispersed away from airfields that might be primary targets for nuclear strikes.

The Gloster Aircraft Company was another UK manufacturer that began work on designing V/STOL warplanes which in their case, might be regarded as descendants of the Javelin fighter. By the end of the 1950s, the Company had produced some solid proposals. The first was a STOL combat aircraft with the reference P.505 that had a fuselage showing some similarities in appearance to a Javelin. It was powered by a single Rolls-Royce Conway turbofan, with an anticipated thrust of 17,150 lb (76.28 kN). Four centrally-positioned, upright mounted RB.162-86 turbojets would provide extra lift for STOL, with each engine delivering a maximum of 5,250 lb (23.3 kN) thrust. Swept wings were chosen for the P.505, giving it the look of a Buccaneer or Scimitar. The cockpit arrangement appeared identical to a Javelin and the aircraft was supported on the ground by a retractable tricycle undercarriage. P.505 had an anticipated all-up weight of 30,000 lb

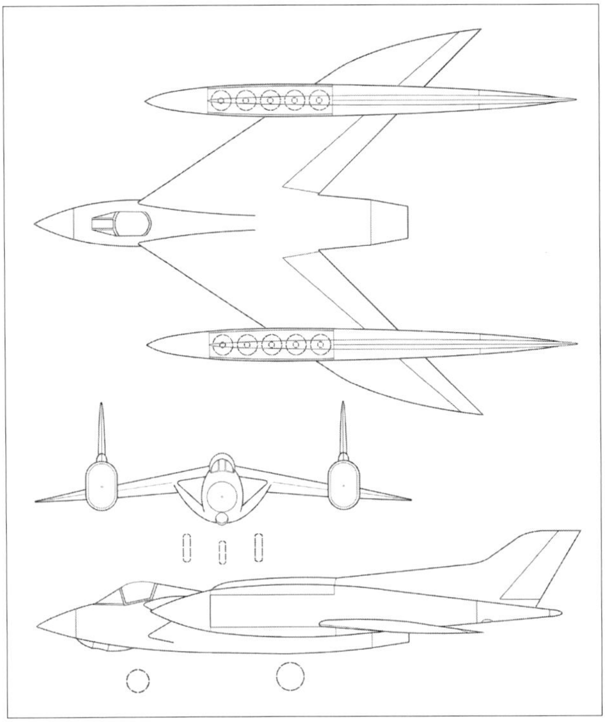

The Gloster P.507, VTOL strike/reconnaissance aircraft, which was probably the last design in this series, which dates from 1960. Powered by a single Rolls-Royce Conway turbofan in horizontal flight, the aircraft would also carry ten RB.162 lift engines for VTOL operations.

(13,608 kg), subsonic performance and was intended for strike and reconnaissance missions. It may have been considered suitable to deliver a single tactical nuclear weapon and because of this, Gloster considered submitting the design for NBMR-3 during 1960, but never progressed that far. Perhaps it was simply outclassed by the competition, or Gloster's parent company Hawker felt that the P.505 might get in the way of their more advanced VTOL designs?

Of the other known military V/STOL studies undertaken by Gloster during the late 1950s, one further design stands out, which is the P.507. This was a swept wing tailless strike/reconnaissance aircraft, also powered in horizontal flight by a single Rolls-Royce Conway turbofan engine and equipped with ten RB.162 lift engines for VTOL operations. These would be housed in very large nacelles built into each main wing section, with all the turbojets mounted in upright positions. The nacelles would also be fitted with substantial fins and rudders, while probably also accommodating fuel tanks. The all-up-weight of the P.507 would be slightly greater than the P.505 at 32,400 lb (14696 kg) and this single seat aircraft would be supported on the ground by a retractable tricycle undercarriage.

The only available drawing would seem to suggest that outrigger wheels might have been necessary. The aircraft would probably carry stores externally beneath the fuselage, and/or inner wing sections, with the P.507 being considered suitable for naval operations. The study was completed in late 1960, but progressed no further. Plans were now underway to merge Gloster Aircraft with Armstrong Whitworth (soon to become the Avro-Whitworth Division of Hawker Siddeley Aviation) and the V/STOL studies were probably the last major projects undertaken by Gloster's design office.

Boulton Paul

With all the major UK aircraft manufacturers exploring ideas for military and civil V/STOL aircraft by the mid-1950s, Boulton Paul's Wolverhampton design office began catch-up studies on a range of ideas with broadly similar capabilities, including the widely favoured delta wing.

Boulton Paul initially concentrated on VTOL designs with military potential under the company umbrella designation P.130. There are known to have been at least twelve separate P.130 studies undertaken between 1954 and 1955, but most of the documentation has been lost and the only remaining information covers the Mk 6 and Mk 8 designs. The Mk 6 was a proposed experimental delta wing design powered by five Rolls-Royce RB.108 engines, providing power for horizontal flight and also driving a centrally located 54 inch (1.37 m) contra-rotating fan generating lift. The aircraft was fitted with two downward positioned fins with rudders, which also carried the fixed main wheels of a tricycle undercarriage. The front wheel was fully retractable. This arrangement would ensure adequate clearance for the fan's airflow.

The Mk 8 was an improved military specification prototype that evolved from the Mk 6. It was powered by two Bristol-Siddeley Orpheus turbojets, providing a combined thrust of 9,700 lb (43 kN). These would be linked to a centrally positioned 75 inch (1.9 m) contra-rotating fan and three smaller fans in the nose and wings used to balance the system.
Unfortunately, the details of this layout are not shown on the original drawing. The same type of downward fins and undercarriage that had been proposed for the Mk 6 were used, but the Mk 8 would have provision for two inboard cannon in the wings, pylons for stores and folding wings for naval hangar storage. It is assumed that this design would be capable of conventional take-offs and landings.

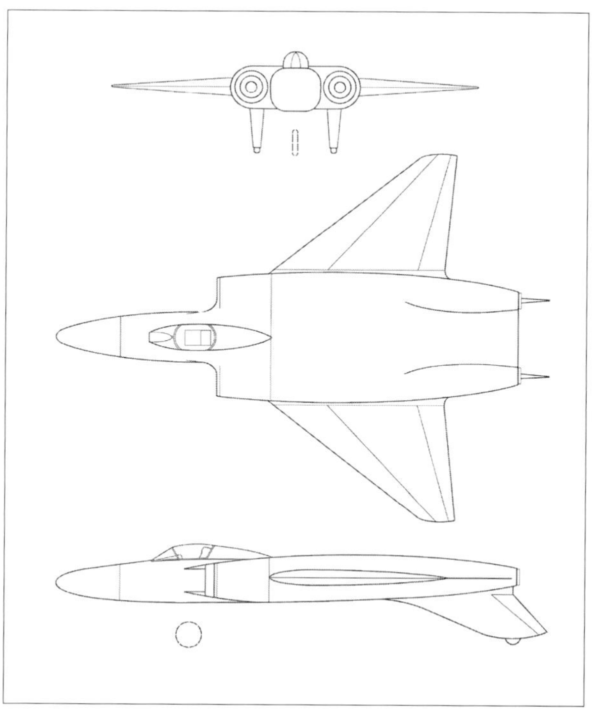

Boulton Paul's Mk 8 design under the P.130 series of studies, for a delta VTOL experimental aircraft. The two unusually positioned fins were intended to improve airflow beneath the aircraft during VTOL and also form part of the tricycle undercarriage arrangement.

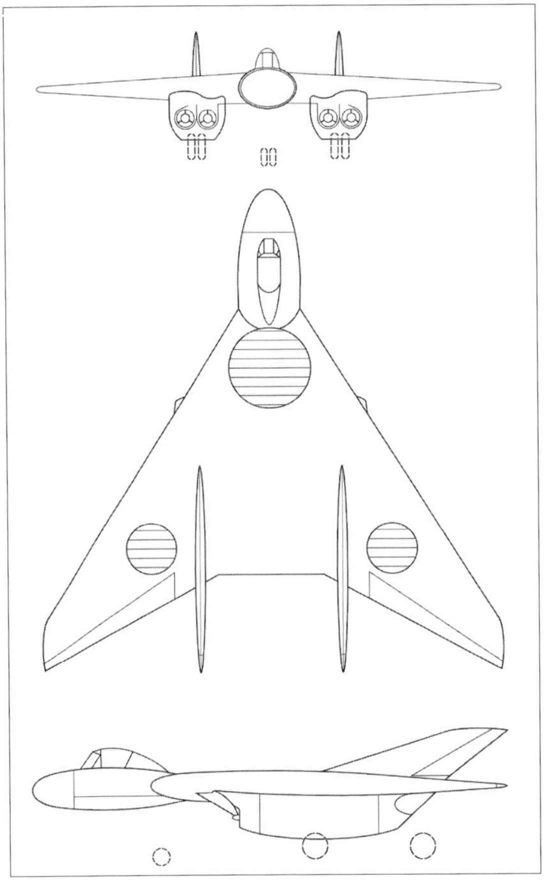

General arrangement of the Boulton Paul P.132 fan lift VTOL concept.

Detail of the propulsion system of the proposed Boulton Paul P.132, showing the turbojets and positions of the lift fans. (*Boulton Paul*)

Nothing is known about the designs which followed the Mk 8, but it seems probable they were further refinements of this series or variants intended for specific tasks.

The next design study in this VTOL series was fan-lift concept, with the reference P.132 (the P.131 was not a VTOL design). This was completed at the beginning of 1956 to meet MoS specification ER.166D for a fan lift prototype. P.132 was a delta design with a leading edge sweep of 57.5°.

The fuselage section was mounted mostly ahead of the wing's leading edge and this is described in available documentation as egg shaped. Twin fins with rudders were fitted above the rear of the wing, with substantial nacelles below, which each housed a pair of Armstrong Siddeley Viper Mk-103 ASV.9 turbojets, individually rated at about 2,000 lb (8.89 kN) thrust. These would be connected by shafts to a series of lift fans, with the largest at the front just behind the cockpit, two smaller fans in the wings, outboard of the fins and a further two smaller fans at the rear of the engine nacelles. In level flight the fans would be shut down, with the engines providing power for level flight only.

There does appear to have been several slightly different fan layouts considered and this design was regarded as suitable for development into a VTOL fighter. P.132 had a provisional length of 40.5 ft (12.34 m), a wingspan of 39 ft (11.88 m) and a height of approximately 11.5 ft (3.5 m). It has not been possible to locate authentic documentation showing planned weight and performance at the time of writing. Scale models of this proposal were built and wind tunnel tested, but it soon gave way to an upgraded version with the reference P.135. Somewhat similar in appearance to the P.132, the first study was completed in May 1957. It was planned to power the aircraft with two Bristol-Siddeley Orpheus turbojets, each rated at 4,850 lb (21.5 kN) thrust. These would be carried in large nacelles below the aircraft. Four lift fans driven by the turbojets were envisaged, with a large central fan behind the cockpit area, another towards the trailing edge and a further two in the outer wing areas.

There are several known versions of the P.135. The P.135A was designed with a Draken-style double delta and the P.135B was a highly swept delta. Models of these proposals were built and wind tunnel tested by the RAE, with the 3/25 scale model of the P.135B undergoing lengthy trials in the 13 ft × 9 ft (3.9m × 2.7 m) wind tunnel at the National Physical Laboratory. Despite considerable interest in the design, it seems there were a number of technical issues that came to light during tests, which may have been responsible for discouraging further development and bringing these particular studies to an end.

Running almost parallel to the Boulton Paul P.132 and P.135 studies were several rather different designs for military combat aircraft with V/STOL capabilities. These came within the overall P.133 company reference and much of this project was undertaken in 1956. The aim was to produce a supersonic VTOL fighter that could be configured for use by the RAF or Royal Navy. An initial proposal for a single-seat fighter utilised some research undertaken by the RAE on fan lift for VTOL and was a delta shaped aircraft powered by two afterburning de Havilland Gyron Junior turbojets rated at 10,000 lb (44.48 kN) dry thrust. These would be connected to six lift fans for VTOL, with the turbojets providing propulsion for level flight when the fans were disengaged. In addition to the turbojets, it was suggested that a Spectre rocket engine was a possibility. This initial design evolved into the P.133A which was fairly similar, but only utilised four lift engines. This was followed by the slightly larger, two-seat P.133B which was primarily configured for naval search and strike operations, with a re-arrangement of lift fans to accommodate the internal carriage of weapons.

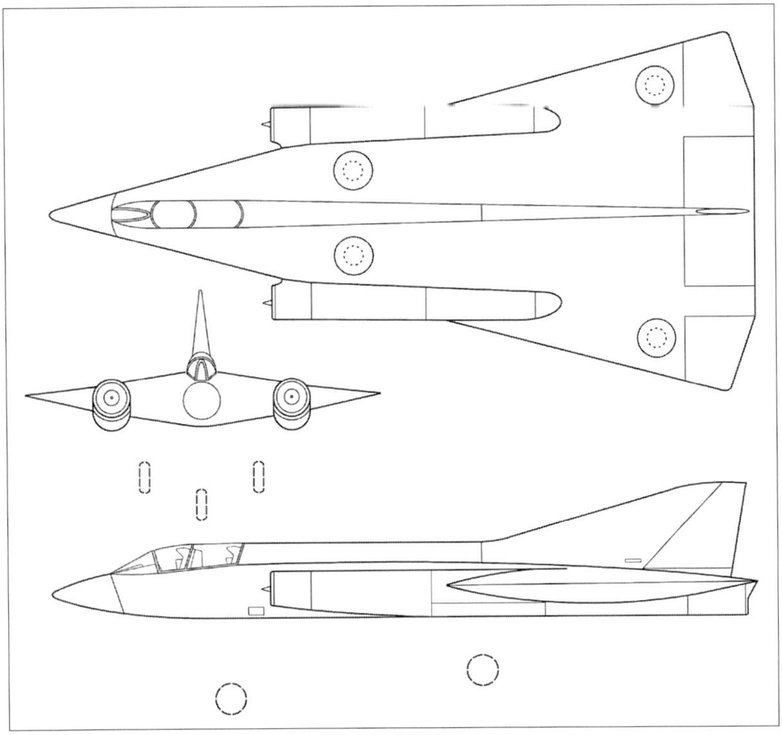

The two-seat Boulton Paul P.133B V/STOL search and strike aircraft, primarily intended for use by the Royal Navy.

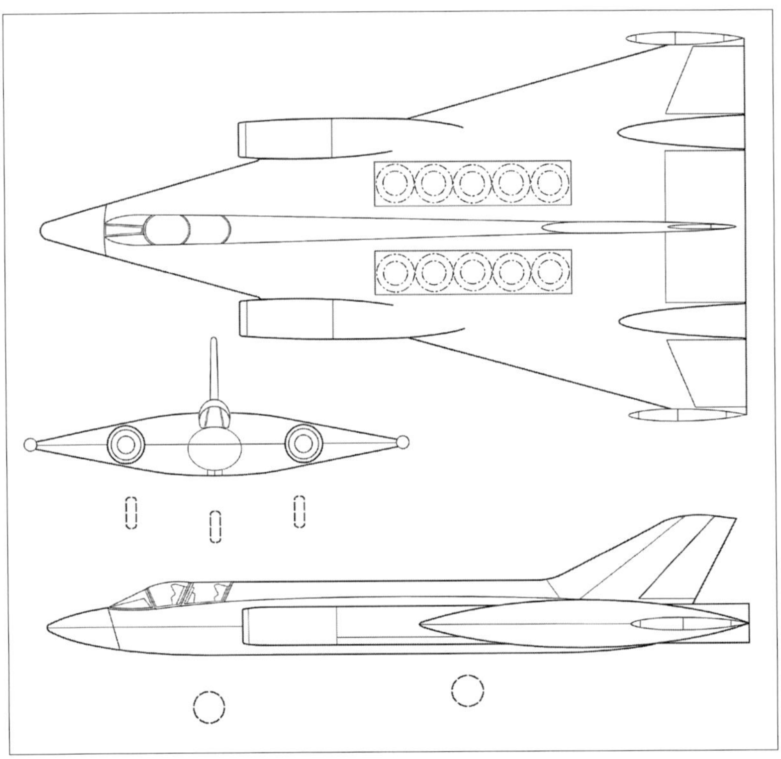

Another Boulton Paul V/STOL proposal for a naval multi-role combat aircraft, the P.137 would be equipped with ten centrally located lift fans adapted from RB.108 turbojets and two de Havilland Gyron Junior engines for level flight.

The P.133B proposal was completed in late 1956 and retained the same highly swept delta configuration with a single tailfin and rudder. Power was provided by two Gyron Junior engines, but there was no provision for an additional rocket engine. Designed to meet naval requirement NR/A.39, it would be fitted with a fully retractable tricycle undercarriage and suitable for carrier catapult launch and normal runway operations. Weapons would be carried in a central bomb bay section, with various configurations for conventional bombs, a single low yield free fall nuclear weapon or possibly rocket packs. The design now utilised four 32 inch (81 cm) lift fans between the engine inlets and towards each end of the trailing edge, just ahead of the elevons. An all-up-weight of 40,120 lb (18,198 kg) was suggested, with the possibility of increasing this to 45,000 lb (20,412 kg) when using a catapult for take-off. The proposed dimensions of this aircraft were 57 ft (17.4 m) in length, a wingspan of 28 ft (8.5 m) and a wing area of 841 ft^2 (78.2 m^2). A maximum speed of Mach 1.4 at sea level was suggested, but there is no further information to indicate the aircraft's expected ceiling or range.

In early 1957, Boulton Paul's designers completed a further study with the reference P.134 that was closely based on the P.133. This was a single seat, supersonic VTOL fighter powered by two Bristol-Siddeley Orpheus BOr.11 turbojets. Four lift fans would be employed for VTOL and the maximum speed is quoted as Mach 1.25 at 35,000 ft (10,688 m). Probably the final design in this series was the P.137. Broadly similar to the P.133B, a two-seater for naval operations, but in this case, using ten centrally located lift fans developed from RB.108 turbojets and using two de Havilland Gyron Junior engines for horizontal propulsion. None of these VTOL combat aircraft were accepted by the MoS for further development, although the idea of using fan lift never entirely went away.

Today, the Lockheed-Martin F-35B STOVL fighter uses a Rolls-Royce developed forward lift fan driven by the F135 turbofan engine, which also employs thrust vectoring to balance the system while the fan operates. A significant problem with using jet engines for VTOL lift is hot gas ingestion and a fan avoids this problem. It seems likely that this system will have more applications in the future.

One other Boulton Paul design study in this overall series was the P.136. This single-seat, twin-engined supersonic VTOL delta was conceived in 1957 and has many features found on similar proposals from this period. For lift, the aircraft would use six centrally positioned Rolls-Royce RB.108 turbojets, located in a row at the centre of the aircraft. Presumably, air bled for these engines would be used for control and stabilisation during VTOL. Two Bristol-Siddeley Orpheus BOr.11 turbojets would be used for horizontal flight. The aircraft would be fitted with a fully retractable tricycle undercarriage and capable of normal runway take-offs and landings. Described as an experimental aircraft, it appears to have intended for development into a fighter, or strike aircraft. Models may have been wind tunnel tested, but the project went no further.

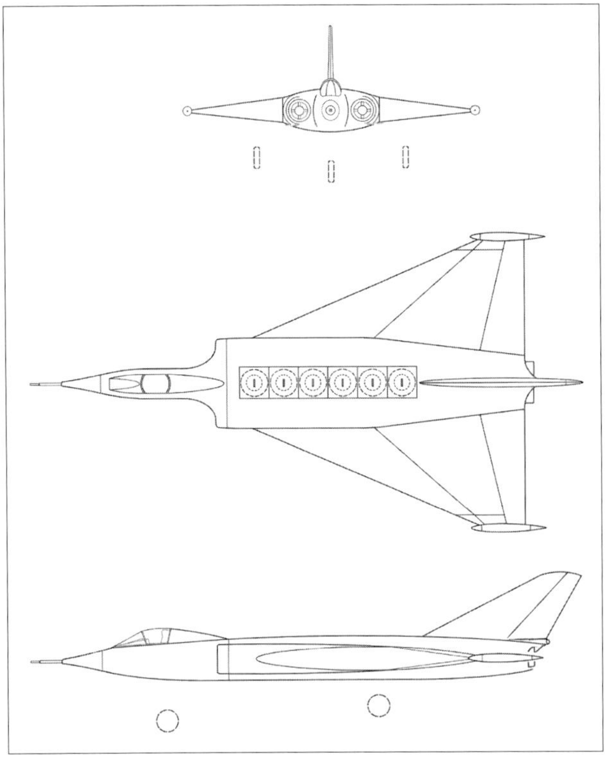

The Boulton Paul P.136 was a delta design with similar features to various designs by Shorts and Rolls Royce.Six Rolls-Royce RB.108 turbojets would provide liftduring VTOL operations and two Bristol-Siddeley Orpheus BOr.11 turbojets were proposed for horizontal flight. Like all the other Boulton Paul VTOL proposals, this concept went little further than engineering studies and possibly model tests in the wind tunnel.

De Havilland

Towards the end of the 1950s, Britain's Admiralty began to look for an advanced carrier-based strike fighter/reconnaissance aircraft with STOL performance and perhaps variable geometry capabilities. This would be a follow-on to the Buccaneer and Sea Vixen, with an introduction to service at the start of the 1970s. There was also official interest in a broadly similar version of the aircraft suitable for the RAF. This would lead to a formal request for proposals that were outlined in OR.346. A driving factor behind OR.346 was the Royal Navy's desire to upgrade its carriers and equip them with more advanced aircraft during the late 1960s. The new carriers were allocated the general designation CVA-01. They would be larger and more sophisticated than any of the RN's existing carriers, which were now showing their age. It was proposed that CVA-01 would replace HMS *Ark Royal* and HMS *Victorious*, while there would be a CVA-02 and CVA-03 to replace HMS *Eagle* and HMS *Hermes*. These new carriers all had a projected displacement in the region of 53,000 tons and a flight deck of 963 ft (293.5 m). The CVA-01 series would represent a significant step forward in terms of the UK's power-projection capability.

Naturally, the Admiralty wanted a more advanced multi-role combat aircraft to accompany its new carriers. They considered Spey main engines the best choice, along with secondary lift turbojets. A maximum speed of at least Mach 2 was required, Mach 0.9 cruise at sea level and the ability to deliver a tactical nuclear weapon over a considerable distance. Several aircraft contractors responded to this requirement and designs were submitted that included the Blackburn B.123, Hawker P.1151, P.1152, P.1153 and de Havilland DH.127 and DH.128.

These last two Hatfield designed aircraft are of particular interest as they were both very similar tailless deltas. The DH.127 was intended for RAF use and the DH.128 was primarily for naval carrier operations. This version had some structural strengthening, arrestor landing gear, folding wings for hangar storage and possibly some changes to the avionics and an allowance for the carriage of different stores. Both aircraft would have much the same capability, with a Mach 2+ performance at altitude, a Mach 0.9 cruise capability at sea level and a ceiling of about 60,000 ft (18,288 m). Able to carry a substantial amount of internal fuel, these aircraft could deliver a single 2,000 lb (907 kg) free-fall nuclear bomb to a target within a radius of 1,600 miles (2,574 km) and the range could be extended to 1,726 miles (2,777 km) with underwing drop tanks.

In a conventional strike role it was anticipated that an 8,000 lb (3,628 kg) payload was possible, comprising of free fall bombs or AGMs. Daylight photo-reconnaissance was another option and configured as an interceptor carrying Red Top AAMs, the DH.127/8 would (under the right circumstances) be capable of engaging an enemy aircraft travelling at a speed of around Mach 3 at 80,000 ft (24,384 m). Furthermore, the aircraft would be able to remain on patrol for 4 hours. The airframe was to be mainly fabricated from an aluminium copper alloy and this was considered the best choice for a very strong structure. A major feature of the DH.127/8 was the STOL performance. Primary propulsion was provided by two Rolls-Royce Mk 202 Spey turbofans (subject to model change) producing an anticipated static thrust of 12,140 lb (54 kN) and 20,500 lb (91.18 kN) with afterburning. Air for the engines would flow through inlets on each side of the cockpit with variable geometry centre bodies. The Spey engines would also be equipped with deflector nozzles fitted at the turbine end of each engine allowing some downward exhaust (when required) for improved lift. In addition, to balance this somewhat unusual feature,

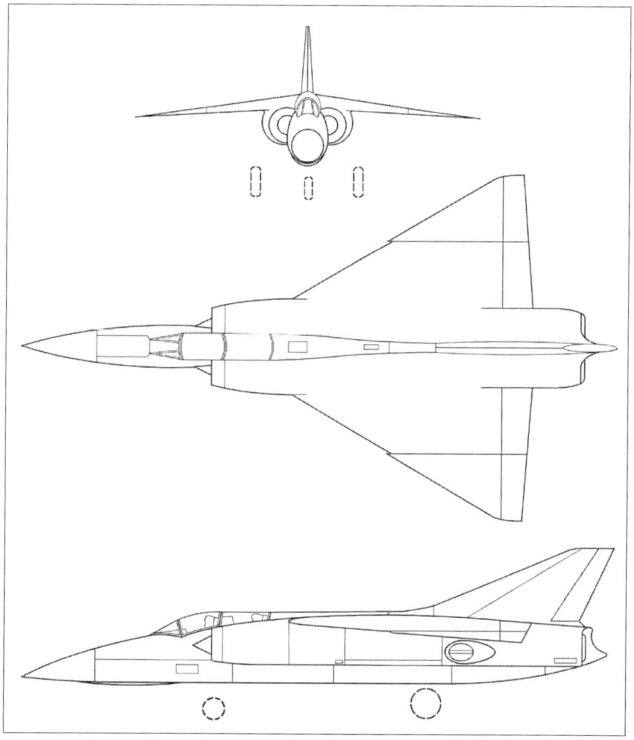

De Havilland (HSA) DH.127 was a design study for a supersonic STOL tailless delta powered by two Spey turbofans, with exhaust diverters and two upright RB.162 turbojets to facilitate STOL.

two compact Rolls-Royce RB.162-31 turbojets, each producing 4,409 lb (19.61 kN) of thrust would be mounted vertically in the fuselage just ahead of the cockpit. The aircraft would have a conventional tricycle undercarriage and a centrally located bomb bay. However, despite being quite an impressive, well-designed aircraft, the DH.127/8 and all the other OR.346 proposals came to nothing. Then in the mid-1960s the RN decided to adopt a UK modified version of the McDonnell F-4 Phantom as its new supersonic combat aircraft to replace the Sea Vixen. Plans for the series of RN supercarriers were also dropped and the RAF were encouraged to take the Phantom as a Lightning replacement.

As things turned out, the Royal Navy would have to wait more than half a century before two state-of-the-art multi-billion-pound aircraft carriers became available, along with a fleet of very expensive high-tech American STOVL stealth fighters.

Vulcan VTOL

An extraordinary proposal from the early 1960s was a VTOL version of the Vulcan B.2. It remains unclear just how serious this idea was, but a highly modified version of the bomber would be fitted with 10 upright mounted turbojets in the central bomb bay area. The aircraft would carry one air-launched nuclear missile in the Skybolt class under the wing and a large balancing fuel tank on the opposite side. One reference mentions an Avro Vulcan 768 VTOL weapon systems, but it's hard to say if this is genuine or even the same concept!

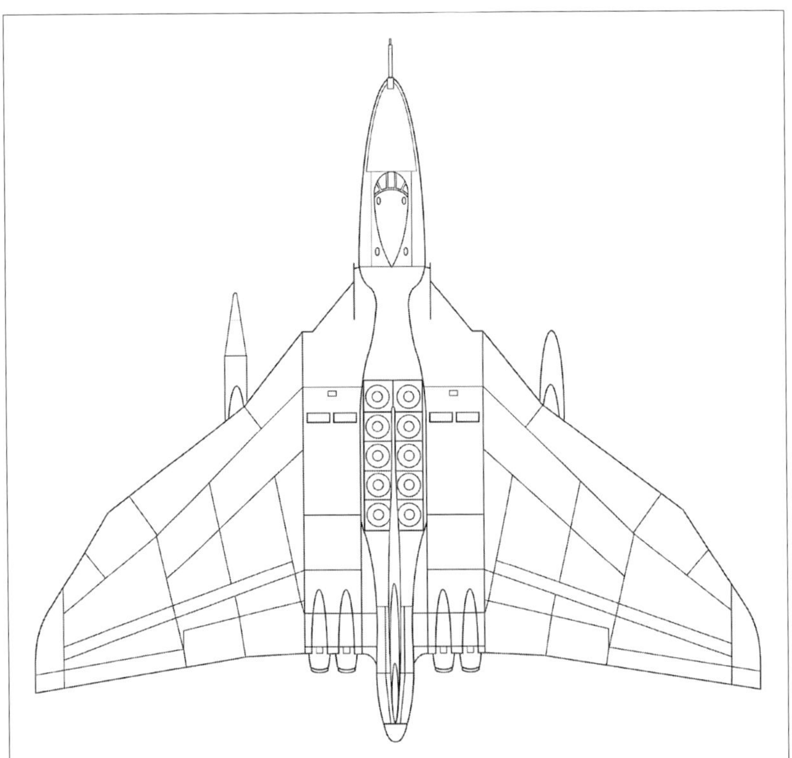

This drawing is based on artwork showing a proposed VTOL version of the Avro Vulcan B 2. It is impossible to say if this concept was seriously considered or not. Ten upright turbojets would be contained in the bomb bay area and the aircraft would carry an external fuel tank and a single air-to-surface nuclear tipped missile such as Skybolt.

Davidson's Aerobus

During 1952 a project was started at Britain's National Gas Turbine Establishment (NGTE) to see if it might be feasible to produce a system of directing the exhaust from jet engines through a wing's trailing edge to improve low-speed performance and hopefully provide a good STOL capability. The idea was not entirely new and the German aerodynamicists H. Hagedorn and P. Ruden had noted interesting trailing edge effects during boundary layer control research in 1938. Similar conclusions were also reached by Valensi in France. Having examined the data from these earlier wind tunnel tests, NGTE scientists decided to undertake their own elementary experiments with small desktop sized models. This confirmed that increased initial lift and thrust could be created by ducting a certain amount of jet engine exhaust to the wing's trailing edge.

It seemed that a thin jet sheet produced behind an aircraft could be used in much the same manner as a hinged wing flap, leading to the term 'jet flap.' Ivor Davidson (1924–2008), who headed the NGTE jet flap project, soon began to consider practical uses for this technology. Various ways of directing the jet flow were clearly possible, such as long slots, nozzles and simply positioning flaps made from suitable metal in the jet flow.

At cruising speed, an aircraft using jet flaps would behave like a conventional fixed wing design, but at low speeds, when the jet flow was directed downwards, this would provide good STOL performance. Nevertheless, it was obvious that any wing capable of vectoring the jet flow along most of its trailing edge would present some substantial engineering challenges and Davidson recognised that there would be difficulties maintaining control of an aircraft in the event of an engine failure.

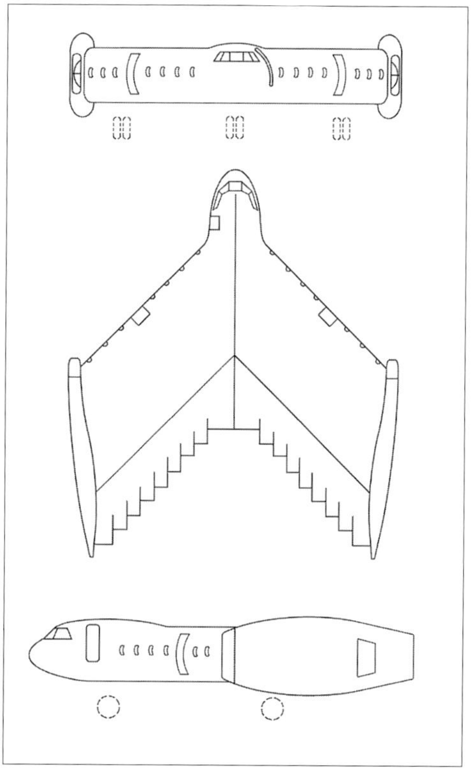

A proposed layout for the Aerobus jet-flap transport aircraft.

The research programme continued, with Ivor Davidson presenting an outline of jet flap development to the Royal Aeronautical Society in October 1955. The idea was sound, but it was clear that this technology could not be applied to the majority of existing fixed wing designs and an entirely new type of aircraft was needed. By the end of the 1950s, Davidson had outlined a compact, tailless transport aircraft called Aerobus that would take advantage of laminar flow aerodynamics and use the jet flap system. This all-wing design had a wingspan of 50 ft (15.24 m), a wing area of 1,240 ft^2 (115 m^2) and a length of 57 ft (17.37 m). Propulsion would be provided by a total of four turbofans in wingtip nacelles connected to 16 trailing edge outlets via ducting. This short-haul aircraft would cruise at approximately 444 mph (716 kph), with a cruising altitude of 20,000 ft (6,096 m). The Aerobus project continued into the early 1960s, with the operating cost initially estimated at 1.2 pence (UK old) per passenger mile.

Aerobus would be supported on the ground by a retractable tricycle undercarriage and the gross weight (as an airliner) was estimated at 64,000 lb (29,030 kg) with the anticipated payload being 100 passengers and their luggage. This aircraft would have considerable military potential in the transport role, with possible adaptions to other uses, but the design went no further. However, the state-funded NGTE continued to develop jet flap technology, having already requested the construction of a proof-of-concept aircraft during the late 1950s. This finally received Ministry of Aviation approval and Hunting Aircraft of Luton, Bedfordshire, were issued with a contract in June 1959 to build two small demonstrators. The first prototype known as H.126 (serial XN714), undertook its maiden flight at RAE Bedford on 26 March 1963, with Hunting's Chief Test Pilot Stanley Oliver at the controls. The second prototype which had a slightly different amount of wing dihedral was allocated the serial XN719, but the RAE no longer considered this aircraft necessary and a decision was made to cancel it in mid-1962, with the partly completed airframe being scrapped.

The Hunting H.126 prototype, built in the early 1960s to demonstrate the viability of the jet flap system.

The jet flap system used on the H.126 utilised 16 nozzles located along the wing's trailing edge, releasing approximately half of the jet engine's exhaust gas. A small amount of gas was also ducted to the wingtips for low speed control and the remainder was exhausted on each side of the lower fuselage. The H.126 was a compact, single-seat aircraft, built around its turbojet engine. The cockpit was located in a forward position, offering good visibility and the tricycle undercarriage was of a simple, fixed position design. Trials were mainly undertaken at RAE Bedford between 1963 and 1967, with no serious problems occurring and the aircraft was then loaned to NASA, who conducted wind tunnel tests at the Ames Flight Research Center during 1969. H.126 was returned the following year and is now on display at the RAF Cosford Museum.

The jet flap experiments showed that the idea could be made to work, but it also became apparent that the nozzle system was too complex to be practical and the power requirements were much greater than originally anticipated. A related, although much simpler system using air ducted from the compressor stage was utilised by several 1960s combat aircraft to improve low speed performance. A form of 'blown flap' can currently be found on several transport aircraft.

Fairey Type K Fighter
Crew: 1
Wingspan: N/A
Wing area: N/A
Sweep (leading edge): 41.5° estimated
Length: N/A
Height: N/A
Empty weight: N/A
Gross weight: 13,500 lb (6,123 kg)
Estimated maximum speed: 650 mph (1,046 kph) at sea level
Ceiling: N/A
Range: N/A
Powerplant: 2 × Rolls-Royce AJ65s (the proposed Avon), each producing 6,500 lb (29 kN) of static thrust
Armament: 2 × 30 mm cannon

Fairey FD.1
Crew: 1
Wingspan: 19.5 ft (5.94 m). Initial Type R specification: 15.33 ft (4.67 m)
Wing area: N/A
Sweep (leading edge): 47.5°
Length: 26.25 ft (8 m).
Initial Type R specification: 28.67 ft (8.73 m)
Height: 19.5 ft (5.94 m)
Empty weight: N/A
Gross weight: 6,800 lb (3,084 kg)
Estimated maximum speed: 628 mph (1,010 kph)
Practical maximum speed: 345 mph (555 kph)
Ceiling: N/A
Range: N/A
Powerplant: 1 × Rolls-Royce Derwent 8 turbojet, providing 3,600 lb (16 kN) static thrust
Armament: none

Avro P.724 Single Engine
Crew: 1
Wingspan 16 ft (4.87 m)
Wing area: 192 ft^2 (17.8 m^2)
Length: 32.5 ft (9.9 m)
Take-off weight: 18,000–20,000 lb (8,164-9,071 kg) estimated.
Maximum speed: Mach 2 at altitude
Ceiling: 60,000 ft (18,288 m) approximate
Powerplant: 1 × Rolls-Royce RB.106 with an anticipated static thrust of 15,000 lb (66 kN), rising to 21,800 lb (97 kN) with afterburner
Armament: 2 × Air-to-air missiles

Avro P.724 Twin Engine
Crew: 1
Wingspan: 24 ft (7.3 m)
Wing area: 375 ft^2 (34.8 m^2)
Sweep (leading edge): 60°
Length: 37 ft (11.2 m)
Take-off weight: 24,500 lb (11,113 kg) approximate
Maximum speed: Mach 2.5
Ceiling: 60,000ft+ (18,288m+).
Powerplant: 2 × Rolls-Royce RB.106, each with an anticipated static thrust of 15,000 lb (66 kN), rising to 21,800 lb (97 kN) with afterburner
Armament: 2 × Blue Jay (later called Firestreak) heat seeking air-to-air missiles

Short Brothers SC.1
Crew: 1
Length: 25.5 ft (7.77 m)
Wingspan: 23.5 ft (7.16 m)
Height: 10.66 ft (3.25 m)
Wing area: 211.5 ft^2 (19.65 m^2)

Sweep (leading edge): 54°
Empty weight: 6,260 lb (2,839 kg)
Loaded weight (CTOL—Conventional Take-Off & Landing): 8,050 lb (3,650 kg)
Loaded weight (VTOL): 7,700 lb (3,490 kg)
Powerplant: lift: 4 × Rolls-Royce RB.108 turbojets, each rated at 2,130 lb (9.47 kN) thrust
Horizontal flight: 1 × Rolls-Royce RB.108 turbojet, rated at 2,130 lb (9.47 kN) thrust
Maximum speed: 246 mph (396 kph)
Ceiling: 8,000 ft (2,440 m)
Range: 150 miles (240 km)

Short Brothers PD.17D VTOL Lift Platform/Freighter/ Airborne Tanker
Crew: 1
Wingspan: 50 ft (15.24 m) approximate
Wing area: N/A
Sweep (forward leading edge): 73.5° approximate
Length: 80 ft (24.3 m) approximate
Height: 14 ft (4.26 m) approximate
Empty weight: 46,050 lb (20,888 kg)
Loaded weight: 150,000 lb (68,038 kg) carrying a P.17A/ TSR.2 strike aircraft
Powerplant: 44 × RB.108 fixed turbojets each rated at 2,130 lb (9.47 kN) thrust and 16 × RB.108 tilting lift turbojets each rated at 2,130 lb (9.47 kN) thrust. Plus 10 × RB.108 or alternatively 10 × RB.145 (rated at 2,750 lb (12.23 kN) thrust) with a 60° exhaust deflection
Maximum speed: N/A
Ceiling: N/A

Short Brothers PD.34 VTOL Lift Platform
Intended to carry an adapted Folland Gnat armed with a tactical nuclear weapon.
Crew: 1
Wingspan: 23–24 ft (7–7.3 m) estimated
Wing area: N/A
Sweep (forward leading edge): 73.5-75° approximate
Length: 35 ft (10.6 m) estimated
Height: N/A
Empty weight: N/A
Loaded weight: N/A
Powerplant: 8 centrally located lift engines, possibly Rolls-Royce RB.162-31 turbojets, each producing 4,409 lb (19.61 kN) of thrust. 2 × unspecified turbojets for horizontal flight
Maximum speed: N/A
Ceiling: N/A

Short Brothers PD.40
Very similar to PD.34 but carrying the slightly larger and heavier Fiat G.91 strike fighter

Short Brothers PD.56
Crew: 1
Length: 54.6 ft (16.6 m)
Span 28 ft (8.5 m)
Sweep (leading edge): 60°
Wing area N/A
VTO take-off weight: About 23,000 lb (10,433 kg)
All up weight: 29,700 lb (13,472 kg)
Powerplant: 8 × Rolls-Royce RB.162-31 turbojets, each producing 4,409 lb (19.61 kN) of thrust. 2 × afterburning Rolls-Royce RB.168-IR turbofans, rated at 12,140 lb (54 kN) thrust and 20,500 lb (91.18 kN) thrust with afterburner
Maximum speed: Mach 1.08 sea level. Mach 1.95 at 40,000 ft (12,192 m)
Ceiling 50,000ft+ (15,250m+)
Range: VTOL combat radius of 250 miles (400 km) travelling partly at supersonic speed, which could be improved to some extent with speed reduction
Ceiling: 50,000ft+ (15,240m+)
Armament: underwing Bullpup air-to-surface missiles or free-fall bombs, Firestreak or Sidewinder missiles, possibly air-to-air rockets or 30 mm ADEN cannon. A single tactical nuclear weapon

Armstrong Whitworth A.W.171/2
Crew: 1
Wing Span: 17.5 ft (5.36 m)
Sweep (leading edge): 83°. AW.172 76°
Length: 70 ft (21.59 m)
Gross weight: 16,309 lb (7,398 kg)
Powerplant: horizontal flight; 2 × Bristol Orpheus turbojets, each rated at 4,859 lb (21.6 kN) thrust with afterburner. VTOL operations: 10 × Rolls-Royce RB.108 turbojets, each rated at 2,101 lb (9.34 kN) thrust
Maximum speed: 1,483 mph (2,387 kph)
Ceiling 60,000 ft (18,288 m)
Endurance: unknown
Range: unknown

Gloster P.507
Crew: 1
Wingspan: 31.5 ft (9.6 m)
Sweep (leading edge): 55°
Length: 45 ft (13.7 m) approximate
Height 13 ft (3.96 m) approximate
All-up weight of 32,400 lb (14,696 kg)
Powerplant: 1 × Rolls-Royce Conway R.Co 11 turbofan rated at 17,150 lb (76.3 kN) thrust and 10 × Rolls-Royce RB.162-31 turbojets in two wing nacelles, each producing 4,409 lb (19.61 kN) of thrust

BOULTON PAUL P.132
Crew: 1
Wingspan: 39 ft (11.88 m)
Sweep (leading edge): 57.5°
Length: 40.5 ft (12.34 m)
Height: 11.5 ft (3.5 m)
Weight: N/A
Powerplant: 4 × Armstrong Siddeley Viper Mk-103 ASV.9 turbojets, individually rated at about 2,000 lb (8.89 kN) thrust
Range: N/A
Maximum speed: N/A

BOULTON PAUL P.133B
Crew: 1
Wingspan: 28 ft (8.5 m)
Sweep (leading edge): N/A
Wing area: 841 ft^2 (78.2 m^2)
Length: 57 ft (17.4 m)
All-up-weight 40,120 lb (18,198 kg). 45,000 lb (20,412 kg) possible with catapult take-off
Powerplant: 2 × de Havilland Gyron Junior providing 10,000 lb (44.4 kN) dry thrust for forward flight and diving 4 × 32in (81.3c m) lift fans during VTOL operations
Maximum speed: Mach 1.34 at sea level
Ceiling: 55,000 ft (16,764 m) approximate
Range: N/A
Armament: 5-8 air-to-ground rocket packs. 2 × 2,000 lb bombs, 4 × 4,000 lb bombs or one tactical nuclear weapon.

DH.127
Crew: 2
Length: 60 ft (18.28 m)
Wingspan: 33 ft (10 m)
Wing area: 560 ft^2 (52 m^2)
Sweep (leading edge): 60°
Height: 18 ft (5.4 m) approximate
Gross weight: 50,000 lb (22,679 kg). Maximum overload weight: 56,000 lb (25,400 kg)
Maximum speed: Mach 2+ at altitude
Sea level high speed cruise: Mach 0.9
Ceiling: 60,000 ft (18,288 m) approximate
Powerplant: 2 × Rolls-Royce Spey 202 turbofans producing an anticipated static thrust of 12,140 lb (54 kN) and 20,500 lb (91.18 kN) with afterburning. 2 × Rolls-Royce RB.162-31 turbojets for forward lift, each producing 4,409 lb (19.61 kN) thrust
Armament: 4 × Bullpup ASMs, 4 × Red Top AAMs, Sidewinder AAMs, 8 × 1000 lb (453 kg) bombs, 1 × 2000 lb (907 kg) tactical nuclear weapon.

Aerobus (1962 Proposal)
Crew: 3 flight 2 cabin
Wingspan: 50 ft (15.24 m)
Wing area: 1,240 ft^2 (115 m^2)
Length: 57 ft (17.37 m)
Height: 15 ft (4.57 m)
Gross weight: 64,000 lb (29,030 kg)
Cruise Speed: 444 mph (716 kph)
Powerplant: 4 × turbofan engines
Payload: 100 passengers (as an airliner)

Hunting Aircraft H.126
Crew: 1
Wingspan: 45.33 ft (13.8 m)
Wing area: 221 ft^2 (20.58 m^2)
Length: 50.05 ft (15.2 m)
Height: 15.5 ft (4.72 m)
Gross weight: 10,740 lb (4871 kg)
Powerplant: 1 × Bristol-Siddeley Orpheus BOr.3 Mk.805 turbojet, producing 4,000 lb (17.79 kN) static thrust
Maximum speed: unknown, although the H.126 was designed to explore low speed and could remain airborne at 32 mph (51.5 kph)
Ceiling: N/A

7

Space Ambitions

German wartime rocketry was extremely impressive and looked as if it belonged to a future era, which in a way it did. The Allies considered this technology so important, that prior to the cessation of hostilities, they began preparing specialist intelligence units to secure hardware, documentation, engineers and scientists. Only Germany's nuclear and chemical weapons programmes would receive the same priority.

Although long-range German missiles caused many deaths, especially in Belgium and Southern England, the scientists responsible for these weapons such as Dr Wernher von Braun, would eventually be credited with making major scientific advances. Without them, space exploration would have taken far longer. The first manned Moon landing might not have occurred until the early twenty-first century and many of the technological spin-offs we all take for granted like digital electronics, would have taken much longer to develop.

With the war in Europe over, America and Russia began shipping vast quantities of captured rocketry and research material back home and started setting up major programmes to reproduce and develop everything the Germans had accomplished. In addition to acquiring the hardware, many of Germany's top scientists were either tracked down, or they simply approached the Americans or British, having no wish to be captured by the Russians. The Second World War might have ended, but a fearful arms race was now underway between the East and West, with the objective of buidling long range rockets eventually able to carry atomic warheads. Despite German scientists showing what was possible, the technical challenges of moving up to the next level were considerable and the balance of global balance power was now at stake. While the Soviets were unable to match America's wealth and resources, they were just as eager to make full use of German rocket technology. They had several of von Braun's former scientists working for them and a fierce determination to succeed.

It began to seem as if 'push button warfare' involving long range rockets carrying atomic warheads would eventually become a practical proposition and this idea gained considerable attention from many British politicans who accepted it as the inevitable way forward. However, the UK faced severe post-war economic challenges and while ambitious rocket and missile programmes were often discussed in Whitehall, the kind of technology being developed by

America and Russia was realistically beyond Britain's reach. That said, there was certainly interest in guided missiles capable of shooting down aircraft, new battlefield or naval weapons and perhaps medium-range rockets capable of delivering atomic warheads. For this reason, a suitable test area was needed, although the UK was mostly unsuitable. Fortunately, an initial agreement had been struck in 1946 between Britain and Australia to establish a large, test range on their territory and by the following year, an uninhabited area in South Australia had been chosen, about 280 miles (450 km) north-west of Adelaide. This was given the name Woomera in 1947, which rather appropriately is the name of an Australian aboriginal spear-throwing device.

In October 1952, the first British nuclear device was tested and although a weaponised version would arm Britain's V-Bombers, it was recognised that these aircraft would have a limited period of operational effectiveness, before more sophisticated enemy air defences became impenetrable. It was clear that if the UK wished to remain a nuclear power there would come a time in the 1960s when missiles fitted with atomic warheads would be needed to replace these aircraft. While various proposals and ideas begun to circulate within Air Staff circles during 1953, there were no easy solutions on the horizon. As for manned, or civil space projects, the ideas continued to generate public and official interest, but they were little more than sci-fi aspirations that belonged to the next century.

Although Germans were the undisputed leaders in rocket development, it had actually been a team of Britons, who drew up the first plans for a manned Moon mission prior to the Second World War. This had been a British Interplanetary Society (BIS) project which started in 1937 and the group was led by J. Happien-Edwards, and included H. Bramhill, Arthur C. Clarke, A. V. Cleaver, M. K. Hanson, Arthur Hanser, S. Klemantski, Harry E. Ross and Ralph A. Smith. Some of their ideas looks a little quaint by modern standards and there are obvious design flaws, but the basic concept for their rocketship was decades ahead of its time. Many of their suggestions would appear to have inspired America's future Apollo Moon programme, although when the BIS Moon study was finally published, it was considered by many as unaffordable nonsense for another century, which of course it was at that time.

The BIS Moon rocket would weigh about 1,000 metric tons. It was 100 ft (30.5 m) high, with a diameter of 20 ft (6.09 m). The rocket's propulsion system used solid propellants and it carried a lunar lander/command module that accommodated three crew members. This had an anticipated weight of about 2,204 lb (1000 kg).

Launched from the equator, the crew's capsule would be protected by a jettisonable ceramic heat shield able to withstand 1,500 degrees C during the ascent, although no consideration was given to protecting the capsule during re-entry into the Earth's atmosphere. During flights to and from the Moon, it was felt necessary to slowly rotate the vehicle at one revolution per 3.5 seconds to induce artificial gravity. The air supply would be fully re-cycled and navigation would be undertaken with basic instruments. Liquid fuel rocket engines were proposed for adjustments during descent to the Moon's surface, with steam jets for attitude control. Equipped with hydraulic legs, the lander would make a soft touchdown on the lunar surface and the crew would leave the vehicle via an airlock wearing rubber and leather spacesuits designed by Harry E. Ross.

Although most of the hardware was rather crude by modern standards, the pressure suit design utilised most of the key features that would appear in Apollo spacesuits such as an oxygen supply in the backpack, temperature control and a radio. Having completed their stay on the Moon's surface, the crew would lift off and return to the Earth, finally making a parachute descent.

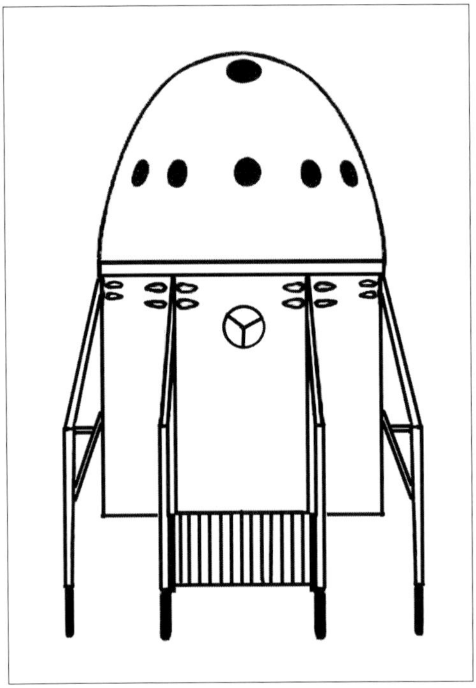

The British Interplanetary Society Moon lander, based on an original pre-war drawing. Strictly speaking it doesn't really belong in this book, but it is interesting to see just how technically far ahead this small group of British designers were in the 1930s.

Some aspects of the proposal were clearly unworkable, but considering that these plans were conceived in the 1930s, it is hardly surprising that nobody was able to suggest any improvements until 1947. This took the form of a fresh BIS study, which re-evaluated the original concept and took into account major advances by the Germans with liquid fuel rocket engines. Of course, no country could have built this vehicle in 1947, but UK interest in rocketry and manned spaceflight would continue at a low ebb, as the Germans had demonstrated what was possible with existing technology and the Americans were visibly pushing ahead with ambitious plans to move things up to the next level.

Perhaps a satellite could be placed in Earth orbit and anyone able to do this would open the door to new types of civil and military technology. So the BIS members kept coming up with new ideas and there was a serious suggestion from Harry E. Ross and Ralph A. Smith to build an adapted V-2 rocket to put a British astronaut into space. Ross and Smith were both engineers who had worked on the Moon rocket project and they believed the V-2 could carry a man to an altitude of one million feet (189 miles; 304 km). This led to their project being given the name Megaroc. Their rocket would be lengthened to accommodate larger fuel tanks; the warhead area would be used to accommodate a pressurised cabin. The rocket's fins would be removed as they served no purpose and the turbopump section would be re-located to impart a degree of gyroscopic stability during ascent. At burn-out, the capsule would separate and finally descend, using parachutes. It was also hoped that the rocket might return to the ground by parachute and some of it could be re-used.

Unfortunately, no consideration appears to have been given to re-entry heating, but the capsule would finally make a splashdown landing and these operations could have been undertaken in Australia.

Plans for Megaroc were submitted to the MoS by Ross and Smith on 23 December 1946 and they received some consideration in early 1947. Perhaps Megaroc could have been built, but scientists lacked experience in this area and there were numerous complex technical issues that Ross and Smith overlooked. These would have taken years to resolve and there was never the finance to start a project of this nature. So it is hardly surprising that the MoS soon shelved the idea. However, in 1948, Ross and Smith began work on the design of a compact wheel shaped space station, based on a proposal made in 1928 by Hermann Noordung (1892-1929). Again, this BIS idea had no prospect of progressing any further, although it would maintain interest in manned spaceflight and future possibilities.

Ross-Smith Space Glider

The next project to be undertaken by Ross and Smith was a large multi-stage rocket capable of carrying a spaceplane into orbit and a preliminary study was completed in August 1951. At this time, Smith was working as a draughtsman for the Rocket Propulsion Establishment at Westcott and would continually discuss technical aspects of this project with scientists and colleagues at work. Clearly, the rocket owed a great deal to wartime German designs, drawing on the A-4 (V-2) and the proposed A-10/11. A series of powerful liquid fuelled rocket engines each equipped with A4 style graphite steering vanes would lift each stage. The first three stages would also be fitted with parachutes and it was hoped that they might be recoverable, allowing refurbishment and re-use. The complete rocket would have an overall length of 165 ft (50.3 m), a fin span of 59.5 ft (18.1 m), a maximum core diameter of 28 ft (8.53 m) and the gross weight of the rocket was set at 2,300 metric tons.

The rocket would lift a small delta winged spaceplane into orbit. It was generally referred to as a Space Glider although the term glider referred to the way it would return Earth, involving the use of braking parachutes and possibly retro rockets. It is also unclear if Ross and Smith had considered the need for a thruster system to allow manoeuvring outside the atmosphere.

The Space Glider would carry a crew of three and there appears to have been no provision for them to escape in the event of a major launch incident. There would be a small payload bay

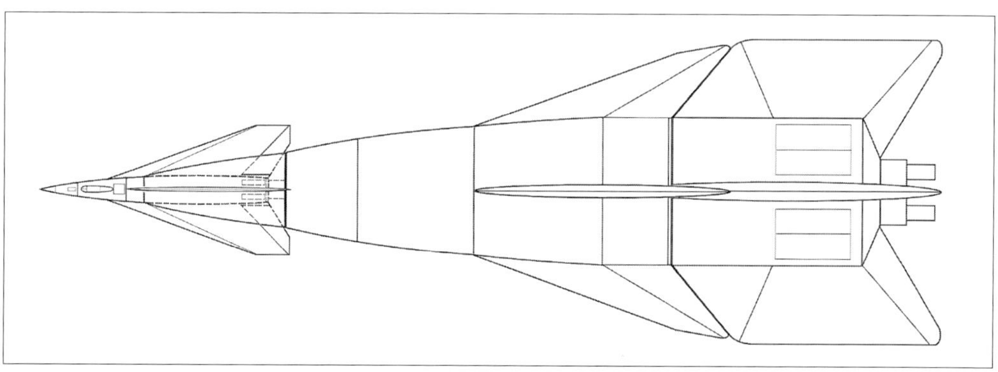

A sophisticated five-stage rocket based on wartime German rockets and liquid fuel engines. Designed by BIS members Harry Ross and Ralph Smith, it would, carry a re-usable, manned, delta winged spaceplane, or a payload container into Earth orbit.

and the rear section would house a single liquid fuel rocket engine. The estimated mass was expected to be about 6 metric tons. The Space Glider would have an overall length of 50.25 ft (15.3 m) and a span of 27.83 ft (8.47 m). The starting point for this delta winged spacecraft were the experimental Avro high-speed research aircraft designs, although at this time, nobody seemed to appreciate the extreme heat generated during re-entry into the Earth's atmosphere and because of this, the space glider stood no chance of making a safe return. An alternative expendable cargo container was also considered and this would be able to deliver about 5 metric tons to orbit. Launched from an equatorial site, it was estimated that either vehicle would be able to achieve an orbital height of about 500 miles (800 km).

Another orbital spaceplane study was completed in America by von Braun just after the Ross and Smith proposal and it utilised broadly similar principles. Von Braun envisaged a much larger three-stage vehicle, with a height of 265 ft (80.7 m) and a multitude of engines fuelled with more than 5,000 metric tons of hydrazine and nitric acid. Von Braun also intended to store hydrogen peroxide in ring shaped tanks that would be mixed with a catalyst to produce steam to drive the turbopumps that fed fuel into the rocket engines. After launch, the first stage of von Braun's huge rocket would be expended very quickly and it would descend by parachute, hopefully being recovered from the sea and eventually refurbished. It was also considered worthwhile to attempt recovery of the second stage which would descend much further downrange from the launch site, although this was probably regarded as an unrealistic proposition after further consideration.

The most important part of this vehicle was the third stage, which was a six-man spaceplane intended to reach orbit at an altitude of 1,075 miles (1,730 km), delivering a proposed cargo payload of 32.6 metric tons. The spaceplane was fitted with five rocket engines and these were identical to the many more used in lower stages.

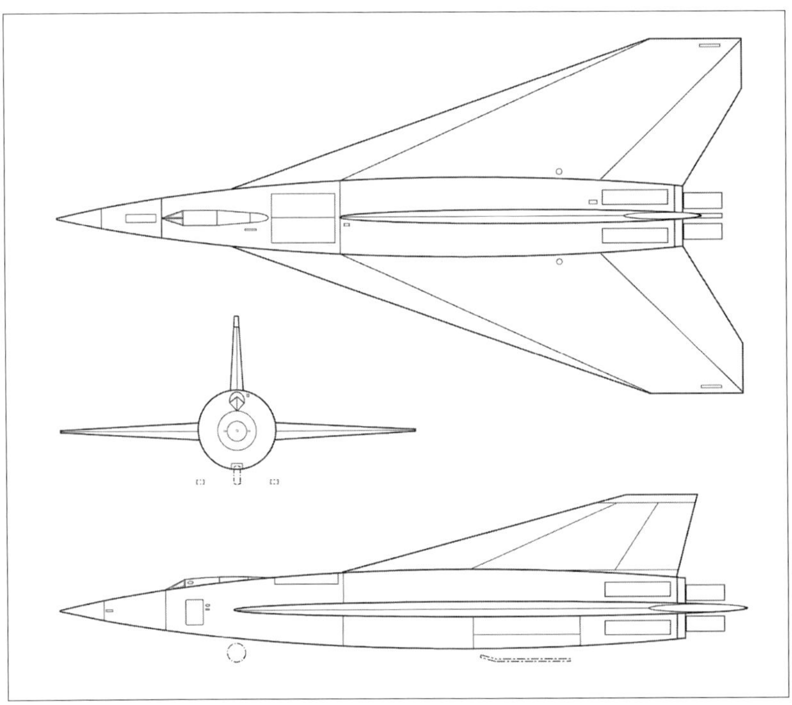

The three-man orbital space glider designed by BIS members Ross and Smith. The ultimate development of an Avro Delta?

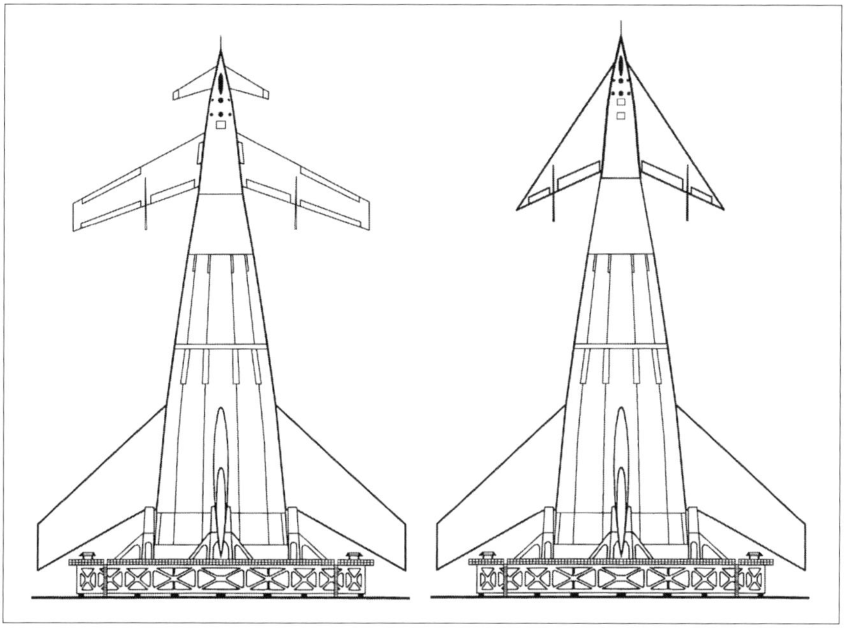

Drawings of two massive von Braun manned rockets based on his ideas stretching back to the Second World War. As this concept evolved during the immediate post-war years, von Braun made a number of modifications, perhaps influenced by the BIS concept. Having moved to a delta configuration for the spaceplane, this would continue to evolve, with alteration to the delta wing's trailing edge and the addition of a tailplane assembly. Runways landings would take place using a fully retractable tricycle undercarriage. No provision appears to have been considered for protection against the extreme heat of atmospheric re-entry. (*US Army/Bill Rose*)

One of the later von Braun delta spaceplane designs in orbit above the Earth.

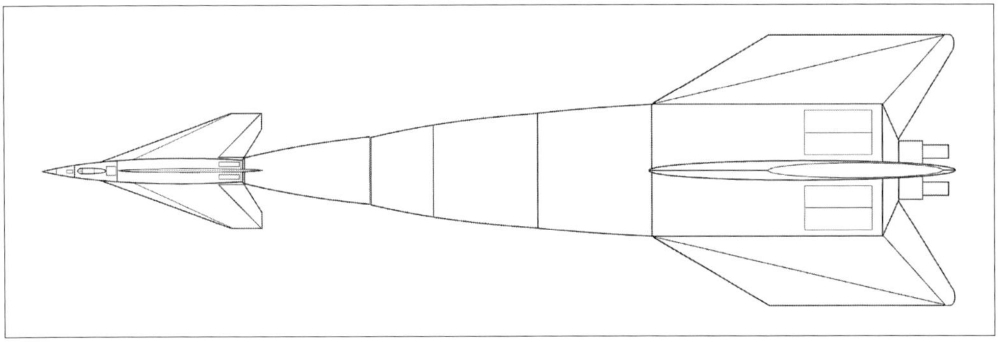

An alternative three stage version of the Ross/Smith rocket which was briefly described in a book written by Arthur C. Clarke in 1954.

Uniformity was something von Braun considered important for mass production. The empty weight of the first spaceplane design was just over 70 metric tons and it was equipped with a canard wing layout using stabilising fins in the main wing. The wingspan was 156 ft (47.5 m), showing there was almost no understanding of atmospheric re-entry requirements at that time. I have included these details, because the general concept is similar and it seems very likely that von Braun studied the Ross/Smith design in considerable depth and came to the conclusion that his third stage, canard winged spacecraft required a slightly more compact delta wing, initially fitted with stabilising fins, which were finally replaced by a tailplane assembly.

Ross and Smith continued to work on their launch vehicle, producing a simplified version with fewer stages. However, these designs went no further. Although the ideas put forward by Ross and Smith were very impressive, the UK could not afford to develop this kind of technology and by early 1953, there was only serious official interest in long range surface-to-surface guided missiles. It would need a range of at least 2,000 miles (3,200 km) and be capable of carrying an atomic warhead. There was now acceptance that by the 1960s a new strategic weapon was required and somehow the government would have to find ways to fund its development and introduction into service. By the middle of 1953, there were high-level discussions taking place which concluded that nuclear missiles would be the only way of effectively fighting a future 'all-out' war with the Soviets.

However, it was obvious that development of a strategic nuclear missile would be technically challenging and very expensive. The Americans had made considerable progress in this area, but Britain had fallen way behind them and could not expect US assistance with a parallel strategic weapon programme. Nevertheless, many major technical issues would need to be addressed as the type of weapon envisaged would have to be several steps ahead of the V-2. It would require an accurate guidance system, more advanced propulsion, perhaps new types of fuel and there would be various metallurgical considerations. Then there was the issue of building a suitable warhead. Britain had exploded its initial low-yield plutonium device in 1952 under Operation Hurricane, but the design was fairly similar to the American Fat Man bomb and relatively crude, with a weaponised version weighing in the region of 10,000 lb (4,500 kg) making it unsuitable for a missile warhead.

The overall size needed to be dramatically reduced and while scientists believed it was possible to do this and also increase the yield, it would represent yet another major challenge. Ideally, any future warhead would have a physical mass of no more than about 3,000 lb (1,360 kg) and be a thermonuclear design with an explosive yield of at least one megaton. This was the requirement for future military credibility and there was no way any adversary could defend against an inbound warhead. Of course, it was probable that the Soviet Union and perhaps eventually Communist Chinese would develop long range ballistic missiles with thermonuclear warheads, taking the world towards a disturbing era of possible confrontation that could have no winners. But having an effective nuclear capability was essential if some kind of strategic balance was to be maintained, along with the UK's status and credibility. So the stage was finally set to start spending huge amounts of money on the next generation of ultra-lethal weaponry. By 1955, there was official agreement to proceed and OR.1139 was issued that sought proposals for an Intermediate Range Ballistic Missile (IRBM). Initially, it would have a minimum of about 1,700 miles (2,730 km) and ideally a maximum range of 2,400 miles (3,862 km).

Clearly inspired by American technology, this IRBM might be considered a reduced size 'Atlas' missile and development was secured by de Havillands, with Rolls-Royce providing the LOX/kerosene RZ 2 rocket engine. The IRBM would have a length of 61.5 ft (18.74 m), a diameter of 10 ft (3.04 m) and a total launch weight of 198,000 lb (89,811 kg). The project soon received the name Blue Streak and it was going to cost plenty. Consideration was also given to using the Blue Streak as part of a military and civil launch system for satellites, probably with at least one additional upper stage. However, as work on Blue Streak progressed, many unforeseen issues became obvious. Possible launch sites in the UK were very limited, although a test site was established at Spadeadam Waste in Cumbria. No launches were ever made from this location, although it was seriously considered, despite being politically undesirable.

Another UK location briefly used to test engines for Black Arrow, Black Knight and Blue Steel rockets was High Down on the Isle of Wight and some of the facilities remain intact. Two other areas secretly discussed were remote parts of Scotland and the Norfolk Coast, but nowhere in the UK was especially suitable for the construction of launch facilities and making test flights. However, an even bigger problem soon reared its ugly head when it was estimated that fuelling the rocket prior to launch would take at least 15 minutes. This significantly reduced its effectiveness as a weapon, with the UK IRBM finally being scrapped during 1960 in preference to the solid fuel, air-launched Skybolt missile.

It had been another ill-considered waste of taxpayer's money on an over-ambitious military weapon that was unsuitable for the country's needs. But to save face on this project, Whitehall decided that Blue Streak could be used as the first stage of a proposed satellite launch system that made use of a Saunders Roe research rocket called Black Knight for the upper stages. The new assembly was given the name Black Prince and the project proved rather costly and soon slowed to a halt. Then the European Launcher Development Organisation (ELDO) was formed, with Blue Streak being chosen for stage one of a new satellite launcher called Europa. This used French and German upper stages. Ten launches were made from Woomera, but the site was not suited to putting space platforms into geostationary orbit. The programme was then re-located to the French launch site of Kourou in South America. Several test launches followed, but ongoing technical issues finally brought the Europa Project to a close in the early 1970s.

Another British rocket dating from the mid-1950s was the Skylark sounding rocket first tested at Woomera in 1957. Originally designed by the RAE at Farnborough, this 25 ft (7.62 m) long rocket was extremely successful, being used by a number of international customers, with the last launch taking place in 2005. The other British rocket already mentioned, was Black Knight, again conceived by the RAE and fully developed by Saunders Roe. Somewhat bigger than Skylark, with an overall length of about 38 ft (11.5 m) depending on the version, Black Knight was manufactured to test re-entry vehicle designs suitable for Blue Streak. This rocket proved to be very successful and was briefly considered for development into an IRBM and later as part of a satellite launcher as already mentioned.

These very brief background details are only here to set the scene for how rocketry was developing in Post-war Britain and it is not my intention to move too far away from the main theme of this chapter, which deals with ideas for British manned (mostly) delta shaped spacecraft. However, there was one proposal for a small spaceplane that created considerable interest using a new rocket somewhat larger than the Blue Streak as a launch vehicle.

Armstrong Whitworth's Pyramid

In the late 1950s, Dr Bill Hilton, who was the chief aerodynamicist for Armstrong Whitworth Aircraft began to investigate atmospheric re-entry requirements for a manned spacecraft. He had already proposed the idea of flying saucer and rectangular shaped craft with smooth undersides at a conference attended by BIS members, the Royal Aeronautical Society and the College of Aeronautics at Cranfield in July 1957. Perhaps his most significant proposal was an ability to control the spacecraft as it plunged through the upper atmosphere along the glide path. Soon after this, Russia successfully launched the first orbital satellite Sputnik 1 and senior management at Armstrong Whitworth decided there might be a future in space after all. So it was agreed that an office would be set up to investigate Dr Hilton's ideas and explore proposals for spacecraft, under the overall control of the company's Technical Director Henry R. Watson.

A decision was then taken to request assistance from Britain's leading aerodynamic expert Professor Terence Nonweiler (1925–1999). He headed the Department of Aeronautical Engineering at The Queen's University of Belfast and worked as a consultant for several aircraft contractors. Nonweiler readily agreed to become involved in designing a spaceplane and it was agreed that the circular and rectangular designs presented too many technical challenges to be viable. The concept now evolved into a unique pyramid shaped vehicle, with a flat triangular underside, short wings and stabilising fins fitted with control surfaces. Up until this point, the spacecraft had been called The Manned Satellite, but the new shape immediately led to company adoption of The Pyramid.

Nonweiler's primary intention was to reduce re-entry temperatures by low wing loading, with the heat being conducted upwards through the fuselage and released into the cooler airflow above the spacecraft. At the rear of the vehicle was a vent to ensure that no air remained trapped within the fuselage that might interfere with the transfer of heat.

The initial dimensions for Nonweiler's Pyramid was 25.25 ft (7.69 m) long, with a height of 9.25 ft (2.81 m), a span of 29.5 ft (8 m) and a wing area of 332 ft^2 (30.84 m^2). An estimate of gross weight was approximately 4,122 lb (1,870 kg), gives some idea of the required launch vehicle. Over the years, this has been consistently assumed to have been a significantly upgraded, version of Blue Streak missile. Now it appears that Watson's team were fully aware that Blue Streak was inadequate for the delivery of a satisfactory payload to Low Earth Orbit (LEO) and were considering the use of a substantial 3-stage rocket which they would design, in collaboration with Bristol Siddeley Engines Ltd.

Pyramid spacecraft with image fairing mounted on a 3-stage vehicle on the launch pad.

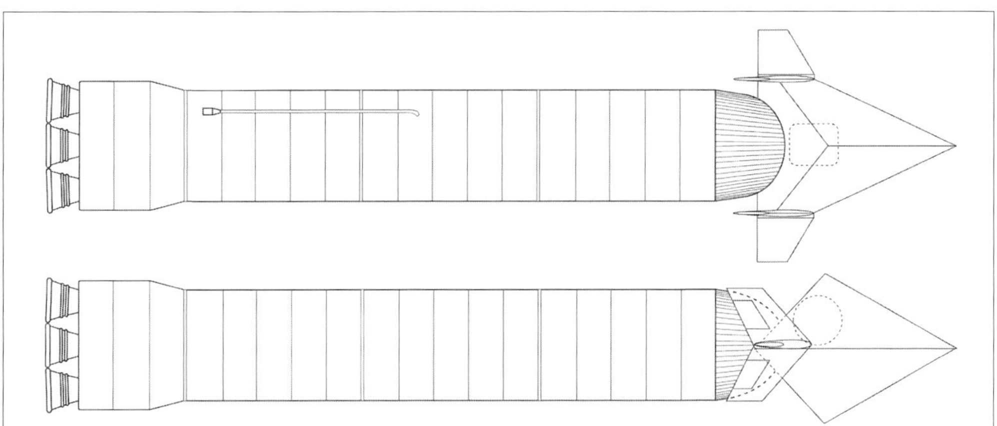

It has been widely assumed that the launch vehicle intended to lift the Armstrong Whitworth Pyramid into space was a heavily adapted version of the Blue Streak missile. but it now seems likely that the AWA designers anticipated using their own ideas for a more powerful three stage launch vehicle developed in conjunction with Bristol Siddeley Engines. This drawing is based on original artwork produced by *Chris Gibson* to give an impression of how it might have looked.

Another feature designed to provide aerodynamic symmetry during launch, was a lightweight 'image fairing,' looking like a duplicate of the pyramid spacecraft attached to the flat side of the vehicle. This carried extra fuel and would be discarded once the Pyramid separated from the booster. After separation from the launch vehicle and fairing, the spacecraft would utilise an attitude control system for manoeuvring.

Essentially, the craft was little more than an aerodynamically configured shell, carrying a fully pressurised drum-shaped capsule of about 5 × 6 ft (1.5 × 1.8 m) in size. This would accommodate two crew members in very tight conditions, or some form of cargo/military payload. The capsule was located at the vehicle's centre of gravity and one option considered was to eject the capsule rearward from the pyramid after re-entry to make a parachute descent. This might also have been used for an emergency escape procedure in the event of a launch failure.

Re-entry and descent through the atmosphere would have been undertaken at a high angle of attack said to be about 45° and if it was decided to release the capsule for a parachute landing, this would require small aerodynamic surfaces. However, there were other proposals for the Pyramid to touch down on smooth water, or suitable ground using skids and the landing speed was expected to be about 88 mph (141 kph). Clearly it was hoped to gain full official sponsorship of the project, with the initial proposal to launch an unmanned test vehicle on a sub-orbital flight, probably from Woomera in Australia

Towards the end of the 1950s, various wind tunnel and scale models of the pyramid had been tested and various modifications were made to the design. Subsequently, the company applied for a patent in 1960, naming Nonweiler and Watson as the designers of the spacecraft, with the details being eventually published in 1963 (Ref: GB936458).

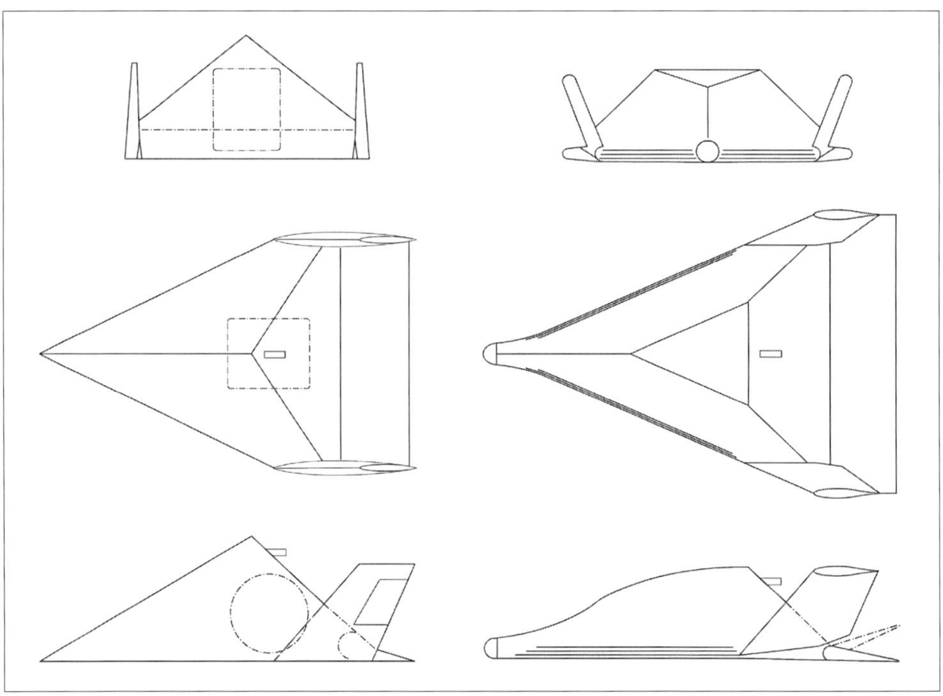

The initial Armstrong Whitworth Pyramid spaceplane proposal (left) and a more advanced version (right).

A different tail configuration was considered, the short wings were removed and two substantial flaps were positioned at the back of the craft between the vertical stabilisers. Then a second design emerged with a blunt nose, more rounded leading edges and a flatter upper surface. A single control surface was fitted to the rear of the vehicle and these changes were intended to address various issue of drag at subsonic speeds. But the Pyramid spacecraft never progressed much further than a detailed study. Nonweiler officially left the project at the end of 1958 and by 1960, the project had been cancelled.

One other manned spacecraft proposal from the beginning of the 1960s originated within the BIS and it briefly outlined a highly modified Blue Streak/Black Knight amalgamation, capable of carrying a capsule into orbit that contained a single astronaut. This idea appears to have encouraged the making of a low-budget movie called *Capsule*, which was set in 1959 and portrayed a secret manned space project that ran into trouble. The film was released in 2015 to mixed reviews.

Air Launched Rockets and Missiles

The starting point for launching rockets of a substantial size from an aircraft can almost certainly be traced back to the first air-drop of an unpowered A5 (a smaller version of the V-2 rocket) from an adapted Heinkel He 111 bomber in September 1939 at the Peenemünde Test Site in Northern Germany. Released at an altitude of 23,000 ft (7,000 m) the A5 fell rapidly, pushing through the sound barrier at 3,000 ft (1,000 m) just before a series of parachutes were deployed. While the general idea of launching substantial rockets from aircraft developed no further at that time, the Germans had already recognised the potential of being able to launch guided bombs like Fritz-X and rocket powered guided missiles of a similar size such as the Henschel 293 series, which were operationally tested in the anti-shipping role. It was then decided that trials should begin launching the more substantial Fieseler Fi-103 (V-1) cruise missile from aircraft. This would not only extend the weapon's range, but remove the need for launch ramps which were prime targets for Allied bombers. Again, the Heinkel He 111 bomber was the aircraft of choice for this role and several were modified to carry an underwing V-1 for airborne launch. Mainly flown by KG.53, the success rate of these operations was judged unsatisfactory due to technical issues and Allied interception. Had the war in Europe continued for longer, there were plans to use a highly modified four-engined version of the Arado Ar 234 Blitz jet bomber for V-1 air launches. The V-1 would be carried by a cradle on the back of the aircraft and just prior to launch, the cradle would hydraulically lift the V-1 about 8 ft (2.4 m) so its pulsejet was adequately clear of the aircraft's tail and ignition could safely take place. It is not thought that this idea progressed much further than an initial proposal and whether it would have been viable is rather debatable. However, the idea of launching substantial missiles from aircraft quickly caught the attention of the Allies and the Soviets. Despite its relative crudeness, the air-launched V-1 had set the stage for aircraft carrying cruise missiles and there were many other obvious possibilities.

In the immediate post-war period, America was pushing ahead with development of supersonic rocket powered experimental aircraft. These would progressively set more and more world records, leading to an air-launched rocketplane that would technically become a manned spacecraft. Using an aircraft as a launch vehicle would clearly never allow the placing of large payloads into orbit, but it would be possible to launch modest sized satellites and military payloads, or possibly small

This rather badly framed photograph shows a modified Heinkel He 111 bomber carrying an unpowered A5 rocket just prior to an air-drop test in early 1940 at the Peenemünde Test Site in Northern Germany. The chalk writing on its side of the A5 reads "Kehrnieder Erika – Come down Erica!"

A German Luftwaffe Heinkel He 111 bomber capable of carrying a Fieseler Fi 103 (V-1) flying bomb beneath its wing. A number of these aircraft were adapted to an air-launch role (H-22 spec) and the majority were flown by KG.53 based at Gilze Rijen in The Netherlands during late 1944 onwards. This allowed attacks against England to continue after the launch sites in France were no longer available. Generally, these operations were not judged to have been an outstanding success by the Luftwaffe due to numerous technical issues and strong defence from the RAF. (*Restoration by Bill Rose. Original image from USAF archives*)

manned spaceplanes that should be fully re-usable. Furthermore, these two-stage systems could probably be operated from suitable conventional runways at a fraction of the cost required for big multi-stage rockets on launch pads. It was also considered possible that given enough time, these craft would be replaced by single stage to orbit (SSTO) spaceplanes.

V-Bombers as Rocket Launch Platforms

In an earlier chapter, I outlined how the Avro Vulcan bomber was adapted to carry the Blue Steel nuclear missile and how there were plans to replace this with the American made Skybolt missile that would be carried underwing. Skybolt was a far superior weapon on paper, but endless technical problems finally brought development to a close and Britain then secured the submarine launched Polaris missile as the country's next nuclear deterrent. Interestingly, there was some serious consideration given to adapting the advanced Polaris strategic missile for carriage by the Vulcan, but this never progressed very far, despite probably being a viable concept.

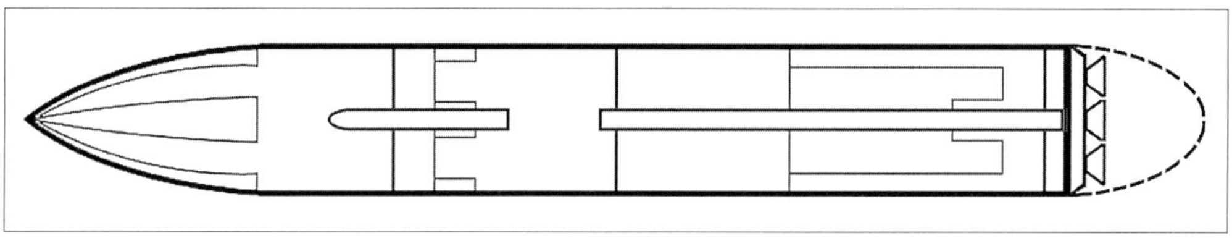

Possible appearance of a modified (normally submarine launched) nuclear tipped Polaris ballistic missile, proposed for air-launching by the RAF's Avro Vulcan bombers. It would probably have required a jettisonable tail cone to improve aerodynamics during carriage.

Beyond Blue Steel

The Avro Vulcan was the best suited of the three V-bombers to carrying a missile or rocket, as it had considerable clearance beneath the aircraft. As the Blue Steel became a reality, there were indications that the aircraft could probably air-launch larger and more advanced missiles without too much difficulty. These included a longer range nuclear missile, a research rocket capable of reaching the edge of the atmosphere and perhaps a multi-stage rocket able to place a small satellite in LEO. Consequently, John Allen, who was deputy chief engineer at Avro's Weapons Research Division (WRD) began a series of studies in 1958 to determine what might be technically possible. His starting point was identification of a high altitude region known as the Flight Corridor which exists between 100,000 ft (30,480 m) and 400,000 ft (121,920 m). At the lower level, hypersonic flight is viable without extreme thermal issues and at the top of the corridor, there is virtually no atmosphere, so no air resistance. But at this altitude control surfaces serve no function and these would require replacement with an alternative system. Soon, this study had produced a series of extensively modified air-launched versions of Blue Steel intended to explore the Flight Corridor that began to significantly evolve away from the original stand-off missile.

The first notable proposal to emerge in May 1959 was the Z.47, otherwise referred to as The Fringe Research Vehicle. Designed to reach a maximum altitude of about 400,000 ft (121 km), this rocket would be powered by a single American built, Rocketdyne A-6 engine, running on alcohol and liquid oxygen. Four strap-on Raven solid fuel boosters would be added to improve initial performance. The second stage of this rocket would be powered by an Armstrong Siddeley Snarler rocket engine. Release from the Vulcan would take place at about 50,000 ft (15,240 m). The length of Z.47 was initially set at 38.4 ft (11.7 m) and the finspan is quoted as 17 ft (5.18).

Later variants would have the ability to reach a higher altitude and included an anti-satellite (ASAT) or reconnaissance capability and perhaps a version capable of placing a 400 lb (181 kg) payload into orbit. To achieve this, the ultimate rocket in this series was to be the three-stage Z.124, proposed in 1962 and designed in association with Hawker, which became known as the Vulcan Orbiter.

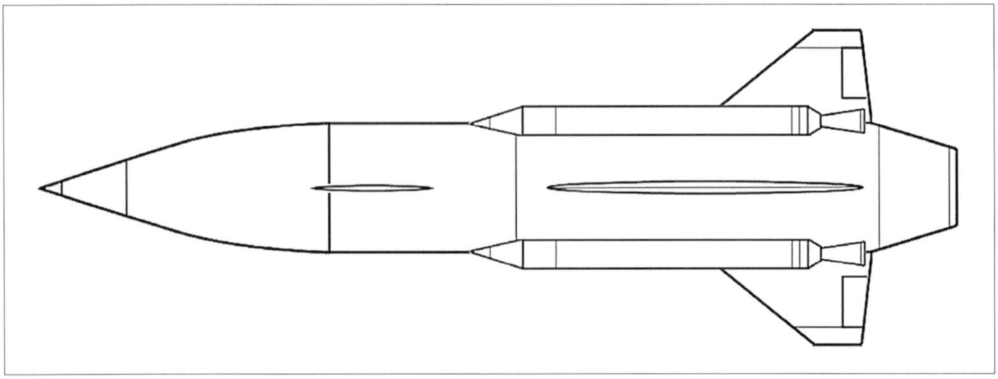

The proposed Z.47 Fringe Research Vehicle, designed in 1959.

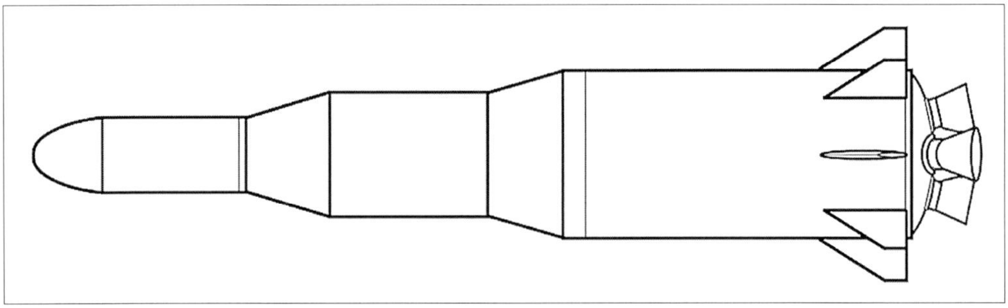

The final development in the Vulcan "Z" series of air-launched rockets was the proposed Z.124 Vulcan Orbiter designed in 1962.

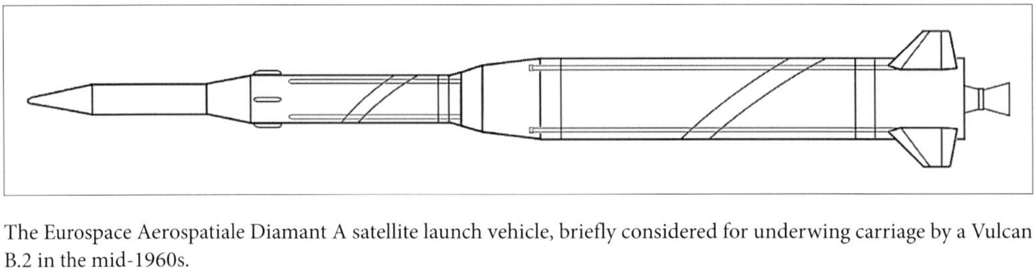

The Eurospace Aerospatiale Diamant A satellite launch vehicle, briefly considered for underwing carriage by a Vulcan B.2 in the mid-1960s.

Bearing no significant resemblance to the original Blue Steel missile, this substantial rocket had a maximum suggested weight of 40,000 lb (18,143 kg) and was expected to deliver its payload to a 345 mile (556.6 km) high orbit. Carrying this rocket beneath the Vulcan would have required extensive modification to the bomb bay area, with the tail end of the Z.124 partly recessed inside the aircraft. But this was not to be the final proposal in a series of air-launched rockets to be carried by the Vulcan. At some point in the mid-1960s, there were suggestions that a Eurospace Aerospatiale Diamant "A" satellite rocket might be launched from a Vulcan B.2. In the end, none of these concepts progressed beyond the design stage and construction of a few small models, although it seems possible that they might have been successful.

Manned, Air-Launched Rocketplanes

Unquestionably, the most interesting and unusual classified proposal developed from the Blue Steel missile was a manned version designated Z.101/35, which received serious consideration during late 1961. Had this idea gone ahead and worked without major incident, it might have been disclosed to the public. It is certainly easy to imagine the headlines that would have been carried by British newspapers. Regarded as a possible UK rival to the American X-15 rocketplane, the Z.101/35 was a significant re-working of the Blue Steel missile. A cockpit carrying the pilot replaced the substantial inertial navigation unit, while larger HT peroxide and kerosene fuel tanks would be fitted. The Z.101/35's Bristol Siddeley Stentor BS St.1 rocket engine was essentially the same as that fitted to the Blue Steel missile. It utilised two chambers providing a fixed thrust of 24,000 lb (106.75 kN) and a variable cruise chamber with a maximum thrust of 6,000 lb (26.68 kN). The Z.101/35 had an expected length of 35 ft (10.66 m) and a launch weight of 16,480 lb (7,475 kg). The Z.101/35 would be air dropped from a modified Avro Vulcan bomber at 55,000 ft (16,764 m) at a speed of about Mach 0.85. After engine ignition, it was expected to attain a maximum speed of about Mach 4.5, reaching an altitude of 290,000 ft (88,392 m). The issue of landing once the mission was completed was not entirely resolved. It was initially thought that because of its shape, the Z.101/35 would make an extremely fast touchdown in excess of 200 mph (320 kph) at a very high angle of attack. A retractable nose wheel would be extended, along with two rear mounted skids, probably combined with a small braking parachute.

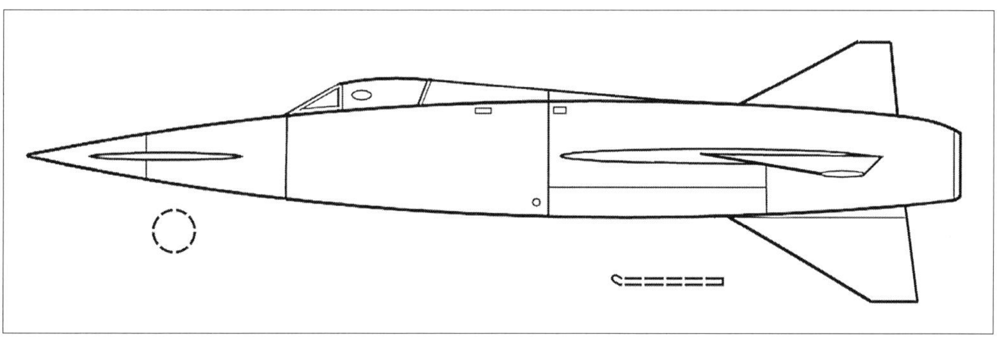

A secret 1960s proposal designated Z.101/35, for a manned version of the Blue Steel missile, which would be launched from a Vulcan bomber at high altitude. The lower (folding) tail fin would be jettisoned prior to landing. This illustration is closely based on an original Avro drawing.

Nevertheless, this arrangement was considered less than satisfactory and it seems that the deployment of a parawing was finally anticipated as the best solution for a safe landing. Each rocketplane built would undertake 10 missions from Woomera in Australia before retirement. These would be released above the test site and travel about 300 miles (482 km) down range, to a choice of two secretly selected landing sites. Both of these locations were dry clay pads and the preferred location was Lake Carringallana.

Prior to any manned missions taking place, there were plans to test recoverable versions of the modified Blue Steel. The first of these was the Z.99 fitted with a parachute system and the second was the Z.100, which would be equipped with a retractable nose wheel and skids to make a remote controlled landing. However, John Allen's team did not stop with the Z.101/35, but moved on to consider a possible upgrade, which would be called the Z.101/38. This would have a stretched fuselage, allowing the installation of a larger kerosene tank. The overall length of the rocketplane would be 38 ft (11.58 m), with an increased launch weight of 18,186 lb (8,249 kg). The Z.101/38 would be truly hypersonic and capable of reaching Mach 5 and an altitude in excess of 300,000 ft (91 km). Possible further modifications might have been the use of two or four strap-on Raven solid fuel boosters. Had there been any serious official interest in the Z.101 rocketplane, it is unlikely to have flown before the middle of the 1960s, but nothing came of this or any other Blue Steel based projects, which were filed away and largely forgotten about for many years to come.

Aircraft Converted to Spacecraft

When Minister for Defence Duncan Sandys revealed his unexpected White Paper on 5 April 1957, the ruthless cuts to advanced military aviation projects came as quite a shock to many contractors and their staff. This included Saunders Roe, who were preparing for production of the advanced SR.177 mixed propulsion interceptor. It would lead to massive redundancies, although senior management did everything possible to prevent the company from going under. The SR.53 was still awaiting trials at RAE Boscombe Down and there was now an attempt made by Saunders Roe management to interest the RAE in a very advanced research aircraft based on this prototype. This proposal was for an entirely rocket powered version that would be launched from the back of a Vickers Valiant V-Bomber at 50,000 ft (15,240 m). It would then climb under rocket power to 250,000 ft (76,000 m), while attaining a speed of about Mach 3–4.

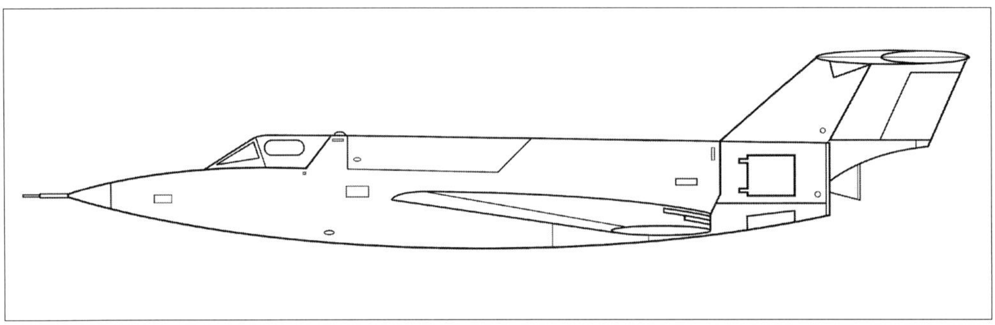

Possible appearance of an "edge of space" rocket powered development of the SR.53, which would be launched from the back of an adapted Valiant bomber.

Saunders Roe also suggested that with a programme of rolling improvements and a rocket engine upgrade, it might be capable of hypersonic performance, competing with the North American X-15 (Project 1226) rocketplanes that were already under construction in Los Angeles. An originally secret, official paper from 1958, held at the Public Records Office suggests that the aircraft might eventually be capable of reaching an altitude of 100 miles (160 km), effectively making it a spacecraft.

However, an SR.53 able to reach near space was an impossibility. Saunders Roe would have needed to build a new aircraft, perhaps retaining some similarities in appearance to the prototype mixed propulsion interceptor, but very different in most respects. An SR.53 would require an airframe built from a metal like stainless steel, with a possible weight penalty or perhaps something like Grade 5 titanium alloy. The overall length of the aircraft would also need to be increased to accommodate extra fuel storage and the aircraft would require a new powerful rocket engine to replace the existing propulsion system. A Bristol Siddeley Stentor BS St.1 rocket engine comes to mind as it was under development for the Blue Steel at that time. The aircraft's skin would need to be fabricated from a suitable material and a reaction control system would be required for ultra-high altitude flight. The cost of developing this new aircraft would have been substantial, it would have taken years and was fraught with major technical issues that seem to have been glossed over.

Air launching from the back of a Valiant might have presented various problems, already recognised by the German engineers who considered launching V-1s from Arado jet bombers.

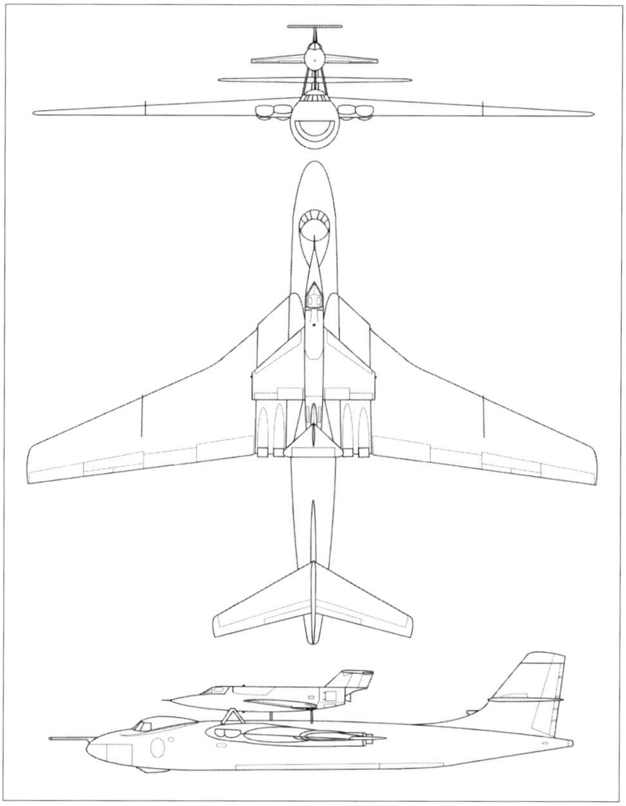

A high altitude development of the SR.53, which would be launched from the back of an adapted Valiant bomber. (*Chris Gibson*)

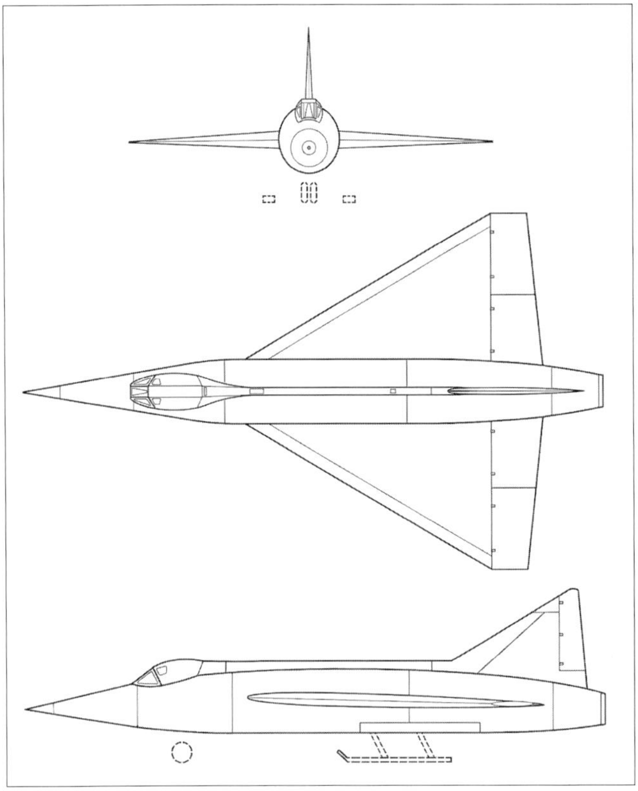

A proposed rocket powered ultra high-altitude version of the Avro 720. It would be air-launched from an Avro Vulcan and perhaps capable of reaching the edge of space in a similar manner to the US X-15. Like the special SR.53 concept, this design would be very different from the original aircraft, being built from more suitable metals and probably having a fuselage stretched to accommodate extra fuel. Strap-on boosters may also have been considered.

Then there was extreme atmospheric heating on return from a mission. In actual fact, the idea of this rocketplane was not completely crazy as extensive high-performance modifications were briefly considered for the USAF's air-launched Bell X-2 rocketplane in May 1952. These were expected to take it to the edge of the atmosphere and achieve a speed of about Mach 4.5. Nevertheless, the RAE showed no interest in the Saunders Roe proposal.

It also came to light that Avro considered making similar modifications to their delta 720, converting it into a manned experimental rocketplane capable of operating within the Flight Corridor. Perhaps Ross and Smith had some influence after all? The lack of information about this proposal makes it very difficult to do much more than speculate. But the modified 720 would have been air-launched from an Avro Vulcan at high altitude and after the mission, it would glide back to land. Much of what applied to the Saunders Roe proposal would apply to a broadly similar Avro design, which also met with rejection.

RAE Space Fighter

From its establishment in 1959, the newly formed UK Ministry of Aviation (MoA) began to take a serious interest in the Boeing X-20 spaceplane, which was under development as a multi-functional military asset for the USAF. It would initially be capable of long range sub-orbital flights utilising boost-glide principles, but was expected to achieve orbital capability with a suitable booster upgrade (Titan IIIC was the final choice). In addition, several air-launched proposals had been considered such as a massive eight engined supersonic delta winged aircraft. British officials viewed the X-20 with a degree of envy, although it was technology beyond their financial reach. Furthermore, even if Britain could develop an affordable system like this, where could it operate from? Launching rockets from almost any part of the UK was a major problem due to insufficient suitable territory and Britain's location in the northern hemisphere, alongside the European mainland raised further issues. If there was going to be the need for military spaceplanes in the near future, launches might just be possible from two locations in the UK, but realistically, operations would need to be conducted at a suitable overseas RAF base. Having determined that this was the only realistic way to proceed if funding ever became available, the RAE were asked to initiate a series of studies which would be referred to as The Orbital Fighter Proposal.

The brilliant mathematician Sir Michael James Lighthill (1924–1998) had been appointed as director of the RAE at about the same time as the MoA was established and he became heavily involved with the MoA's ideas for a military spacecraft. Under his direction, this became a significant project with research continuing for several years. Then in September 1962, Professor Lighthill revealed to aviation journalists that an RAE study was underway to determine the viability of a large Mach 7 aircraft for military applications. This impressive design would be capable of reaching altitudes in the region of 120–150,000 ft (36,500–45,700 m), with a range of about 4,000 miles (6,400 km). Professor Lighthill went on to explain that such an aircraft also had the potential to launch a smaller vehicle capable of achieving Mach 12–14 at an altitude of 180,000 ft (55 km) and eventually. It might be able to reach orbit with an adequate propulsion upgrade. Further RAE estimates suggested that the ideal release altitude for a smaller craft and its rocket booster would be at about 75,000 ft (22,860 m).

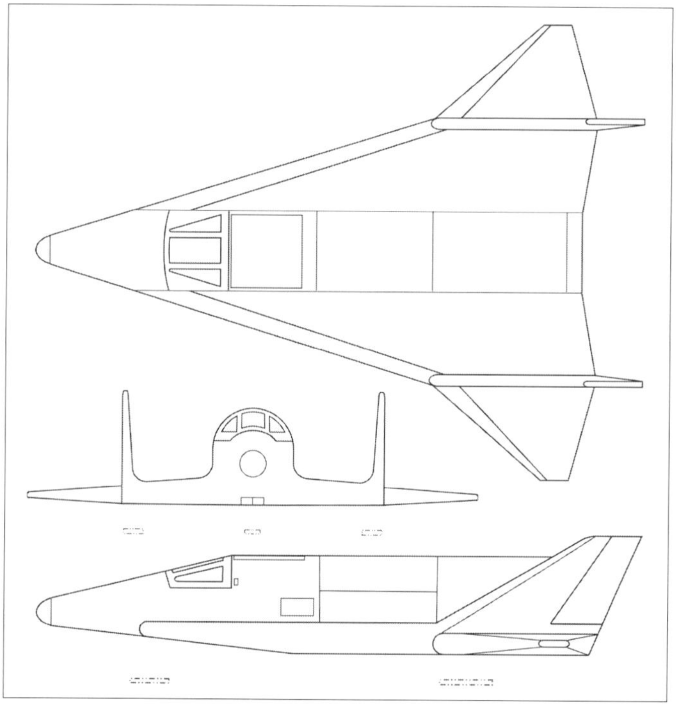

The most favoured RAE proposal for a "Space Fighter," bearing some resemblance to the American X-20.

A mock-up of the Boeing X-20 spaceplane which inspired the RAE space fighter concept. (*Boeing*)

Not surprisingly, the appearance of the air-launched spacecraft bore some resemblance to the lifting body Boeing X-20 spaceplane and there were suggestions that it might carry a crew of three. Like the American spaceplane, the RAE proposal would be capable of long-range reconnaissance missions across the Soviet Union that could not be intercepted. It was hoped that the development of a more powerful booster stage would carry the space craft into LEO, where small satellites could be launched and ASAT missions might be possible.

It was now decided to determine if the project was a realistic proposition and the MoA chose to involve BAC at Preston, who were contracted (Ref: KD/2X/2CB7(c)) to produce a detailed report on the overall concept. This was completed by the end of 1963 and submitted to the MoA in January 1964. BAC provided suggestions for the construction of a large, high performance double delta, provisionally accommodating a crew of two. While intended to be the first stage of the spacecraft system, it could be adapted for other roles. The aircraft was assigned the designation EAG 4396 and while its anticipated dimensions remain uncertain, a rough estimate suggests a length of about 160 ft (48.76 m) and an overall wingspan of approximately 130 ft (39.6 m). The double delta was to have a leading edge sweep of 73° and 50°.

However, the Preston team had scaled back expectations of the carrier craft's performance after determining that near-term engine technology and the use of suitable metals for construction would limit maximum speed to Mach 4, with a ceiling of about 90,000–100,000 ft (27,500–30,000 m). EAG 4396 would be powered by six Rolls-Royce or Bristol Siddeley turbo-ramjet engines housed in a ventral pack and these would run on conventional aviation fuel. Much of the airframe would be fabricated from titanium alloy and a substantial tricycle undercarriage was required. If the aircraft was developed for the sole purpose of operating as a launch vehicle, its gross take-off weight was expected to be about 500,000 lb (226 metric tons) and the optimal release altitude would be 84,000 ft (25,600 m) at an angle of 20°. A number of wind tunnel models were tested by BAC,

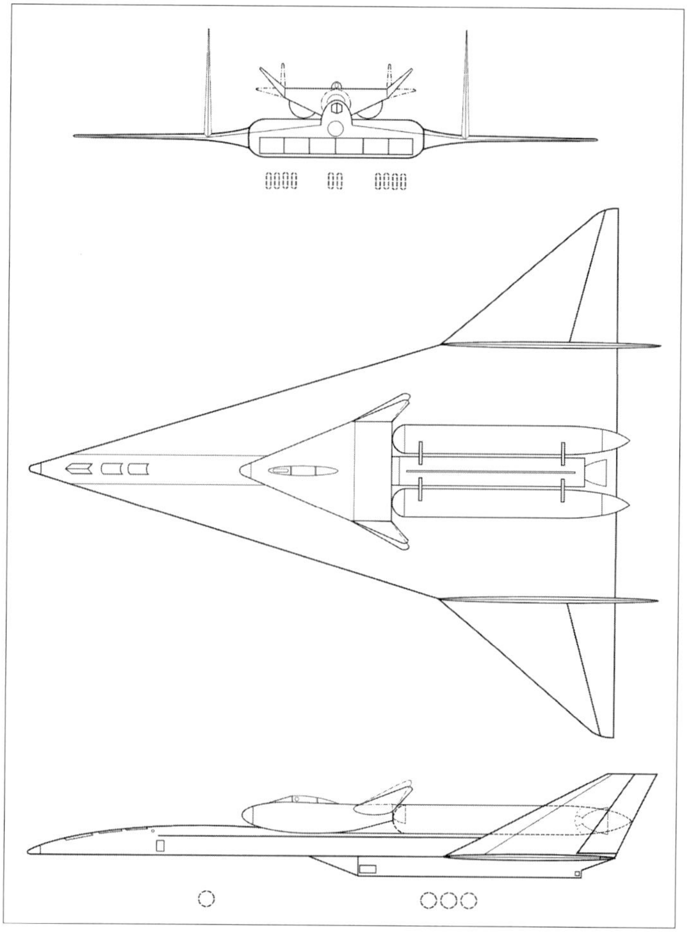

EAG.4396, a Mach 4 double delta turbo-ramjet aircraft proposal, developed by BAC at Preston as the first stage in an orbital spacecraft concept. Shown in this drawing with the piggyback spaceplane and booster attached. This illustration is closely based on BAC artwork.

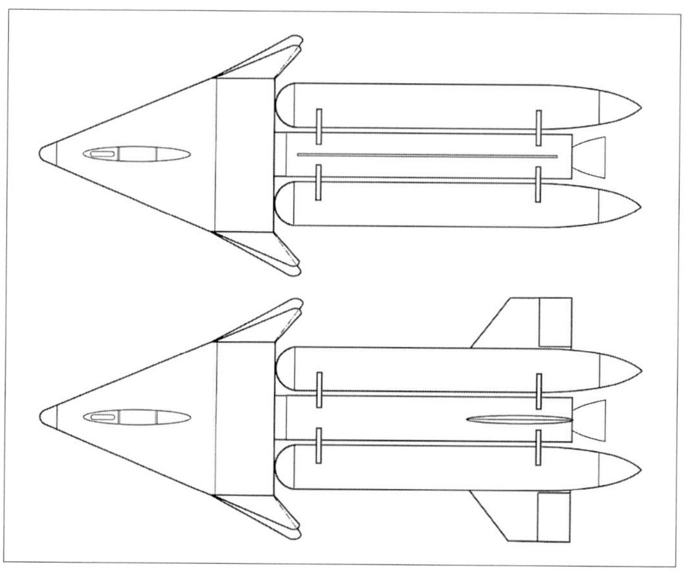

The second stage for EAG.4396, showing the orbital spacecraft attached to fuel tanks and a rocket motor. The spacecraft appears to have formed the basis of later MUSTARD designs and several configurations were considered for the rocket booster section, with and without stabilising fins.

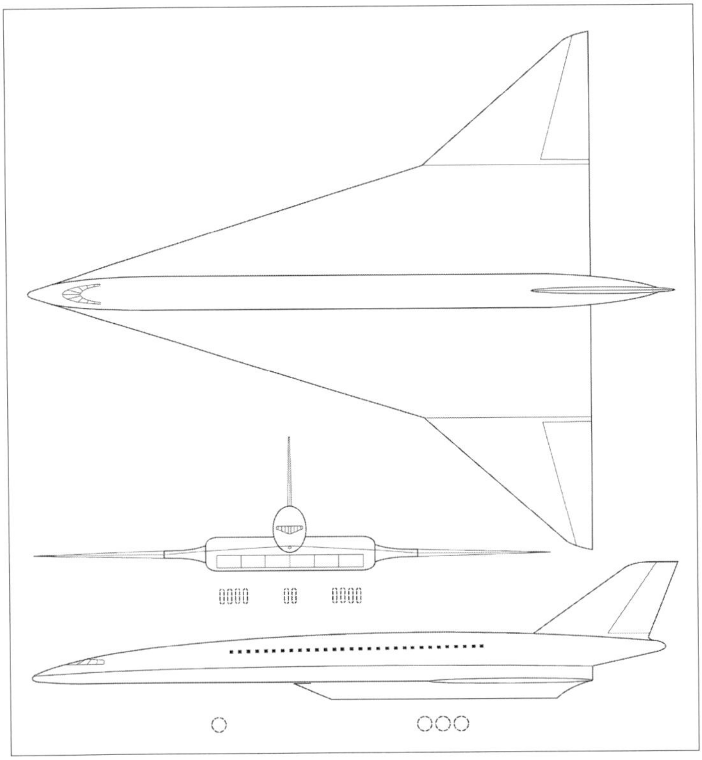

EAG.4397, a proposed high performance transport aircraft based on the EAG.4396 launch vehicle.

with favour shifting back to a simple straight delta wing. Ideas were also forthcoming for several alternative roles this aircraft might perform. One possible development was EAG.4397, a high performance military transport aircraft. Like Concorde, the propulsion layout would have made the design difficult to configure as a bomber or strike aircraft. However, it might have been able to operate as a high performance reconnaissance aircraft, assuming sufficient money had been spent ironing out the many anticipated technical issues.

BAC also examined a number of alternative lower cost launch vehicles. These included the VC10, Avro Vulcan and the American supersonic Convair B-58. All these aircraft would have required substantial modifications, but the B-58 was considered the best choice from this group. Perhaps BAC designers knew that the B-58 had been considered as the carrier for a secret Mach 6 spy plane or an air-launched ballistic missile?

This resulted in BAC indicating in the report that this was their preferred choice and it was allocated the company reference EAG.4409. The straightforward plan was to carry the spaceplane and booster section beneath the fuselage. While EAG.4409 was an unmistakable version of the B-58, the engine layout used twin engine nacelles under each wing as was once proposed for the B-58. This was probably decided on to provide adequate clearance around the spaceplane and booster. Carriage beneath the fuselage was the only option for this aircraft and probably safer than mounting it on the back of a large high performance aircraft like EAG.4396. Although EAG.4409 had a maximum speed of about Mach 2.2, it became apparent as the study progressed that a greatly reduced launch speed was more acceptable and a Mach 0.9 version of this aircraft known as EAG.4412 was suggested, which would allow the carriage of a greater weight.

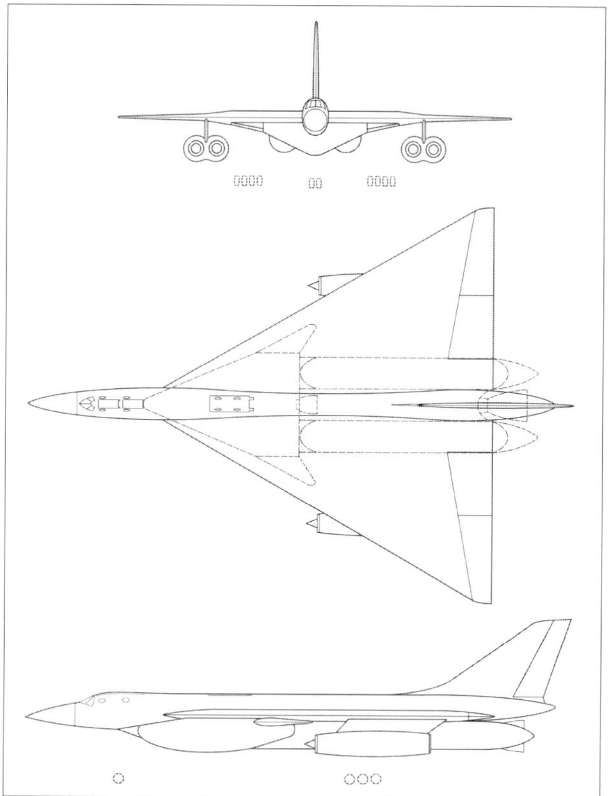

EAG.4409. A Mach 2.2 aircraft considered by BAC in the early 1960s for use as the first stage in an orbital spacecraft system. The spacecraft and booster stage were broadly similar to the EAG.4396 design.

An early mock-up for the Convair B-58 Hustler supersonic bomber with twin engine nacelles (later separated), which BAC intended to develop as a Mach 2+ launch aircraft for their spaceplane and booster.

BAC also provided a detailed study of suitable spaceplanes, having started out with a design that was broadly similar to the original RAE Space Fighter. This evolved into a more compact lifting body vehicle designated EAG.4413, which was fitted with variable position tailfins, a reaction control system, an X-20 style heatshield over the cockpit windshield, an ejection capsule for one or two crew members and skids for horizontal landing. The expendable second stage booster used to lift the EAG.4413 spaceplane into orbit took the form of two large cylindrical fuel tanks containing liquid hydrogen and LOX on each side of a central section housing a Rolls-Royce rocket engine. A single cylindrical booster was considered at one stage, but it was felt that the side by side configuration was far more satisfactory for carriage and air-launch. I will just add that several different stabilising fin arrangements were proposed, which would depend on the launch aircraft.

The MoA had indicated that high-inclination polar orbits were a requirement, although the military role they envisaged remains somewhat obscure. There are several possibilities that include photographic reconnaissance, the release of small satellites and just possibly the ability to undertake a nuclear strike with a space-to-surface missile. The BAC study finished by suggesting that there were no overwhelming technical challenges likely to impede this project, but failed to mention that it would have been immensely expensive to undertake and might generate massive public opposition.

There was still the issue of where UK military spaceplanes might operate from. The MoA accepted the need for a base in an equatorial region, but wanted a prime centre for operations in the UK. One or two existing bases or locations suitable for development might have been found in Scotland, but in their infinite wisdom the MoA decided that a new facility at Brancaster Bay in North Norfolk was better. This location had been secretly earmarked as a Blue Streak missile site and a major test facility for rockets, with the idea remaining popular in Whitehall because of the convenient distance from major UK aerospace facilities.

There are no significant land masses between Norfolk and the Arctic, so this location appeared to be a passable choice for launches, although there was the possibility of objections from the Norwegians. However, the UK is not well suited for any of this and proposals to build Brancaster Spaceport were finally dropped in 1966 because of the growing number of oil and gas platforms operating in the North Sea that might be put at risk, the anticipated public opposition and massive cost of the project. Perhaps the whole thing was a crazy idea from the outset?

At the end of 1963, the X-20 was scrapped and this should have sent a very clear message to UK government officials about, mission creep, over ambition, runaway costs and whether there was actually a need for such a high-status defence project.

BAC Delta Winged Spaceplane

However official UK interest in manned spaceflight persevered, despite all the previously described projects coming to nothing and there is said to have been ongoing discussions in Whitehall about the idea of putting a British astronaut into space. It is even rumoured that the RAF considered the idea of buying a Gemini capsule from the Americans. Presumably, this would be supplied with a suitable rocket and the UK would either build an appropriate launch and control site somewhere, or make use of NASA's facilities? Assuming the Americans were willing to allow this, it is still hard to see this kind of arrangement taking place, but stranger things have happened on occasion. Nevertheless, interest in developing an affordable small British spacecraft, capable

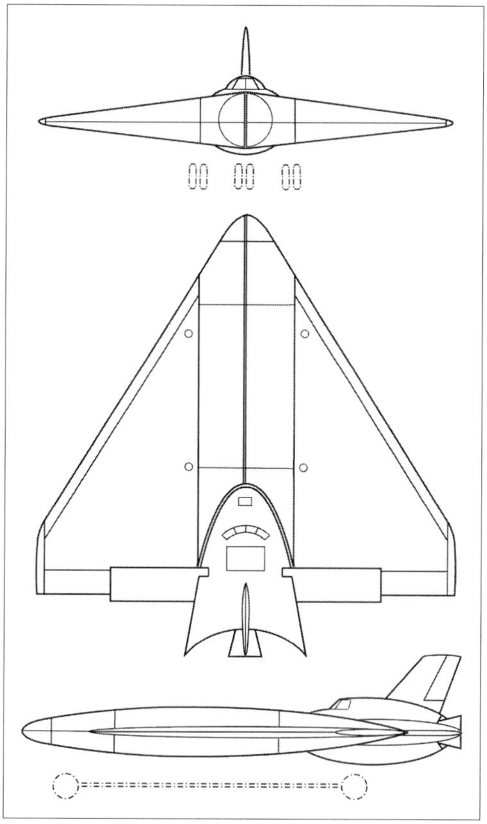

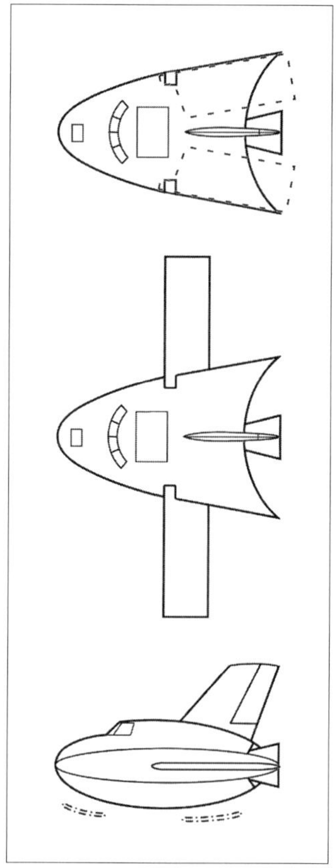

Left: An unusual early BAC concept for a large two-stage delta winged spacecraft. The delta wing would be little more than a large aerodynamic fuel tank, carrying a small orbital spacecraft that included the propulsion system. This fitted into the delta wing's trailing edge.

Right: The upper stage of the BAC delta winged spaceplane system, showing the wings retracted and extended for landing.

of some sort of runway take-off continued, with studies continuing at BAC's Preston Division. Heading this was Geoffrey F. Sharples who had been employed by English Electric Aviation Ltd during the 1950s as an undercarriage specialist and was involved in the Lightning interceptor's development. After English Electric was absorbed into the BAC conglomerate during 1960, Sharples was assigned to spacecraft design and he started working on ideas for a two-stage orbital vehicle that could take-off and land on a conventional runway.

Designer Ken Pocock had developed proposals for a compact lifting body spaceplane that utilised a variable geometry wing feature, housed within the body of the vehicle until after re-entry. The company reference for this craft was EAG.4414 and it would be lifted into orbit by a substantial multi-stage rocket. Sharples examined Pocock's design in detail and adapted it to become part of a runway launched two stage spaceplane system. This took the form of a substantial delta that was supported on the ground by a large launch trolley. The delta provided lift, but internally, nearly all the space was taken up with fuel storage. The orbital stage was fitted into the trailing edge of the delta, carrying the crew/payload and the vehicle's propulsion unit, which comprised of one or more liquid fuel rocket engines. During and after launch, all the fuel would be supplied by the delta wing. Once this was exhausted, the delta stage would separate from the smaller spaceplane, split into two sections and fall back to the surface. It was not intended for re-use.

The EAG.4414 spaceplane was fitted with stubby swing wings that could act as elevons during the ascent, when fully extended at 90°, in line with the delta's trailing edge. However, just before separation, these would swing back into the body of the spacecraft. For the remainder of the flight into orbit, the main engine, or engines would be fed with fuel carried within the spacecraft, or as another option, a forward tank that previously formed part of the delta wing. It is probable that Sharples envisaged a two-man crew in the forward located pressurised cabin equipped with a Shuttle style windshield. There would also be provision for a small payload bay. Unmanned flight by remote control with a larger payload was also considered. A reaction control system would be used for manoeuvring outside the atmosphere and it was suggested that the wings might be fitted with solar panels and extended while in space to generate extra electrical power. The dimensions for the EAG.4414 spacecraft are clearly quite different to Pocock's original proposal and after making some simple estimates based on the BAC drawings, the EAG.4414 spacecraft would require a larger fully extended wingspan than its predecessor (which was 50 ft (15.2 m) and in turn, the delta would need to be large enough to accommodate sufficient fuel to lift the entire craft high altitude.

The rather bulbous looking lifting body spacecraft would be fitted with a tail fin and rudder to provide control after re-entry and the wings would again be extended, allowing a controlled glide to the landing location, ideally something like a dry lake. Final touchdown would be made on extendable skids and perhaps accompanied by a braking parachute. Sharples suggested that it might be possible to use the rocket engine to assist with landing, although retaining any fuel at this stage could present a number of potential hazards.

It was hoped that the spacecraft which carried the propulsion system would be refurbished and remain usable for a number of flights. Exactly what Sharples had in mind as missions for this spacecraft are unknown, but military operations immediately come to mind, such as reconnaissance and anti-satellite missions. It is understood that scale size models were built and some wind tunnel testing took place. In 1964, BAC applied for a UK patent which outlined this craft and it was finally published in February 1967. To be honest, I cannot see a great deal of advantage to this design over a rocket booster and the only feature of interest seems to be runway lift-offs. It would certainly have been expensive to develop and operate for the occasional mission. Nothing indicates there was any official consideration given to this unusual concept, although it probably helped to maintain a reasonable amount of UK interest in manned space projects throughout the decade.

Hawker Siddeley TSTO Concept

In 1964, BAC's UK rival Hawker Siddeley Aviation (HSA) at Kingston began to examine ideas for a fully re-usable Two-Stage-To-Orbit (TSTO) system that would be capable of operating from a conventional runway (in Europe). The Advanced Projects Group led by Hugh Francis was following on from research undertaken by the RAE and responding to the Junkers Raumtransporter, which was conceived by the spaceflight pioneer Dr Eugen Sänger (1905–1964). The fairly wide-reaching TSTO study by HSA was regarded as an important project within the company, as they had just formalised an agreement with SNECMA and Junkers to form Eurospace and needed to retain their status as a high-tech company.

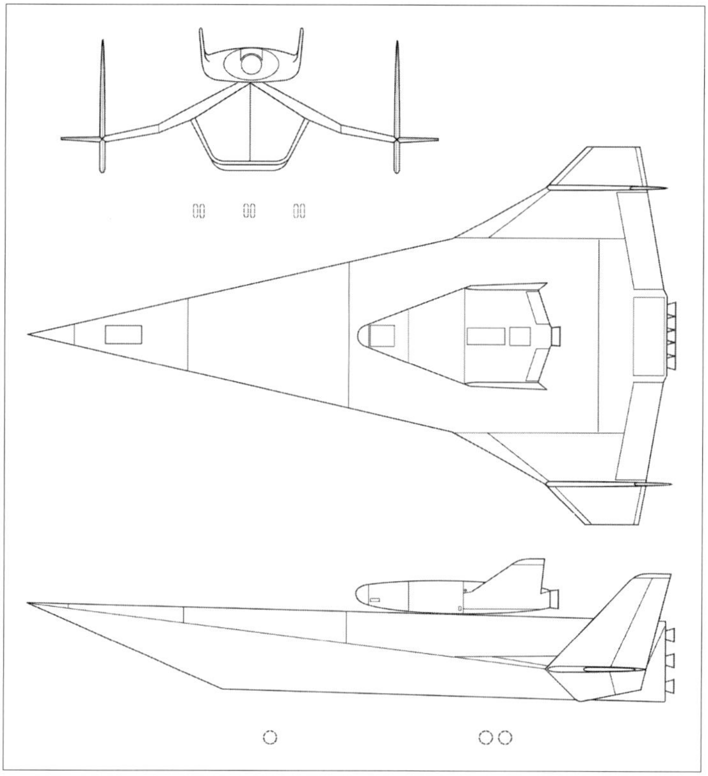

Hawker Siddeley's Spaceplane System: A proposal for a double delta vehicle capable of hypersonic performance for use as an orbital spacecraft launcher.

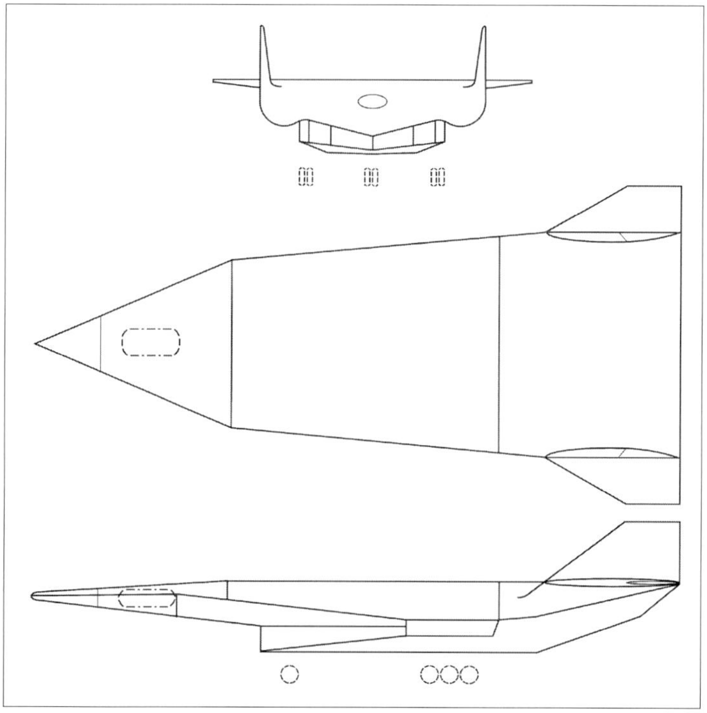

One of several Hawker Siddeley designs for an air-breathing hypersonic launch vehicle. The artwork is based directly on a British Aerospace drawing.

A series of different studies were started under this design project, with two or three of these proposals chosen for further refinement. One of the two-stage concepts known as System A would have been very substantial in size and weight, requiring quite elaborate handling facilities and a very long runway.

The first (probably manned) stage of this proposal was a very large double delta shaped vehicle, with an approximate overall length of 200 ft (60.9 m), a span of 121 ft (36.8 m) and a height of 41 ft (12.5 m). Estimated gross weight would be about 400,000 lb (181 metric tons) and the aircraft would be equipped with a hefty tricycle undercarriage. There is confusion about the propulsion system for this vehicle, probably because several alternative systems were considered. One suggestion was to power the vehicle with six liquid hydrogen/LOX fuelled rocket engines, but there were also proposals to use turboramjets capable of propelling the vehicle to Mach 5.5, supplemented by scramjets (when technically feasible) which would provide Mach 12 performance. Because this was just a study, there were various possibilities considered, but the HSA design team working under Hugh Francis were aiming for a maximum speed of about Mach 6.5, with a proposed ceiling/separation point between 150,000 ft (45 km) and 250,000 ft (76 km). A revision of the design had been completed by 1967, resulting in a slightly smaller aircraft with an overall length of 188 ft (57 m) and a span of 98 ft (29.8 m). Propulsion would be provided by ten turboramjet engines. Further developments might have led to a long-range hypersonic reconnaissance vehicle or a bomber, with Nonweiler waveriding characteristics. A second somewhat smaller, manned first-stage hypersonic aircraft was also proposed alongside Series A. This was an air-breathing design, powered by ram-rocket engines, fuelled with liquid hydrogen and LOX. Overall length was expected to be 157 ft (47.8 m), with a span of 80 ft (24.3 m). Weight was estimated at 375,000 lb (170 metric tons). Maximum speed was expected to be Mach 11 and the craft would be released at 120,000 ft (36,576 m). The launch aircraft would also be equipped with turbojets for use when returning to base.

The HSA, lifting body spaceplane was a separate development and may have originally been considered suitable for use with several different launch vehicles. It was powered by a single liquid fuel rocket engine capable of delivering the craft into LEO after release. The estimated maximum payload was 8,000 lb (3,628 kg). Dimensions were 57 ft (17.4 m) in length, with a span of 34.5 ft (10.5 m) and a weight of 89,900 lb (40,777 kg). Two vertical stabilisers and trailing edge control surfaces were fitted for atmospheric use and the vehicle would be flown by a crew of two or by remote control. Landings would be made on retractable skids, undoubtedly at a fairly high speed due to the design of the craft. A smaller version of the spaceplane was proposed for the more compact launch vehicle, which would have a length of 45.75 ft (14 m) and a span of 25.33 ft (7.7 m).

The RAE, BAC and Hawker Siddeley all maintained considerable interest in waveriders throughout the 1960s. While the RAE sponsored tests of at least one small rocket launched waverider at Woomera and undertook wind tunnel studies, Hawker Siddeley developed plans that now tend to appear somewhat unrealistic, although there were some proposals for mini-shuttles based on 2½-stage launch systems produced during the 1960s that have the look of viable designs. Needless to say there was little enthusiasm in Whitehall for any of HSA's ambitious space projects, there were no commercial backers with very deep pockets and the various concepts were soon forgotten.

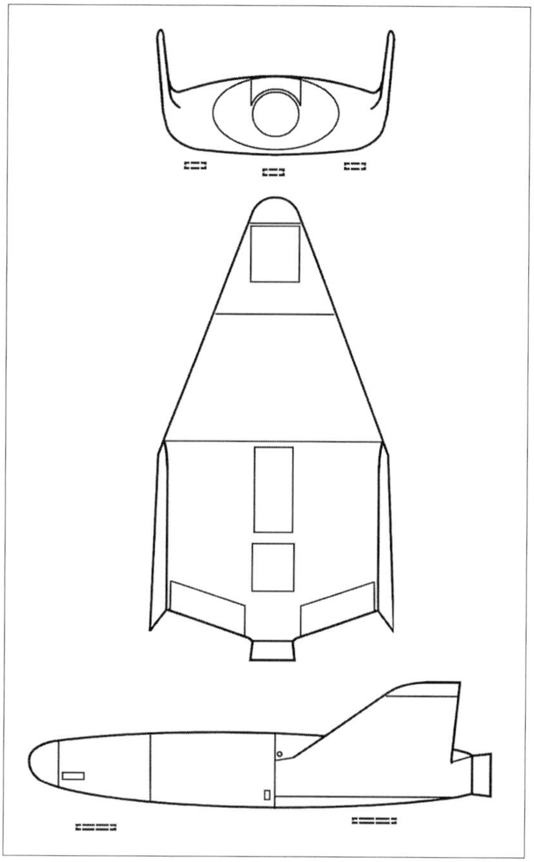

Hawker Siddeley's proposal for a small spaceplane, launched from the back of a supersonic mothercraft at high altitude.

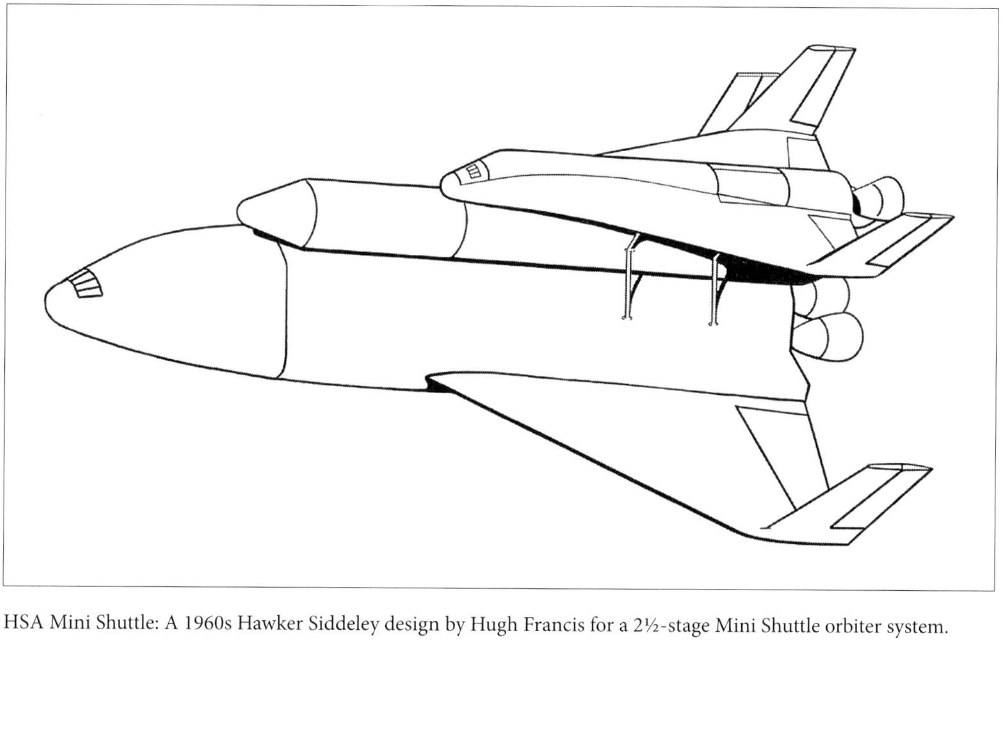

HSA Mini Shuttle: A 1960s Hawker Siddeley design by Hugh Francis for a 2½-stage Mini Shuttle orbiter system.

MUSTARD

Having worked on several hypersonic and spacecraft concepts during the early 1960s, BAC's Aerospace Department at Preston moved to a new government funded study that examined the possibility of developing a fully re-usable, cost effective manned spacecraft, that would be capable of fulfilling a number of civil and military roles. As a manned spacecraft it would be used for scientific research, studying the Earth, placing modest satellites in orbit or undertaking experiments in space. Military uses for this system would include the re-supply of a 10-man orbital space station (details unknown), reconnaissance, satellite inspection and near space control.

A Single-Stage-To-Orbit (SSTO) vehicle was considered technically too demanding, but the designers had come up with an interesting new idea that employed several fully re-usable fly-back boosters.

This project was co-ordinated by the company's chief aerodynamicist Thomas William Smith (1927-2012), who was assisted by Gerald Walley and Robert Wilson. Initially secret, the spacecraft known as Multi-Unit Space Transport & Recovery Device (MUSTARD) was finally revealed to members of The Royal Aeronautical Society on 2 March 1966 by BAC's Managing Director Robin Inskip (1917-1999). The MUSTARD spacecraft drew on some of the design work undertaken

Artwork produced in 1966 showing the most favoured launch configuration for the MUSTARD space vehicle system using a stack. These are three of the later twin tailfin Scheme 15 designs finished in a white ablative silicon coating that would be tested the following year on NASA's X-15A-2. This material helped the X-15A-2 to reach the record speed of 4,520 mph (Mach 6.7), but it didn't behave as expected and was never used again. In the case of MUSTARD, the designers returned to an unpainted fuselage. Also note the substantial number of rocket engines being used, which was either the artist's idea or intentional to avoid giving away too much accurate detail. *(BAE Systems)*

during the Space Fighter programme and various American lifting body proposals, but the unusual launch system was a revolutionary concept that typically used three craft attached to each other. During the vertical ascent, fuel would be transferred to the primary vehicle keeping its tanks full and separation would take place at about 200,000 ft (60,960 m) when two-thirds of the launch fuel had been used up. Now the fully-fuelled (upper stage) MUSTARD vehicle (supposedly launched from a suitable location in the UK) would continue to polar LEO, carrying a payload of approximately 5,000 lb (2,267 kg) which would then be placed in a higher orbit of 345 miles (555 km) above ther Earth. According to BAC, the unusual system of transferring fuel from one vehicle to another during ascent would permit more ambitious possibilities, perhaps eventually even missions to the Moon.

After separation, the two MUSTARD spacecraft that assisted the lift-off would return to base, making conventional runway landings. It was expected that this could be undertaken with manned or unmanned craft. Landing would be assisted by the use of two retractable turbojets that ran on liquid hydrogen drawn from the vehicle's main fuel tank. These would be replaced in later designs by a single turbojet, also in the rear dorsal section of the rocket engine bay. With production costs in mind, one common airframe would be used and one standard propulsion unit selected. Smith and Walley believed that all the craft should be of identical design and interchangeable. However, it was accepted that the MUSTARDs used as boosters would not require the same amount of heat shielding as the space vehicle and this would have made some obvious cost cutting possible.

Many different launch configurations were examined, from two vehicles upwards. One heavy-lift concept proposed the use of six spaceplanes assembled around an extra fuel tank, with a large rocket stage on top. As the study evolved, the usual launch configuration for a routine orbital mission became three similar vehicles in a stack or triangular arrangement.

The spacecraft went through numerous changes as the lifting body shape evolved, often being referred to as a flying wing design in the earliest technical literature. MUSTARD was initially expected to carry a crew of two or possibly three, along with the payload housed in an upper bay behind the crew compartment. In space, the MUSTARD vehicle would be controlled by

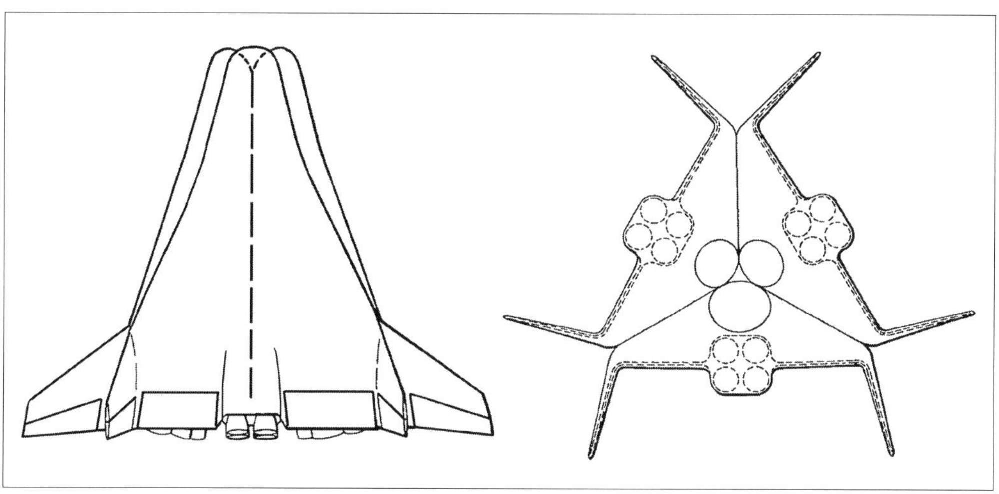

The second launch configuration choice of three BAC MUSTARD spacecraft in a triangular assembly.

gimballing the rocket engine(s), plus the use of a reaction jet system. The eventual configuration for the MUSTARD spacecraft bore quite a resemblance to the upper stage of a 1963 Douglas proposal for a fully re-usable spacecraft system called Astro. The similarities ended there because the Douglas concept would have been launched into space on top of a slightly larger lifting body booster stage. But it is possible that some exchange of technical information took place between Douglas and BAC during this period.

Initially, MUSTARD's two upright control surfaces could be turned outwards to provide additional lift following re-entry. This would increase the aspect ratio, shifting the aerodynamic centre rearwards and boosting the lift/drag ratio. However, the design evolved fairly quickly due to the wind tunnel testing of scale models at Warton and the layout was re-configured from three fins to two fixed upright fins. One problem that is known to have been identified at an early stage involved the fuel connections between vehicles during ascent and it remains unclear if this was ever resolved. Specifications for the MUSTARD space vehicle are to some extent approximate, with the length of the earlier MUSTARD designs being set at about 104 ft (31.7 m). By the time Scheme 14 (EAG 4477) arrived, this had been reduced to 98.5 ft (30 m) with a span of 65.5 ft (20 m). For the final Scheme 15 (EAG 4478) design which underwent considerable weight reduction measures, length was shortened again to 83 ft 25.2 m), with a span of 56 ft (17 m). The appearance remained very similar and the main section of leading edge wing sweep was 65°.

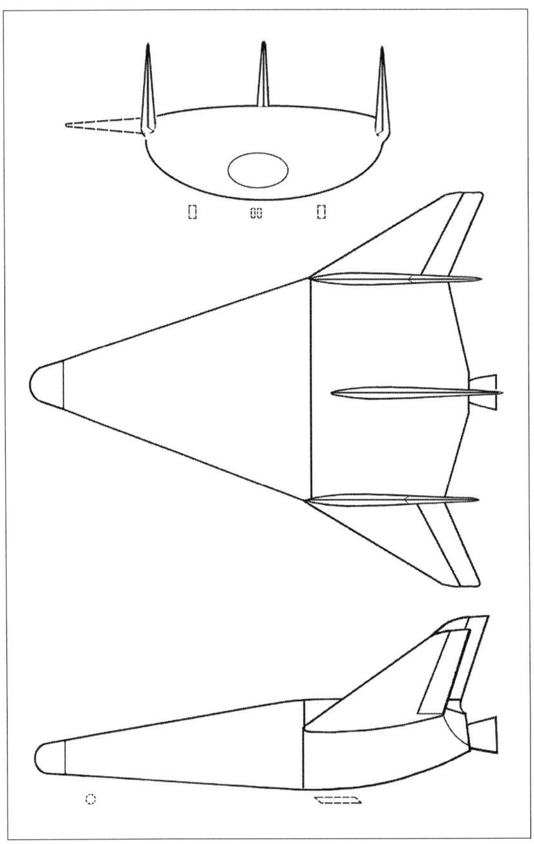

One of the original designs for a MUSTARD spaceplane. Closer in size to the American Space Shuttle, this concept evolved from earlier lifting body studies and was equipped with a central tailfin and fold down outer fins. A single rocket engine was proposed and the cockpit was flush with the forward fuselage section.

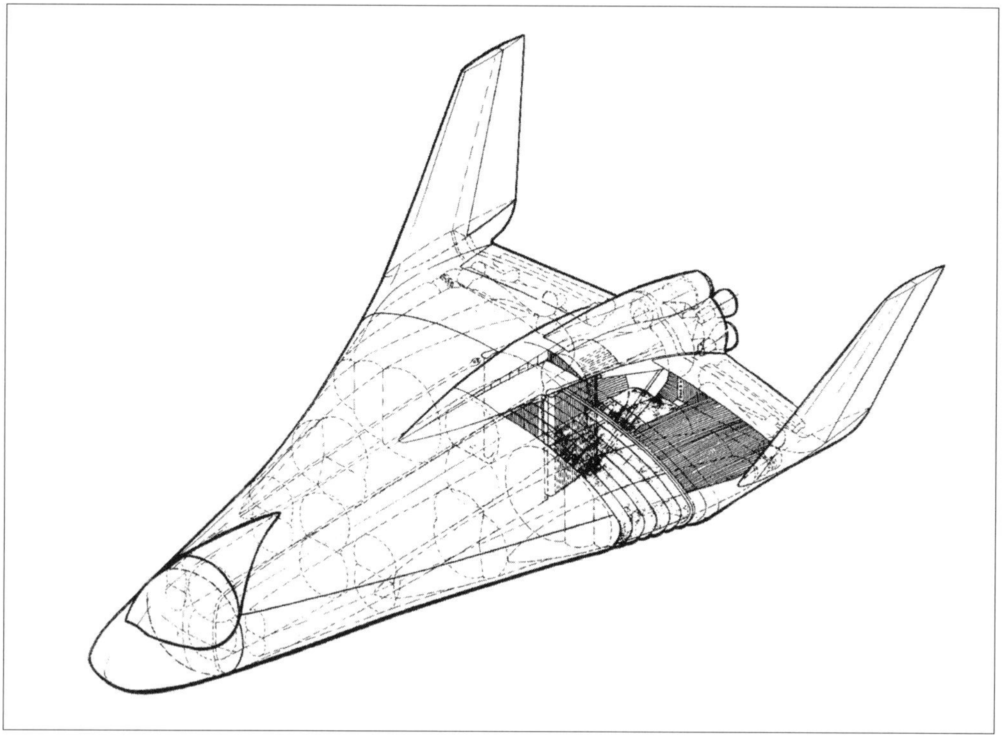

The Internal layout of the final version of MUSTARD showing the fuel tank locations and propulsion system.

The initial choice of propulsion for each vehicle was a single rocket engine using liquid hydrogen and LOX. This would produce an expected thrust of 485,017 lb (2,157 kN) and burn for 215 seconds. The combined take-off weight was calculated to be 935,740 lb (424,444 kg) and the lift-off thrust from all three vehicles, would be 1,077,818 lb (4,794 kN). Later drawings for the Scheme 14/15 proposals show the use of four engines. Scheme 14 had an estimated empty weight of 59,990 lb (24,943 kg) and a gross weight of 313,462 lb (142,184 kg). Scheme 15 was a degree lighter and had a lower engine thrust of about 400,000 lb (1,779.28 kN), although the same 5,000 lb (2,267 kg) payload capability. Unfortunately, some of this information is rather confusing and like many initially classified, studies that went through considerable development and alteration, the details are just reasonable estimates. The spacecraft's airframe and upper surfaces would be mainly fabricated from titanium alloy and the underside would be made from nickel-alloy panels. This was possible because the vehicle would experience lower re-entry heating rates than the later US Shuttle. Steel and titanium would be used for the LOX and LH2 storage tanks inside the vehicle. Separate forward and aft payload bays were a feature of the final design and although this was a less than ideal arrangement, the locations were probably dictated by fuel storage and weight distribution requirements. The main cockpit would accommodate two crew members and a lower linked cabin area would be used to carry additional personnel or specialised equipment. Drawings show this area being used to accommodate a substantial camera system that could be used for civil mapping and military reconnaissance in daylight conditions. MUSTARD could also be equipped with a

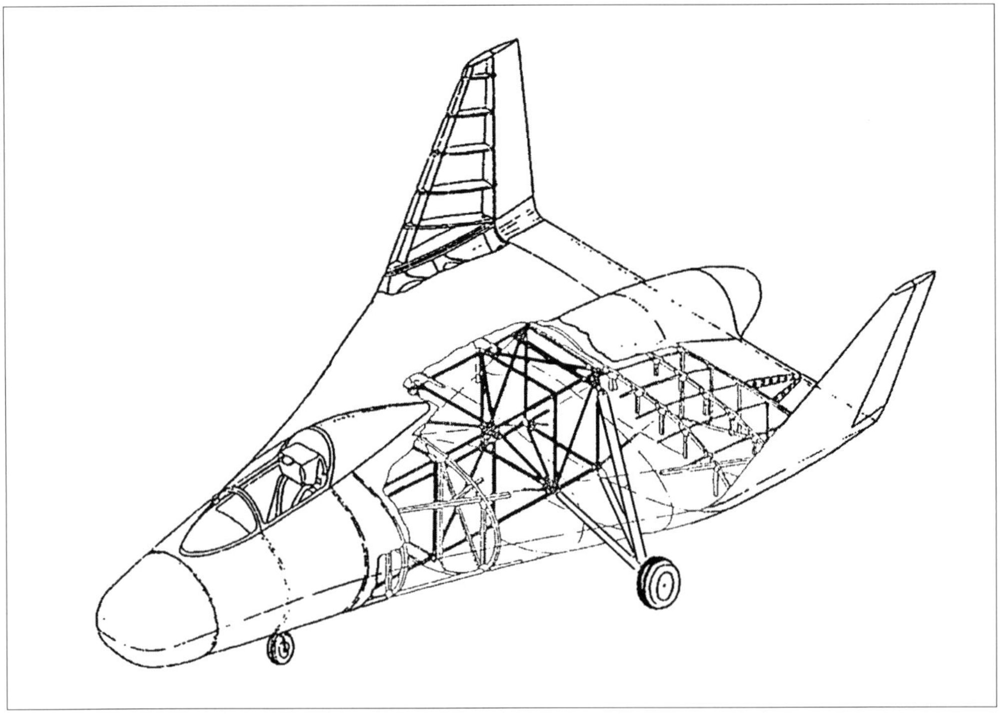

The proposed MUSTARD single seat aerodynamic research glider.

further three survey cameras behind the cockpit, that were installed as required. In the case of the vehicles used to assist the launch, these would be fitted with a much simpler one-man cockpit and no forward cabin area.

From an early stage of the project, it was hoped to build a small, scale size manned MUSTARD lifting body glider. This 26 ft (7.92 m) long aircraft would have been fabricated from a welded tubular steel framework covered in plywood, with a fixed tricycle undercarriage and there was provision to fit a small rear-mounted propulsive unit at a later date. It is understood that the glider was formally discussed with the RAE at a meeting in Farnborough during 1967, but there was no additional funding forthcoming. The Warton Aerospace Department also hoped to receive official support for the construction of (presumably several) 13 ft (3.96 m) long models of the MUSTARD spaceplane, weighing 1,500 lb (680 kg). These would be launched on a sub-orbital flight using Black Arrow rockets, with the overall length of the vehicle and booster being 35 ft (10.6 m). Details of this proposal were disclosed to BIS members at their first annual meeting in 1968 during a talk given by Derek Pritchard-Jones from BAC Preston.

Although the project had not developed much further than wind tunnel tests of models, Gerald Walley addressed the major issue of vehicle mobility by designing the means to convert a MUSTARD spacecraft into a temporary aircraft able to undertake runway take-offs and landings. MUSTARD vehicles would be equipped with one or two low-powered, on-board jet engines to assist landings and utilised a lightweight tricycle undercarriage for craft with nominally empty fuel tanks, but these were unsuitable for conventional transfer flights. To solve the issue of mobility, Walley conceived a specially constructed trolley undercarriage unit containing jet engines and their own fuel supply.

It would allow the vehicle to make short flights between manufacturing or maintenance facilities and launch sites, while also proving an essential recovery item following an emergency landing at an alternative airfield. Full control of this module would come from the spacecraft's cockpit. It is also possible that the trolley might have been used for some ground tests and handling operations. At the same time, it was determined that a single MUSTARD vehicle could almost certainly be launched vertically to high altitude during the development phase and for training purposes.

Finally, it is clear that the Americans took a close look at MUSTARD, recognised its potential and determined how far they could go in developing similar technology without directly copying it. Both the Convair Division of General Dynamics at San Diego and Lockheed's Skunk Works undertook design studies in the mid-1960s, which were based on the vertical launch of a three vehicle stack. This work was undertaken for the USAF's classified Integrated Launch & Re-entry Vehicle (ILRV) programme (AF33-615-67-C-1885), which examined the possibility of developing a fully re-usable spaceplane system. Initially designated as the T-18, the Convair spacecraft differed considerably from MUSTARD lifting body design. It was semi-cylindrical in appearance, with a flat underside and considerably larger than the first MUSTARD proposals with an overall length of 149.5 ft (45.5 m), a height of 31.4 ft (9.5 m) and a span across tailfins of 46.1 ft (14 m). T-18 also carried folding wings that would be extended after re-entry to improve landing performance. These would have a span of 107.5 ft (32.7 m). Also assisting landing would be two pop-out turbojets housed in the forward fuselage. Two (larger than those used on the boosters) liquid fuel rocket engines would be accommodated in the tail and the spacecraft would be supported on a properly wheeled tricycle undercarriage. The weight of this spacecraft would be substantial, with one estimate suggesting 1.5 million pounds (680 metric tons).

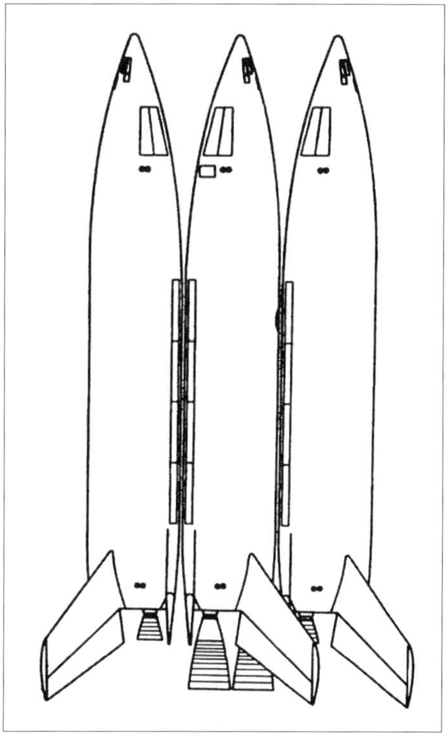

Starting in the mid-1960s, the Convair Division of General Dynamics began work on a stack spaceplane system known as the T-18 Triamese. This fully re-usable concept had many striking similarities to MUSTARD.

The launch method was very similar, using three identical vehicles with liquid fuel transfer taking place during ascent. These Convair studies continued until the end of the 1960s and concluded with the FR-3/4 designs. A similar series of proposals were undertaken by Lockheed for a Triamese spaceplane system, using two booster vehicles fitted with the addition of podded external jet engines and lifting what appears to be a fairly typical Lockheed delta shaped spaceplane rather like their proposed Starclipper. This also failed to secure government funding for further development. Some years later, there were denials that there had been any formal links between the US and UK involving MUSTARD, but it remains hard to dismiss the possibility that a certain amount of unacknowledged technology transfer took place.

By 1970 the MUSTARD project had been abandoned. It was never going to be a realistic proposition for the UK government and could only have been developed further with foreign partners. While somewhat unconventional, MUSTARD was innovative and might have been made to work if sufficient money had been spent on it.

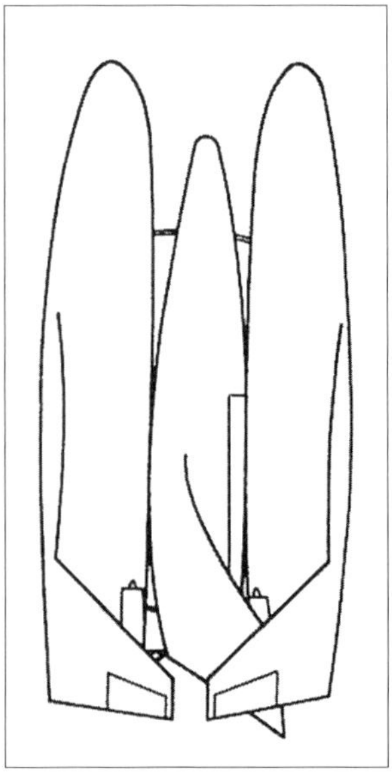

Left: Company artwork depicting the Convair three vehicle T-18 space system separating at high altitude.

Right: The Lockheed Triamese spaceplane concept utilising three stacked lifting body vehicles, with larger boosters carrying externally mounted jet engines to facilitate controlled landings.

8

Some Final Thoughts

In the space of little more than a century, flying wings, tailless aircraft and deltas have evolved from unusual, mostly experimental contraptions into mature machines capable of fulfilling many different, often demanding roles. By the second half of the twentieth century, British designers were producing ambitious proposals for variable geometry bombers, hypersonic aircraft and re-usable spacecraft, with many of these concepts based on flying wing, delta and tailless configurations. Unfortunately, the majority would never progress much further, being too advanced for their time, relying on unproven technology and in most cases, requiring a king's ransom to develop.

This was also a period that saw enthusiastic support for the development of nuclear propulsion for military aircraft. Various forms of this new technology were being promoted by the Americans, who believed atomic energy was capable of solving many existing problems. This enthusiasm for something new would find its way across the Atlantic and resulted in designs that generally took the form of delta shaped aircraft. While scientists in Britain undertook considerable research into building compact nuclear reactors, it became increasingly apparent that although atomic powered aircraft had some attractive possibilities such as almost unlimited range, flying around with a nuclear reactor on-board was incredibly dangerous and these projects were soon abandoned, with no prospect of them ever being revived.

British politicians also aspired to lead the race into space, with major contractors being encouraged to work on plans for suitable vehicles during the early 1960s. While the UK had many brilliant scientists, designers and engineers at its disposal, the quest for a manned (predominantly military) presence beyond the Earth's atmosphere was far removed from the UK's financial capability and it remains that way today. Placing satellites into orbit is one thing, but developing space fighters, manned orbital platforms and perhaps even reaching the Moon were never realistic aspirations. Such projects require massive funding, thousands of technicians, the application of cutting edge technology, a few scientific breakthroughs and realistically, can only be undertaken from overseas locations as the UK is simply not the right place to make space launches. Of course, it would be a mistake to say things can never change. Perhaps 50–100 years from now, there will be technology available that makes manned spaceflight readily available to all wealthy industrialised nations, with Britain able to take full advantage of it. Nevertheless, the days of rapidly progressing from ambitious ideas to the assembly of full functional hardware using affordable parts and low-cost labour are long gone. In the past, an experimental or military aircraft could progress from design to construction in less than a year, but this is no longer the case. Today, the development of a sophisticated combat aircraft or a new airliner will require thousands of highly skilled staff, supercomputers, exotic materials, cutting edge assembly methods and intense testing at every level. The cost can be astronomical and it may take decades of development.

Both civil and military aircraft are expected to perform exactly as specified, which means substantial manufacturing costs. You can add expensive spare parts, continual upgrades and the highest standards of maintenance, requiring carefully selected, fully trained, degree level technicians. Advanced military aircraft will be expected to operate reliably in demanding conditions with their service life measured in decades. Expectations will be equally high for the next generation of armaments carried by these aircraft, along with advanced electronic warfare systems and sophisticated sensors. Yet another factor that usually arises is mission creep, where a military system is expected to function in ways it was never intended to and as a consequence, poor compromises are made. In the case of a new combat aircraft like the Lockheed-Martin F-35, which has been adopted by the UK, this is so expensive, it remains beyond the reach of many economically smaller nations who have previously opted for very capable, straightforward supersonic combat aircraft like the F-16. Today, less than a handful of nations can develop their own military aircraft and even the American F-35 involved international partners, including the UK.

It seems to come as a surprise to some people that the majority of aircraft contractors draw on a range of parts produced by other companies. An aircraft described as indigenous can comprise of many different components, often sourced from foreign manufacturers. These can be the radar and communication systems, undercarriage units, maybe the cockpit canopy, an ejector seat and perhaps the propulsion system. This is the way things have been done since the start of the last century and during the Second World War, many British aviation contractors became reliant on specialised components manufactured in the US. Today, a company like Boeing will source parts for their 787 Dreamliner from the UK, France, Japan, Sweden, Canada and South Korea. Nevertheless, we still regard this aircraft as being of American manufacture. On the other hand, development of any new aircraft is a massive undertaking, regardless of who you buy basic components from and as far back as the early 1960s, it was clear to British officials and major UK aviation companies that the cost of producing a new indigenous military aircraft would become prohibitive, with further large-scale projects requiring the involvement of other nations. It was during this time that BAC began negotiations with Dassault Aviation in France to develop and build a multi-role variable geometry combat aircraft, but for various reasons this progressed no further. However, in 1969, Panavia Aircraft GmbH was formed in West Germany, by BAC, Messerschmitt-Bölkow-Blohm and Fiat Aviazione (which became Aeritalia shortly afterwards). The initial aim was to produce a fighter capable of matching the most advanced Soviet combat aircraft. This would steadily evolve into a multi-role supersonic fighter, with the emphasis on low production costs. By 1970, the single seat version of this aircraft was being called the Panavia 100 and by 1974, the first prototype had become the Tornado. The European aircraft contractors responsible for the Tornado would come together again in the 1980s to form Eurofighter GmbH based at Hallbergmoos, Bavaria, Germany. Their objective was to develop a new state-of-the-art supersonic fighter that would out-perform the next generation of Soviet combat aircraft. The first proposals to meet this need had already been produced in Britain and West Germany during the late 1970s and an amalgamation of the design features led to a twin engined cranked delta, canard design that would become the Typhoon. The first flight took place in 1994 and the level of this aircraft's sophistication was perhaps reflected in the cost of £125 million per unit, which falls within the same overall development and manufacturing cost as the F-35. Because the Typhoon is a European project as opposed to predominantly British and it has a canard configuration, it did not seem right to include it in this book. I also decided not to delve into the recent unmanned experimental Unmanned Combat Aerial Vehicles (UCAVs) developed by BAE Systems as my aim has been to cover manned aircraft. However, Britain still has a very capable aviation industry and BAE Systems have proposed a new 6th Generation stealth fighter as replacement for the Typhoon. Work on the project began in 2015 and this advanced delta winged multi-role fighter would undertake manned or unmanned missions. Powered by advanced adaptive cycle engines, the Tempest would be primarily armed with directed energy weapons. So far, companies supporting this proposed fighter are BAE Systems, Rolls-Royce, Leonardo S.p.A. and MBDA, with Sweden having expressed an interest in 2019. So it is just possible that the Tempest might be ready to enter RAF and AMI (Italian) service by around 2040.

The future of all military aircraft beyond this time period is impossible to predict, although some familiar designs will still be in operational service by the middle of the twenty-first century. However, it is conceivable that by then, unmanned drones could be the dominant type of warplane. These may well use flexible autonomous AI (Artificial Intelligence) to undertake complex and very dangerous missions, although there will be concerns about sci-fi style killer robot machines on the loose that could turn against the humans using them. This may be a reason why they are never allowed to carry nuclear weapons.

Artwork showing the proposed BAE Systems Tempest. This is a sixth-generation multi-role supersonic combat aircraft and the current objective is to begin development with an international consortium. The Tempest would be stealthy, equipped with advanced engines, enjoy supercruise and as a fighter, it would be armed with high-power directed energy weapons and AAMs. Primarily intended for manned flight, the Tempest could also fly unmanned, perhaps almost autonomousy by means of artifical intelligence. A mock-up of the aircraft was exhibited at Farnborough 2018 and should this design be given the go-ahead, it might enter RAF service by 2040. (*BAE Systems*)

BWB deltas may well become the larger commercial aircraft of choice perhaps mainly flown by AI systems. In military form, the BWB could be relatively stealthy and adaptable to many different roles. With more efficient aerodynamics and improved engines, there should be lower operational costs and many payload advantages. The BWB design would be suitable for various transport operations, airborne command platforms, specialised reconnaissance, in-flight refuelling and perhaps as a laser weapon platform or arsenal aircraft carrying nuclear and/or conventional stand-off missiles.

Whatever happens to the British aviation industry during the next 50 years, it is still a certainty that aircraft will continue to evolve and the delta, flying wing and BWB design will become increasingly significant shapes in our skies.

Tempest showing underside. (*BAE Systems*)

Artwork produced by Boeing which portrays the general appearance of a future twin-engined BWB aircraft that would be used for air-to-air refuelling. A similar aircraft might be developed in the UK.

Primarily developed by BAE Systems at Warton, with assistance from Rolls-Royce, GE Aviation and QinetiQ, the unmanned Taranis shown in this picture, is one of several BAE Systems prototype demonstrators to reach the flight testing stage. Very similar in size to a BAE Systems Hawk and quite stealthy, the compact flying wing is said to have cost about £185 million to develop and is closer to a future military design that previous test vehicles, having internal accomodation for missile. It first flew at the Woomera Test Range in Australia during 2013 and is powered by a single Rolls-Royce Adour turbofan, providing an unconfirmed maximum speed of about Mach 1. Some elements of the design will be shared with the French who are working on a similar craft and a derrivative of the Tranis could be in RAF service by 2030. (*BAE Systems*)

The BAE Systems Magma is an experimental unmanned demonstrator, developed in conjunction with the University of Manchester, the NATO Science and Technology Organisation and the University of Arizona. It employs very unusual flight control systems using air drawn from the engine. One method involves blowing air at supersonic speed through narrow slats in the wing's trailing edge and the other is called "fluidic thrust vectoring". This uses blown air from the engine to deflect the exhaust. While Magma retains conventional control surfaces, the ultimate aim is to develop an aircraft with no moving components for this purpose. The first phase of flight testing concluded in late 2017 and further trials have continued. BAE Systems have suggested that a successful application of this new technology will reduce maintenance, weight and make the aircraft stealthier. (*BAE Systems*)

Select Bibliography

Alexander, W & Street, A. Metals in the Service of Man. Pelican. 1977.
Anderton, D & Batchelor, J. Jet Bombers. Phoebus. 1976.
Baker, D. In Valleys of Shadow. Part 1. Air International. September 1995.
Baker, D. Wizard Wars and Air Power in the 21st Century. Part 1. Air International. September 1994.
Barnes, C.H. Shorts Aircraft since 1900. Putnam. 1989
Barr, L. Wing Warping Aircraft Makes First Flight. Air Force Research Laboratory. Public Affairs Release. November 19 2002.
Bono, P. & Gatland, Kenneth. Frontiers of Space. Blanford. 1975.
Buttler, T. British Secret Projects – Jet Fighters since 1950. Midland Publishing. 2000.
Chamberlain, G. Materials Shape Aerospace Future. Design News. Sept 6 1993.
Collier-Webb, D. Tailless Trials. Part 1 & Part 11. Aeroplane Monthly. December 1997, January 1998.
Dabrowski, H.P. Horten Flying Wings in World War 11. Schiffer. 1991.
Ethell, J & Price, A. The German Jets in Combat. Janes. 1979.
F.A.S (Federation of American Scientists). Numerous technical and scientific military papers on this website: fas.org
Flightglobal/Archive: www.flightglobal.com/pdfarchive/index.html
Fulghum, D. Seek and Destroy. New Scientist. December 4 1999. (Stealth Detection)
Fulghum, D A. Missile-Killing UAV Makes Initial Flights. Aviation Week & Space Technology. August 23 1993.
Gatland, K. Space Technology-Second Edition. Salamander. 1989.
Gibson C & Buttler T. British Secret Projects- Hypersonics, Ramjets & Missiles. Midland Publishing 2007
Gibson C. Vulcan's Hammer: V-Force Aircraft and Weapons Projects Since 1945. Hikoki Publications 2011
Global Security. Numerous technical reports on military issues at this website site: globalsecurity.org
Graham-Rowe, D. Nuclear-powered drone aircraft on drawing board. New Scientist. February 19 2003.
Green, W. Famous Bombers of the Second World War, Vol 2. Macdonald. 1960.
Green, W. Famous Fighters of the Second World War, Vol 1. Macdonald. 1958.
Green, W. Rocket Fighter. Macdonald. 1970.
Green, W. Warplanes of the Third Reich. Macdonald. 1970.
Gunston, B. Fighters of the Fifties. PSL. 1981.
Gunston, B. Future Fighters. Salamander. 1984.
Gunston, B. Jet Bombers. Osprey. 1993.
Gunston, B. The Jet & Turbine Aero Engines (Second Edition). PSL. 1997.
Herwig, D & Rode, H. Luftwaffe Secret Projects – Bombers 1939-1945. Midland Publishing. 2000.
HMG. Code of Practice on Access to Government Information. House of Commons Deposited Paper No 4373 (3s) Second Edition. 1997.

Hobbs, D. Space Warfare. Salamander. 1986.
Jones, B. British Experimental Turbojet Aircraft. Crowood Aviation Series 2003.
King, J.B & Batchelor, J. German Secret Weapons. Purnell. 1974.
LeBlanc, Captain N. German Flying Wings Designed by the Horten Brothers.
USAAF Technical Intelligence Report F-SU-1110-ND. Wright Field Air Materials Command. January 10 1946.
Masters D. German Jet Genesis. Jane's Publishing 1982
Ministry of Defence. The Defence Advisory Notices, A Review of the D-Notice System. Document No 93/06. House of Commons Deposited Paper No 9563. 23/07/1993.
Morgan, E. Delta Developments. Aeroplane Monthly. 1996.
Mullins, J. Secrets of a Perfect Skin. (Aerodynamics) New Scientist. January 1997.
Pelletier, A J. Towards The Ideal Aircraft Air Enthusiast July/Aug & September/October 1996.
Price, A. Eric Bachem's Snake in the Sky. Air International. July 1996.
Price, A. The Last Year of the Luftwaffe. MPG Books. 1991.
Rogers M. VTOL Military Research Aircraft. Haynes Publishing 1989
Rose, B. Secret Projects Flying Wings & Tailless Aircraft. Ian Allan Publishing 2010
Rose, B. Secret Projects Military Space Technology. Ian Allen Publishing 2008
Schick, W & Meyer, I. Luftwaffe Secret Projects – Fighters 1939-1945. Midland Publishing. 1997.
Smith, J.R & Kay, A. German Aircraft of the Second World War. Putnam. 1972.
Whitford, R. Fundamentals of Fighter Design. Part 7: Structure. Air International. March 1997.
Whitford, R. Fundamentals of Fighter Design. Part 9: Avionics 11. Air International. July 1997.
Whitford, R. New Shapes in the Sky. Air International. April 1998.
Windle, D. Top Secret Stealth Jet Revealed. New Scientist. October 21 2002.
Wood, D. Project Cancelled. Bobbs-Merrill. 1975.

Glossary

AFB	Air Force Base
AAM	Air-to-Air Missile
AGM	Air-to-ground missile
ASAT	Anti-satellite
AI	Artifical Intelligence
BAC	British Aircraft Corporation
BAe	British Aerospace
BAE Systems	Formed from the merger of British Aerospace (BAe) and Marconi Electronic Systems (MES) in 1999
BAT	Baynes Aerial Tank
BIS	British Interplanetary Society
BLC	Boundary Layer Control, a method of drag reduction
BLT	Boundary Layer Theory
BWB	Blended Wing Body aircraft design
Black Projects	Highly classified, secretly funded programmes usually involving the development of new military systems. These can remain hidden for years, perhaps decades, sometimes progressing no further than studies
ETPS	Empire Test Pilots School
Geostationary Orbit	An orbit that keeps exact pace with the Earth's rotation and allows a spacecraft to remain in a fixed position above the planet
HTP	High Test Peroxide
Hypersonic	Generally accepted as a speed above Mach 5 (Mach 1 – the speed of sound)
Kt	Kiloton. Normally used to describe the explosive yield of a nuclear weapon. 1 Kt = 1,000 tons of TNT explosive
Hypersonic	Generally accepted as a speed above Mach 5 (Mach 1 – the speed of sound)
HSA	Hawker Siddeley Aircraft Co
LEO	Low Earth Orbit
Lifting Body	A re-entry vehicle utilising lift, which falls somewhere between a semi-ballistic shape and a winged craft
LOX	Liquid Oxygen
Luftwaffe	German Air Force
MAP	UK Ministry of Aircraft Production
Mission Creep	The expansion of a project or mission beyond its original objectives

MoA	UK Ministry of Aviation, 1959–1967
MoD	UK Ministry of Defence, 1964-Present Day
MoS	UK Ministry of Supply, 1939–1959
Mt	Megaton. Normally used to describe the explosive yield of a nuclear weapon. 1 Mt = 1,000000 tons of TNT explosive
MUSTARD	Multi-Unit Space Transport And Recovery. UK Space Shuttle Study
NACA	US National Advisory Committee For Aerodynamics, the forerunner of NASA
NASA	US National Aeronautics & Space Administration
NATO	The North Atlantic Treaty Organization. An intergovernmental military alliance based on the North Atlantic Treaty that was signed on 4 April 1949
NBMR-3	1961 NATO Basic Military Requirement 3. Contest for a VTOL strike aircraft
NGTE	National Gas Turbine Establishment (UK)
NORAD	North American Aerospace Defence Command
Payload	Normally cargo or equipment but can refer to military ordnance
PCB	Plenum Chamber Burning
QRA	RAF Quick Reaction Alert aircraft
RAE	Royal Aircraft Establishment
RAF	Royal Air Force
RATO	Rocket Assisted Take-Off
Reaction Control System	System of gas jets used to adjust the orientation of a vehicle in space
Sesquiplane	A type of biplane where the lower wing is significantly smaller than the upper. This can reduce drag and weight.
SSTO	Single Stage To Orbit
STAC	The UK Supersonic Transport Aircraft Committee, set up by the RAE in 1956
Stealth	Low-visibility technologies
STOL	Short Take-Off and Landing
STOVL	Short Take-off and Vertical Landing
Sub Orbital	A high-altitude rocket flight that does not achieve orbit
Tons/tonnes	Throughout this book the value for 'ton' equates to an American short ton, which equals 2,000 lb. The metric tonne is 1,000 kg, and the conversion factor is 0.9072
TSTO	Two Stage To Orbit
USAAF	United States Army Air Force
USAF	United States Air Force
VTO	Vertical Take-Off
VTOL	Vertical Take-Off & Landing
V/STOL	Vertical/Short Take-off & Landing
Walter RII-203b rocket engine fuel	*T Stoff: Concentrated hydrogen peroxide *Z Stoff: Calcium permanganate liquid catalyst *C Stoff (replaced Z Stoff): Methyl alcohol, hydrazine hydrate and water mixture catalyst
Waveriding	This is an aerodynamic principle developed by Terence Nonweiler of the Queen's University, Belfast in the early 1950s. A suitably shaped aircraft can employ this at hypersonic speed to improve the lift-to-drag ratio by using the shockwaves it creates to generate compression lift

Index

Aircraft

People

Engines (Propeller/Jet)

Rocket Engines/Fuel

Rockets/Spacecraft

Organisations

Locations

Requirements/Specifications/ Operations